MY
ISRAEL
Trail

Finding Peace in the
Promised Land

ARYEH GREEN

PLAIN SIGHT
PUBLISHING
An imprint of Cedar Fort, Inc.
Springville, Utah

ISBN 13: 978-1-4621-2201-1

Published by Plain Sight Publishing, an imprint of Cedar Fort, Inc.
2373 W. 700 S., Springville, UT 84663
Distributed by Cedar Fort, Inc., www.cedarfort.com

LIBRARY OF CONGRESS CATALOGING-IN-PUBLICATION DATA

Names: Green, Aryeh, 1963- author.
Title: My Israel trail / Aryeh Green.
Description: Springville, Utah : Plain Sight Publishing, an imprint of Cedar
  Fort, Inc., [2018] | Includes bibliographical references and index.
Identifiers: LCCN 2018004369 (print) | LCCN 2018006992 (ebook) | ISBN
  9781462128969 (epub, pdf, mobi) | ISBN 9781462122011 (perfect bound : alk.
  paper)
Subjects: LCSH: Green, Aryeh, 1963---Travel--Israel. |
  Hiking--Israel--Anecdotes. | Israel--Description and travel. | LCGFT:
  Autobiographies.
Classification: LCC GV199.44.I75 (ebook) | LCC GV199.44.I75 G74 2018 (print)
  | DDC 796.51095694--dc23
LC record available at https://lccn.loc.gov/2018004369

Cover design by Shawnda T. Craig
Cover design © 2018 Cedar Fort, Inc.
Edited by Deborah Spencer and Jessica Romrell
Typeset by Kaitlin Barwick

Printed in the United States of America

10 9 8 7 6 5 4 3 2 1

Printed on acid-free paper

Praise for

MY
ISRAEL
Trail

What a fascinating journey Aryeh presents us with and takes us on. This book is a beautiful exploration of self and identity; the movement of his body through Israel echoes the movement of his spirit from loneliness and fear to strength and fulfillment. What a metaphor for so many of our journeys in this life!

—MAYIM BIALIK, actress *(The Big Bang Theory, Blossom),*
author, activist (Grok Nation), and neuroscientist

In his new book about walking the Land of Israel, Aryeh Green unabashedly demonstrates his love of the Land of Israel, the state of Israel, and the people of Israel. His passion, persistence and curiosity shine through in this user-friendly, engaging new book.

—NATAN SHARANSKY, chairman of the Jewish Agency and
former Israeli deputy prime minister and Soviet dissident

Walking alone through a beautiful country is conducive to thinking creatively. Aryeh Green's wonderful description of his 42-day hike throughout Israel will make every reader think hard about the state of the nation-state of the Jewish people at this critical time in its history. It's a worthwhile literary journey on which to embark.

—ALAN DERSHOWITZ, former professor of law
at Harvard Law School

Deeply moving and profoundly thoughtful, *My Israel Trail* is a must read for lovers of Israel, nature, and the human spirit. Aryeh Green has done an immense service to us all.

—MICHAEL OREN, Israeli deputy minister and member of Knesset, former Israeli ambassador to the US, and historian and scholar of the Middle East

Aryeh Green's book is so vivid, the first time I went hiking after I read it, I had flashbacks to his text, his story, his insights. The book takes readers on a wonderful journey, with a stunning landscape, emotional and physical challenges galore, and a pleasant, insightful narrator who is charming, self-deprecating, honest, and wise. The book makes you really want to hike the Israel trail. If you can hike it, hike it. If you can't, reading this book is the next best thing.

—GIL TROY, historian and author of *The Zionist Ideas* and *Why I Am a Zionist*

For Peter, who loved Israel
—the country, the people, the land, and the ideal—
and me.

And for all seekers of peace
in the world—
those who humbly
and gratefully
accept,
forgive,
and dedicate their lives
to a higher purpose.

CONTENTS

GLOSSARY

HEBREW TERMS

Aliyah—Moving to Israel; literally "going up" or making a pilgrimage

Bracha—Blessing

Challah—Special braided bread served on the Sabbath and Festivals; Plural, *Challot*

Davka—Slang, specifically or purposefully, indicating intention, as in "He *davka* bumped into me"

Daven, davenning—to pray, in Yiddush

Gat—Wine press

Gemara—Later element of the Talmud, discussions of the Mishna, from about 200 to 400 CE

Har—Mountain

Kfar—Village

Kibbutz—A cooperative socialist community with shared/common ownership and responsibilities

Kiddush—Sanctification, of the Sabbath or Festivals, a prayer/blessing usually made over wine

Kippa—skullcap or yarmulke (Yiddush) worn by Jewish men as a sign of respect for God

Kol HaKavod—Good for you; Respect!

Ma'ayan—A fresh-water spring; *Ein* is another, related word, used as a prefix as in Ein Gedi

Mikdash—The Temple, lit. the Holy Place, in Jerusalem

Minyan—Jewish prayer group of ten, required for certain aspects of services

Mikvah—Ritual bath; Plural, *Mikvaot*

Mishkan—The Tent of Meeting, carried and set up as the Israelites walked through the desert, then in Shilo and elsewhere in the Land of Israel until it was brought to Jerusalem by King David and the Temple was built

Mishna—Earlier element of the Talmud, from around the time of Jesus

Moshav—A cooperative community with private work and property

Nachal—Stream, or creek

Peyot—Side curls of hair, conforming to the biblical injunction not to cut the "corners" of the beard

Shomron—Samaria, the biblical and geographical/cartographical name for the mountain region north of Jerusalem overlooking the coastal plain and the Jordan Valley. Includes Beit El and Shechem ("Nablus"). See *Yehuda* below.

Siddur—Prayer book

Shabbat—the Sabbath

Shul—Synagogue (Yiddush)

Shvil—Trail/path; the Shvil refers to Shvil Yisrael

Shvil Yisrael—The Israel National Trail; *Shvilist* is one who hikes the Israel Trail

Simcha—Joy, happiness; also, a celebration; Plural, *Smachot*

Tallit—Traditional Jewish prayer shawl

Talmud—Central corpus of Jewish thought and tradition, based on the Hebrew Bible

Tanach—The Hebrew Bible (Lit. "Torah, Nevi'im, K'tuvim" or Torah, Prophets, Writings)

Tefila—Prayer

Tefillin—Leather boxes containing parchments with related Torah passages, with straps; "Phylacteries"

Torah—The five books of Moses which begin the Hebrew Bible; literally, the scroll hand-written on parchment. Often refers to the entire collection of all Jewish thought and practice, as in "a Torah perspective" or "Torah-observant."

Yehuda—Judea, the biblical and geographical/cartographical name for the hill and desert region south of Jerusalem between the coastal plain and the Jordan Valley; named for the tribe of Judah/Yehuda, one of Yaakov's twelve sons. Includes Bethlehem and Hebron as well as Masada and the Judean Desert. (Judea and Samaria are often referred to jointly, as the heartland of Jewish history in the region and the areas of the "disputed territories" otherwise referred to as "the west bank," a Jordanian term geared to connecting their "east bank" of the Jordan with the western side. Judea spans both sides of the pre-'67 armistice lines of 1949, including the Jerusalem foothills where my town, Beit Shemesh, sits.)

Yishuv—"Settlement" or community—a Hebrew term for any small residential community, whether village, moshav, or kibbutz, whether in pre-State or pre-1967 Israel or in Judea & Samaria.

PLACE NAMES IN ISRAEL AND THEIR ENGLISH OR ANGLICIZED MODERN USAGE

Galil—Galilee

Hevron—Hebron

Kinneret—Sea of Galilee, also known as Lake Tiberius

Shechem—Nablus

Shomron—Samaria

Tiveria—Tiberius

Tzfat—Safed

Yerushalayim—Jerusalem

Yehuda—Judea

A LIST OF "CHARACTERS"

FAMILY:

Aryeh—Age 51 at the time of the hike

Karen—Aryeh's former wife of twenty-eight years, age 54

Netanel—Aryeh's first-born son, age 27 (nickname: Nati)

Tehila—Netanel's wife, age 26

Merav—Aryeh's second child and first-born daughter, age 25 (nickname: Meravi)

Meira—Aryeh's youngest daughter, age 22 (nickname: Mimi)

Bini—Meira's boyfriend at the time of the hike, now husband, age 23

VARIOUS CLOSE FRIENDS MENTIONED FREQUENTLY:

Moshe

Zvi

Aaron & Hadas

Mandy & Jeremy

Deborah & Michael

Yaakov & Shalva

Rebecca

Ken

Nomi

Leonie & Chaim

Michal (Aaron & Hadas's daughter)

BIBLICAL HEBREW NAMES:

Avraham—Abraham

Moshe—Moses

Shaul—Saul

Shlomo—Solomon

Yaakov—Jacob

Yehoshua—Joshua

Yeshayahu—Isaiah

Yitzchak—Isaac

Yosef—Joseph

PRELUDE

I'm scared, standing on a thin ledge on the side of a cliff. To my left is a sheer rough wall; to my right, a drop of 30 feet or so to the river bed below. But directly ahead an angry tree blocks the way. (How does it hold to the side of the rock?) It seems threatening as it jumps in the hot wind. With about 50 pounds on my back, I'm too afraid of falling to turn around. Turn to the right and my backpack hits the rock face; turn to the left and the weight of the pack puts me off balance. And the boulders down below aren't very welcoming.

What to do?

The trail leads into an abyss. Literally. I guess I've lost the path, which, while it's happened before, has never been such a problem. Usually you just retrace your steps, find the last trail marker, and then pay a bit more attention to discover where you missed the next one. But here, on a cliff in Nachal Amud, the Stream of the Pillar connecting the holy city of Tzfat (Safed) with the Kinneret, the Sea of Galilee, it's just not that easy. Even with the backpack on (including the small guitar hanging from its side), just a minute or so ago I pretty nonchalantly leapt over a three-foot gap in the ledge a few paces back. But I just know—with all my casual confidence built up over the preceding weeks of hiking through Israel's desert mountains and northern reaches—I can't do it again. That is, if I can even turn around on this one-foot-wide ledge.

It may be the perfect metaphor.

Sometimes you reach an impasse. Not only is it unclear what the next step is, but you're also not sure how the heck you got there and are too scared to move. All the alternatives you can imagine are dangerous, or unpalatable, or frightening. You're stuck, and the panic starts to rise.

Times of personal hardship, relationships, work situations, and other challenges we face test our mettle. Rabbi Herschel Schachter taught that the biblical "value" of a person in Vayikra, the Book of Leviticus, is calculated by his or her response to suffering and adversity. Elie Weisel and Victor Frankl took the personal and national horror of the Shoah/Holocaust and translated their experiences into timeless lessons for humanity. In *Man's Search for Meaning*, Frankl stresses the importance of having a goal to strive for, pushing us to move ahead, to take the next step, and the next.

My goal that day was to get to the Kinneret by nightfall (and not to plunge down the cliff face onto the rocks below). My grander goal was to finish what I'd started, hiking the Israel National Trail ("Shvil Yisrael") from one end of our tiny country to the other. (It's not that tiny—the Shvil runs some 1000 kilometers or 600 miles from the Red Sea in the South to the border with Lebanon in the North.)

And after my devastating divorce, my ultimate goal was to get my life back on track, or to find a new track for myself.

I take three deep breaths—thank you, Thomas Crum—to calm down, focus, and discover the possibilities open before me; then I make a decision. Not moving my feet an inch, I lower the pack slowly to the ground, managing to lean it against the rock. Freed from the weight of the bag, I turn carefully and retrace my steps along the narrow path on the side of the cliff—jumping over the breach—and yes!—find the trail-marking high up on the rock face above an almost invisible foothold carved into the cliff. I did that ledge once with the pack, I know that; all I have to do now is convince myself I can do it again, this time in the opposite direction.

Retracing my steps, it's funny, but when I (carefully!) heft the pack on my back, it seems somehow lighter, more manageable. It hasn't changed; I have changed. Or rather, my attitude, my sense of self and sense of direction and purpose, my confidence and belief in my ability to walk the path, has changed.

It's not that I'm no longer afraid; I just know I have it in me to keep going.

Sometimes we need to set aside our baggage and re-evaluate. That's what this book is about. My hike along the Israel Trail—or *my* Israel Trail as I'm calling it—enabled the discovery, or rediscovery, of a number of essential truths for living. All come from the ancient wisdom of the Torah and the rest of the Hebrew Bible and Jewish tradition, but at the same time they are universal and universally relevant for anyone seeking peace.

I began to consider the concept of peace on three levels: inner peace (tranquility and wholeness); harmony and beauty in relationships (whether personal or work-related); and even conflict resolution between nations, regions, or countries.

I set out on a journey to "find peace in the holy land." And in my search for inner serenity while walking the Land, I realized many of these truths helping me on my personal journey could perhaps be helpful to others.

I was overwhelmed by the daunting challenges facing me—on the Trail, in my life, and at the national level. Every day brought a new difficulty, from scorching heat and impossible inclines to aching loneliness and crises of confidence, from news of family problems to news of terror attacks. I meditated on mountaintops and cried in dry creek beds; I wrote anguished journal entries and composed songs to lift my spirits. I looked back, and inward, and up to the night sky, and over the valley to the next mountain range, and down at the ants in the dirt, and back along the trail to see how far I'd come.

What I discovered on the Shvil was a sense of self, a sense of personal and national history . . . and a perspective of sorts on the human condition. These are my reflections, a meditation as it were on existence, relationships, happiness, challenges, and hope.

INTRODUCTION

I am no philosopher. I'm a normal guy trying to adjust to a number of life situations: some normal, some less so—divorce, loneliness, war, loss, terror. Seeking "peace," I found it while walking ten miles a day across Israel. But what helped me find the internal tranquility I sought wasn't just the solitude or the exercise; it wasn't just the moving history I stumbled across or the phenomenal views. It was the realization that—for me, perhaps for you, maybe for all of us—there are a few basic concepts which, when understood and acted upon, can make our journey on the Trail and in life successful, enjoyable, and meaningful.

Divorce has become so commonplace in modern life that it seems mundane; well over fifty percent of marriages in America end that way. I suppose that's like saying death is commonplace; it doesn't make it any easier to bear, though, does it? I was happily married for almost thirty years. "Happily" is hardly the word: ours was an epic love, an aligning of the stars, a bringing together of disparate worlds and two individuals who were destined for each other and who were emblems of all that is right with the world and of what real love is. Our friends and our children—and our friend's children and childrens' friends—looked to us and our relationship as a paradigm of what a loving, romantic, blissful, supportive, equal marriage is.

When Karen, my British wife of twenty-eight years, said she wanted a divorce in the Spring of 2012, it was as if everything I'd built my life on—my understanding of the dedication that is part of the institution of marriage, my commitment to Israel, my religious observance, my belief in the power of love—disappeared into an abyss. Over the course of the next eighteen months, through various stages of counselling, tears, confusion, anger, discussion, attempts at understanding, and eventual acquiescence, my life was literally turned inside out.

In the midst of the separation, as Karen was moving out, I attended a three-day silent meditation retreat soon after my son's wedding. It was a transformative experience, and it began a process enabling me to move forward. Then, later that year, with the lessons from the retreat undeniably on my mind and the divorce imminent, at the climax of an excruciating and exhilarating hike with my youngest daughter to the top of Half Dome in Yosemite, California, I made a decision. "I'm going to hike the Shvil!" I told my daughter, referring to the Israel National Trail—*Shvil Yisrael* in Hebrew, or just the Shvil or the Trail for short. Six months later—six weeks after handing Karen her *Get*, the Jewish religious bill-of-divorce—I stepped through the revolving door of a hotel in Eilat on the

Red Sea and headed into the desert, with nothing but a backpack and two walking sticks to accompany me.

My Israel Trail is the story of what I came to understand while walking the Land of Israel, its length and breadth, over the course of eight weeks, in forty-two days of hiking (I keep Shabbat, the Jewish Sabbath, and didn't hike from sundown Friday evening through stars-out Saturday night). Of those 42 days, 40 I walked alone. I hiked either entirely alone (reviewing my journal entries, there were twelve days during which I didn't come into contact with a single soul on the trail) or with no companion save an occasional nod or exchange with others along the way or at rest stops, stores, or hosts for the night. Forty days of contemplation—of life, of destiny, of priorities, of the human predicament, of God, of fate, of politics and love and history and philosophy. It wasn't exactly the 40 days and 40 nights of Moshe (Moses) on Mt. Sinai, nor the 40 years of the Children of Israel's wandering in the desert—but it felt like a little of both.

And though I don't pretend to have discovered the secrets of the universe, I did uncover the secrets of *my* universe, finding or recognizing a number of truths and tools that not only enabled me to overcome the challenges of the actual physical difficulties of the trek, but inspired me to move forward with my life and to conquer my anguish and despair. And at the same time—or rather, soon thereafter—I recognized how these few simple truths may well be of value to others facing hardship. (I also saw ways to apply these approaches to our Middle Eastern quandary and the hostility Israel has faced since before its founding—a subject to which I hope to return one day.)

None of these concepts are new—but some were new to me. Like the importance of looking back when on the Shvil, taking stock of how far I'd come and enjoying the very different perspective this gives on the present and future direction I was taking. None are even particularly deep, truth be told: but the truth in them, when told, is profound enough to warrant, I believe, the review offered here. Rabbi Moshe Chaim Luzatto, the Ramchal, intoduces his seminal work "The Path of the Just" by noting that the study of known truths can be incredibly powerful, and helpful, and important.

I might humbly suggest that such could be said of this effort. What is original here is the combination of these ideas and how I reached these conclusions, how they connect to each other, and an innovative application of them to the hardships I was facing and the challenges we all try to meet in our lives. (Much of what follows refers to God because for me God is real and active in history; but it can also be understood from the perspective of fate or providence.)

Put simply, I learned on the Shvil that there are five fundamental elements that combine to create the framework for real peace and harmony, whether personal or national.

Combining these five elements on a hiking trail helps immeasurably. A life philosophy based on these five can lead to incredible happiness—the kind we all yearn for.

The first thing I learned was **humility** (and an understanding of our place in the universe). Humbly recognizing how little we really control in our lives, how insignificant our concerns really are, when compared with the vastness of the universe or the suffering of others, how our intelligence and understanding is not as vaunted as we might think, enables us to approach challenges with an openness and creativity that otherwise eludes us.

Acceptance (of reality, of the world as it is and not as we'd like it to be) is the second element. Accepting what is—it's hot, it's steep, it's lonely—allows us to focus on what we need to do and to enjoy the experience. Acknowledgment of reality as it is—divorce, death, war, flood— rather than insisting on changing it or berating ourselves for our part in making it that way, is simply liberating. I wanted and needed that freedom so badly it hurt, though I didn't know it.

The third lesson was **gratitude** (appreciation for what we have and what the world offers us). By accepting any given situation with minimal or no complaint, we open ourselves up to see the incredible miracles we otherwise ignore or take for granted—from our health and children to the very existence of our country and the wonders of nature.

These first three elements—humility, acceptance, and gratitude—are connected. On the first day of the Shvil, I made a terrible decision, taking a steep, perilous route up Har Shlomo (Mt. Solomon) overlooking the Gulf of Eilat. (Perhaps had I known the Hebrew word "תלולה" in my guidebook—"t'lula—extremely steep"—I might have chosen to stick with the regular route. Duh.) Imagine: first day out, searingly hot with an occasional drizzle, nearing sunset, climbing hand-over-foot up a sandy, rocky, slippery incline. "What have I done?" I asked myself. "Why am I here?"

As I began to recognize not only my growing fatigue but the imminent onset of darkness, I stopped the self-criticism, took myself in hand, and looked again at the map. "OK: you made a bad decision, you're an idiot—accept it; you can't change it; now make a good decision and move on."

This is not to say we can't or shouldn't work to change our reality; it is simply the first step in mapping our path toward that change. That pithy folk aphorism about accepting the things I cannot change gets it exactly right: acknowledge that there are aspects of life over which we have no control.

One of the greatest strengths of Moshe was his humility; our sages teach that this was his defining characteristic, and the primary vehicle enabling God to help him lead the people of Israel to freedom. Recognition that we are not truly in control of every aspect of our life—or even many—is a large part of that humility. And it was the lack of gratitude demonstrated by the Children of Israel in their complaints in the desert which most distressed Moshe—and which provoked God's anger at the time.

The Jewish people's daily and festival prayers, which include continuous motifs of gratefulness even at commemorations of national disaster, reflect this connection between humble acknowledgement of our relative powerlessness, acceptance of what is, and deep thankfulness for the wonders of the universe and the miracles in our lives.

Yet how can this be achieved, practically? I developed a meditative practice, to be described later, focused on the very first of God's names used in communicating with Moshe: "אהיה אשר אהיה"—"*Eheye Asher Eheye*—I am as I will be."[1] For me, this was a constant reinforcement of the first and second principle, something I'd discovered a year previously while on that silent meditation retreat in the Judean mountains, that God controls the world, not me. It could have been frightening, acknowledging how small and insignificant we are in the vast universe and course of history. But it was and is wonderfully comforting, and liberating, to humbly accept life as it is.

This was immediately followed by a focus on "מודה אני"—"*Modeh Ani*—I am thankful," the traditional Jewish prayer on waking. I'd often sing it on the Shvil, sometimes quietly, sometimes at the top of my voice, making the transition from acceptance to appreciation, expressing my incredible, deep gratitude for everything good in my life. From the last Snickers bar to my daughter-in-law's walking sticks, from the help I'd received the night before from a perfect stranger to the breathtaking panorama spread out before me, for my family and friends and—yes—for the wonderful, beautiful years I had shared with my wife in building a faith-filled home in Israel, I was incredibly grateful.

I include time for meditation, not least with a focus on *Eheye* and *Modeh,* in my daily morning *Tefila* prayers. And starting each day appreciating the incredible kindnesses and gifts God has given me made the Trail—and life—so much easier and more enjoyable.

Of course for me, the gratitude for my 28-year marriage wasn't easy to achieve, marred as it was by my wife's leaving. But accepting the reality, and pushing myself to remember and appreciate all the wonderful aspects of the life we'd built together, enabled me to reach a level of forgiveness, the fourth element.

---

1   Translating such a powerful concept from the Hebrew is a fascinating challenge. Three words only, this "Name of God" is one of the ways He describes Him/Herself, a phrase He gives to Moshe to use in explaining who God is to the people of Israel. It is a deep meditation on existence, translated above as simplistically as possible. God exists (or rather is existence, actually), and the word "to be" or "is" is expressed in biblical Hebrew in the future tense—"will be" ("Eheye אהיה")—which itself includes the letters of one of the more explicit names of God, Yah! The middle word, אשר, (Asher) is a conjunction which can mean "as," "what," "that," or even "when" or "who." So this pithy phrase is really best translated as: I am/will be what/that/as I am/will be. Hence its power as a focus of our meditative experience.

Forgiveness (of those who have hurt us or are perceived to have harmed us) is a tremendously powerful idea. When hiking over an extended period, there are many things—and people, and situations—to complain about. I've mentioned the heat and the steep inclines; more consistently, I found the directions provided in "The Red Guide," the authoritative reference for Shvil Yisrael, to be frequently misleading and unhelpful. Usually, it would underestimate the time and effort required on any particular section; sometimes it was just wrong or confused. It was hard to humbly accept or appreciate, but even more to forgive, the author, while sweating in 100-degree heat retracing my steps three hours after I'd expected to arrive at my destination. And that challenge to forgive was only at the most mundane level.

Allowing ourselves to forgive others who have caused us pain, or whom we feel have hurt us, whether personally or communally, individually or nationally, is an essential part of moving ahead with our lives and developing cooperative, harmonious relationships. It's not necessary to "forgive and forget"; but even if we "forgive and remember" we must certainly forgive in order to put behind us historical grievances and reach real peace. Leo Buscaglia, who taught a class called Love at USC for years, stresses the importance of forgiving our parents, for instance, for their very humanness, in his book *Living, Loving & Learning*. And he passionately advocates moving on and exploring all the alternative paths available to us in any situation—as Gandhi did before him.

The fifth element is **purpose** (a sense of meaning, and direction). Having forgiven, and looking toward the future, the various possibilities open for exploration have to be anchored in some set of overriding principles, leading to a sense of purpose, a goal or goals that make life worth living. Clearly for me on the Shvil each day, and the trek itself, this fifth aspect was obvious. I had a concrete, physical goal—to climb to the top of that mountain, to reach the destination planned for that day, to finish the Trail itself. And just as clearly, following my divorce I had new goals to set: getting my life back on track, finding my life's partner, and various other personal aspirations relating to family, community, professional and career moves, and the like.

But on a more general level, I recognized while on the Trail—rediscovered, as it were—the spiritual, national, human goals I have pursued since being a young adult. It was no coincidence that I found walking the Land of Israel immensely uplifting, as it combined so many of my personal values in one activity. Walking in nature, in the land of my people—where our prophets and forefathers lived and worked, fought and died, and introduced the ethical monotheism of Jewish thought and tradition to the world—at a time of re-established independence, was, as my friend Moshe suggested, "one long meditation."

Hiking the Land combined my love of the outdoors with a deep emotional identification with the Zionist enterprise and a powerful aim to enhance and improve my spiritual and religious practice and commitment. And without question, I was able to recommit to my personal and national sense of mission and meaning in being part of what I like to call this "experiment" in Jewish sovereignty in the Land of Israel after two thousand years of dispersion. ("Zionism" is understood best as simply the national liberation movement of the Jewish people re-establishing our sovereignty in our ancestral homeland. It is merely the name given to the modern political movement expressing that 2000-year-long desire and intention.)

In *Man's Search for Meaning*, Victor Frankl suggests that a person can arrive at meaning in life in three ways: acting or creating, in a love relationship, and in personal growth and change. Yes! I was walking, a continuous "act"; I was moving away from one relationship and anticipating another; I was certainly growing and changing personally.

Put together, a person with a sense of purpose has more motivation to forgive, more to appreciate, more reason to be grateful, and greater incentive to accept historical and present reality, if only because he/she or they just want to get on with things, to achieve their goals. And part of this is recognizing and being willing to consider all the possible alternatives that present themselves; being able to, and wanting to, explore all the opportunities inherent in the various paths one can take in pursuing those goals.

Having an objective beyond mere survival, and embracing and exploring all the avenues available to reach it, is the key. It was true for me on the Shvil; it is true for me in my life; it can be true for others seeking solace and direction.

As a direct descendent of one of the first Jewish families to arrive in the American colonies (around 1690), I represent a wonderful, complex, somewhat unique combination of identities. I am an American-Israeli-Jew; a member of an Orthodox community observant of Jewish tradition who grew up in a staunchly Reform[2] Jewish family; a man who is an ardent advocate of the equality of women; a radical moderate politically, with both conservative and liberal opinions competing for my intellectual fealty; and an eternal optimist and idealist who is fully cognizant of the importance of realism in our present circumstances.

Having decided more than thirty years ago to throw my lot in with my people in our ancestral homeland, I've developed an intense love for Israel: the country, our people, our history, and our land (despite the frequent criticism I and many others have of various governments and their policies). All this came to play in my trek along the pathways and dirt roads, hills and valleys of the Shvil, and it informed my interactions with all those I met: Jews and Arabs, Christians and Muslims and Druze, Israelis and tourists and all others.

---

2 "Reform" Judaism is the more liberal stream of modern Judaism; "Orthodox" is the normative continuation of traditional Judaism; "Conservative" is a liberal stream adhering to more of the traditional rituals—in greatly simplified terms.

This book is not merely a travelogue—though I'll enjoy sharing some of the many inspiring experiences, amusing anecdotes, and fascinating people from the trail as launch pads to explore the personal and communal challenges we face. And it is not just another self-help book of inner/outer exploration and personal growth—though I am confident the path I discovered can be of enormous help to others facing similar challenges and decisions, based as it is on time-honored wisdom and the works of giants, from Talmudic sages to modern psychologists, teachers, and writers. Rather, these threads are woven together, relevant to and supportive of the other. As we discover the Land and strengthen the self, we can apply the five elements as related in the context of my two months on the Shvil.

I hope you enjoy the journey, and that it may offer some encouragement for journeys of your own.

"There is a difference between knowing the path and walking the path."

—Morpheus in *The Matrix*

(As quoted by my son Netanel, in his farewell note
given to me on the morning of the first day of my trek.)

A note on names: This is a true story; everything in this book took place as related here. The names of some people have been changed to protect their privacy.
A note on style: Two "voices," or styles, are used in the book:

Standard text, for description/discussion
Italics for thoughts/feelings as experienced while on the Trail

Additional items: In addition, occasionally we'll include the following:

> These highlighted boxes are *verbatim* excerpts from the journal kept on the trek.

> These outlined boxes are quotes from my weekly Saturday-night Facebook posts.

Transliterations of Hebrew terms are *italicized*; frequently-used or well-known Hebrew terms, like Shvil or Shabbat, are *not* italicized; **Hebrew place names** are *not* italicized.

THE ISRAEL NATIONAL TRAIL MAP

Chapter One

DESERT: HUMILITY

[Week One]

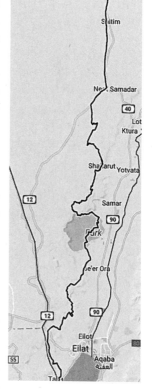

The truth is, I had no idea what I was doing. I'd been on hikes before, of course—many, in Israel, California, Italy, England, and elsewhere—but this was different. Different? This was insane.

Setting out in the drizzle of that early Sunday morning in February, walking literally from the entrance to The Orchid Reef, that lovely little hotel on the Gulf of Eilat where I'd spent Shabbat with my friend Zvi, I wasn't really aware of the magnitude of this endeavor I was embarking on. It soon became apparent.

These are the first steps I'm taking on a new journey; walking the path, as Netanel wrote me in the note he emailed this morning. Here I am, moving ahead. But toward what? This initial trail is more like a dirt truck route, with only a slight rise; yet when I look up I see the mountains (hills, really, but I have a 50-pound pack on my back) as well as the rain clouds ahead. They are stunning in the morning mist and light, brown and gray and red and hovering ahead, menacing and inviting at the same time. I'm humming to myself, partially to tamp down the growing panic and aloneness and partly in rhythm with my steps. I have to stop looking back all the time; the sun shining on the water is sparkling and lovely, and I can still see Zvi walking back to the hotel and wave to him twice . . . and suddenly I just want to turn around and head back.

What am I doing? I'm 51 years old, not 21! What kind of reaction to a divorce is this—some play on Cheryl Strayed's Wild *or Elizabeth Gilbert's* Eat Pray Love? *I'm thinking of the pool and the sun and the incredible breakfast at the Reef, and how Zvi would smile wryly if I showed up back there and just accept the decision to turn back as just another Aryehism. . . . The preparation, the equipment purchases and route planning and advice sessions with friends' kids (and kids' friends) and food/water burial were all good fun, a project of sorts. Here I am trying to use walking sticks for the first time, my shoulders already hurt after 15 minutes, I'm sweating in the 26°C (82°F) heat, striding up a dirt road I once drove along with the kids and my folks for a lark—and I really just can't believe it. I'm DOING THIS.*

So I turn around one last time and wave goodbye to the hotel, to Eilat, and to a certain extent to my former life, in many ways. I really believe I'm going to do this, I'll get through it, I'll make it. I am taking charge of my life, my destiny, and even though I realize it's all hyperbole and self-absorption, I start singing at the top of my lungs. "Oh What a Beautiful Morning" and "Zip-a-Dee-Doo-Dah" and "I've Got Six Pence" from my childhood and camp hikes, and then "I Will Survive" and finally Passenger's "Let Her Go" and I'm crying and walking faster and laughing and feeling wonderful and miserable, jubilant and pathetic all at the same time.

Then it starts to rain.

The funny thing is, I was prepared for rain. I just didn't think it would actually happen, and certainly not on my first day out (this was Eilat after all, with about two inches of rainfall annually). The business of finding a tree under which to lower the backpack to the ground (why did it seem so heavy when not on my back?), finding my rain poncho (calling myself an idiot—I saw the forecast; didn't it occur to me to put it somewhere accessible?), unraveling the raincover (how does that work?), and then getting the pack back on, was pretty exhausting. And then the drizzle stopped. Or was it the remarkable tree I was standing under? I wished I knew the name of it (Acacia; I looked it up later) but I knew from my years of reserve duty patrols along the borders with Jordan and Egypt that these unique flat-topped desert trees capture moisture and absorb it through their leaves as well as from the roots, so that most of the drizzle never reached me underneath it. Amazing.

Setting out anew, the path begins to rise into the hills—and I'm hot now. How do I balance protection from the rain and the heat at the same time? It's quite unexpected; I usually wouldn't hike in the rain. Hmmm. My first inclination is—and I say it to myself—"whatever: so you get a little wet, so what?" But on second thought: if my shirt and shorts get wet, what if they don't dry by tomorrow? Have to think this through . . .

OK, I tell myself, You paid enough for this rain jacket with air holes; keep it on to stay dry, and just accept that it's going to be hot and you'll sweat. I'm bored even thinking about it; just keep moving. I'm now on a trail; the dirt road has ended, I have to be really careful with the rocks and stones in the way—that'd be a laugh, having to call Zvi or worse, the nature authority people, to come get me with a twisted ankle or something. The loneliness, and the philosophizing, dissipates as the path rises and I focus on each step, the rhythm, breathing, sweating . . . and feeling the growing pain in my calves.

Now I'm remembering the Ibex we saw on that family trip a few years ago here; now I'm recalling another time we had a flat tire on this very dirt road, taking a "short cut" down the mountain. I'm marveling at so many shades of yellow and yellow-brown and yellow-red on the hillsides to my right and left and ahead. It's sort of weird—striking and a little frightening—how the trail seems to end ahead, and when you get there it just turns a bit into another narrow crevice between the hills. And then the path splits.

Here's the thing. It's now 3 p.m., I'm pretty hot and tired but I have energy and have gotten into a rhythm. I can hear voices up ahead of two guys I passed and who then passed me earlier—Israelis, young, fit, tanned, out for a day hike. Lord knows what they thought of me with my gray hair, American accent, ill-fitting rain poncho, rain cover, and, of course, middle-age belly and a pack clearly more than a third of my body weight. But it seems to me they took the red path to the left. I consult the Red Guide, half of which I tore out to schlep with me, and the map seems to show two relatively equivalent trails. The red path follows and then meets the road; the blue heads to the right toward Har Shlomo. I don't really want to meet the road; the blue meets up with a black trail which leads to the same night camp at the end of the red, which is where I'm headed.

The Red Guide says the views from the top of Har Shlomo are "breathtaking." That clinches it. On my first day, how can I miss that?

My eyes skimmed over, and my brain registered but didn't really compute, the phrase "קשה ותלולה" (hard and exceedingly steep). So I was blissfully unaware of what awaited me. My kids had convinced me to take the Hebrew version of the guide along with me, rather than the English. It made sense: I've lived in Israel for some 30 years, I speak the language fluently, even if reading speed is slower than in my native English. After all, this is the Israel Trail—Shvil Yisrael—not the Appalachian Trail. And anyway, the Hebrew version was up to date, a 2013 edition, whereas the English was published/updated only in 2011.

But as it turns out, it didn't make that much sense. "Fluent" can mean many things; I function perfectly in my positions in government and business, in the non-profit sector and in high-tech companies, where specific terminology is easy to learn and adopt and my conversational and even professional Hebrew is smooth and almost without accent. But having not bothered to study (or even think about) the terms related to hiking, climbing, slipping, rappelling, falling, tripping, gripping, sliding, ascending, descending or the like, maybe I was a little unprepared. Or not maybe. "Steep" was one of those words I never learned in Ulpan (Israel's famous center for accelerated acquisition of Hebrew).

I had, in fact, read through the entire English version in the preceding months as preparation, so I was familiar with the basic contours of the terrain and had planned out a rough schedule. What I hadn't really digested was (1) the true meaning of words like "difficult," or the true length of a kilometer when carrying a 50-pound (25 kilos or so) pack; and (2) that the author of the Red Guide,

Yaakov Saar, didn't necessarily have the likes of me in mind when creating his guide to the Israel Trail. He is an experienced hiker and—as I discovered when I tracked him down to complain/comment by phone much later—a somewhat haughty, grizzled Israeli about twenty years my senior. Saar apparently based his time and distance estimates on young day-trippers in top shape; not on a reasonable estimate of the abilities of 50-year-olds with 50-pound packs. (In fact, a few days later, a "Trail Angel" [to be described] told me that 22-year-old veterans from crack combat units have arrived at his doorstep "on their knees and in tears" having tried to follow the book's instructions. That made me feel a bit better.)

Heading up to the right, along the blue trail, I turn into an ever-narrowing canyon, and I can see ahead of me a path winding a few meters up the hill among the rocks. Looking up at the sky I see only a few clouds; it's still hot and the rain has stopped, so I rest a bit at the edge of a wall in a slice of shade, and listen to bird calls I can't identify from somewhere on the left. Is there shade over there, and trees? Maybe water? I'm not sure but can't be bothered to look at my map; having made the decision to go this route, I'd better start out. Packing away the rain cover, I hoist the bag on my back (how can it be getting heavier if I'm drinking the water I'm carrying?) and get a move on.

Almost immediately I realize something's different. Every step now takes an effort—because it's an ascending trail, I'm well into my sixth hour, and I'm completely out of shape, as my various muscles (back, shoulders, arms, buttocks, thighs, calves, ankles, feet . . .) remind me each time I move them. Yes, I feel them all, separately and together; depending on my movement, I can actually identify each one straining against the pull of gravity. I wonder: is this what a weight lifter feels when working on a particular set?

Now I'm scrambling to keep my balance and not fall (backwards too!) as I pull myself up and over huge boulders; looking up I really can't believe the sight. The blue trail markings are clear and terrifying: up, up, and more up, on an incline of stone and dirt and huge rocks resembling more a Matterhorn on the moon than a pleasant ascent like I used to climb as a kid in the hills of the San Francisco Bay area. What am I doing here? Am I insane?!?

Okay—I can do this. Map says it's only two or three kilometers or so to the campsite—that can't take more than an hour, and it's not all an ascent. . . . So I keep going, and in continuing, I repeat to myself the childlike mantra that one step at a time, one pull up at a step, I can do, each one a single effort, which is manageable. And I do it, again and again and again. I'm sweating so much it could be raining; I broke a fingernail literally trying to hang on to a jagged rock and prevent myself from falling; but I fell in the end, and twice more. And finally, as the light begins to fade with the sun hiding behind a peak, I reach the meeting point of the blue and black paths.

I had heard of Har Shlomo a few times; in fact, I have seen photos from a recent trip Nati (as I sometimes call my son Netanel) took with his then-girlfriend now-wife, Tehila. Truly the views from the top are magnificent (the Red Guide doesn't lie). I was pretty committed to climb up, and I decided to leave my backpack on the ground at the trail crossing since I'd have to return to get on the trail to the night camp, which I thought was clever, figuring this would be a slightly difficult but brief 40-minute ascent to the summit to enjoy the view.

It was at this point, as I began to climb hand-over-heel up the face of the black rock to the next trail marker, that I started to think a bit. I had been so focused on the climb, the pack, the weight, the heat, the pain, that I hadn't given any real thought to the wider picture. What time was it? How much left to go? If I misread the map on the way up, not realizing how steep and difficult it was, might I have missed something regarding the "easy" and flat last leg to the night camp? When is sunset anyway? And how important is the view of the Gulf of Eilat, however "breathtaking," compared to arriving at the campsite to set up while it's still light, let alone avoiding hiking in the dark?

Pulling back; taking stock; re-thinking; looking back and looking ahead. These were the processes I hadn't really pursued in the previous four hours, and I realized at that point how crucial a mistake it would be just to push ahead. I literally sat down—I could see the top of the mountain, some 150 meters up— and spent about 30 seconds calculating. I had to accept it: the responsible thing, the mature thing, the rational thing, was to forget the view and go back to get moving along the new trail to the campsite. It wasn't easy: I had to give up on the view and take the teasing I'd surely get from Netanel and Tehila and the comments from others. And more, I had to accept the fact that I had to leave the trail I'd chosen and known and conquered with some effort, to embark on a new, unknown trail.

And thank God I did.

Having clambered down from the ladder-like rock face of the peak, a bit scraped and battered, I stand at the trail crossing and shoulder my pack with some reluctance. Down to my left—unthinkable!—is the steep climb I'd done just to get up to this point; to my right that trail continues down and north to points unknown. Don't look at the map to see if maybe it ends somewhere near the road to Eilat and civilization. Don't! I look; it does; I hesitate.

In front of me is the trail I'm to take—and it starts, I realize dejectedly, with another sheer hand-over-heel climb up a jagged rock face. Déjà vu all over again. But I feel a sense of purpose and strength; I took the mature decision to set out for camp and relinquish the desire for the great view—having made the impetuous choice to come this way in the first place—and know from the map that this last section is relatively flat and easy.

Except it's not.

Forty-five minutes later, I sit on the ground in despair. I'm actually crying. Not quite "sitting"; crouching, precariously, with my pack still on, leaning against the rock wall of this mountain (Har Yehoram), looking straight down to the rocks about

6 meters, or 20 feet, below me. After the initial few hundred meters of intense boulder-navigation and climbing up and down the large rocks on the path linking Har Shlomo and Har Yehoram, I find myself walking a path winding along the side of the mountain—and it becomes narrower and narrower. I see it continuing on ahead—what, is this a goat path? A mouse trail? Indeed, the map is correct: it is relatively flat. But my God! I can't keep my balance, and one step just a few centimeters to the left and I'll fall into this crevice and break my neck!

I keep saying to myself: you are not the only person to ever have done this, others have passed here before you. This is a marked trail, schoolchildren from Eilat probably walk here. If something were to happen, you have a cell phone. But then I keep thinking that few do this with a heavy pack, or at 50, or in the late afternoon, or after a rain, or alone, or . . . and I'm really panicking. I can't take another step—and even as I crouch down I recognize what a cliché that is. But I just can't.

So I start to fantasize: I'm on the cell phone with Netanel, asking him to call in 669 (the air rescue unit); I'm calling Zvi to come find me; I'm walking back to the trail crossing, which at least is on a level part of the mountain, and setting up my tent there for the night. I have just enough water; I can always pick up what I buried at the night camp when I get there in the morning. And in the morning all this will look different—brighter, easier, more passable.

And then it hits me: Aryeh, you are here. You are alone. This is your reality and, no, in the morning the only difference would be you'll be tired and frustrated, disappointed, and hundreds of meters back from where you are now. It's not dark YET. This path is your path; you know this.

Netanel's note comes back to me: there is a difference between knowing the path and walking the path. Frankl is right, it's all a question of attitude. Forget the fantasizing as you forget the overdramatizing of the dangers and the narrowness of the path and sharpness of the rocks. It is what it is, as Nati's friend Zachy said once, and your "is" is here and now and ahead. Deal with it; get to it.

So I get up and look ahead. Clearly, I was right: I really do have to be careful. But I can do this; and I start, slowly, keeping my weight to my right, with my hand on the rock face and walking sticks dragging and bouncing from my left hand as they hang over the edge . . . and I make it, some 500 meters or so, wow, to a small pass where the trail widens and I collapse on the ground, literally, a bundle of nerves and exhilarated emotion. I did it!

There's an amazing thing about our ability as humans to reinterpret, or reassess, events in our past. In the immediate aftermath of this traumatic first day out on the Trail, and then months after I'd completed the trek, my perceptions of the danger and difficulty, of the heat and discomfort and weight and—yes—despair, were overcome with the excitement and feeling of accomplishment of getting past that harsh ascent and treacherous mountain-precipice path. It wasn't merely the physical act of conquering the mountain (Mountain? Serious hikers, please refrain from chuckling, but from sea level to 700 meters is a bit more than a hill.), nor even the psychological victory of overcoming my terror. It was, I've come to realize, an emotional, almost spiritual recognition of my ability to persevere, and of my capacity to focus on a goal, find a reasonable path, ignore or subdue my fear of failure or injury or of the unknown, and move forward. And this all on the first day out.

It's not that I didn't still hurt from the effort—my muscles wouldn't let me forget. And later, it's not that I didn't remember the pain. But the hardship seemed to fade in importance, both immediately following, and then as time passed. The sense of triumph grew and became dominant. At the time, and then periodically through the trip and following it, this gave me pause: what is it about the human psyche that allows us—in fact encourages us and almost forces us—to focus on the positive and diminish the negative? And how can we harness this, purposefully, to help us rise above our personal or societal challenges? Then, and now, it reminded me of all the stories of childbirth I've heard (as a man and a father)—"It was a difficult labor . . . but look at this beautiful child!" Without the latter emotion overcoming the former painful experience, would any woman agree to give birth (or to have another child after the first)? How does this work, and is there a way we can cognitively train ourselves to use this capacity to overcome hardship, address problems, change our lives? I wondered about this continually through and after the most challenging days of my trek.

From here, I can see a long, flat path along the ridge—not easy but certainly easier than it's been up to this point. About twenty minutes along this path I come across a small plaque, and I wish my cousin Tamar (a PhD in geography) is with me (remember to message her). It says this is a unique place on the face of the earth. I'm standing at a point where the granite rock on my right, and the sedimentary layer of earth to my left, emerged some 500 million years apart, and apparently, the juxtaposition of the two in one location is extraordinary. I feel privileged, and rather small, to just stand there for a few moments. It's tremendously humbling to realize how brief our stay on this planet is, how insignificant a part we play in the vast symphony of the history of the cosmos. It kind of puts my problems in perspective.

A few steps later I arrive at an unexpected sight: a panoramic view looking north to the Arava, east to the hills of Moav/Jordan, and south to the Gulf of Eilat. So perhaps I missed what Saar says "some consider . . . the best panorama in Israel" at Har Shlomo—but this is incredible! And more so in the gentle light of the fading day. And most so in the afterglow of the feeling of achievement I still can't (and don't want to) shake. This is Har Yehoram, which means I'm close to the night camp. I take another break here too, appreciating the view and the sunset, though I'm increasingly aware that I mustn't pause too long, having lost all confidence in my map-reading abilities (and in the Red Guide's time and distance estimates). I don't want to tear myself away: I'm somewhat overcome with awe and gratitude for the beauty, the silence, the majesty of the mountain, the sunset, the magnificent vista and in many ways the entire day. I wish I had someone to share it with. But I'm glad I'm here alone too. Confused, yes; emotional, certainly; ready to get to the campsite—definitely.

That's really the end of my first day on the Trail; the mundane aspects of arriving at the night camp, digging up the water and treats I'd planted a few days prior, setting up my tent, etc. need little description. Except perhaps that it took some 20 minutes in the fading light to set the tent up—why didn't I practice this at least once after buying it? By day three I had it down to 4 minutes. . . . And I suppose I should explain the term "night camp." The campgrounds of my childhood in the Sierras, and the organized campsites in Israel too, usually have running water or at least a stream nearby, field toilets (at a minimum), and sometimes even electric outlets or a mini-store. On the Trail, a square of dry dirt is demarcated by a few stones or perhaps a simple wood fence on one side. Sometimes a rusty old sign warns you not to sleep outside its perimeter. (The surrounding area often serves not only as a nature reserve . . . but as a tank training field for the IDF [Israel Defense Forces] tank corps.)

I was so tired and beat that I couldn't bother to cook the quinoa or boil water for tea. In fact, I was so devoid of energy (and it was cold, and starting to drizzle again) that I could barely be bothered to leave the tent. (Note to other campers: kneeling at the entrance of your tent to urinate is not the best of ideas, particularly in a slight breeze and with the ground sloping gently toward you. . . .)

In my tent, as the rain started again (and how grateful I was for the tent, however heavy; I had considered not schlepping it!), I wrote in my journal: "Two lessons learned: (1) do not blindly follow the Red Guide; (2) respect elevation markings on the map. It was terrifying—what am I, a mountain goat?"

Even though I was dead tired, and aching, I reflected on the experiences of the day: "The silence is a bit overwhelming, oppressive even, heavy—but then liberating, it becomes a quiet solitude, breathing . . ."

Regarding the ascent and then the perilous mountainside "goat-trail," I finished my journal entry with a bit of a celebration.

Looking later over my journal entries, I'm taken by how much I experienced and felt in that first day. "What the hell were you thinking" I wrote, reflecting on the choice of the steep trail to Har Shlomo. But on the other hand, I had consulted with the Nature Authority that morning and heeded their advice not to take an alternative route out of Eilat with steep granite slabs which were dangerously slippery in the rain. "Providence!" I wrote that night. "God sent the rain to make me take the "easier" Nachal Shlomo trail . . . or so I choose to believe. The rain prevented me from attempting the [more] difficult route."

The following morning—day two on the Trail, though it already felt like so much more—I set out in rising heat to descend from the heights of the Eilat Mountains through the Shechoret Canyon. Knees, feet, back, and shoulders were all still stiff and aching from the previous day's exertions. This clearly wasn't going to be easy.

It's hot, even at 7 a.m. as I pack up my tent. The oatmeal I cooked and coffee I drank with it was like a five-star breakfast—I'm so proud of myself for packing it, buying the one-person mini gas and pot and all, and bringing Splenda with me too! *Thus fortified, I'm now prancing (lurching) downhill from Har Yehoram, and the hills are again changing color. From the light browns of Eilat's hills (and then dark browns and even blacks and grays of Har Shlomo and Yehoram), the descent brings me into a wide expanse of peaks in various hues of yellow and light brown, almost golden in the morning light. And heat. I hope I have enough water—have I really screwed up here? I was too lazy, and anxious to get to Eilat on Friday afternoon before the onset of Shabbat, to bury water at the night camp in Shechoret. I might have to walk an extra 2 kilometers each way at the end of the day to find water. Sheesh, what a thought.*

Hours later, I'm still going downhill. "Hill" is a euphemism: First, this is a huge mountain (at least from the perspective of a tired and battered hiker with pack). Second, it's hard going on the knees, in the heat, with no real idea whether my estimates of time and distance are any more on target than they were yesterday. And third, the descent includes periodic sliding, jumping, and slipping down giant granite slabs in the river bed which is the route.

At one point I can't make it through a crevice going down a 10-meter cliffside. I can see the markings, so clearly this is the way. I can squeeze through, but not with my pack on. The pack is too heavy to carry in front of me or behind. I take it off to consider, drink a few gulps of water, eat one of my truly disgusting, sickly sweet protein bars—it's only the second day and I am already SICK of them—and look over the side of the cliff.

And it comes to me—I have the string Netanel insisted I take with me from his days in his combat unit in the army! Gratitude again fills me up almost to tears: the little things, these, which are so big when they happen. I quickly riffle through the stuff in the top compartment of the pack (which I've dubbed the miscellaneous section, holding an assortment of matches, bandaids, Wet Ones, a compass, bandana, journal, maps, hair clips, gum, toilet paper, my siddur [prayer book] and more) and find both the strong black string and a few straps I had thrown in at the last moment in case. Tying them together, along with a doubled-up set of shoelaces, I attach it all to the top clip of the backpack and slowly let it down over the side of the cliff.

What a brilliant idea—I'm a genius! Except I'm holding it with my arm extended . . . and it reaches to about 3 meters above the ground. Should I let go? What might break (a water bottle? The Camelback itself inside the pack? Flashlight?) . . . and what if the pack itself rips? Maybe I can swing it over there to rest on the rock jutting out a bit above the bottom . . . holy crap it's too heavy. I'm dropping it. I can't hold it! . . . It falls almost in slow motion, bounces against the rock I'd tried to steer it toward at the last minute, teeters and falls head first into the next rock below.

I'm in a complete panic now. Doesn't sound like anything broke but I can't be sure, and I'm suddenly and profoundly aware how alone, isolated, vulnerable, and STUPID I am to do something like that without thinking. I scramble down the cliff, into and out of the crevice . . . and find myself looking UP at my pack, stuck about a meter above my head, just out of reach, with no visible means of access. And there's something leaking from it, slowly, down the sandy rock face.

Suffice to say I managed to find a foothold, knocked the bag off balance, didn't stop its fall to the ground, as it was too heavy, found no tears or breaks, and discovered the leak was only from a small water bottle with a top that had simply popped off. So I was soon back on track and in the swing of the rhythm of my steps on a gentle sloping descent following the stream bed. I started to sing—what a marvel the mind is, all panic and self-critique gone, feeling on top of the world—and kept up a resounding chorus of "Zip-a-dee-doo-dah," must have been at least twenty minutes. The rest of the day, including sliding down a few more dry waterfalls, was glorious. At one point I found myself at a 120-degree bend in the trail/river: behind me was a narrow channel in gold and blonde sand, ahead of me another canyon in shades of light brown, and to my sharp left, with a beckoning tri-colored Shvil marking, was a phenomenal path bracketed by walls with a combination of almost jewelry-like sparkling onyx and dark jade-colored rock.

I was all alone; but feeling content, peaceful, and full of amazement to find myself in this almost monastic quietude. I was in a cathedral of nature, with the sun low enough to be almost cool but not so low as to worry me that it might get dark soon. I stopped, lowered my pack, and took stock. Here's a good place to *daven mincha*, I thought—to pray the afternoon service, which, to be honest, was not necessarily my everyday practice. (At my age I've stopped pretending that I—or any Jew for that matter— fully practice all the commandments required by our tradition. I'm a spiritual person and do my best to follow as many as I can at any given time.)

Shechoret Canyon

Breaking camp up on Har Yehoram, I had been both anxious to get started with the heat increasing and distracted by traffic on the nearby road and school groups tramping through on their (so easy from here!) day hikes. So I had said my prayers that morning in something of a hurry—and not without some hesitation and self-questioning about lugging my *Tallit* and *Tefillin*[3] with me to add to my weight. (Weight, yes; and "weight" too, with great religious and personal

---

3 *Tallit* is a traditional "prayer shawl," the four-cornered garment with *Tzitzit*, the ritual fringes mandated in the Torah; *Tefillin*, or phylacteries, are the small leather boxes placed on the forehead and wrapped around the arm with leather straps commanded in Exodus and Deuteronomy. Both serve as "signs" and reminders of God's commandments, and of the Exodus of the Children of Israel from Egypt. *Tefila* means "prayer."

significance, important enough for me to do so without really thinking about it, as I do even when traveling light on my business trips abroad. I carried my [ex-]father-in-law's prayer shawl, smaller and lighter than my usual one, and the phylacteries I've used since becoming more observant some 30 years ago.)

But there in Shechoret Canyon, I was blissfully away from all distraction. I was—literally—at one with nature. And not a sort of nature I was used to, growing up in California and loving the details and joys of the coastal range, not to mention living the last thirty years in the green center of Israel. This was a nature which was somehow more serene, less busy . . . soundless. As I started my *tefila,* the prayers began to speak to me in ways I hadn't experienced in some time. "Great, Valiant and Awesome God . . ." who "makes the wind blow and brings down the rain"; "give me understanding, knowledge and enlightenment"; "see our suffering, fight our battles, as you are a mighty redeemer"; "bless our year as the good years" became more than mere phrases recited often by rote.

I won't say I felt in the presence of God. Not least as I've always felt that, in some ways. In other ways, I've never truly felt it. How can one? But there was certainly a poignancy to the combination of aloneness and one-ness with all that is, in that canyon halfway down the mountain. What I began to feel was a sense of kinship with all things, however cliché or bombastic that may sound.

I was developing a certain שלווה (*shalva,* tranquility), as the peace of the desert settled around me. It's hard to describe or perhaps understand from this remove. The intensity of that first day was balanced by the relative relief of the descent (however hard at times) on the second day, and then challenged by another difficult ascent up Mt. Shechoret. Together, these initial 36 hours combined to create and set the tone for the rest of my three weeks in the desert.

There was something powerful about the aloneness, and I began to reflect on the word, and the concept. Aloneness is not necessarily negative. In an eastern and Sufi teaching I recalled learning at Berkeley, aloneness is also, or can be, All-One-Ness. Almost meditatively, as I listened to my boots crunching the stones and sand under foot, I repeated that mantra—we are all one, I am not alone if I am all-one or part of the All and the One. Somehow this engendered a growing sense of humility, of recognition that my existence is caught up in the much larger existence of the universe. It made me pause, but did not depress me; rather, it bolstered my confidence, my feeling of connection with God and my people, my land and my country . . . and my world. *My* world, *my* people, *my* land, *my* Trail—however small a part I play, I am part of the larger whole.

Though I am more than just me, I continue to feel the smallness of self. Surrounded by majestic, stark, frightening, magnificent mountains, I am tiny. I begin to think about my place in the long march of geological and biological creation: I am nothing, not even a recognizable speck of dust.

Especially as I look up to the top of this mountain. The Red Guide lists the descent and ascent through canyon and Har Shechoret and then the ascent up Maale Amram and hike along Nachal Racham as a one-day section. Seriously? I had already decided to split it up into two days but as I'm now climbing up the foot of Har Shechoret I'm asking myself can they be for real? Who did they plan these sections for? Day-trippers in tip-top shape, clearly. I'm feeling fed up; I didn't come looking for a challenge-course, or a survival-in-the-wilderness experience. I want to feel the lay of the land, yes, but not so strongly that it hurts! And this hurts. Everywhere. I'm almost incapable of enjoying the views (which are, if I'm willing to admit it, stunning), struggling up the steeper and steeper side of this next mountain, clambering over rocks bigger than the ones yesterday on Har Shlomo. It's terrifying. And I'm asking, for the twentieth time at least, what am I doing here? Why am I doing this?

At the top, after a rest (and the rush of elation accompanies my arrival, something I'm beginning now to recognize and, if not anticipate, at least enjoy when it comes), I begin to appreciate an answer of sorts. I am here because I choose to be; I am doing this because it is what I want to do. It's funny—it's been a day and half (only! And yet it feels like an eternity) and I guess due to the intensity of the experiences and the concentrated focus on myself, my thoughts, my feelings, my very steps, I'm already in a different place mentally, emotionally, and spiritually than I was when embarking yesterday morning. The silence is so very powerful; the aloneness so consuming, and so moving, and so thought-provoking. I listen carefully as I walk—the scrape of my steps on the stones and the knock and echo of the walking sticks; the rustle of wind through the canyon or in the occasional bush and tree; the calls of birds I wish I could identify.

As I near the end of this, my second day in the desert, I enter a new and unfamiliar phase of working through my pain and exhaustion, the heat and tedium. I try to embrace it, and to embrace my part in it, and this begins to give me both strength and pleasure. I'm noticing how awareness of time, and of space, changes, not only with this humility but with familiarity with the rhythm of hiking. I listen almost meditatively to my footsteps, and it seems like the time it takes to walk a kilometer, or the feeling of the distance itself, changes according to many factors: mood, weather, thought processes, terrain, vistas, wildlife and more. But mostly it's the overarching silence that plays tricks with your perception of time and space. I bet astronauts experience something like this; I should look it up.

This smallness I feel is exhilarating. I may be a tiny speck but I am part of something larger, immense, beautiful—the vast stretch of life and living.

I emerge from the last part of this exquisite shimmering narrow winding rocky canyon into a sandy flat creek bed opening into a broad expanse before me, and begin to think of (and look for) a place to camp for the night. I realize I need water. I really can't face the idea of that extra 2km to and from the small community mentioned in the Red Guide; sun is going down also.

But what's that I hear? Music? About a half-kilometer ahead at the Shechoret Canyon night camp area, I see a group, a truck, a bus . . . and keep walking (stumbling a little) toward it. Following the riverbed as it slopes gently down to the Arava/Jordan Valley, when I look up I can see, and even enjoy, the hills of Ammon/Moav/

Jordan in the distance. Approaching and passing through the group, it's clearly a school overnight outing, done the typical Israeli way: a hired company is setting up tables, stoves, music speakers, lights, etc. The teens gather in small groups near their tents and wrestle or joke loudly, like teens across the world, to impress the others around them. And they have water! Yes! I approach one of the counselors, a twenty-something young man with dreadlocks and, explaining that I'm hiking the Shvil, ask if I can have/use some water. Omer is his name, and he's sweet in his enthusiastic agreement.

I'm too exhausted to relate much to the teens, though normally I would; I dunk my head under the tap of the water tank trailing behind their van, fill up my bottles and Camelback, and trudge back up the riverbed in the growing dusk. So tired I can't really see straight, with my feet and legs hurting even more than they did yesterday (surprise?), I realize I'm actually in a bind here. I don't want to spend the night listening to teens partying; but it's against Nature Authority regulations to camp outside a designated night-camp.

That didn't take too long to decide, though; having passed 50 I'm not too scared of the authorities. After a little more than a kilometer, I can't hear or see anyone anymore; and at this point my fatigue really dictates my next moves. I just plonk my bag down in the darkness next to a tree right by the trail, and begin to set my tent up actually on the path itself, as it's the only flat place around. I fall asleep quickly after reviewing maps for tomorrow and sorting food for supper and breakfast. This time I remember to relieve myself before getting into the tent for the night.

It's a strange thing to realize: it takes almost as much time to relate the events of each day as it did to experience them. (It takes longer to write it, that's for sure.) Looking over the above, I'm aware that we've only related the first two days, and yet some of the themes of the entire journey have already been established, from humility to acceptance to appreciation, and so much has already been accomplished and felt, experienced and lived.

And looking back, this next day, my third of the trek, was perhaps a watershed. It was long and tiring; it included a steep ascent up Maale Amram and a lengthy grind along the wide and majestic Nachal Racham riverbed (following a picturesque descent, which included clambering down two dry waterfalls). It was glorious and beautiful and hot and interminable and silent and exhausting

Shechoret Canyon

and exhilarating . . . and it just was. That's why it was a watershed. I had passed through the first two days of "beginning"—asking myself why I'm doing this and whether I could or should or would carry on—and was simply continuing. I was DOING THIS. I started to feel that at the top of Har Shekhoret, looking out across an expanse of desert hills and mountains behind and in front of me, seemingly never-ending; I took a video (Video 1), and just said "I guess I go that way." And kept on.

Walking that third day along the river bed of Racham, where for the first time I had before me and behind me an expanse of flatland as far as the eye could see, I was accompanied by a hawk of some sort for about an hour or so. I watched as it glided and circled, and somehow I connected its search with mine, its journey with mine, its existence with mine. It was at that moment that I understood I could and would make it to the end of the Shvil. Somehow I just knew that I had it in me to complete the journey.

I've planned the day pretty well; having divided the one-day absurdity described in the Guide into two, I'm now nearing the end of a protracted stretch of Nachal Racham, with the hills of Timna already in sight. I'm tired (what's new), hot (same), haven't showered in three days (it's Tuesday) and so I'm glad to see the trail markings pointing to Be'er Ora, a small community where I think I can stay with a Trail Angel and get water. I'm just a little perturbed that the path goes up a small hill—after three hard ascents in three days (and the last one, Maale Amram, the most difficult yet), I'm a bit deflated by the prospect of even this small incline. Discovering that Be'er Ora is some 2 kilometers off the trail doesn't help either.

I hesitate: might I have enough water? Just camp out here under this tree, save myself the 4 kilometers there and back, and continue on in the morning? Maybe someone or a group will come by and I can bum some water off them? Yesterday worked out pretty well that way . . .

I guess in my old age, and with the wisdom that comes from (all of) three days on the Trail, I've become a responsible adult. I set out up the hill toward Be'er Ora.

It turns out I underestimated again the size and length of the hill, darn it; I'm so tired and all my muscles ache. Keep going. Finally I arrive at the back gate of the small community, where there's a sign with a phone number. Zohar (his name, which means "incandescent," "radiant") says to walk around to the main entrance. Doesn't he understand what he's asking? It's at least another two kilometers to circle around the perimeter fence and then walk into the community from the main entrance! I've got 50 pounds on my back for crying out loud and have been hiking all day. I seriously can't believe he can't or won't come out to unlock the back gate. After rejecting the idea of climbing over (just too tired to figure out how to get the pack over; otherwise I would have), I simply start to trudge along the fence. Forty minutes later, I arrive at Zohar's . . .

Truth is, I now understand why he didn't come to open the gate. A resident of the community and something of a (radiant?) character, a guide and nature/hiking enthusiast, just in the 20 minutes I spend with him he gets four calls asking to open the gate (and he's just a volunteer). He hosts groups at their home for a small fee; unfortunately, tonight he has "no room" since there's a school group coming. I use his sink in the garage to wash my hands and face (and dunk my head under the tap too for good measure), fill up my water bottles and the Camelback and gratefully accept his offer to drive me to the back gate. I have no shame: it's a small relief. Zohar unlocks the back gate and wishes me well. It's a nice community, built along ecological principles, and as my first contact with real civilization in three days is a welcome entry point back into the "real world"; but I'm actually relieved not to be staying with them, and to return to the solitude of the desert.

Tired and filthy, I set up camp near a small grove of trees in a "zula" Zohar told me about (where the community's teens sometimes hang out). I'm cold but happy to sit by the fire and write for the first time since Sunday night; so very strange how time is so malleable, so confusing—much has occurred but it's still only two days later, and only three since I set out. Just uncanny. And now I have this sense of purpose, renewed or rather reinforced; not sure why but I've got to a place inside where I am certain—CERTAIN—that not only am I going to finish this, not only that this is the right thing for me, but that this is good for me, good for my soul, good for my life.

Wednesday morning I slept a bit late because I expected the walk to and through Timna would be (relatively) less difficult than those first three days ("late" meaning staying on the hard ground in the cold tent a few extra minutes and getting up about 6:45 a.m.). It was a real treat having the fire the night before and just for fun—didn't really need the warmth—I re-kindled it and heated the water for my coffee and oatmeal over it. Packing everything away, I couldn't find the tent bag. I looked everywhere, thinking perhaps the wind had blown it away—until out of the corner of my eye I spied a flash of bright orange . . . on the edge of the fire ring.

Sure enough: it had blown into the fire just minutes before, as my back was turned while I focused on the packing. It was just gone. That was a good, and fortunately almost painless, way for me to learn three lessons: Be careful with fire. Weigh things down against the wind. You don't really need a sack to wrap things with—it's just stuff.

With that in mind—in fact using that small setback as a bit of an uplifting reminder to take things as they come—I walked back to the trail to start my fourth day, and headed for Timna national park. Looking at the map—and learning from Har Shlomo, Har Shechoret, and Har Amram to pay attention to mountain elevations!—I decided to take a "long"-cut. Rather than climbing back up and then down to the point where I left the Shvil, I could go around the small hill on a longer but flatter dirt road, to meet up with the Trail on the other side.

What I met was a new friend.

I am so incredibly brilliant! Yes, I skipped a few hundred meters of the Trail, but avoiding that incline and descent just made my morning. The sun is shining but not too hot—just took off my fleece—and I can see Mt. Timna in the distance. It feels great to be back in the field. Though I appreciated some aspects of seeing Zohar and using his faucet, I had this kind of "cheating" sense last night and I'm glad to be heading back into the desert. And proving both my map skills and cleverness has brightened my mood further.

I see ahead of me, as I round the corner of a small rise, a little yellow minibus that I think I remember from Shechoret—and outside it two guys, one older and one younger, whom I said hi to a few days ago. Not too friendly, as I recall, kind of gruff Israelis. Then again, it was at the end of the day and I wasn't the most social person on the planet either at that point. Anyway—walking right past them, at least I can nod and say good morning.

"Boker Tov!" I say. "Good morning!" "Boker Or," says the older fellow. "Morning Light," a rather arcane response which only previous generations even learned, let alone use. I keep striding as I come alongside them, not unfriendly but not planning to engage them in conversation. But that's when the younger man asks me whether I'm heading to Timna; I stop and reply that yes, and beyond, to the night camp north of the park. He says, "So am I! Let's walk together. . . ." Without really thinking about it—yes, I like my solitude, but hey, here's a chance for a slightly new experience, and anyway the first stage is only a couple of hours to the park entrance and the lake there where I plan to stop to rest . . . all of which runs through my mind in less than a millisecond—I just smile and say, "Sure!" Consulting his map, we agree to head across a sandy river bed to meet the Trail a few meters away; he says goodbye to the older man and we start to move out.

We introduced ourselves while walking ahead; Yaron was about 43 or so and it turned out that the other fellow was his father, accompanying him on some of his hike. It was a great arrangement: Yaron walked with a day-pack and his dad met him at the end of the day with food, water, the tent (sometimes already set up) and more. His dad, an avid biker who apparently did much of the Israel Trail by bicycle some years ago, sometimes met him for lunch midway if there was a connecting trail he could find. Our initial few moments set a wonderful pattern for the next two days—and a foundation for an enduring friendship.

At turns talkative and taciturn, with a rather wicked sense of humor and irony, Yaron was a perfect hiking partner. He's one of those amazing and not-so-rare Israelis (we spoke in Hebrew of course) who are not particularly observant religiously but who have a keen interest in and knowledge of Jewish sources, as well as a deep attachment to the Jewish people and the Land of Israel. In our first minutes he impressed me with the names of a few desert plants as well as an understanding of which ones are edible and which poisonous. (After hearing him describe the similarity between a certain poisonous berry and its edible lookalike, and his story of a school group taken to the hospital for eating the wrong one, it took something of a leap of faith for me to pop a little fruit nut he took off the bush next to where we stood to rest at one point.)

We alternated between conversation and companionable silence, and between walking together and slightly apart. It was fascinating to me to walk behind him for a while; though we were different physically, I found looking at him to be akin to a sort of out-of-body experience, realizing that what I saw was what someone following me would see: the pack, the dust, the strides, the stumbling, the weight and heat, the sticks swishing back and forth. It was like watching myself, and not.

Those first two hours were pleasant, and they passed more quickly than the seven kilometers or so would have alone. I learned that Yaron had recently left a senior management position in a high-tech company and was contemplating his next steps in life; he heard a bit of my story, though in no real detail. It was non-threatening, enough to create a connection but not so much as to be invasive; there was something strangely intimate in the intense and private exchanges we had while in the middle of a vast desert landscape. We were alone but not alone; and I felt, personally, a comfortable companionship that didn't compromise my aloneness.

On arrival at the southern park entrance we discovered that while I planned to rest, eat, and get organized (and swim or shower) at the artificial lake and campground, Yaron planned to push on to climb Mt. Timna. Coincidentally, but perfectly, that suited me fine; I had already decided I didn't need that challenge and was happy to be on my own again. Proud of my morning skirting around the hill by Be'er Ora, I had found a trail on the map around the bottom of Mount Timna, which would lead me to the night camp with less effort—or so I thought.

Yaron wants to climb Mt. Timna; I can't be bothered. With Mt. Amram behind me and "the Milchan" ahead, I'm okay with an easier day today. When we walk into the park, I mention to him the life-size model of the Mishkan, the ancient Tabernacle of the Israelites which accompanied them through their desert wanderings, which is right up ahead next to the lake, and he says he's never seen it. So we walk over, ease our packs off (Okay—crash them to the ground, with enough noise accompanied by moans and sighs to bring the attendant over), and peek in. I explain (in English— turns out the attendants are visiting Christian Americans) a little about the Israel Trail, Yaron and me, and ask sweetly whether we might take a quick walk inside. Though they usually charge, he lets us in.

I've been before, but this time I find it strangely moving. It's a walk-through facsimile of the Tabernacle. It includes well-constructed models of the altar, the copper water basin, the Tent of Meeting, and even the innermost sanctum of the Holy-of-Holies with the Ark of the Covenant containing the tablets of the Ten Commandments surmounted by the two gold Cherubim (angels) facing each other with their wings stretched out one toward the other, almost touching. It's all pretend; it's all plastic and metal and cloth and imported wood, not the original leather and copper, gold and sheepskin; and of course it's just a tourist attraction. But it's life-sized—we walk in past the altar, take in the attention to detail in the colors of the outer perimeter skin (cloth) wall and posts, and enter the Tent of Meeting, where two mannequins stand with copper trumpets and (real) ram horns to call the nation to assembly—and I feel a tug of recognition, of affinity, of meaning.

Yaron feels it too. We are two Israelites walking through the desert; this is our home and our focus, these are our national symbols and ancestral inheritance. It probably means more to us than to that Christian group—no offense intended. It means more to us than the majestic mountains and desert riverbeds and all the flowers we've been identifying and discussing. We don't discuss it—perhaps because we'd both be embarrassed to admit we even think to make the comparison—but I know we're both thinking to ourselves how we're walking across the desert, as children of Israel. It makes the act of joining together on this day all the more poignant.

And then, with a casual wave and informal Israeli banter we part ways, sure in the knowledge we'll meet up again—so fitting for the Israel Trail.

Near the Tabernacle reproduction is the Timna Lake and campground, and a rustic and surprisingly well-stocked food-and-trinkets visitors shop. Arriving there I felt as a shipwrecked sailor reaching landfall in Manhattan might feel: civilization! Espresso! Salad! Ice cream! And . . . it was all kosher too. It was paradise. Like a kid in a chocolate shop, I grabbed a huge bowl of minestrone soup, a handful of fresh pita bread, a wide plate of hummus topped with olive oil and Zatar (the marvelous Israeli hyssop-and-sesame seed herbal mix that I love), a salad of fresh lettuce and tomato such as I hadn't seen in the lifetime I'd lived in the past four days—and went to sit down.

Got a few funny looks. I did wonder at one point: was it the obviously filthy hiking clothes? The unshaven face? The gray/whiteness of the hair more likely, combined with the backpack, Israeli flag, walking sticks, maps, and enough food for three people scattered all around me. I know it wasn't the smell—I think I know that—though just to be sure, I sat far away in a corner of my own, where I could spread out. Seems that word got around that an old guy was walking Shvil Yisrael; I could see people pointing and talking, and a few approached me to ask questions.

The young staff in the café and shop were incredibly helpful; "supportive" even. They gave me extra food and drinks, brought stuff to me (it's not a table-service spot), and wanted to know more and more about the trek. Then I asked about showers, knowing there were some in the campground. After a few minutes of consultations between them and a call apparently to a manager—or even a manager's manager it seems—they came and told me they'd open up the shower building specially for me. (I had thought to just jump in the lake, though it didn't look too clean.)

As any hiker—or soldier, or student at exam time—knows, three or four days without a shower, not least when hiking twenty or more kilometers a day, is something not taken lightly. I wasn't just filthy: I could feel the sweat and dirt and bugs and dust and food remnants and tears and I don't know what all over me. I walked into the changing room—a dusty, cement-and-tile hut with steel pipes and naked light bulbs—and I couldn't have been more ecstatic were it a five-star spa. I stood under the hot water—hot water!—for what felt like hours; scrubbed every inch, washed my hair three times, and basically pretended I was finished with this crazy trek and on my way home.

The shower, the food, the rest, the interaction with the day-trippers while I repacked my stuff, left me incredibly ambivalent. It was wonderful to be back in civilization; I couldn't wait to be back on the Trail.

As I look around the large restaurant room, with its hubbub and people, low Bedouin-style chairs and sofas, I feel a strange tug. I want to move on; I want to walk. It's not claustrophobia; certainly no lack of appreciation for the enthusiasm and help of the staff and interest of the tourists. But I'm beginning to get that old feeling: lonely in a crowd. I remember sitting at a Shabbat table on one of my US trips last year, as the divorce was becoming imminent, surrounded by about twenty others happily chatting and singing—and feeling so very much alone. I take a last look around— should I buy another Snickers?—and throwing my pack on, sort of just run out. Weird. Now—five minutes away and facing the decision whether to climb the ascent up Mount Timna or go around—I guess I'd better take a look at my map again and figure out where I'm heading.

This is the fourth day of hiking. I've climbed (and descended) Har Shlomo, Har Yehoram, Har Shekhoret, Maale Amram, and more. As I told Yaron a few hours ago, I really don't feel the need to climb Har Timna. Let's see if that blue path I noticed earlier on the map might actually allow me to skirt the mountain and rejoin the Shvil on the other side. I might save a few hours; I'll definitely save a lot of pain. Yes: I have become expert in making up any excuse to take the easy way . . .

"The easy way"? Not exactly, but it was indeed less steep. I ended up following a dry stream bed with old and clearly no-longer-used trail markings, clambering over boulders and sliding down slabs of granite the size of houses. But I was rewarded with the feeling, when I found the Shvil three hours later, that I'd at least saved myself the more strenuous climb up and down Har Timna. And I was rewarded, more, with the tranquility of the quiet of the path-less-travelled-by. Joining the Shvil again, I met a few people coming and going, and though acknowledging them with a nod and "shalom" and even a smile, I wasn't really interested in interacting with them. I was more intrigued by my reflections on the Children of Israel passing this way with the Tabernacle—and by the fascinating variations in the stone and rock and the shadow and light as I walked.

Timna was mined in the time of Solomon; walking through it you can readily understand how it drew the attention of any who passed. In one crevice, I could distinguish between at least four separate kinds of stone—dark brown almost earth-like; light brown harder granite; semi-transparent yellowish crystal; and orange-red sparkling quartz—not that I could identify them by name. Aside from the geological curiosity, I found the variety of color and shade, shape and substance, oddly intriguing. It was frustrating not to know what they were; why they were different;

how they came to rest side by side in the cracks of this ancient mountain. My mind wandered a bit—was it the heat?—and I kept confusing the wanderings of the Children of Israel with the journeys of Frodo and his companions of the Fellowship of the Ring in Tolkien's *The Lord of the Rings* trilogy. I'm not sure whether I thought I was Frodo or Sam or Joshua or one of the leaders of the tribe of Judea, but I had this recurring sense of déjà vu. I felt a sense of kinship with my good friend Reuven who had walked across Ethiopia and the Sudan to come home to Israel . . . or with Odysseus in Homer's *Odyssey*. Yes—it was beginning to sound even to me more like sunstroke, so I decided to rest a bit in the shade of a large rock and take a break. After ten minutes of rest, I kept moving.

Turning a corner as I climb a slight rise in the sandy path with 30-meter chalky cliffs on each side, I abruptly come upon a parking lot with a few low buildings at the far end. I've reached the northern entrance to Timna, the main tourist entry point. I don't know why but it's a tremendous letdown, almost makes me angry. I did enjoy my shower and lunch at the lake; I did appreciate the smiles and help of the staff and friendliness of the people there. But I'm not ready—not yet, not now—for more civilization. Seriously. I just want to be out in the desert. Stopping only long enough to refill water, I don't even take my pack off. I nod to an older couple I had passed and said hello to two days ago at Canyon Shekhoret—was that only two days ago?—but without being rude, just walk by. Thankfully, they're on the phone and don't seem to want to talk anyway.

I keep walking along the flat dirt and sand, putting as much distance between me and the Timna visitor center as possible before stopping to take a leak. I'm noticing, but not over-analyzing, that I hesitated to stop for over 40 minutes, holding it in, to get to the point where, when stopping, I couldn't see the entrance any more. That Ah! feeling of relief that is so familiar is even more powerful: Ah! I'm back with the shrubs, with the sand and rocks, with . . . myself, is what I'm thinking as I get rid of all the water I gulped down back at the visitor center.

It's getting late; I keep looking at the map, trying to decide: Should I press on to the night camp in the valley a few kilometers from tomorrow's hard ascent up the Milchan? Or should I turn east and get to Elifaz, the small kibbutz where I can find a Trail Angel to put me up, buy some stuff, have another shower? It's so strange, this contradictory set of impulses. Don't want; yet having had that shower (and sweated the better part of the day since), and sat on a soft sofa/mattress at Timna, I feel the pull of those little tastes of normality. Sun sets in about an hour. Time to make a decision.

Standing by a small, unusually shaped hill called Sasgon, unique in its siltstone and shale deposits (I'm reading in the Guide), I consider climbing up it. Though it's really too late in the day for that, I've decided: I know that I'll get a shower tomorrow before Shabbat; I know I'll reach a (form of) civilization then; I know I want to get an early start tomorrow and the extra two kilometers from Elifaz will make a differ-ence. But mostly I know I want to stay in the field. So I walk on—and am rewarded with a combination of stunningly beautiful scenery, a breathtaking sunset over the desert mountains, and . . . just as I arrive at the night camp, a warm welcome from Yaron and his father, setting up alongside their van.

I really didn't want to socialize, so said a quick hello, and we compared notes. Yaron was jealous of my solitude and adventure going around the mountain, I was jealous of his sense of accomplishment in climbing Mt. Timna, dedication to sticking to the trail, and the views he described. But not too much. I walked a hundred meters or so away to set up my tent next to a large acacia tree. I took a photo or two of the moon drifting above the hills behind my tent, and thought of my Grandma Helen. Once, when my son was about four, we visited my grandmother in Florida, and she said to Netanel, "Look up at the moon. When you see the moon, know that I can see it too, from way over here on the other side of the world!" It was a wonderful way to connect, halfway around the globe, and between the generations. And it is a concept which has never left me—and never fails to be associated with Grandma Helen whenever I look at the moon.

Having made camp, I took my little one-person gas burner and REI one-person pot and fork-on-one-end-spoon-on-the-other utensil and walked over to where Yaron and his father, Eilon, were preparing their dinner. (They had invited me to join them, and I felt it would be a little churlish not to. Besides, Yaron and I had discussed the idea of walking together the next day, and I wanted to finalize plans.) I felt a little distracted; the next day's climb was already weighing on my mind, as I recalled Shani telling me how the *Milchan* is one of the most difficult ascents on the Shvil. And I was conflicted about joining them. Yaron's father, Eilon, had strung up lights connected to Yaron's van, and they had a set of burners hooked up to a gas canister, with a pair of folding chairs and some music playing. It was nice; it was jarring; it was sociable and friendly but somehow out-of-sync and off-putting.

But I made the best of it; used their gas rings to cook and heat my tea, as they were bigger and stronger, and borrowed some spices. I enjoyed their choice of music—very Middle Eastern. We tasted each other's food and complimented each other on it—all lies, but all in good spirits. Then the older couple joined us and I took my leave, with the genuine excuse that I wanted an early night—and not least as Yaron insisted we set out at 7 a.m.

After brushing my teeth—I'd hung the Camelback on the tree, and knowing I could refill from Yaron's van in the morning, enjoyed the luxury of washing my face and brushing my teeth with more than a half cup of water—I sat down on a rock near my tent. (The tent and the tree blocked out the light, and most of the sound, still coming from Yaron's van and the conversation there, for which I was very grateful.) The moon had now fallen behind the hills to the west, and looking up I was a bit overwhelmed: it was as if a blanket of glitter had been strewn across the deep blue-black evening sky, and there were so many stars it brought tears to my eyes. Not as a figure of speech; I started to tear up, and a few dropped down my cheek. I wasn't exactly sure why. I was seriously tired, but that wasn't it. It seems the toll of the last four days—I guess the last few years—was catching up with me. I was crying, but I wasn't feeling self-pity, or even sadness really.

Overwhelmed, indeed; I felt small. Insignificant. Not in a personal or self-deprecating way; not compared to other people. But I was beginning to feel a new and unique combination of real humility, and of a deep and simple acceptance of my very inconsequential place in the universe. It put the difficulty of the incline, the heat of the day, even the pain of the divorce, in an ever-wider perspective. I felt small, yes, but that did not make me feel helpless, or unimportant, or afraid. Sitting there looking up at this demonstration of the vastness of the universe, I felt a strong sense of comfort; of embrace almost. Yes there are a million billion trillion stars; but however small I may be, I am a part of this incredible thing called life. I have a place here; I too belong. I began to sense myself, and all of us, all of life, as inhabiting that still small space and time of the inflection which is the here and now. Which is God, fate, reality. All existence is in us, and we hold in each of us the entirety of the universe.

Those were my thoughts as I went to sleep in my tent, with the vision of the night sky still clear before me even when I closed my eyes. I chuckled a bit—playing the philosopher-king to yourself can get rather heady, since you're pretty much willing to listen to even the most bizarre and pompous meanderings of thought, as an adoring audience of one. But as I drifted off to sleep, I remembered a saying of Rav Simcha Bunim of Peshischa, which charges us to ponder a strange contradiction: "The world was created for my sake; I am but dust and ashes."

There is a deep Jewish understanding that all things are connected, revealed most movingly in the mystical ideas of the Kabbalists; and there is a strong Jewish insistence that God controls the universe and continues to be involved in human endeavor. At the same time there is a fundamental Jewish concept of the power and responsibility of individual autonomy and the import of our behavior and personal decisions. These positions seem contradictory; yet I was coming to recognize how understanding this paradox can help me grasp my place in this world—and that awareness could bring with it a sense of serenity and inner peace. As I drifted off that night I remember thinking, "This is hard; it's been hard and will be hard . . . and that's really okay."

At 6:50 a.m. I walk over to Yaron and Eilon, who are just finishing breakfast and chatting quietly. I'm pretty impressed with myself: I awoke early, said my tefilot with particular intensity—a continuation, clearly, of last night's contemplations—and packed up quickly. I'm glad I came over. For whatever reason, I've warmed to them—even to Yaron's father, a somewhat gruff, weather-beaten man of few words, and those few are mostly sarcastic—and I accept their offer of fresh coffee. (Botz, or "mud" in Hebrew, as it's known, is a delightfully harsh way to start any morning: ground coffee heaped into boiling water with lots of sugar, re-boiled till almost over-flowing, then served without filtering.) Waiting until the grounds settle and it cools a bit, I sip it slowly as I make my oatmeal—again taking advantage of the water in

Yaron's van both to luxuriate in a larger serving of mush and to drink a second and third cup of tea.

As we make our last-minute adjustments and consult the maps (Yaron has two, I have three), Yaron suddenly turns to me and says, "Why don't you give your pack to my dad?!"

I'm a little taken aback—what? Why? How? And I say, "No, thanks, that's okay . . ." and continue to adjust my hat, the belt at my waist, leaning to the right and left to make sure the tent and water are balanced properly.

Yaron looks at me like I'm an idiot. "What are you, crazy?" he says. ("מה, אתה דפוק?") He goes on to explain that he's arranged for his dad to meet him—as usual, and as I already know—at the end of our day's hike; that today is the longest day yet of the Shvil, at 28 kilometers (which I know too); and that the Milchan is not just long and steep but SERIOUSLY long and steep and hard. Which I also know. The idea begins to sink into my consciousness: I am being offered a chance to hike without those 25 kilos on the hardest climb so far. AM I an idiot?!? So I ask him, "How does this work?" Obviously yes, I'm just stupid. I have some subconscious sense of loyalty to the Shvil—some sort of a purity of arms or something—which at the time made me feel guilty for skipping that bit leaving Be'er Ora, and not climbing up Timna. And now I'm wondering if giving my pack to Yaron's father is cheating. I decide it isn't, though not casually: I don't feel Yaron is doing any less of the Trail than I am.

So it's settled; I quickly detach my day-pack from the backpack—bless Shani and Shuki, I've already thanked them a hundred times each day for loaning me his backpack; and I knew somehow the attached day-pack would at some point come in handy! I had anticipated side-trips, not this, but still—what a concept. I place a bit of food into the pack (we had just prepared a few cheese sandwiches, again from Yaron's storage bin in his van, his father had stocked up yesterday—amazing), along with my Camelback and water bottles, sunscreen and a power bar, and my headlamp and windbreaker in case it takes longer than planned, and WOW, how LIGHT it feels putting it on my back!

It's like wearing nothing; I feel like those old videos of Neil Armstrong bouncing almost weightless on the surface of the moon. Wow! I'm grinning like a lunatic; toss my backpack in the back of the van (well—"toss" is entirely too light a word, more like struggle to lift it and shove it up and in). I give Yaron's father a spontaneous hug and "Todah" (thanks)—and, checking our watches, we stride off. It's 7:10 a.m. on day five of the trek and I feel like it's a new world.

It's hard to describe, each time anew, the beauty and the difficulty of each ascent. Each day was incredible; each was hot and exhausting, serene and interesting, wonderful and powerful. The Milchan on that Thursday was no different, just harder. Of course without my pack it should have felt easier. I suppose that's like saying taking the bar exam after studying for two months is easier than after studying for one month. Not only was it easier; I can't imagine having to do it with that pack on my back. I said as much to Yaron, about twenty times. But even so, it was excruciatingly, painfully grueling. It was without doubt the most demanding day yet: a 600-meter ascent over 1.7 kilometers, on the hottest day so far, on much too little sleep and not nearly enough food. I felt faint after the second hour on the trail.

Yaron and I had agreed to take the day as it came; meaning, to sometimes walk together but not always, to wait for each other but not if we didn't feel like it. It worked out better than I'd imagined it could possibly have, in my quest for solitude. Yaron and I were indeed well-matched for the Trail. Somehow we both seemed to know when the other wanted or needed quiet, or space. And in the intervening times, we talked of everything under the sun—not least our struggles in our personal lives.

In the most demanding moments, early on climbing up the Milchan, when I really thought I might not make it to the top and entertained fleeting fantasies of walking down the "escape" trail to the valley on the eastern stretches of the mountain, I saw Yaron way up ahead, at some summit-like juncture of the trail, and I wanted to catch up with him. (Yes, on the climbs he was almost invariably ahead of me. He's taller, has longer legs, is younger. What?) A few times he waved to me; just being friendly, not at all patronizing nor even purposefully encouraging. But it had that encouraging effect.

I was first to reach the actual summit though, just coincidentally, having strode off following a rest stop where he'd waited for me. I found myself looking back at the valley where the night camp was, Timna, Har Shekhoret in the distance, and a glimpse of the Gulf of Eilat shimmering in the morning sun. I turned on my phone and took a photo, and a video, to capture the moment. I knew at the time that it couldn't possibly do justice to the tremendous sense of accomplishment I felt, or to the strength of my feelings of friendship and camaraderie toward this almost-stranger-now-soulmate who shared my feat of endurance. We stopped and put a few rocks on a Rumjum—a desert pillar of stones—which others had built there. I stared in silence back at the incredible heights and distance I'd covered already that morning and over the past five days, and Yaron did the same. Then we turned and headed out toward the long stretch ahead of us.

Maybe it's a sort of bonding resulting from the sweat and pain of the ascent up the Milchan; or maybe just the sense of shared accomplishment. But no question that at this point Yaron and I are true friends; perhaps also due to the easy way we've settled into reading each other's moods and given each other space over the past few hours. Now, as we move into a new element—long stretches of relatively flat walking, with an intermittent rise and fall offering the occasional challenge—we fall into an almost relaxing, if aggressive, pace. We both know three things: we have a long way to go—over 25 kilometers still—and so must push ahead; the hardest part is behind us; and talking as we walk keeps our spirits up and seems to make the time pass more quickly.

We pick up where we left off and share our personal stories. Or, rather, Yaron turns to me just as we heft our packs on to set out along the flat river bed immediately after the summit, and says (in Hebrew, of course), "Nu Aryeh, seriously, I don't understand. How have you managed to live without a woman for a year and half?!!?" Like I said: a blunt Israeli. So we talk: about marriage, about careers, about security and insecurity, about our love for our children and our wives and extended families. He's so intrigued by me, it makes me start to think how my life looks from the outside. He grills me about becoming observant 30 years ago; then about my philosophy of moderate normative Judaism and Zionism; then about the global media's hostility toward Israel; then about my work with Natan Sharansky in the prime minister's office and Arab democracy activists. He's especially interested in the environment on college campuses in the US, as he's never been but has heard rumors of the antipathy to Israel and keeps asking about the new anti-Semitism and my experiences speaking at universities around the world, not least when I travelled with Natan to 65 campuses across America and Europe.

Finally, after about two hours—out of weariness with hearing myself speak, let alone a sort of emotional exhaustion, and a natural curiosity about Yaron and his life—I turn the conversation to him. I'm keenly aware of how different we are, and of his fascination with my reality, so different from his. And though I may be more familiar with his cultural milieu than he is with mine, I'm still incredibly interested in his journey. I find myself filled with admiration for his dedication—to his family, to our country, to himself and his professional integrity—and enjoy his descriptions of his kids and Ayelet, his wife, and a few amusing stories about his father.

Yaron has a strong sense of identity as a member of the Jewish people, and loyalty to Israel as the nation-state of the Jewish people. We argue politics—my pragmatism sometimes overcoming his left-leaning ideology, his idealism sometimes reminding me to reclaim my own. We agree on much; not least about the paucity of intelligent, strong, moral, idealistic leaders in our political system. But at base we just enjoy the back-and-forth, the getting-to-know-you, the interaction between two very different but very similar people, two men from seemingly unrelated worlds wandering the same desert trying to find their way together separately.

At one point, as the afternoon wears on, we found ourselves walking along the edge of the mountain ridge overlooking the Arava—the southern section of the Jordan River valley, which stretches from the southern tip of the Dead Sea down to Eilat on the Red Sea. At this point we couldn't see the Red Sea—we were amazed at how far we'd walked—but the view across the valley to the hills of Moav and Ammon in Jordan, lit by the sun behind us, was gorgeous. Looking down we could see a few Israeli settlements scattered below.[4] These communities

---

4   Not "settlements," as the word is used pejoratively to label the Jewish towns and villages in Judea and Samaria as somehow illegitimate. Rather as the generic term "*yishuv*" ("settlement") is used, referring to all small Jewish Israeli communities wherever located, on both sides of the 1949 armistice line, since the beginning of the Zionist enterprise over a century ago, including Rosh Pina, Tel Aviv, Petach Tivka, Be'er Sheba, my home town of Beit Shemesh, etc. Sort of like Salt Lake City, San Francisco and Seattle were once "settlements," as Americans settled the West. Herein, I use the word for all small Jewish villages.

looked like Lego creations spread out on the sand, as toy cars and little ant-like people scurried around them. It was a bit disconcerting: on the one hand, we were in the middle of one of the most inhospitable, inaccessible points on the Trail—and enjoying the contemplative desert silence and alone-ness. On the other hand, it felt like we could just reach out and touch civilization, or call to it if we could yell loudly enough. Weird.

Twenty-eight kilometers and eleven hours on, we arrived at the small yishuv/community of Shacharut ("Dawn" or "Morning"—fitting, as it sits on the edge of a cliff where you can enjoy the sun rising over the mountains of Moav every morning). It's less inspiring than the name, or the concept—a bit rundown, no store, no real facilities. As we were resting, I realized I really didn't want to stay there overnight. The map showed a night camp about 10 kilometers along, near the Gei Cholot sand dunes. That looked more welcoming, and I even thought I'd prefer the solitude once again. Walking around, trying to find some water, I ran into a boy and girl sitting on a low wall in the main circle of the yishuv—playing a guitar! Asking if they'd mind (they didn't), I took the guitar and put it on my knee, my foot on the wall. It was an old, beat-up, nylon-string toneless instrument—and it felt so very good. I played for only a few minutes—but it reminded me gently of how I missed playing. In preparing for the trek, I had bought a little guitar but decided it was too heavy to carry. Now, I promised myself I'd find a way to take it when I headed North.

We met Eilon, Yaron's dad, dumped our stuff in the back of the van, and drove out. I felt absolutely no guilt whatsoever in bumping along the rough road descending gently toward the plain of Uvda; I had done my bit that day, and the next day was Friday. With Shabbat coming in by 4:30 p.m., there was no way I could make the entire schlepp from Shacharut to the Desert Ashram at Shitim, my Shabbat destination, in time. When they dropped me off at the night camp, Yaron and his father gave me some bread and cheese . . . and apples and oranges . . . and carrots . . . and wood for a fire. I was so thankful—it's the small things, and not-so-small, which really get you on the Trail. I kept refusing; they kept refusing to accept my refusals. And of course, later that night, savoring the flavor of the simple yellow cheese and brown bread (with a little of my Zatar sprinkled on it), sitting by the warmth of the fire burning the logs they tossed out of the car earlier that afternoon, I thought of them with appreciation—and even love.

On the one hand, after the intensity of the last two days—of the hiking, and of the conversations—I was glad to be on my own again. On the other hand, I was strangely a little frightened of being alone, as it had been some 36 hours since I had teamed up with Yaron.

I'm sitting by the fire, near my tent. Like back in Shekhoret Canyon, my tent is a little bump sitting on a vast flat expanse of dirt—though this is flatter, and devoid of any vegetation. Back there in the canyon, the tree next to the tent, shrubs not far, hills and mountains in the distance made it seem less alone. Here, there's nothing but flat earth and rocks for hundreds of meters in every direction. I miss my companions—Yaron and his father, the trees and bushes, even the occasional bird or beetle. The airport at Uvda has shut down for the night too—it's a conspiracy to make me feel alone.

Looking up at the stars, instead of being inspired as I was the night before, I'm feeling insignificant, and a bit scared; tired, lonely and agitated. I shake myself a bit, add another log to the fire, take out my map, and figure out tomorrow. My first Friday hiking, it seems a bit far for a half-day and leaves little time to prepare for Shabbat. I'm abruptly aware that there's no way I can hike the entire length—though it's relatively flat—from here to Shitim. So that's simple: I'll hike through Gei Cholot—the only true sand dunes in all of Israel—and then since the trail follows the road, grab a ride to the rest stop at the Neot Smadar junction, and depending on the time, either walk the last 7 kilometers or hitch another ride.

For whatever reason, the planning itself calms me. And then I remember something wonderful, as I climb into my sleeping bag, zip up the tent and turn off the lantern-flashlight (thanks Nati and Tehila again, amazing): I'm going to see Meira tomorrow! My youngest daughter, age 21, Mimi (as I often call her) is driving down to spend Shabbat with me at the Ashram, and bringing supplies. It's just incredible how our psyche plays games with our emotions. I'm overcome with a wave of powerful feelings, my eyes fill up, I'm happy and anticipating and tired and relieved and impatient and ecstatic and melancholy all at once. But as I drift off to sleep, the simple gratitude returns—for Meira, and Yaron, and all the rest, and that's a comfort.

I was woken up by a plane engine roaring nearby; I didn't quite realize how very close this night camp is to the runways of the Avda airport. Between the plane, and then multiple trucks passing on the nearby road, it was pointless to try to sleep more. ("Sleep" in this sense is a relative concept, as I learned after a week on the Trail. My new and so-advanced special REI half-sponge, half-air mattress lost its bounce and cushioning after about two hours every night. And the ground was hard, really hard, on the hips and shoulders and back.) The morning was seriously cold; I didn't want even to wash my face. Once up, I seriously contemplated not even bothering with the trail and the dunes, and just flagging down a passing vehicle and making for the Ashram. I heard echoes of the previous night, feeling small and insignificant—what's the point? But on the other hand, I thought to myself, if I'm not important in the wider scheme of things, who cares? Just do it.

At that moment, three young men came into view, recently-released soldiers, whom Yaron and I had come across the day before and who had slept at Shacharut. They passed by a few hundred meters away, and headed toward the dunes. Well—I wasn't about to wimp out now. I piled the remaining wood neatly for use by the next camper to come along, wolfed down the last of the cheese and bread and a granola bar, and set out. After an hour of dirt and rocks, climbing a small rise, I came across something out of a Lawrence of Arabia story (or a film set): rolling hills of sand, with those indentations and waves so familiar from every painting or photo of the Sahara.

It was a bit unnerving, as if I'd been transported to North Africa and left to search for an oasis. Though I knew I was only a few hours from a road; though I had heard and then seen a group of jeeps passing by; though I was half-expecting to run into those boys who passed me earlier, or other hikers; though I could see on the map I was only 15 kilometers or so in each direction to various communities . . . I still felt a bit lost in the middle of nowhere. Surreal is the only word for it, even after a week of desert mountains, valleys, dry river beds, and vast stretches of dry earth and rock. I was looking out over an expanse, as far as the eye could see, of huge mounds and bowls of yellow-gold sand. I could almost see the camel caravans carrying spices to the Orient. I thought of Yosef (Joseph, in the book of Genesis) being taken by the Midianite traders and then sold to the Ishmaelites and imagined the procession before me.

Standing on the edge of the highest rise, next to a large boulder clearly placed there by the Shvil caretakers to mark the continuation of the Trail (as there are of course no trees or markings otherwise), I actually did picture the ancient Children of Israel in various permutations—not only Yosef and his brothers but Yaakov (Jacob) being brought down to Egypt, and 400 years later the nation coming back up through the Sinai. It was romantic and colorful and entirely fanciful, considering that these dunes are hardly typical of the terrain they crossed. But it worked for me—something psychological about dunes being equated with the ancients. I felt connected and had a sense of belonging. This is my land; this is my people's trail; I'm retracing their steps. And so I walked on.

It's my sixth day on the Shvil. Last time I showered was Wednesday midday at Timna—it feels like a month ago. I feel hot and sweaty, slimy and sticky, and crusty and dusty all at the same time. The only reason I'm not panicking is that I know I'll shower soon. I hope. As I trudge down the hill from the dunes, back to the long boring tedious flat brown and gray rocks and dirt part of the Trail toward Shizafon junction, I begin to worry a bit about my set-up for Shabbat. Yesterday I called to confirm the reservation I had made a few weeks ago at the "Ashram BaMidbar" (Desert Ashram) in Shitim, which their website describes as a meditation and spiritual retreat—with showers, grass to pitch a tent on, and veggie food. There's even a discount for hikers on the Shvil. But now I'm thinking—what do I even know about this place? Maybe it's a complete dump! I trudge on.

With the airfield behind me and to my left, and the long straight road to my right, I realize I've kind of had enough. Enough heat, enough hurt, enough walking, enough contemplation, enough challenge, enough boredom, enough singing, enough praying, enough sun, enough alone. I'm tired. And my legs hurt. And my feet, toes, ankles, knees, hips, lower back, upper back, shoulders, neck—even my forehead. (Have to stop squinting in the morning sun.) I hear a car coming; reflexively, as if it's the most natural thing in the world, as if it's a done deal, as if I made a decision after weighing all the pros and cons . . . I put out my hand to catch a ride.

I was really glad I did. The two guys who picked me up were nice; more than that, they were impressed, saying "*kol hakavod!*" ("Respect!") repeatedly. Since they were young hikers themselves, wishing they could join me, their excitement raised my flagging spirits, renewing my energy and enthusiasm. They dropped me off at the junction, and though I knew (hoped) I had a shower waiting for me at the Ashram, I went in to the little store/restaurant there to splash some water on my face and use their bathroom. With Shabbat coming, I bought a few treats—organic granola and fruit bars made locally—but couldn't allow myself the wine and cheese and amazing jams from the nearby kibbutz Neot Smadar, as I knew I had to carry them.

Or not. When I put my pack back on, it weighed about 100 times what it did 15 minutes earlier. Or somehow that's how it felt. I began to walk . . . and crossing the highway, about 50 meters along the road I came to a bus stop. I took the pack off, leaned it up against the bus stop shelter, and sat down. Looking at the map, I realized, first, that it's 12 kilometers of straight walking on a dirt track alongside the highway. That would take almost 3 hours. Second, it's 4 hours before Shabbat. And third, it's okay to hitch a ride. I can look out the window to enjoy the scenery . . . and it's getting hot. This was a considered decision, and a good one it turns out. (A car stopped for me within minutes.)

Arriving at the Ashram, I'm tickled. I didn't know really what to expect—I've never been to India—but had I imagined it, and described what I had hoped for, this is what it would feel like. A cross between summer camp and rustic resort (though that may be pushing it). My first impression is of a peaceful sense of tranquility, as I see a few young people lounging on mattresses and a hammock on the lawn, one playing guitar (a guitar!), while others wander around, some just walking quietly, others clearly making preparations for the evening but very calmly, slowly. And then—ah, what's that?—the scent of marijuana. Never had THAT at summer camp. But really the most amazing thing, as I walk toward a tree where I think I'd like to pitch my tent, is noticing the feel of walking on grass. I've spent the last six days walking on dirt and rock, sand and stones—and I can't wait to take my boots off.

So I do, and it's such a sensuous feeling I'm not sure whether to shout or smile or cry or sing. It's not even especially soft grass—more like sharp crabgrass—but I swish my feet over it and curl my toes around it, and it's incredibly lovely. I am so happy to be here.

But now it's time for discipline; I can enjoy the grass and the quiet (or not) over Shabbat; I have to get started. There's only 3 hours left. I start to unpack—again, amazing to be on grass, I can lay my stuff out all over and not worry about it getting all dusty and dirty—put up the tent, and sort out my clothes and food. Then I wash my underwear and socks (I had washed one pair at Timna), wearing my swimsuit, and hang them out to dry, and jump in the shower. Turns out I showered during the women's time in the shared outdoor shower house—oops—but fortunately I was alone throughout. What an AMAZING feeling, hot water and all.

I put on the Shabbat shirt I'd been carrying since Sunday and the lightweight "trousers" which had doubled as my PJs but are blue and dark enough to look nice enough for Shabbat (in a way), and walked around the place. It turns out they have "Tzimmerim"—rooms in little huts with beds and outdoor but private showers attached—wish I had known! But no—I'm really quite happy with my tent on the grass. Sleeping out on the ground and granite for five nights will do that: pitching a tent on grass becomes the definition of luxury. I pass a small pond with a fountain and a bubbling stream flowing from it into a nearby smaller pool, with sofas and chairs arranged around it; a covered meditation/class area with pillows and mattresses; and a larger tent enclosure with a bar. I find my way to the office and kitchen. All sorts of notices, and political cartoons and slogans too, dot the walls and whiteboard and bulletin board, some funny enough to make me chuckle.

The people managing the place are less welcoming, and less warm, than I'd expected. What—aren't spiritual truth- and wisdom-seekers supposed to talk and smile and radiate love and peace like Gandhi or Rabbi Arye Levin or Mother Teresa or the biblical Aaron (he of the title "seeker of peace and lover of all creation")? I guess not—they're just individuals running a (mystical, vegan, meditative) hippie retreat center. But the guy in charge of the kitchen is great—apparently he either was observant or just knows a bit, as he launches into much more detail than I really need about the kashrut (they don't even allow meat or fish on the premises, let alone cook with them). He then demonstrates incredible sensitivity by both pointing out to me what's being cooked now (before Shabbat, and therefore permissible for me to eat on Shabbat) and saying that he'll try to bake a few challot (Shabbat bread) prior to the onset of Shabbat, just for me. It's so very considerate of him; I really am so glad to be here.

Heading back to my tent—by then it was an hour before Shabbat—my phone rang. I had wondered what was up with Mimi, on her way to join me for a relaxing Shabbat with all sorts of supplies. I had decided not to bother her, because she was driving a good three hours plus and I did not want her to feel pressured or to talk on the phone while driving. She'll get here when she gets here, I said to myself—though I was getting a little concerned. Among other things, she was bringing the large four-person tent as one of the special treats I had prepared for myself the week before, and I knew it would take some time to erect prior to the onset of the Sabbath.

But the call wasn't from Meira; it was from Bini, her boyfriend. "Don't worry; Meira's fine, but she's been in an accident. She's all right, not too far from where you are, but the car can't move . . ."

I'm a very calm person—always was, even before I started meditating regularly. As a medic in a combat reserve unit in the Israel Defense Forces and in other experiences, I had learned to deal with emergencies efficiently, keeping my composure; very cool. But I have to admit, as a father, this got to me, and I felt my heart flutter. I spent far too may seconds imagining Meira lying bleeding on the asphalt of a twisting mountain road . . . and then pulled myself together. Hanging up with Bini, I called Mimi—and after saying, "I'm okay," she started crying. After a few moments, we covered the basics; I gathered she was about 15 minutes away—but that hardly helped when I had no car. It was by then less than an hour until Shabbat was to come in (driving, calls, all sorts of things aren't allowed on the Sabbath unless there's a life in danger), and she was stuck on the side of the highway in the middle of nowhere.

I ran to the office to ask if I could borrow their (or someone's) car—a business like this MUST have a vehicle for supplies, etc.—but no: their office car was "in use," and no appeals were compelling enough to warrant even making a call to see if it was nearby. And the young adults running the place had no cars to their names—of course, it's an Ashram. Who needs the trappings of this world, the "stuff" of modern existence? I ran out into the parking lot, yelling loudly to no one in particular, "Anyone have a car I can borrow? Is there anyone who can help me?!?" in Hebrew and English, over and over as I half walked, half ran around the dusty lot, afraid people would think I was on drugs or doing some sort of therapeutic exercise.

I was on the verge of panicking—very unlike me—and considering running out to the highway to flag down a ride (not hitch, but stand in front of an approaching car to actually STOP them). I began the thinking process whereby observant Jews look to find justifications in Jewish law to enable them to perform a usually not-permitted act on Shabbat, in this case driving and carrying, etc. to bring Meira to the Ashram even after Shabbat had commenced . . . when a concerned and kindly face came into view.

A woman, perhaps only a few years younger than me, walked toward me and I trotted to her, stopping a few feet away so as not to scare her. Quickly explaining, I saw her hesitate—and then decide. Thank goodness, I had found not only a sensitive, intelligent, and sympathetic person who happened to have left her meditation session for a break—"happened to"—but a mother of three to boot. Her name was Maya; as she went to call her husband Eli out of their group, I ran to get a few things and throw my stuff into my tent. Then, with Eli driving and Maya in the passenger seat, we were off.

It turned out a young and irresponsible driver had passed Mimi, swerved back into the lane in front of her, leaving no room, and then suddenly slammed on his breaks. Apparently he thought his accelerator pedal was stuck, and panicked. Needless to say, she hit him from behind; fortunately, neither was hurt, if both were shaken up. After a few more tears and many hugs, we quickly got down to business. My car (which Mimi had been driving) incurred enough damage to make it inoperable; the guy's car had some dents in the rear but was drivable. We exchanged details, took some photos, and got on with the business of transferring to Eli and Maya's car all the stuff—so much stuff!—that Mimi had packed into the trunk. ("We're using a car, what difference does it make if we bring more than needed? I can always schlepp it back." Famous last words . . .)

Eli and Maya were so kind—not only for the ride, and interrupting their session, but for intuitively understanding that what was needed on the ride back was to allow Meira and me to talk quietly in the back seat, processing what had happened. They offered an occasional word of wisdom and experience without condescension or judgment. They spoke as I did: it wasn't Meira's fault; her alertness averted a worse outcome; an accident like this is an important lesson in the dangers of the road and the importance of taking those dangers seriously.

I shared with them (and Meira, though not for the first time) my father's "ABCD" dictum, based on his father's: presume other drivers on the road are either *A*ngry, *B*lind, *C*razy or *D*runk. We laughed and breathed a sigh of relief. On arrival back at the Ashram they helped us drag to the grass the huge tent, boxes of food and equipment and clothes and books and more for my re-supply and for Shabbat, and returned to their class. My feelings about the Ashram, the people there, and the spirit of the place, returned to the positive side of the scale.

With a few minutes to spare, Meira and I quickly put up the large tent (with two rooms!) and riffled through the boxes of resupplies (more granola bars and those disgusting energy bars? Oy . . .). I then sat alone under a tree in the welcome coolness of the late late afternoon, as Meira took a quick shower. With the peace of Shabbat descending, I marveled at the wonders of the universe. "Humility" doesn't begin to describe my feelings of a complete nothingness, a dimunition and yet transcendence of self and of all reality.

I felt the weight of a limitless inability to comprehend anything. Meira's arrival, the accident, and the commencement of Shabbat combined to affect me greatly.

Meira is my youngest, and the child who lived with me through the years of distress and separation and divorce and beyond. I'm privileged to enjoy a special relationship with each of my children—including my first-born and only son Netanel, and my first little girl, Merav (who is most like me in many ways, including but not merely physically). But at that time I was closest, naturally, to Mimi. The idea, very notion, of anything happening to her filled me with a frightening sense of powerlessness I barely contained.

A memory came to me of the "graduation" of her unit in the IDF intelligence corps, a somewhat clichéd ceremony with marching, traditional songs, motivational speeches, and the requisite calling out of "אני נשבעה" (*Ani Nishba'ah*—"I pledge") with a rifle in one hand, the Hebrew Bible in the other. Somehow I connected her service to our country with her support for me; her swearing-in ritual with our ritual bringing in of the Sabbath. I sat pondering her dedication, and her various decisions in growing up—and my thoughts shifted to her choice to have a more involved Bat Mitzvah than most of her peers.[5]

I felt at her Bat Mitzvah that what Meira was doing was good and right—words and themes which were in fact part of the Torah portion read that very week of her Bat Mitzvah. Pushing the envelope of Halachic[6] observance was just one way which Meira adopted, and improved upon, my approach to balancing between the progressive/liberal values I was raised on and the Jewish people's historical adherence to practices, rituals and philosophies introduced to humanity thousands of years ago in the Mosaic code. It was a central element of her place in the family; and it tied us to each other more each day, aside from our sharing the house for the past year. Meira and I share a combined experiential, mystical and text-base approach to our traditional practice, whether learning or sharing, praying or hiking.

I sat under that tree marveling at the twists of fate, the matter of seconds involved in the difference between her being there with me or not. The time for candle-lighting and the beginning of Shabbat arrived. In a hurry, I changed clothes, and we set up a flashlight lantern to hang from the tent roof and sent a few last-minute phone messages. And then it was Shabbat . . . and a unique, unforgettable Shabbat it was.

It's actually a nice way to bring in Shabbat, this—a small group, about thirty or so mostly young men and women, sitting in concentric circles on pillows and mattresses in the dining room, singing and humming and chanting. Now we're singing in English . . . now in Hebrew . . . simple folk tunes on various themes of nature and water, meditation, and the oneness of being. One of the women with a guitar invites a visiting woman to light candles—without a blessing, but I do feel a hint of Jewish content.

I'm aware of my internal conflict: On the one hand, I wasn't raised in an Orthodox Jewish home. I grew up with non-conventional observance of Shabbat,

---

5   In the observant Jewish world, boys at 13 are called to read in synagogue from the Torah. *Bar Mitzvah* literally means "son of the commandmant," and this act throughout the ages symbolizes joining the community of adult males, upon whom the commandments fall. By tradition, only men join a "minyan," or prayer group of ten—an interpretation of Jewish law which more modern Reform and Conservative branches of the Jewish faith have expanded to include women, or dismissed altogether. My daughter Meira took our philosophy of "modern Orthodoxy" and made it her own, and very real, by choosing to read from the Torah in a prayer group of women, at the traditional age of 12 (for girls). Modern Orthodoxy is the stream of normative Judaism that attempts to combine science, culture and the trappings of the modern world (from university studies and film to mixed dancing and rock music) with the traditional observance of the commandments (such as observing Shabbat and eating only Kosher food, dressing modestly, being scrupulously honest in business, and not speaking ill of others). Meira chose to have a Bat Mitzvah which expressed not only her love for our Jewish heritage, but her insistence that where allowed in Jewish law it was incumbent on women to fully participate in Jewish life. She embraced and acted upon this very modern concept, which she learned on our knees.

6   "Halacha" (הלכה) is the Hebrew term for Jewish law (lit. "the Way"); "Halachic" is an adjective describing something which accords with Jewish Law.

riding my motorcycle to a hilltop with my guitar as the sun sets, and I so enjoy the spiritual depth of these seekers-of-meaning. On the other hand, as an observant Jew now for over thirty yeas, and as one who believes deeply in the universal truths and beauty of Jewish thought and tradition, it pains me so to sit here, in the desert of the Land of Israel, with Jews seeking religious inspiration who ignore the very themes of Judaism. Traditional Shabbat observance is rich with Jewish practices and liturgy expressing exactly what these American songs from the '60s do. They're singing "Close your eyes and the world disappears," a motif reminiscent of a number of other-worldly elements of Shabbat, from shutting our eyes while making the blessing after lighting the candles, to "מעין עולם הבא," "taste of the world to come" imagery of Shabbat prayers and songs.

I say so to Meira, quietly. And yet, ironically, she, born in Israel and raised Orthodox, is much more tolerant and accepting of it than I am—mister California, live-and-let-live liberal that I am. I find that fascinating, and meditate on that for a few minutes even as I realize that the song they're singing now, about a river flowing into the sea, is suggestive of one of the Psalms traditionally sung on Friday night by Jews around the world. I want to stand up and sing or shout: "We—YOU—have such incredible, meaningful, beautiful traditions of our OWN—explore these, in your own backyard! We/you don't need a re-creation of an Indian ashram in the Negev; you can find it all in the various mystical streams of Judaism!" Or, I think, you could infuse this India/Ashram setting with deep and resonant themes from our tradition. . . . But I am calming down, and with Meira's encouragement, relax into the moment, and enjoy it.

It's becoming clear that this is exactly what both I and she needed. Isn't that amazing? For me, it's yet another experience on the Trail. On the one hand, it's a perfect combination of rustic ambience and still "roughing it," which is not far removed from the Shvil (not even physically, as the Shvil literally runs right by the Ashram). On the other hand, just a little bit of luxury: a larger tent on grass, a mattress, a shower with hot water, a toilet, hot food . . . and of course the company of my youngest daughter, who has supported me, laughed with me, cried with me, grown with me over the past two years in ways unimaginable before then. And for Mimi, after her car accident, it's a real chance to re-group, understand how lucky she is, allow herself to be afraid and then to recover, in the embrace not only of her father but of a group of warm and friendly strangers.

Well—warm and friendly, yes they were. Also pretty unusual. Downright bizarre in many ways. The Shabbat developed into a strange combination of amazing vegan food, drawn-out and profound contemplative prayer (on the grass, on my own), deep meditation (twice), enjoyable interactions with various travelers and participants in workshops at the ashram, and wonderful, rewarding, fun, and light conversations with Mimi. It also included off-the-wall occurrences like watching a few people literally scream obscenities at each other at the top of their lungs; a man and then a woman challenging each other to take off their clothes in the dining room; and various others apparently in the same "let it all go" workshop wandering around half-naked all afternoon.

Some of these experiences helped Mimi and me figure out that the sign above the door to the kitchen saying נא לא להיכנס למטבח ערום ("Please do not enter the kitchen naked") was not a joke. There were cartoons and caricatures on the bulletin board right next to this sign, so naturally it seemed to be an attempt at humor. Clearly, it was not. It must have been a requirement of the health authorities, and necessary more frequently than one might have expected.

By the time Shabbat was coming to a close we had settled into a welcome Shabbat-mode of thought and behavior: relaxed, accepting, somewhat contemplative. We were somewhat sad to see the end of Shabbat nearing, yet glad to be thinking of moving on as well. We sat by a bubbling fish pond, with a bit of pot smoke wafting over from the thatched-roof smoking area nearby (I wanted to ask my rabbi: is that allowed on Shabbat? I think not—on many levels). I spoke with a few of the post-army young men who'd caught up to me along the Shvil, one of whom played some slow and expressive tunes on his harmonica. And we just enjoyed the quiet. (The screamers had moved back into silent meditation exercises. Thankfully.)

I was so very happy to have Meira with me; I missed her, and the rest of my kids, terribly. The loneliness of that first week was and is something I wouldn't experience again on the Shvil, and I was glad it was over. As Shabbat went out, I shared with Mimi something I hadn't mentioned yet. I'm not sure why this thought came to me, but as I crossed the highway at the Shizafon junction on the previous day, Friday, I simply realized: I'm going to do this. I'm really going to hike the entire length of the country.

I remember thinking, explicitly, to myself: this isn't a promise, and it's not a declaration of intent. Nor was it a calculation, at least not a premeditated one, as in "if I could do this past week, I can do the rest." I just knew I was going to finish. And somehow that gave me an inner peace which carried me into Shabbat—even with Mimi's accident and the intensity and emotion it engendered—and through Shabbat . . . and then into the coming week.

That night—*Motzei Shabbat*, Saturday night, after Shabbat went out and after Meira left to head back home—I took a walk out behind the Ashram, into a part of the desert sand/dirt that had been laid out as a meditative space, with rock-lined paths meandering up and down small rises and depressions in the valley. There was a bright crescent quarter moon, in a phenomenally clear night sky, with a thousand shining lights seemingly embracing me in the warmth of the evening. I was again aware of the vastness of the cosmos and my own very smallness. I, Mimi, the Trail, the accident, even the divorce seemed just to fade into insignificance in comparison.

In that first week in the desert, I began to appreciate the importance of humility. I recognized how little we really control in our lives, how inconsequential our concerns really are when compared with the limitlessness of the universe or the suffering of others. I started to grasp how our intelligence and understanding is not as exceptional as we might think. Perhaps counter-intuitively, this admission enables us to approach challenges with an openness and creativity that otherwise eludes us.

הִגִּיד לְךָ אָדָם מַה־טּוֹב וּמָה־יְהֹוָה דּוֹרֵשׁ מִמְּךָ כִּי אִם־עֲשׂוֹת מִשְׁפָּט וְאַהֲבַת חֶסֶד וְהַצְנֵעַ
לֶכֶת עִם־אֱלֹהֶיךָ:

He has told you, O mortal, what is good, and what the Lord requires of you: just to do justice, act with loving-kindness, and walk humbly with your God. (Micha 6:8)

From my Facebook post on that Saturday night (Feb 22):

Miss my family and friends very much and I do appreciate all the concern and good wishes—and (just a beginning here) thanks so much to Shani & Shuki for the pack and guidance, Tehila for the walking sticks (Omg couldn't possibly manage without them), Bini for the צווארון & hat, wear them every night (it's . . . COLD in the desert!), Mark for the lentils & Quinoa, they were my staple all week (2 nights just ate the leftovers cold in my tent, too exhausted & freezing to even cook—or brush teeth or anything else, don't ask), Mimi & Bini for the Leatherman and Netanel & Tehila for the light/lantern, Zvika for taking me down to Eilat (& buying the beers with me for Ethan and Jeremy, our US Marine buddies from the ship at the 3 Monkies pub) & for waving me off at Nachal Shlomo, and Hadas for worrying ☺ . . . and my crew at MediaCentral for the shirt I wore all week (yes, I washed it Friday; still, doesn't look like it . . . sorry). All for now—hope to see you soon on the trail . . . Shavua Tov

Chapter Two

DESERT: ACCEPTANCE

[Week Two]

I'm not at all sure this was such a good idea. "This" being everything combined: standing out here on the highway in the heat trying and failing now for almost an hour to hitch a ride; spending Shabbat at the Ashram with Meira and the feeling of home she brought, with all the luxuries involved; expecting to make it all the way to Mitzpeh Ramon in one day; starting out as late as I did. Watching the cars pass me by I'm wondering if I should try a new tactic, and wave one down as if I'm in trouble. But I'm not really comfortable doing that—it would be dishonest.

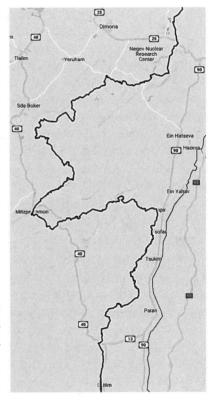

Just as I begin to consider alternatives—perhaps walk back to the Ashram and see if any staffers or guests are planning to drive north, maybe change the goal and just start walking along the trail and make camp at the Zichor junction where I'd buried water and munchies anyway, before I made the plan to get to Mitzpeh Ramon today—a yellow van honks as it passes by going south, in the opposite direction. Yaron! He pulls over with a screech. Big hugs, and with Eilon. Reuven and D'ganit, the older couple we'd met a few days before too; they even invite me to their son's wedding taking place in a few months, sweet. For no good reason, seeing Yaron and his little yellow van makes me optimistic. Sure enough, a minute later a car heading north sees me, stops, and I'm on my way.

The couple in the car were heading for Modi'in, a town very near my home in Beit Shemesh. I remember thinking to myself, "Wha . . . ?!!?" I wanted to go home, it would be so easy, and it's so near, only about a three-hour drive. Getting back to the trail was emotionally difficult, adding weight to the heat and the climb. Having had a slow start (including losing my maps at the Ashram—was that subconscious perhaps? At last I found them), it was about 11 a.m., and already hot and dry and dusty. After sharing the idea with them—they said "Sure, we can drive via Beit Shemesh!"—I dismissed the thought as just passing fancy.

They let me off near the center of the Ramon Crater, and after about an hour of walking I made for a lone shade tree mentioned in the Red Guide. There, in the middle of the massive natural bowl, some 40 kilometers long and 9 kilometers across, which scientists suggest is probably the site of a meteor smashing into the earth, I stopped for a bit of granola bar. Some say this cataclysmic event—an impact equivalent to 100 nuclear bombs exploding at once—was responsible for the disappearance of the dinosaurs, as the dust and ash blocked the sun for a period of years. Others claim it was the cause of a massive tidal wave, which explains the "holding back" of the Red Sea just as the Israelites were crossing it in the Exodus from Egypt. I didn't really care at the time about the theories; I just knew it was enormous.

At the large tree, I met a couple of young hikers just out of the army. Within about six seconds we had covered the six degrees of separation, discovering that just a few weeks ago we'd both been at the wedding of my friend's daughter—with whom the young man had served in the IDF. Under the bows of the *Shita* (Acacia) tree—the name of the street I lived on for 13 years in Beit Shemesh—I sat quietly, eating another granola bar, watching them walk away south, thinking about what a small country this is and how lucky I am to be part of this ingathering of exiles from around the globe.

I stretched and dawdled as I tried to gather my strength for the long flat walk across the crater, and then the steep climb up its side. It was like a threatening mirage. Eventually I pulled my pack on and stumbled out onto the trail. Just then I noticed a young guy, about 40 meters ahead, pulling *his* pack on and staggering a bit; and so, with a brief "shalom," we started walking together. Segev was 22 and from a Kibbutz up north. After a few minutes of who/what/where exchanges, he asked me, "Why do 30 percent of marriages now end in divorce in Israel?" Suddenly I'm the world's expert. Reminding him of the relatively positive nature of that number in comparison to the rates in the US and Europe, I mentioned a few factors, from women's empowerment to more relaxed attitudes toward the institution of marriage. I said I thought it wasn't necessarily a bad thing, not least as Israelis tend to marry younger than other westerners, not to mention a worrying incidence of abusive husbands and fathers. But I told him truthfully that I didn't really know and didn't really want to talk much about it. Segev then launched into a passionate defense of polygamy (!) and wanted to know my views—at which point I was ready to allow him to walk ahead faster, and we parted ways as we neared the cliff. It was a hard climb up the edge of the crater; higher (400 meters or so) and longer than it looked from far away. What a surprise.

I reached the top and wound my way through the small, quiet, somewhat poor town, and wondered not for the last time what people thought of the backpackers who wander past their doors. And not least what locals made of this gray-haired, unshaven, dusty and sweaty old guy with a funky hat and a little Israeli flag fluttering from the back of his pack.

Making it to the "Desert Shade Eco Lodge" before sunset—I made it to Mitzpeh Ramon in one day after all—I was pleasantly surprised to find a set of mud huts with enough modern conveniences to make the Ashram seem primitive. I was improving my situation every day! Here was a wooden platform with a mattress on it—with sheets and blankets! A heater! And the hot shower came with shampoo right there. What could be better?

Well, wine, for a start. What drew me to the Eco Lodge initially was the invitation of the founder of the Rujum winery there, who had told me about the place and said it was right on the Shvil and that "we host Shvilistim all the time!" ("Shvilistim is the plural term for those who hike the Shvil.) I've made wine as a hobby since 1997, so was of course interested. On arrival I was given a wonderful little room in the earth-and-natural-materials hut, a towel and a glass of warm tea . . . though no wine (yet). After my shower and a little getting organized, I walked over to the industrial area of the town where I found a cute little shop with a fireplace, had a pizza and coffee, and walked back quickly in the increasingly cold night. The heater in my room was a welcome extra, that's for sure.

In the morning, I prayed just after sunrise, overlooking the cliff and the crater itself, and took a long walk along the escarpment where huge wind chimes welcomed the rising sun. As I enjoyed a modest Israeli-style breakfast of fresh bread, scrambled eggs, and salads in the common room, a few wild desert sheep wandered through and by the site. So even with the trappings of luxury I still felt I was on the Trail. Ziv, part-owner of Rujum and manager of Desert Shade, with whom I'd spoken a few times by phone prior to my arrival, came over and introduced himself. He walked me through the small (5,000 bottles or so a year) and clean winery, and we tasted a few of their more recent blends. Very impressive, full of flavor, if a bit harsh and young, with a dusty sort of feel. (No, I didn't just imagine that.)

There and then I decided to find and visit any and all wineries along the trail, something I managed to do with some frequency from that point on. Ziv and I discussed a number of wine-related issues, not least the unprecedented step they took to arrange for kosher supervision from the *Masorti* (Conservative) branch of Judaism rather than Orthodox; we agreed I'd buy a few bottles to be shipped home for Pesach (Passover). (My opinions regarding the esoteric complexities of kashrut and wine can be summarized easily: there's the Law; there's Tradition;

and then there's "*shtut,*" or idiocy, to quote the Vilna Gaon, the eighteenth-century rabbinical sage, in a different but not unrelated context regarding *kitniyot* or legumes, on Pesach. What is actually permitted to the kosher-observant Jew, versus what is now dictated by Orthodox authorities, is worlds apart. Further explication must await another opportunity.)

And then it was time to go. But I was hesitant; the intensity of that first week had caught up with me, and the steep ascent from the bottom of the crater had been more than I'd bargained for. I had already decided, the night before, to skip the "new" route of the Trail. (The new route is an additional set of sections off the original path of the Shvil, including a four-day segment down to the Arava from near the Ashram, and another two-day segment in the hills and valleys between the northern edge of the Ramon Crater and the Akev spring just south of Sde Boker. I figured I was spending enough time in the desert as it was—three weeks—and had a schedule to keep to if I was going to finish by Pesach. And in any case, I hadn't arranged for water drops or resupply, and the extra sections dive deep into the desert and are impossible without preparation.)

So that Monday morning I elected to take a bus to my next stop, the small community of Sde Boker, on the straight road alongside the Shvil. I have to admit I guiltily enjoyed the bus ride, purposefully looking out the window to catch the tricolored Israel National Trail signs at the side of the road, pretending I could enjoy it from the comfort of the air-conditioned bus as much as I could walking along it. I couldn't, and didn't, but I did take pleasure in the views and scenery whizzing by. And it did, in fact, put into relief the incredible difference between the pace of walking and that of driving—a difference most of us acknowledge intellectually but rarely have the chance to really experience.

Thirty minutes or so later we had covered the 33 kilometers, which would have taken a whole (boring, hot, interminable) day, and I jumped off the bus happily, looking forward to a little break exploring Sde Boker, the home and final resting place of Israel's first prime minister and founding father, David Ben Gurion. Finding the "Shvilistim" room among the small dorm pods at Midreshet Ben Gurion took a while; "almost as long as walking there might have taken from Mitzpeh Ramon!" I said to myself. I was a little taken aback on entering: nine beds, stacked in tiers of three, in a small dark room with a little table in the middle. On closer inspection it was nicer than it looked, with coffee and tea and assorted munchies left out, and a little box to put contributions to support the upkeep and electricity costs. I chose a bed—thankfully on my own it seemed—and went out to look for food and guidance. I'd been in touch with Haim Berger, a tour guide and desert expert, over the past few days, by phone; now I went to meet with him to discuss water drops and plans for the week. I'd already discovered in the Red Guide that a few of that week's routes were some of the hardest on the Shvil; and I knew there was no chance of resupply from Monday through Friday, and similar the following week.

I found Haim in his home office near the buildings of Ben Gurion University's campus in Sde Boker, and he was warm and helpful, almost comforting in his casual familiarity with the terrain and the logistics. We arranged to have him prepare and leave water for me in four locations. It felt like a bad take on a James Bond film when he described where to find them. "A few meters from the trail where it crosses a dirt road, you'll find a break in the small embankment; walk through there, continue for about 10 meters, and you'll see a small set of rocks on your left about shoulder-level. The water will be under/behind those rocks." I suppose if the water was there when I arrived, I could laugh about it. Spoiler alert, as they say.

I was, though, comforted at the time to hear details of the Trail from him, suggestions for where to rest and sleep and the like. I then wandered through Sde Boker, impressed by the expansion of Ben Gurion University (when I studied for my masters in business at the main campus in Beer Sheva, they had no branches in Sde Boker, or Eilat, or elsewhere as they do now). Ending up at the grave of David Ben Gurion and his wife, I was strangely moved both by his choice to end his days living in Sde Boker (bravo for a leader who acts on his values) as well as by the location of the graves. They overlook Avdat Spring and Tzin Valley, which I'd be walking through the next day, and looking out from from far above, the hues of the desert change even as you're watching the sun drift behind the hills.

The combination of the modern leader of Israel perched on the edge of Midbar Tzin, the Tzin Desert, where the ancient leader of the children of Israel, Moshe, is said to have led them in our wanderings in the desert, is poignant. Historically accurate or not (I struggled over the course of these weeks with the geographical and biblical challenges involved in establishing the historicity of just where the Israelites walked), I found it touching and uplifting to ponder the audacity, the idealism, and the power of Ben Gurion's dedication to resurrecting the nation of Israel and creating our modern nation-state.

By the time I got back to the room, it was dark and I was tired. But I had to eat and didn't feel like making more quinoa, so I walked over to the little area of shops and found a bar/café/restaurant where I could order a salad and pasta. They were holding, it turned out, a sort of community arts event, so I watched and listened as a few local artists made presentations of their rather unusual sculpture and painting—it's a pretty radical, secular kibbutz, and their art fits the desert, nonconformist nature of the community. Finishing my drink, I went back to the room and after spending another hour looking at maps and planning the week, fell into a deep sleep.

The next morning—Tuesday, really the beginning of my week in some ways—I enjoyed saying my prayers outdoors amid the bustle of the young students making their way to breakfast. I took a shower, and walked out into the sun. At the little pizza place in the shops area, which doubled as a morning-coffee-and-breakfast nook, I grabbed a shakshuka for breakfast. (Shakshuka is an

Israeli specialty, highly recommended: whole eggs slow-cooked in tomato sauce with various vegetables and spices.) The advice of the friendly Russian couple who owned the place, and their daughter, was not too helpful, but I appreciated their interest and enthusiasm. Setting out, I stopped at the "ranger station" visitor center info desk at the nature reserve entrance—and they were equally unhelpful, as will be seen. Finally, with a goodbye visit to the last toilet I'd see for three days and a fill-up of my water bottles and camel-back, I set off down the incline into the Advat valley, which I had gazed down upon from Ben Gurion's grave.

Yes—I'm off! It's not too steep but I have to keep reminding myself to keep my balance, as it's been two days since I did any serious hiking with the pack on. Starting to sing as I descend, I'm belting out what's becoming a theme song for me: "רבות מחשבות בלב איש, ועצת ה' היא תקום"—*"Rabot machshavot b'lev ish, v'etzat HaShem he takum"—"There are many thoughts/intentions in a man's heart, while God's guidance/wisdom will prevail . . ." I'm singing at the top of my lungs, alternating between melody and harmony, and it feels great. Until someone starts clapping just as I finish. It turns out that a group of three boys/young men are sitting on a boulder around a corner of the trail; I didn't see them. They applaud and call for more (they're below me, about 70–80 meters away); I laugh and just keep bouncing down the hill. As I am passing them, they ask me to sing again, but I just smile and say, "Another time perhaps"; when they see the flag on my back one calls out "Shvil Yisrael?!?" and I nod and wave toward them, not breaking stride; they hoop a bit, yelling "kol hakavod" ("good for you") and it makes me smile.*

Setting a good tempo, though it's getting hot, I'm really enjoying the scenery of a bit more greenery and exquisite rock formations, looking almost like waves as I walk by. I drop my hat and (thankfully) notice not too long after; heading back, I reprimand myself, as I had felt something was amiss but paid no heed. "If you know it, ACT on it" I tell myself. Could have saved a half hour of retracing my steps. But I'm glad I turned back when I did; it would have been much worse had I continued to ignore it.

It's really beautiful, and being back on the trail is very welcome; not least as I need this time to myself. I'm singing, and saying various tefilot (prayers), and allowing my thoughts to wander. The scenery is truly spectacular, and I take a moment to make a video of this segment (Video 2). Hearing the crunch of my steps in the sand and rocks, I turn this way and that so the camera captures at least a sense of the expanse of hills and valleys, the river bed and the rock formations, some smooth from years of flood waters and some jagged from years of dry desert winds, as well as the silence as the clouds drift by far above. I'm feeling like this is a little taste of paradise—even if it is the middle of the desert.

A Nature Authority ranger stops in his jeep as he drives by; we chat a bit and he warns me to be out of the reserve by 4 p.m. so the animals can drink (as the first did in the information hut up at the entrance to the reserve). He offers no advice or guidance—though I explicitly tell him my plan is to visit Ein Akev (the Akev spring) and then to head to Hod Akev cliff to climb down it to reach the night camp before dark. He doesn't respond to this plan in any way; neither did the other for that matter, and I think nothing of it.

Arriving at Ein Akev, I remember Bini urging me: go in every spring you pass. Here, I don't need his instruction: I'm hot, the water is clean and clear and cold, and though I showered this morning, I'm already sweaty and dusty and ready for a wash. I'm not alone—though it's quiet, thankfully—and I take a minute to consider. Deciding, I approach the family sitting by the edge of the water and politely explain that I can't find my swimsuit (or, really, can't be bothered, but I don't say that), and would the mother mind closing her eyes as I jump in the water, since I promised my daughter's boyfriend that I'd go in to every pool I passed?! They smile and as she pulls her hat over her eyes, lying in her husband's lap, he says he'll ensure she doesn't peek. (They're religiously obser-vant, so it's a funny joke.) I then walk over to a French couple sitting a ways away and have a similar conversation—in English—though I realize it's probably unnecessary as (1) they're facing the other way and (2) they're French, after all.

I quickly strip out of my clothes and dive in. The water's FREEZING but exhila-rating! I swim over to tread water under the water fall, and then back and climb out pretty fast as my limbs are getting numb—but not before I get a boy to take a few photos of me (one of which is just about okay for sharing). Sitting afterward, I remember, "Hey—I have lunch packed!" and take out the cheese, tomatoes, mustard, and whole wheat bread I bought this morning, and enjoy a veritable feast. Then it's time to move out.

What happened next has become one of the two or three worst and best stories of the Trail for me. Though I continued to walk at a good pace, it took well over two hours to reach the top of the plateau next to Hod Akev, the small mountain above the night camp I was to stay in. It was a pleasant walk—alone but agreeable, singing, quiet, an occasional bird, enjoying again the solitude of the desert and the rolling hills as I tramped onward. I've tried not to overuse the word "suddenly" in these descriptions, but here it's utterly appropriate: With the peak of Hod Akev to my left, striding forward happily, I suddenly found myself at the edge of a cliff and almost walked right over it.

Imagine driving an 18-wheel truck and having to stop on a dime. That's what it felt like, as I just about managed not to let my 25 kilo/50 lb backpack roll over the top of my back and pull me over the precipice. Yes, I wasn't paying attention. No, I'm not an idiot. Yes, it was a close call. I was singing, and looking up and forward, and to the left at the peak, not down. I took a breath, and looked over the edge, struggling to keep my balance. The first part looked difficult but not impossible, a rocky cliff with a few iron hand- and footholds for assistance; I fig-ured I could manage that, if just, with the pack hopefully not dragging me away from the cliff side and carrying me down the mountain. I could see the trail then drift off to the right, into the side of the mountain. It seemed to disappear, then reappear, but literally down the side of the chalky cliff, about a foot wide if that.

Much as I tried, I couldn't see where one could walk, let alone how it's possible to do so with a huge, unwieldy, heavy, cumbersome backpack. As I considered the situation, I sent an emergency sms to Michal, daughter of my friends Aaron and Hadas (the one who helped me save some kilos of weight before the trip, throwing stuff away for me, who had done the Shvil the previous year), to ask whether she'd descended this cliff successfully. Then I saw a couple of guys far below, about two hundred meters away down the mountain.

I yelled to them and asked (in Hebrew) "Is this truly possible?" One called back "Yes—but it's really scary!" "With a 25-kilo pack?!!?" "No!" came the answer. "It's really dangerous! Don't do it—danger of death!" (סכנת מוות!)

I took another few minutes to evaluate. Others before me have done it. They're probably younger by half, in better shape by a lot, probably with better equipment, lighter packs, more experience. Do I walk back and around—10 kilometers at least, maybe three hours—or just do it on my backside? I'm so close (you can see the night camp at the bottom!) and am getting tired—and it's already past 3 in the afternoon. I felt stupid—both as I should have read the elevation diagrams and asked more questions, and I could have spent less time at the spring. And I was angry: at the author of the Red Guide (again), at the two rangers who perhaps could have thought to *mention* something to this old guy with gray hair and huge back-

Hod Akev, overlooking the cliff

pack when they heard he was thinking of climbing down Hod Akev, even at the guide Haim, who didn't say anything. And of course at myself for not planning better, knowing better, thinking more clearly. But there are some advantages to being fifty-one; and one of them is (sometimes) knowing what the right thing to do is, even when you're angry and tired and frustrated.

So I did the mature thing, and after taking some photos and even a video for posterity (Video 3), turned around and started the schlepp back along the way I came. As I walked—quickly, knowing it would be getting dark soon—I kept thinking how much I wanted one of those rangers to come along and reprimand me for being in the reserve after 4 p.m. "Let the animals wait—or go thirsty!" I wanted to say to them; "You want me to die trying to slide down a cliff so their watering hole isn't bothered?" I was ready to tell them to arrest me—or better yet, to give me a lift to the night camp. But no such luck—there's never a ranger around when you need one it seems.

(For the record, Michal—my friends' daughter—had not descended the cliff. Hadn't even tried. As I discovered since, most of those I've spoken with didn't bother, but just hiked out from Ein Akev around the mountain to the night camp. I've since posted a note on the Shvil site warning others . . .)

Of course, the story can't end there. I arrived at the night camp after sunset, where the two men to whom I had called earlier down the cliff were happily sitting around a fire with another three or four, old friends from school who had come out for a few days hiking and camping. Dumping my pack, in the growing darkness I took my headlamp and went looking for the water according to Haim's 007-like instructions. I went down the dirt road, found the break in the low dirt rise, walked along the "corridor" as instructed . . . and found nothing.

After an incredibly irritating 30 minutes or so, in the (of course) starless and moonless pitch black of the early night, I called Haim (thankfully there was cellular reception). It didn't help: the water just wasn't there. Yet I did have some luck: the men back at camp said they could spare four liters of water; so I was saved.

I sat by the fire with them, made quinoa with a bit of the garlic, onion, salt, pepper, rosemary, and oregano (which I carried with me, so very cleverly I thought, in a pill box with separate compartments) and oil—it was actually quite good, and I shared some with them. They gave me tea, and I had some of their noodles. It was warm by the fire, if a bit smoky, and I welcomed the company for a while. I was grateful for the end of the day; I appreciated the camaraderie, their willingness to share, and of course their water too. I was grateful for my own smarts and wisdom and glad of the decision to go back and around, even as I felt the pain in my legs intensifying from the long day made even longer.

I spoke with one of them about the *Carbolet*—the name for the high mountain rim on the edge of the Large Crater, the "toughest day on the Shvil" according to the Red Guide—awaiting me in two days' time. I wasn't 100 percent sure which route to take; in fact, I wasn't sure I wanted to try it at all. It's steep and dry and windy and dangerous. I was tired and my head hurt, so I crawled into my tent, a little further up the hill from the group, and wrote a bit in my journal (without the amazing hanging lantern Tehila and Netanel had given me—where was it? Darn it! Did I throw it in with the stuff Meira took back with her on Saturday night?).

Journal Day 10—Tues 25 Feb:
 The guys are pretty loud. Hope can sleep . . . Not sure about the Carbolet. But that's okay—nothing is set in stone. Lonely. Others have someone—these guys have each other, friends. While Yaron has his father; Reuven his wife; all the others I've met have SOMEONE. I have no one. I still can't really believe it. Am I running away from facing this reality?

Lying alone in bed in the dark, listening to them talk and laugh, I start to relate to the difficulties along the way in a new fashion. It just comes to me: accept the heat, take the steepness, acknowledge the tiredness, bear the pain, tolerate the rain, endure the repetitive sound of your own footsteps, brave the loneliness: accept accept accept.

It is what it is.

To successfully meet the challenge, the first step is to accept the reality of the situation.

And I immediately connect this to, and can't stop thinking of, a key experience at the meditation retreat I attended following my son Netanel and Tehila's wedding last year.

A week after my son's wedding, I turned off my phones, left my laptop at home, and disconnected from my family, friends, work, and the world at large to attend a three-day silent meditation retreat, as mentioned briefly in the introduction. Combining Jewish mystical traditions with various methods of relaxation, concentration, and introspection, this escape from reality was sublimely timed for me. After a year of talk-talk-talk with Karen and therapists and friends, months of intensive interactions with family, let alone the emotional highs of the wedding and lows of dealing with the fact that my wife wants a divorce. . . . I was so ready for some quiet I could scream. (And I'm a talker, for sure.)

With lessons from the Kabbalah and ancient techniques of sitting, standing, stretching, singing, praying, and more, Rabbi Hillel Lester of the Shalev Center of Jerusalem led our small group gathered in the hills south of Jerusalem, in the small, hippie-ish village of Bat Ayin, to contemplate life, the universe, and everything. Coming together as an ad-hoc community, we created a bond of kinship through our silence and suffering (many of us), through meditation and song and guided imaging, and struggled individually, together. It was a fascinating experience of poignant, emotional personal introspection, each of us alone, while surrounded by a supportive, if quiet, group.

The setting was a square studio-like wood frame living room in the home of our host and the co-leader of the retreat, Rabbi Daniel Cohn, surrounded by tall, strong pine and fir trees, bushes and flowers, with wide picture-windows looking across the valley to the hills leading north to Jerusalem.

One of the most incredible, transformative moments for me was learning the practice of walking-meditation. Taking slow steps across the room, around the garden or along the path on the side of the hill, we were encouraged to use the movement as an inspiration, as a point of departure, in conjunction with a meaningful phrase or mantra to guide or promote reflection. At one point in the Shabbat and *Rosh Chodesh* (new month) prayers I started to relate to my slow steps as somehow connected to my need to slowly move ahead with my life, as I came to terms with the disintegration of our incredibly happy, committed, loving marriage of 28 years.

That's when I experienced an epiphany.

It may be obvious, and we don't spend much time thinking about it (most of us), but each physical step we take has three distinct stages. First, our weight rests on our back foot. Then, we transfer the weight across/ahead and balance in-between. Finally, we rest our weight on our front foot. The first and last stages are well-defined, and stable. But the middle stage is transient, impossible to identify (when exactly does the weight cross over?), unstable. That shift is indefinite, frightening, ephemeral, *un-knowable*. I was transfixed by that middle, in-movement, undefined element. That was *me*, exactly: in the middle, unsure, imbalanced, in transition.

I was profoundly disturbed when I realized this. "This *isn't* me," unsteady and insecure or afraid, I said to myself. Yet rather than giving in to the despair beginning to rise within me, I realized something incredibly powerful. I had been meditating earlier, purposefully, on one of God's names—the very first name of God mentioned in the Bible, אהיה אשר אהיה (*Eheye Asher Eheye*). This translates literally as "I Will Be as I Will Be" or "I Am What I Am" (see translation note in the Introduction). I had seen it very much as a teaching related to an acceptance of reality, a recognition that God controls the universe, not me. In fact, at the burning bush, our tradition suggests, God intended for this to be one of the primary aspects of our understanding of Him—unknowable, inscrutable. I had already begun to relate this in my meditative reflections to the much more casual, almost harsh phrase thrown out by my son's friend Zachy, "It is what it is," which had become something of an ironic reference for my kids and me in recent months.

But now it began to sink in; the walking meditation made it concrete, and my understanding of this aspect of God's essence became so much deeper. That first and last resting point were the "אהיה"—the "I Am/Will Be" of existence, stable and solid; where we are standing and where we are ending up, with the foot on the ground, in contact with the earth; at rest. And those aspects, the existential imperative and omniscient presence of the "I Am" and "I Was" and "I Will Be," are usually the focus of most commentary on this name of God, and are in the prayer/song which concludes every synagogue service. Yet I discovered another, perhaps hidden, aspect which speaks so much more to me: The dynamic mid-point, indefinable, active, inscrutable, "אשר" ("*Asher*"). This is the actual reference to God's essence, the here and now as it's happening, the state of being *in between* the verb(s) expressing that being, that reality.

This distinction is so significant, if so perilously difficult to make or understand. That indeterminate transient moment as the weight transfers from one leg and foot to the other is the "*Asher*," that almost ignored word meaning "as" or "what" or "that" in the phrase "I am WHAT I am" or "I will be THAT which I will be" or "I exist AS I exist." And it is at that *precise moment*, that *instant* of existing in the present, that we are actually living, constantly. That is precisely when we are alive. I could relate so much more to that evolving aspect of God's essence than God's omnipotence.

I thought of a car tire in constant motion: we know that at any instant, however fast the car speeds down the highway, there is a piece of rubber actually touching the road. At that instant, neither the road nor the tire are actually moving: they are stationary, in motionless physical contact—and that is the present moment. This is *Asher*, this is the indefinable, always moving but with no movement, present.

This is life.

And for me, at that moment, this became the source of incredible comfort, and the focus of my meditation, whether walking or sitting. It was, in some modest way, a discovery of that still, small voice of Isaiah. *Eheye Asher Eheye*: *Eheye* (I Am/Will be) on the back foot; *Asher* (As/Which/That/What) in the transition; *Eheye* (I Am/Will be). Breathe in on *Eheye*; breathe out on *Eheye*. Where the inhalation transitions to the exhalation, and where the weight shifts from back to front, is the *Asher*, the transition point, the pivotal instant of progress or change and moving forward even without movement—the Present. Try as you might, you cannot catch that inflection point. If you're not holding your breath, if you're not balancing between two feet, the moment of transition is ephemeral, fleeting, impossible to hold on to.

It is the here and now. It cannot be grasped—we can't define or identify that split second of transition—but of course we are aware when it occurs. It can be noted. It can be accepted. It can be lived. Not "living in the moment"— though that's one application, on the lighter side, and thank you, Jason Mraz, for your song that kept me going through hard times. Rather, it's allowing all the moments of your life to simply be . . . and for life to be the continued and continuous experience of those moments strung together.

This is an acceptance of What Is, and it was this acceptance of reality, of this aspect of God's essence, which was transformative for me on that day at the meditation retreat in Bat Ayin.

And at that point of the Shvil, in the darkness of the desert under Hod Akev, it took on a whole new meaning. I had come full circle, from that epiphany on the meditation retreat to incorporating it no into my life philosophy, and acting on it.

Lying on my leaky air mattress listening to the young men not far off talking and laughing, after writing that brief journal entry, I said over and over to myself: No. I am not running away. I accept that this is my reality; I am using this time to deal with it as my new reality. I fell asleep repeating my new mantra to myself: it is what it is. Not exactly meditation—or maybe yes—but a meditative relaxation exercise which lulled me to sleep, with only a few tears . . . "אהיה אשר אהיה"— Eheye Asher Eheye—"I Am What I Am." "I Will Be As I Will Be." It is what it is. I accept.

Wednesday dawned very cold—so cold I didn't want to even bother to light a fire. I stayed in my sleeping bag in the tent for an extra few minutes as the morning warmed up a bit in the early sun, and then enjoyed a quick cup of tea and some oatmeal, while "the guys" were sleeping (without a tent—weren't they freezing?!? Oh to be young . . .). As on most mornings of the Shvil, meditating on *Eheye*, acceptance, and on *Modeh*, gratitude, was a central part of my *Tefila* prayers.

It was a short, flat, slow walking day—a sort of break between the (frustratingly unplanned long and more-difficult-than-it-should-have-been) previous day and the upcoming serious challenge of the Carbolet. A number of aspects of the day made it truly enjoyable, aside from the ease of the terrain and the relatively late start and early finish.

To begin with, the vistas at the edge of the long expanses of flat or slightly rolling dusty hills were surprisingly pretty. Though not huge or towering, and with relatively uninspiring rock formations, the mountains rising ahead and to my right filled me with a sense of wonder, and of purpose. Though far away, and not small, they seemed to beckon, and seemed manageable. Compared to the mountains of Eilat, *Maale Amram*, the *Milchan* and others from the previous week—which loom directly ahead and above you in a threatening way, engendering a sense of foreboding—these were far enough away, and seemed smooth and almost soft in the morning haze. They made me think of pillows and clouds rather than the jagged teeth of the monsters I'd climbed further south. It felt almost inviting.

The second enjoyable aspect of the day occurred as I slowly walked up a hill . . . and stumbled on an expanse of rocks along the flatness of the plain above the Tzin riverbed. I had just noted to myself how interesting it is that the light tan dusty earth is more and more covered with dark brown and black crystal-like small rocks, when at the crest of a small rise I discovered something incredible, and so fun. Numerous previous hikers had created art in small dark stones on the ground. Some had written poetry; others just their names. Some were enormous productions, others simple listings; many were completely intact, while others half-erased (from erosion/nature or others taking the rocks? I preferred to presume the former). It was a rather impressive display—graffiti in nature, as it were—and went on for hundreds of meters in each direction along the Shvil. It was really a kick, as I continued to walk along the path in between the words/stones/names/shapes. I debated adding my name or a thought, but chose not to; I was happy to just enjoy the others' efforts, including some funny and other poignant poems or lines. I paused to absorb, and then kept on (as one of the stone-poems read: "Keep striding").

And the most pleasurable surprise: a few desert flowers! I knew I'd crossed from the southern Negev into the central Negev by the appearance of bunches of small pink buds and blossoms (not many, but so pretty). It was such a welcome sight; had I not been looking down at that moment, I might have missed them, hidden as they were on the right of the path. Though I'd enjoyed the sandy and rocky mountains, and marveled at the variety of rock sizes and colors and formations, it was an emotional moment, becoming reacquainted with color, with life and growth and nature. As they peeked out from the crevice on the side of the trail, they represented for me the struggle to thrive in a challenging situation. They were a symbol of new beginnings, of rebirth, of the cycle of existence, of Spring and life itself. Oy, I waxed so poetic and philosophical!

By then, the day had become hot, and it was taking longer than I expected; with a headache (perhaps caused by the Hoodia gum I'd bought at the Ashram?), I sat down for an extended lunch break. My thoughts somehow connected the emergence of the flora with new beginnings and regeneration—and linked that to Karen and my beginnings and breakup, as described in my journal entry from later that day, reproduced below.

Still, I arrived at the Nachal Mador (Mador Stream) night camp around 4 p.m., early enough to leisurely set up camp and collect a bit of wood for a fire. This time, I found the six liters of water Haim had hid (yes! Though why

Flowers in Nachal Tzin

did it have to be over 300 meters from the camp? What a schlepp), and then was contented to sit for a bit before sunset on a hilltop overlooking the camp. As before, "camp" was in the middle of a tank exercise area. I suppose the warnings afford a bit more compelling a reason to follow the rules than the mere protection of flora or fauna, or even cautions in Yosemite about bears possibly raiding your campsite.

I could see the Carbolet and its sharp, jagged ridge in the near distance; planning for tomorrow became less theoretical. I took stock of my physical state (pretty tired, hungry, dirty, and in not a little pain in my calves, hips, toes, and shoulders; well, actually, all over, but those were the points of particular hurt). Looking at the maps, I more or less decided to ascend the Carbolet along the Mador Stream bed rather than the ladders-and-boulders eastern route. Slightly less difficult, it was, I felt, the more realistic choice. Images of the pack pulling me off-balance and the potential of having to descend in the dark if it took longer than anticipated—and whatever I anticipated, I just knew it would take longer—convinced me to continue my tradition of maturity and wisdom from Hod Akev.

It began to turn cold as the sun set (behind the accursed Hod cliff face) as I sat on a small rise and reflected on my thoughts during the latter part of the day's walk, and wrote in my journal. My reflections on seeing the flowers had brought on a slew of ruminations which occupied my thoughts for the rest of the afternoon.

Journal Day 11—Wed 26 Feb:

Today walking alone was less lonely, more meditative walking—just going according to the קֶצֶב [rhythm].

Still thinking about things—what could have or should I seen or done? Or not done? Wonder—is Karen happy? What really went on here? What does that mean "I've fallen out of love"? I can't really grasp it. I thought marriage is *forever*. I thought that, when I asked Karen, and I thought it 25 years later, and I still think it now. Why couldn't she just have taken a "break"?

I keep returning to thoughts of her diagnosis of depression or other elements but WHAT'S THE POINT? She is a whole person and whatever part of her motivated her to do this—"right" or "wrong" in terms of what she "really" wants or needs or what is "good" for her or what will answer her unhappiness—is still part of her—and SHE made this decision.

I AM ANGRY at Karen, not just sad and disappointed, bitter + resentful & hurt. [Ed. note: The word "angry" is a bit messed up—seems I couldn't or didn't want to write it, went over the "N" a few times.]

I am ANGRY that (1) she didn't seem to care enough to work through it, (2) she wasn't mature/adult enough to act on her response of "this changes everything" with her diagnosis of depression, (3) she was basically willing to *give in* without a fight—"I don't want to work at it."

I am ANGRY because I see all these as demonstrations of a basic SELFISHNESS which was rather new to Karen. Or not. As generous + giving as she always has been, that self-assertion has been a theme for years— with my folks (and sometimes hers), the kids, me, friends—of "I'll do what's good for ME." This is just the most radical and extreme example.

I can deal w/my anger. But as [our long-time friend] Rebecca asked a few times—why didn't I EXPRESS my exasperation, anger, lack of understanding, incomprehension???

Sympathy for her, before & especially after the diagnosis, is only a partial explanation . . .

OKAY ENOUGH.

Now to hopefully make soup . . .

I had enough propane gas to make soup, with the last of my whole-wheat noodles, what a treat! While making the soup, I thought more about Karen and myself, and about my anger and my acceptance. It is okay to recognize my anger; and it is okay to have focused at the time on helping Karen to deal with her unhappiness and depression. But seriously. I was not only confused; I knew that there HAD to be a better explanation for her misery than me/us. I may not have been the perfect husband or father, but our relationship was without question one of the best either of us were familiar with, among our family and friends. And all other observers knew it too. Only Karen insisted that her melancholy resulted from discontent with us. And in the end, her fixation on that was the undoing of everything we built.

It was a strange sequence of events. Sometimes I wonder if it could have been scripted any more enigmatically. As she told me and others later, Karen had been finding herself crying for no reason at her computer, while driving, and at other mundane tasks. Looking for an explanation, she decided it must be that she was unhappy in the marriage. As a couple, we had our ups and downs of course, including a rough patch as our kids hit the teens, when our different styles of parenting became more apparent. Mine was a more laid-back Californian, Reform/liberal, and soft-spoken approach; hers a more British, Orthodox/conservative, and strict approach. (Once, as an example, our 12-year-old daughter was caught sneaking out of a boys' dormitory window. With her on the phone, us in a supermarket, Karen began to read her the riot act; I preferred to wait until we got home to discuss it. Karen was angry at me for not being more angry at our daughter. She resented my somewhat detached calmness, not even related to any discussion of what approach might be more effective with our daughter.) But Karen was a loving and nurturing mother, with great emotional intelligence, and I was willing to be a stronger disciplinarian when necessary, and we balanced each other well. Even, or especially, when her relationship with our older daughter deteriorated. More important, our love always brought us back together when we found ourselves at odds.

And most important, when she looked for that interpretation of her unhappiness, she was the first to admit there was no specific grievance, nor even a general complaint, directed at me. She said she just didn't want to be married anymore. Not to me, anyway. Coming literally out of nowhere—and coupled with the certainty with which she expressed the desire to split—it prompted in me first sadness, then sympathy, and then a search for solutions. (I'm a man, after all, even if I pride myself on being sensitive, a good listener, in touch with my emotions, etc.) Continuous discussions between us and with friends, counselling as a couple, and Karen's personal therapy did little to amerliorate my agonizing pain. First she moved to another room, and then downstairs to our guest room. We ceased couples counselling after about ten sessions when it became clear she was not at all interested in trying to reclaim our love and repair the relationship.

After six months, Karen received pivotal news. Her doctor gave a name to her ailment: depression. As quoted in my journal above, she said at the time, sitting on our living room balcony overlooking our garden and the Jerusalem foothills as the sun set in the distance over the Mediterranean, "This changes everything." We were ready to embark on a new direction, recognizing that with the diagnosis comes a combination of understanding, treatment, and resolution.

That lasted three days.

Inexplicably, Karen was too committed to her course of action, too enamored perhaps of the allure of living alone, too invested in the idea of divorce to let it go. But I and the few others apprised of the news hoped it would open up new avenues of thought and engender a willingness to re-evaluate. For three days I lived on a cloud of happiness and relief. Depression was something I knew well, from experience with family and friends suffering from that terrible condition where not sadness, but the lack of any feeling, or even ability to feel, creates a black hole of dread and uselessness. As bizarre as it sounds, I was glad she was depressed. At least this we could deal with.

But it was not to be. I have to admit, one of the things I loved about Karen—which attacted me to her in the beginning—was her conviction. Growing up in an Orthodox Jewish home, she had a keen sense of right and wrong, and a strong set of deeply-held principles. These helped to guide her life, including a dedication to observance of Torah commandments and a commitment to Israel as the national home for the Jewish people. Even if this occasionally created friction—and not least with the children—it was always something I admired. Yet in this case it worked against us. Three days after the diagnosis, Karen changed doctors, finding a therapist who would help her achieve her goal of divorce, rather than one who would help her heal . . . or encourage her to heal the relationship. Though she agreed to postpone moving out of the house until after Netanel and Tehila's wedding, as far as she was concerned it was a done deal.

For me, it took another six months—until after the wedding, and that silent meditation retreat—to even begin to accept that the deal was indeed done. The constant talks with friends and family, emails, letters, WhatsApp messages, and Facebook posts over that time have become a running joke, if a somewhat painful one, among my circle of close friends. I managed to go to work, relate to my kids and wider family and circle of friends, pretending there was still a chance. But I'd sit on a bench in the center of Jerusalem and cry, not caring if passersby noticed, as the new light rail trains floated across my vision and people went about their shopping as if the world wasn't falling apart. I found a therapist to help me work through my own issues; we focused for ten weeks on my feelings of betrayal and disappointment, frustration at Karen and myself, resentment of her and empathy for her. I stopped the sessions after a few months, not least as my friend Moshe was a better therapist, and friend. I also had the support I continued to receive from Rebecca and Deborah and all my other friends. If during the first six months after Karen's bombshell my natural optimism allowed me to focus on my hopes to mend things between us, the second half-year was a slow process of trying come to terms with the end of our relationship, even as my son began his own marriage.

I focused on supporting her in an effort to help her explore and discover the true source of her sorrow and despair, rather than being angry at her for not wanting to even try to salvage the relationship. Anger just isn't my default reaction. This therefore became another thing for me to work on "accepting": my failing to be more forceful in expressing my resentment and anger (or even to be aware of it perhaps). In the end, sitting there outside my tent, I accepted her right to decide she just didn't want to be married to me anymore, even if the "reasons" weren't clear to her, me, or anyone else. I accepted my resentment of her for not wanting to make any effort, for just deciding that separating is the only step she can take to be happy. And I accepted my own failings, in the marriage and in the process of the divorce, not being able to change myself even as I couldn't change her. Yes, it is what it is, but also I am who I am too. Not that I think my being angry would have made any difference. It might have enabled me to check that box, too, among the tools I employed in my efforts to save our marriage, but it would have been artificial at the time.

As I made tea, looking up at the stars, I finally, truly accepted all of this, and let go of my anger for that day. I shared some soup with two German boys who, along with a group of six loud Israeli men, had arrived at the night camp while I was writing and shivering on the hill above. I packed up my stuff that evening, to be ready for an early start the next day; lights out at 7:30 p.m.! I was tired, bothered, sticky, cold, and the pains in my hips and shoulders were only exacerbated by the defective air mattress which lost air almost immediately. It was a COLD night; the Israelis made a lot of noise; the wind rattled the tent almost constantly. Needless to say, I didn't sleep much.

Having set an alarm for 5:45, I was woken before that by the (loud—such a surprise) men. I yelled at them from inside my tent, "Guys! You're not alone here! A little CONSIDERATION!" That helped some, for a while. I finally braved the cold when my alarm went off; it was a bit surprising that even having packed up all I could the night before, it still took me a full hour to break camp—without any breakfast. On the trail by 6:45, just as the sun rose in the mist, and it was hard going almost from the outset.

Just as it started getting steep enough to warrant a stop for a drink and to take off my overshirt, I came across an incredible array of spring flowers. White daisies, yellow stars, purple circles with dark centers, magenta and pink and light purple and lavender cones or tube or bulbs, as I described them (and drew little pictures) in my journal; bushes with white petals/fingers with brown edges (poisonous according to Yaron, as I recalled), peculiar shrubs with grape-like fuzzy fruit, even a few red poppies! I took some photos to share and to ask Flo, my former mother-in-law (an expert in all things floral) to identify. And then I began the real climb.

Yes this is hard. I kind of understand why the author of the Guide wrote that it's the most difficult section of the Trail. And I'm only halfway up. Seriously—this refrain of "why exactly am I doing this?" is getting a little tiresome.

I keep going. The occasional stumble, and near-fall, and increasingly frequent halts to sip water and just catch my breath, are continual reminders: be careful, take it easy, you're 51 not 21, the only way you can do this is to take one step at a time. But you CAN do this.

Now that I'm nearing the top, I have no doubt I made the right decision to climb the Nachal Mador path. If this is considered "easier" than the Nachal Efron ascent then I'm certainly glad I'm here and not there. But in this small valley near the summit of the climb, I think I'll leave my pack here in the shade of a boulder, and climb up toward the south to the crest of the ridge at the top of the other route, just to say I did.

Fuggedaboutit. Can't really say much more. I'm sitting on the side of the mountain, I can see the path stretch up above me—and up, and above, just about says it all. So far I've managed to find handholds and footholds and to avoid falling. But having stopped to enjoy a family of mountain sheep I startled on the way up, I'm really thinking to myself—forget it. Who's there to either show off to or compete with (or even to help or support or encourage)? Who needs the hassle, and the fright, and the danger? I mouth a quiet goodbye to the sheep—צבי הנגב (Tzvi HaNegev)—and take some photos and a video even (Video 4), as more than two dozen of them, including not a few lambs, wander away along the precipices. They of course don't give even a thought to the danger of a slip or injury to themselves. I'm jealous! And also of their peacefulness.

Arriving back at my pack, I shoulder it and move forward, heading north to the where the Shvil actually follows the edge of the ridge. First, I climb up what's basically a rock face, with just a hint of a path, hand over hand, seriously getting more afraid by the moment that one slip or off-balance move will carry the backpack (gravity being what it is) and me with it, obviously, halfway down the mountain. And then I arrive at the top of the crest.

Looking out over it, it's hard to describe; the Red Guide says it's like walking along the edge of a knife, and that about sums it up. It feels to me kind of like the last half mile to Half Dome's cables—but ten times as long, with blustery gusts of wind, with no cables, on a rocky and slippery uneven pebbly surface . . . and with a 50-pound pack. And of course I'm alone, and blisters are developing on my feet, and there's this blazing sun beating down through my hat. But I keep going.

With the constant strain of trying to balance, it's getting harder and harder here, walking along the rim. It's taking all my concentration not to slip, or get blown off the edge by the fierce gusts of wind coming up from the valley, or fall over the next boulder in the way. As I'm saying my tefila prayers, I'm thinking of the strength needed to persevere . . . and I break down a bit. Just a few tears. Perseverence. Every hardship, every thought, brings me back to the reason I'm even here. Why didn't she have the strength to continue? This walk is a metaphor: when the going gets tough—and this is as tough as it gets—you don't just throw in the towel, call in 669 to send a helicopter to pick you up, walk away! You find a solution; you push yourself harder, you take a break, you adjust your gear, you step carefully, slowly. Sometimes through using the markers as a guide you have to choose your own way which is comfortable or best for you. But you don't just give up! Not without a fight. Not without some reason, and not without making every effort, exploring every possibility, making use of every resource, to continue the journey.

I curse to myself—it's not a metaphor, it's a parallel. So the tears just come—for me, for her, for us. All gone. When I asked her to marry me, it was not only because we were so obviously in love. It was a commitment for the future. It was to grow old together as soul mates (like Tevya and Golda as we watched in Fiddler on the Roof *that night in her folks' living room in London). My folks had asked us what would happen if one of us (me) changed—ie. in Jewish practice, my being newly observant. Karen told them "we'll work it out because we love each other." But when it came to it, she bailed out rather than working to make it work. I'm on the dangerous edge of a windy mountain cliff and can't take another step because I'm crying; not only in sadness but in anger and frustration and exhaustion as well.*

As I step/stumble along the ragged ridge overlooking the Machtesh HaGadol, *the Large Crater, brown and shadowed, of which the* Carbolet *is the southern rim, I begin to pray:*

תן לי כח
כח להמשיך
כח לדעת להבין להשכיל
כח לסלוח
כח לתת
כח לאהוב
כח לשרוד

תן לי בינה השכל ודעת
תן לי אהבה אחווה שלום ורעות
תן לי סבלנות וסובלנות
תן לי כח להחזיק מעמד

It is a prayer for strength: strength to carry on; strength to know, to understand, to perceive; strength to forgive; strength to give, to love, to survive. With words resonating from some of the central prayers of Jewish tradition, not easily translatable, but in a structure and format of my own making, I had been asking those past two years for strength: for wisdom, enlightenment and comprehension; for love, brotherhood, peace/serenity and friendship/fellowship; patience and tolerance. For the ability to hold on. For those familiar with traditional Jewish prayer, some of the words will strike a familiar, perhaps even jarring note, taken as some phrases are from the *Sheva Brachot*, the seven blessings recited at a traditional Jewish wedding ceremony. Others are more intuitively appropriate, adopted from our daily prayers for understanding and harmony. For me, as a personal meditation, it was a mantra which did, as requested, give me some strength to carry on—frequently, and certainly there on the edge of the Carbolet.

By the time I took a break in a little hollow, still along the rim of the mountain, I'd pretty much had enough views, frights, exhaustion, near-falls and challenges for a lifetime. I meditated there in the אוכל (the "saddle') for a while. It was a bit overwhelming; a bit surreal; almost like I was in my own movie. I tried to relax. That was hard, knowing I still had at least three hours of more of the same ahead, with another two or more kilometers of the ridge still to go. In the end, I succeeded. I rested and managed focus, to observe and take it all in, to enjoy. It was glorious.

While I sat there, with tears drying on my cheeks in the wind, I thought about acceptance—of life, of challenges, of differences, of difficulties, of struggles, of unexpected turns of fate or decision. I recognized how even with the hardships I am so incredibly grateful for all the wondrous blessings of my life, not least the opportunity for this journey and all this personal growth. The seed sprouted in my mind of a connection of all this; I started to realize the importance of all the personal les-

Top of the Carbolet

sons I was learning merely by putting one foot in front of the other.

Aryeh at the Carbolet Summit

If humility is the basis for a healthy approach to challenges, as I discovered the previous week, then acceptance builds the foundation for looking forward. The humility which accompanies the understanding that "I'm not in charge here" contributes to a willingness to see reality for what it is—and to not only acknowledge that reality, but accept and embrace it. As I sat at the peak of the Carbolet, I connected these dots without really trying to, not thinking about it so much as allowing the ideas to emerge and coalesce in my subconscious. I may not have been able to articulate it at the time, but I was reaching a point where one thing was becoming clear: The key to my being able to finish the day's hike was my acceptance of the reality I faced: the heat, the incline, the weight, the length of the trail and its difficulty, the time limitations, the pain in my feet/calves/legs/back/shoulders. Once I resigned myself to this state of affairs, once I accepted it as a given, I was able to focus on my next step(s), map out my aim for the remainder of the day, shake off the growing desperation, and move on.

And of course the same was true for my life. Sitting there at the top of the Carbolet, experiencing the thrill of the achievement, I reached a level of acceptance that was at the same time deep and heavy and exciting and relieving. If I could only just acknowledge, even embrace, the reality of my life today—the divorce, the pain, the loneliness, the frustration, the humiliation—just accept it rather than fight it, I could then begin the process of getting on with my life. Somehow, at that moment, I knew not only that's what I should do, and that I could do it; I knew also that this is what I was in fact doing, physically and emotionally. I had reached a point of humble acceptance.

With that awareness came a certain calm. I remember sitting there, staring back over the crest of the ridge I'd climbed earlier, and grasping the significance of the revelation, even as I let the hot wind carry it away over the edge and allowed my thoughts to move on. Just as I succeeded in clearing my head, as the meditation did its magic and brought me to a place of silence and tranquility, another thought popped up. THIS is what's needed in our region. A bit of humility, of course, but more, an acknowledgement by all parties that hey—get over it, accept it, Israel is here to stay, there are Arabs who self-identify as "Palestinians": let's admit it, them's the facts, now let's see what we can do, accommodating that reality, to move forward here.

Permitting those thoughts to percolate, I then let them go. I'd had enough meditation, and enough of these convoluted, somewhat pretentious theories, for one day.

I sent a text message with a photo to the kids, and to Matan, my son's childhood friend and one of my three "other sons" ("*HaMaith*," a made-up word used as both a nickname for him and an exclamation along the lines of "Wohoo!"). Sent an "I'm okay/I'm alive" text to Meira as usual. I ate my carrot and cheese with Zatar and enjoyed a real treat, half a Snickers bar, which I'd saved for the occasion. I got up to head forward, knowing that I'd finish the Shvil. And I knew nothing would be as hard—neither on the Shvil, nor after it. I had learned the lesson of acceptance.

I wrote in my journal that night:

> The CARBOLET!!! !!! הכרבולת
> Aaaaaaaaaaaaaaaghhh
> HAMAITH HAMAITH HAMAITH
> I did it, I f#@%ing did it.
> I am A.W.E.S.O.M.E.!
> Rest of the day was spent trying to stay alive. ☺ Not fall off cliffs or down ravines. Glad I did it; glad it's over. Sang a lot (not only but also to distract by very real fear of imminent death)—
>
> "רבות מחשבות בלב איש, ועצת ה' היא תקום. עצת ה' לעולם
> תעמוד, מחשבות לבו לדור ודור"
> [משלי יט:כא]
>
> Many thoughts lie in the heart of man
> Yet the wisdom of God will prevail
> God's understanding will always stand
> His heart's thoughts prevail for generation to generation
> [Mishlei/Proverbs 19:21]
>
> כי את כל הארץ אשר אתה רואה
> לך אתננה—לך ולזרעך עד עולם
> [בראשית יג:טו]
> לך אתן את הארץ הזאת, את הארץ הארץ הזאת
> וברך כל מיני תבואתה לטובה ותן ברכה על פני האדמה
>
> All of this land which you see
> I will give unto you
> To you and to your descendants forever. [Breishit/Genesis 13:15]
> To you I will give this land
> This land, this very land
> And bless all it's bounty for good, and give a blessing over the
> earth . . . [Popular Israeli song]

From my Facebook post on that Saturday night, two days later (Feb 29):

> . . . the impossibly tortuous, unbelievably frightening כרבולת [Carbolet] overlooking מכתש הגדול [Machtesh HaGadol—The Big Crater] on Thursday. That was a killer. Literally. Remember the scene where Frodo and Sam are pulling themselves up hand-over-hand on the craggy rock-face of Mount Doom, weighed down by their packs (and the ever-heavier ring)? And Frodo says something about being "here, at the end of all things"? That about sums it up—but where was my Sam?
>
> It was harder than Half Dome—longer, more dangerous, more slippery,

> more windy, with a backpack no less, and no cables (and no Meira with me either). And it just kept going! Every time I thought that was it, it's over, there was another treacherous climb to another peak, or tip-toe across a ledge looking straight down into the abyss—literally—of the crater, or crawl and scrape down the edge of the cliff to get to yet another rise. As a lover of nature, I've never been happier to see a phosphorous factory ahead of me, signaling finally the eventual end of the hike.

The truth is, coming down the mountain wasn't as big a letdown (pun intended) as it could have been or as I had anticipated. I met up with a group of young men who had passed me on the Carbolet (and yes, I passing them, even at 51 and with my heavy pack), and we compared notes and shared moleskin as we tended to our blisters. I managed to get to the end of the trail a good half-hour before I thought I would, and waited only 20 minutes or so for a ride that would take me all the way to the entrance of Dimona, a "development town" (a poor and under-developed small settlement) in the central Negev, known mainly for the nuclear reactor nearby.

Dropped off near the entrance to town, I noticed that the 200-meter walk to the Burger Ranch, Israel's down-market version of MacDonalds, felt like a mile. Ridiculous! I went in to use the bathroom and perhaps order a drink. I hate to admit it in print, because I've been a vegetarian pretty much all my adult life, but I ordered and then ate a hamburger and fries; I'm not sure, and don't feel the need really to analyze it too deeply, but I think it was a sort of connection with civilization, with normality, even with "home" in a way, more than the nutrition itself (if you can even call it that). As a vegetarian, I of course felt guilty and hypocritical; knowing that I was about to spend Shabbat happily in a non-meat-eating environment, I asked myself what I was doing. Then, without answering, I just did it, spontaneously and willingly.

The people—staff and other customers—were incredibly kind and enthusiastic about my being in the midst of hiking the Shvil; they don't see too many Shvilistim as it's a bit off the route, and it sure made me feel good. On leaving, I just couldn't bear walking another step, because my pack kept getting heavier (or perhaps the greasy hamburger weighed heavily inside me). So I flagged down a cab and, after getting lost three times (how can this town not have street names and numbers? How can a local taxi driver not know where the street is?), I finally found my way to my destination: the neighborhood of "*Kfar haShalom*," the "Village of Peace." One of the other things Dimona is known for is this neighborhood. Quite unusual, unique in fact, *Kfar HaShalom* is home to the community of the African Hebrew Israelites of Jerusalem, or the Black Hebrews as they are known informally, with whom I planned to spend Shabbat.

One of the group's leaders is a great friend, Prince Immanuel Ben Yehuda. At one of my birthday celebrations, Prince Immanuel had pressed me to promise to let him know when I did the Shvil, and to come stay with them when I did, although it was a ways off the Trail. Why not stay for a Shabbat? I had visited the village, as they call it themselves, before—had given talks there and brought international journalists there—but had never stayed for Shabbat. I didn't quite know what to expect. I admire and respect their religious convictions and way of life, not least as a vegetarian who marvels at their strict vegan diet. Though my friendship with Immanuel had introduced me to many aspects of their ideology, I wasn't too sure how their connection to Judaism and somewhat unusual understanding and interpretations of Jewish tradition would translate into practice. I thought it would be an experience; I was not disappointed.

I'm so thrilled to be here; Prince Immanuel is so welcoming, as are two of his (three) wives and some of his 12 children. Clearly they had been prepared for my arrival, some asking questions about the Shvil, others showing me their pre-Shabbat treats. The Kfar is quiet, though bustling with pre-Shabbat preparation activity; it is also spotlessly clean. Having been moved by the Israeli authorities some 25 years ago into an abandoned new-immigrant absorption center complex in this peripheral and struggling town, they've since established a vibrant and very self-governing enclave including a small garden and park. And they have a guest house!

I am surprised, and a bit touched, as Immanuel and his family compete to care for me. One of his sons shows me where I'm staying—in the official "tzimmer" or B&B of the Village, a small apartment with four bedrooms, a shared toilet and shower, large living/dining room, and full kitchen. Another child, an older daughter, brings me a drink and some cookies. Another, a younger boy, arrives and instructs me to give him my laundry (in a bag he provides) so they can wash it. El-Yaakov his name is, about 9 years old; he waits while I undress in the other room, and gives me a shirt and shorts from Immanuel to wear in the meantime. So very, very sweet—and quiet, courteous, well-spoken, as all the kids in the Kfar are. "Dayenu!" I write in my journal, each aspect "would have been enough," full of gratitude for all the small kindnesses they extend to me.

The shower is AMAZING (or is it that any shower is amazing when you've been walking/stumbling/ climbing/tripping/sweating for three days straight?) and the bed looks so welcoming that I almost just climb in once I'm clean. But I have stuff to do; I write, send messages, and take a quiet walk around the grounds, enjoying the peacefulness and the neat rows of flowers between the single-story hut-like structures and caravans, with their erstwhile additions of plasterboard and tin and cinder blocks. Some of it has a very temporary nature, as if to say, "we're moving to more permanent housing soon," though it's been over two decades. I'm really looking forward to spending Shabbat here.

When I do fall into bed, my last thoughts are that I can't believe my luck, or my great planning: I'm going to be in the same place, and the same bed (a bed! first time in 11 days!) for three nights in a row. I then drop l into the most sound sleep I've had in two weeks.

How to describe the beautiful, eerie, spiritual, bizarre, inspiring, wonderful, uplifting, mind-blowing *MISHMASH* (crazy combination) which is this community? I suppose that about does it.

I slept amazingly, for nine and a half hours or so, until 8 a.m. My *tefila* morning prayer—accompanied by music outside wafting over from a nearby home—was focused and rewarding, more than usual. Breakfast in the guest house was prepared by a tall, stunning woman in traditional African colorful flowing dress and high wrapped (matching) headpiece—another trademark of Black Hebrew society. I enjoyed the fresh strawberries, banana and apple in coconut milk with granola and coconut flakes on top, all vegan of course. It was a serene morning.

I walked to the *makolet* (local neighborhood store) to buy a few treats for Shabbat: wine for Kiddush (sanctification of the Sabbath day), a bit of cheese, some crackers and munchies. I stocked up on supplies for the next week, including some of the really delicious vegan "sausage" produced at the *Kfar* which I was familiar with from previous visits (and which for some reason you can't seem to get anywhere else in Israel except at specialty stores). After a lunch of cheese and tomato, I showered early for Shabbat (not that I really needed it, but what a luxury!) and started to get organized, both for Shabbat and the week. I made a few calls while packing things up, to say Shabbat shalom to the kids and a few friends. Two more guests arrived, from Holland, and we chatted briefly.

I wasn't surprised when Immanuel called around 4 p.m., since I was waiting to hear from him about when/where to meet at the onset of Shabbat. (It is traditional in observant communities to meet to walk with guests to synagogue, or meet at synagogue, or meet at home for the meal after prayers). But I was quite surprised when he said, "Come on over to join me at the pre-Shabbat meal."

It turns out the Black Hebrews *fast* on Shabbat. That's right: they do not eat each week, on the Sabbath, though they do drink water. This was news to me. At first I panicked; but I relaxed when I realized I had enough cheese and wine to nourish me over Shabbat (what else can one need?), and more so when Immanuel told me that guests are not expected to fast, so we'd be provided with lunch tomorrow. I quickly made my last two calls, tidied up my room because I wouldn't be returning prior to the onset of Shabbat, and (glad that I'd already done my Shabbat preparations) set out for his home.

Walking into Prince Immanuel's small caravan-like house I'm immediately struck by a number of things. It is tiny—compact, cramped even—but tidy, and in a simple way, elegant, with European-style faux antique furniture and soothing landscape photos and curtains on the walls. There are numerous children running around, of all ages; and it's apparent that while some are his, and others not, all are treated as members of the extended family. His wife, AnaYa ("Eyes of God"), whom I've met before, says "Welcome!" A second waves from the kitchen. Immanuel invites me to sit in the armchair next to his, in what seems to be the living room. Through a door into the kitchen, I see at least four girls preparing food. As soon as I sit, one of the teenage girls in a headscarf puts a tray-table in front of me, and another puts a plate of appetizers on it, after putting one in front of Immanuel. He makes introductions; I try, and fail, to remember all the names.

We make a bracha, a blessing before eating; we talk a bit. I listen as he explains that they fast every Shabbat, with a goal of purification and focus on the Sabbath as a day of "rest." I realize quickly that they have basically applied the biblical concept of the Shabbat Shabbaton, Sabbath of Sabbaths. To Jews, this refers to Yom Kippur, or "the Day of Atonement," the holiest day in the Jewish calendar, when Jews fast and avoid other physical pursuits so as to raise ourselves to the highest spiritual level—like angels. Normative Judaism rejects the idea of fasting on a "regular" Shabbat. In fact, it explicitly prohibits it, and promotes various physical pleasures (including eating good food and meat, drinking wine, singing songs, and even making love) to best enjoy and appreciate the wonders of creation on the Sabbath day. Still, I recognize the aim of their undertaking, however foreign it feels to me.

It is certainly a bit strange. Not the eating-before-Shabbat, that's familiar from both Yom Kippur pre-fast meals and occasional times on a business trip when I've been forced to eat supper prior to the onset of a late Shabbat. But rather the fact that we're sitting in a room, being served a four-course meal by any number of teenage and adult women coming back and forth from the kitchen. I suppose this is what ancient royalty did, and perhaps what even today is done for royalty in certain cultures still (in Africa? Asia? Arabia? I'm just not sure . . .). I find it somewhat uncomfortable. Engaging our servers in conversation makes it easier, as the kids and one of the wives are responsive, even talkative, when asked about their lives, school, work, and the like. And when I ask about the food—which is delectable, colorful, varied, natural, vegan, and nutritious!—they really become animated, and that is a pleasure.

As we finish, Prince Immanuel asks me if I'd be willing to speak at their Friday night prayer service. I agree, having remembered a few thoughts about this week's particular Torah portion (Pikudei) which are relevant both to my hiking the Shvil and to their community's approach to conflict resolution (I've spoken at the Village before, actually, at a conflict-resolution conference). As we walk over to the community hall—it's dark already, we must have sat at dinner for about two hours!—Immanuel prepares me (slightly) for the service. Candles have been lit in observance of Shabbat; no electricity is used, including microphones, which is reassuring to me. He tells me it will be a combination of singing, prayer, a sermon, my talk, and communal "sharing." Their Shabbat assembly is a weekly occurrence. They apparently do not gather for prayer otherwise (as traditional Jews do, daily and of course weekly on Shabbat). Instead, community members are advised to pray three times a day on their own.

I am not very prepared for the experience, to be honest; it is different from anything I am used to. Entering, we are greeted by the assembled residents standing and bowing. I'd noticed this earlier, walking through the village with Immanuel: People—men, women, and especially children—bow slightly when approaching Immanuel, or when he passes by. Like so many other practices here, it is somewhat mystifying, and also *endearing. I'm wearing a traditional African robe, which Immanuel offered to me after dinner; I am glad I accepted, though it's still hard to ignore that mine is the only non-dark face among the two hundred or so gathered here.*

I have enjoyed different prayer gatherings in my life, including Zen Buddhist sitting, Hindu chanting, Quaker meetings, Protestant Sunday-morning services, Episcopalian evening Vespers, Catholic Masses, and Jewish Reform camp sing-alongs, Jewish Conservative Friday nights with guitars and female cantors and Jewish Reform Temple services with hug circles and welcome blessings, drums and gay singing rabbis. I'm as comfortable in all these settings, as I am at home in my modern-Orthodox Jewish synagogue as well as at strictly-Orthodox ("Haredi") all-male shuls and shteibels (small "minyan factories"). Yet I am so out of place here that it takes all my inner resources and concentration to bring myself to a point where I can both accept and enjoy the rollicking, American-Southern Baptist revival feel of the service.

Once I do, though—and in no small part due to the welcome I feel from the group, and the fact that much of the language of prayer is Hebrew—I find it incredibly, perhaps uniquely, spiritually rewarding and uplifting. With many of their Hebrew prayers resonating as identical or at least similar to my own, and with many of their songs either using phrases from the Hebrew prophets or reflecting themes from normative Jewish liturgy, I find this experience comparing favorably with the efforts made by the (nominally Jewish) leaders of the Ashram to instill a sense of serenity and spirituality last Shabbat. I close my eyes and, obviously not for the first time, express my thanks quietly to God and the universe for bringing such incredible and moving encounters my way . . .

Prince Immanuel then introduces me—with far too lofty hyperbole—including a mention of the Shvil and that I'd "walked to the village from Eilat, on foot," which generated shouts of approval and a warm and extended round of applause as I climbed the few steps to the podium. By the light of two candles on either side of the stand, I speak fondly of the visits I'd had to the Kfar in the past, and how welcome and "one of the family" I feel, not least with Prince Immanuel and his family. I wax poetic about the varied nature of the people you meet on the Shvil. I compare the peace and calm of the Kfar with walking in the desert north of Eilat, and then connect this with the journeying of the children of Israel and that with the decades-long effort to gain acceptance in Israel by the African Hebrews.

This special Shabbat marks their annual week of "Appreciation"—so appropriate for me and my personal ruminations—and I speak of the importance of acceptance and the connection between humility, acceptance, and gratitude. I relate this to the Shabbat "Shekalim" marked by Jews throughout the world in preparation for the celebration of Pesach, when each Israelite was required to donate a half-shekel toward the building and upkeep of the Tabernacle in the desert. I focus on the equality of each individual and family (none could donate more, none less) and how central this idea of equality before God is to Jews and Judaism. To bring it all together, I use the Shvil and the wanderings of the children of Israel in the desert, the journeys of the African Israelites from the US via Liberia to Dimona (in the desert), to reinforce our brotherhood and affinity while connecting it all with the gratitude I have for my life and the thanks which they express in this week of appreciation in their community.

My remarks are interrupted by sporadic outbursts of "Amen, Halleluya!" and cries of "Say it, brother!" Even as I'm speaking I'm thinking playfully of calling out something similar next time the rabbi gives a sermon in our synagogue in Beit Shemesh, and smile to think how that would be received there. It's a lot of fun, and I simply allow myself to follow along, play the part, with enthusiasm even, and enjoy it while it's happening.

The remainder of Shabbat is much less eventful. With no rabbinical tradition of normative Judaism, the Kfar goes without actively using electricity on Shabbat. This is unlike Orthodox Jews of today, who use "Shabbat clocks," timers set prior to the onset of the Sabbath, among other devices which enable the use of electrical appliances, lights, hot plates, or heaters and air conditioners and the like. It is so quiet as to be almost unreal; I sleep incredibly deeply. In the morning, after some meditative slow walking around the Kfar, Immanuel and I happen upon each other and we sit on a bench and talk for over an hour.

It turns out he has been divorced—something I did not know—and we discuss various aspects of my and his challenging experiences. We go to rest a bit; I look over some maps and then return outside to do a bit more walking meditation in the small garden planted in memory of community leaders who have passed away, along carefully raked paths in the midst of well-tended plants, bushes, and trees. A woman comes into the apartment midday to prepare lunch for the guests, and it is once again a magnificent and scrumptious feast, all vegan, so varied in color and texture.

It's slightly uncomfortable to be eating while she continues to prepare and serve, but knowing this is their practice and once we've discussed it with her and she reassures us, we happily dig in. Veggie sausages (three kinds, and each different!), two different grain dishes prepared prior to Shabbat, and three salads, and I'm ready for a nap. The wine I had bought yesterday helps as well; and I share it with the Dutch man and woman who're staying in the other rooms, and they greatly appreciate it.

After a nap, in the afternoon Prince Immanuel and I took a walk around town; toward the end of the day he invited me to join him and his family—an unusual honor, I learned later—as they held their "taking leave of Shabbat" family gathering. Like so much in the African Israelite's tradition, it had a basis in Jewish practice, hints of Black American Christian custom, and even one or two elements I think may have come from Islamic sources (such as holding the hands out, facing up, slightly away from the body, when saying "Hallelu-YAH"). All the children and both wives were present (the second wife lives on the other side of town, due to space limitations in the village).

To begin, Immanuel asked each son or daughter to describe what they are grateful for from the past week. Then the wives too; then me. And then another round, talking about what the coming week is expected to bring. It was a little artificial at times, especially as the younger children simply repeated a few refrains, such as being "grateful for my mother and my father and for Ben Ami" (their leader). But it was at the same time rather special, as it was clear each had his father's undivided attention, and enjoyed it so. As through most of Shabbat, they try to speak only in the "holy tongue," Hebrew, and that too is special.

By the end of Shabbat I felt rested, enriched, and inspired. As a vegetarian I had enjoyed a number of unusual combinations and products I knew I could and would emulate or find to purchase for my use at home. As an observant Jew, I had been exposed to—and found meaningful and uplifting—a number of new ideas and unique approaches to observance, to Shabbat, to prayer and meditation. As a hiker on the Shvil, I had re-connected to one of the more idealistic, religiously fervent, Zionist communities in Israel—even though they are not, and acknowledge they are not, actually Jewish in the religious sense, feeling themselves connected in a cultural, tribal sense—and through them to one of the more traditional, challenging, and yet also hospitable small towns in the South, Dimona.

There is a great deal of beauty and spirituality in the *Kfar*, a calm and creative, positive undercurrent and energy. It's a real amalgam of West and East, America and Africa and Israel, Judaism, Christianity, eastern traditions, Islam, Rastafarianism, and more—and it seems to work on many levels. One take-away from the weekend was understanding the connection between the humility I'd been pondering for some time, acceptance of God's will and the world and reality, and appreciation for all that is in that world, all that is good in it and with my life. As I wrote in my journal that night, "Truth is everywhere; you just have to look for it to see it."

Certainly, from a humble awareness of our insignificance in the universe and acceptance of the historical realities that face us, the peoples of this region should be able to recognize the many gifts we've been given. We share western and eastern, Jewish and Muslim traditions of hospitality, humility, acceptance, and appreciation. This I know from my studies in comparative religion at UC Berkeley and my reading and discussions since then. That night after Shabbat I began to wonder why so few scholars and rabbis, imams, and political leaders stress the startlingly beautiful simplicity of our common spiritual approach. Fewer still base our pursuit of peace on these concepts. I pondered that as I organized my pack and prepared for bed.

I stayed up far too late; after writing in my journal, I posted an update on Facebook, deciding this could become a regular thing each Saturday night, and enjoyed doing it (from my phone, so amazing this modern technology!). But it's interesting, the aspects of ourselves and our lives we're willing (and not willing) to put out there. I kept it light and talkative—though I was feeling lonely again, a bit down, as the evening continued. "Why?" as I wrote the next night in my journal: "Listened to a song from *Once*, and other reasons—mainly as I would have loved to share all this, especially Shabbat with Immanuel, with Karen." As I let the tears come, I realized there were fewer than before, and the feeling was less intense than previously—I was observing myself, as it were, move through another stage in the mourning period over the loss of my marriage and my life as I knew it.

In that second week in the desert, I came to recognize the centrality of acceptance in dealing with hardship. As I wrote earlier, accepting what is—*it is what it is*—whether on the Trail or in our daily life, enables us to broaden our perspective, to truly live in the present, and to prepare and act appropriately for whatever lies ahead. It reminds me a little of the book *Who Moved My Cheese?* Rather than grumbling over whatever pain, large or small, is bothering us—and it might be major and life-altering or minor and merely aggravating—acceptance provides a basis for gratitude. We are here; we are alive and well, the world is an amazing, wonderful place, and our lives are full of extraordinary blessing if we only can acknowledge it.

This is not to say we should simply accept without complaint hardships that *are* in our power to influence. I'm not suggesting we can't or shouldn't work to change our reality; acceptance is simply the first step in mapping our path toward that change. Again, that cliché about accepting the things I cannot change is so very true: humbly conceding that there are aspects of life over which we have no control. I needed to reach that understanding in order to free myself for the next stage in my healing. And I was well on the way.

Chapter Three

DESERT: TRANSITIONS—FROM ACCEPTANCE TO GRATITUDE

[Week Three]

Sunday morning, March 2, started off slowly; I found myself, again, reluctant to get moving, after sleeping in a bed for three nights in a row. I found a ride (paid an elderly fellow from the *Kfar* to take me to the trailhead) and said my goodbyes to Immanuel and a few of his children, and was on my way by 8 a.m. At the trailhead I hesitated; I procrastinated by sending a few messages to the kids, calling Meira, adjusting my straps, eating some dried fruit—I really just didn't want to get out there again. But I did, at 9 a.m. exactly, and then as I strode down a small decline toward the waterfall at Ein Yorkam I experienced a wonderful surge of energy and enthu-

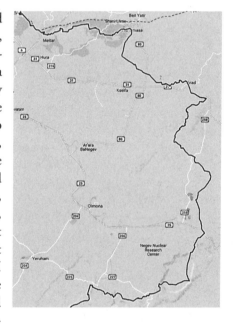

siasm—I was truly excited and thrilled to be returning to the trail. And a good thing that was, considering how incredibly difficult the day turned out to be.

I'm descending through a canyon, following the path of a small river, and I feel a real sense of transformation. The terrain is a wild combination of dirt and sand and multi-layered rock formations, in various shades of brown, tan, yellow and gold; there are more trees and shrubs, and flowers too, than I've seen so far. It's as if from the bleak windswept rocky peaks of the Carbolet I've emerged into a more sedate, living, thriving planet of life and growth. Is it symbolic of my internal transitions? Or am I seeing meaning in small coincidences, interpreting a few green plants and pink flowers in the desert a little too deeply? Either way, it is stunningly beautiful. Ma'ale Palmach, Nachal Chatira (and the waterfalls!) are just gorgeous, a combination of stunning views, arresting patterns in the cliffs and hills, startlingly high and broad wadis, lots of greenery, and of course frightening and difficult climbs, both ascents and descents.

Trying not to panic, or fall over, as I inch my way along a cliff's edge at Ma'ale Palmach, I'm both surprised and comforted in a strange way as I recognize my initial lack of balance, as I go through again the Sunday-morning-here-we-go routine, figuring out for the third time how to walk, step, climb, jump and crawl even with this pack on my back. Knowing—having read in the Red Guide last night—that this part of the Trail was fashioned during Israel's war of Independence by the fighters of the Palmach (the strike force of the Hagana, the pre-state Jewish militia in "Palestine") gives this part of the trek whole new meaning.

And it raises all sorts of questions. First: how did they do it? It's so very steep, and even treacherous in parts, as it winds its way along the cliff's edge and down the precipice to the floor of a massive now-dry waterfall—at least 50 meters in height. And second: how did they manage to get up and down it with equipment, supplies, donkeys even apparently? The ladder I find strategically placed at the steepest point—a cliff side of course—and the iron hand- and footholds, which appear as saviors every now and then along the narrow path on the side of the waterfall—were put here much later. I appreciate their placement; but it only makes me marvel all the more at the feat of engineering, and sheer willpower and courage, which this path represents. And third: why and how can we, as a society, as parents, allow schoolkids to climb up or down this on field trips? It's madness! I wonder if anyone has died along here?

I manage to stay alive to the bottom of the ravine, and take a few photos looking back up at the cliff, humbled that I managed it without falling, and more so that the soldiers of the Palmach managed to hack a path out of the forbidding mountainside.

Ma'ale Palmach, The Palmach Ascent

I'm so glad I got moving, though I'm already tired and my left calf has begun to hurt. I think I didn't rest enough. Must remember to be disciplined: 5 minutes every hour, 15 or so every three hours. But my 5 are up and I press on. It's getting hot, a sharav *heat wave is coming, and I want to make progress before having to take a lengthier break.*

The rest of the morning passed pleasantly, descending the length of the Nachal Chatira dry stream, including a number of contemplative stops to enjoy the expansive desert views. The more frequent appearance of greenery—bushes and shrubs and the occasional tree—as well as small pink and white and blue star-shaped flowers, lifted my spirits. Striking rock formations, deep canyons, and the continued cliff-side climbs and stumbling descents down boulder-strewn hills combined to fill me with a sense of wonder, and accomplishment.

By midday, though, the heat and challenges began to wear me down; the afternoon became tedious and hard. What is it about our psyche which connects unrelated painful experiences? Becoming physically worn down, I returned my thoughts to those ruminations on life and relationships that had occupied me the previous night and weeks (and, let's face it, months and years). Lonely and alone as I trudged along Nachal Yamin, and then up Maale Yamin (the Yamin dry creek and ascent), I kept thinking, WHY? Why did this happen? Was it me? What did I do wrong? We were now divorced, so there was no need to pretend— and she continued to insist there was nothing I did wrong. And yet . . . I didn't know. It was still so confusing.

And this hill—it just goes on forever. I'm hot, now my feet are hurting, in addition to my calves, in addition to my heart. Dusty, dirty, sweaty—I can feel the grit at the back of my neck and under my hat—and my sunglasses are slipping down my nose. And I feel the grit in my soul; I'm lonely. It's only Sunday and I just want to quit. What's wrong with me? Just a few hours ago I was so pleased to be back on the Trail; now I wish I could find a side path to a road. . . . And I can't shake these thoughts about Karen and me, about us, about what was and what was supposed to be, and about how we lost our path. I suppose I don't need *to shake these thoughts off. That's why I'm here, after all, to challenge myself emotionally as well as physically.*

What could I have done? What could have been done? However much Karen doesn't want to admit the depression's connection and responsibility for her decision, it just doesn't make sense. You can't disconnect the person and their depression. But I was a loving and attentive husband; how can I have missed that she was depressed? What kind of soul mate is that? On the other hand, she TOLD you how she hid it from you. I'm trying to be objective here but how is that possible? I'm beating myself up as I trudge up the hill. Stop. There is nothing you did wrong—at least not to provoke depression or justify divorce—and NOTHING you could have done differently, except perhaps get angry (as per Rebecca) and that would not have changed a thing. Get over it. She blew her and your life away, for whatever reason, and you were and are powerless to affect that.

IT'S OVER, ARYEH. Enough. It's behind you; it is past; it's history. ACCEPT it.

We used to tell the story of how God brought us together. It's not like we casually met on a bus or at a party or were introduced by friends; a lot of stars had to align to bring Karen and me together. My visit to Leningrad as part of a student trip to the USSR; Passover; my seemingly casual decision to see if someone at the synagogue spoke English; the invitation to have the Pesach *Seder* meal at a *Refusenik* family whom Karen had visited two years earlier; the wife's suggestion that this London girl and I "would like each other."

Our love was epic. We knew it; our friends and family commented on it. It was special, like no other. It had to be: how else could a Californian from a Reform family and a Brit from an Orthodox family decide to marry, move to Israel, build a family (and a community, or two), and avoid going nuts?

A friend—another American married to a British woman—says there are three things the British don't talk about (Brits not being quite as talkative as Americans at the best of times): money, feelings, and sex. Americans—and Californians in particular—love to talk about all three, and more. Reform Judaism sees our religion as a fine set of traditions from which one can choose those meaningful to oneself; Orthodox Judaism views our laws and customs as obligatory and existential. I was a laid-back liberal on my way to study to be a Reform rabbi, literally riding in on a motorcycle from my studies at the University of Surrey. She was a rather conservative student-dentist on her way to fulfill her Zionist ideology by moving to Israel. We couldn't have been more different; we couldn't have been more in love.

Our friendship started with the Russian Jewry connection but quickly developed, over long conversations, phone calls, and then bi-weekly and sometimes daily letters, into an ongoing philosophy discussion. Exploring issues of morality and values related to God and humanity, from Shabbat observance (why refraining from work and other restrictions are liberating, even if I miss playing my guitar on the Sabbath) to dressing modestly (with me more of a feminist at times than she), our relationship blossomed at the same time as I sought answers to many of the spiritual questions I'd been pondering over my high-school and college years. Traveling through Europe and ending up in Israel to begin the Reform rabbinical program, I found my physical journeys complemented by philosophical wanderings—and our relationship became closer as I discovered new and rewarding ways to express my Jewish identity.

Becoming more traditionally observant, and having left the rabbinical program but deciding to remain in Israel, I visited London on Valentine's Day, for a two-week visit. One week into it, after watching Tevya and Golda sing "Do you love me" on the video of *Fiddler on the Roof* in her parents' home, I asked Karen to marry me. Our friendship had deepened to the point where we were already best friends; I knew I loved her deeply and passionately, though we had never even kissed. I was 22 years old, she 25; I saw myself in 25—or 50 or 75—years living with her, and loving her, and knew we could spend the rest of our lives together.

Growing up with only one divorce in our family circle and virtually none among my parents' friends, I had from a young age wanted to be married; I was always a one-woman-man since starting to have relationships in seventh grade. And I always believed that marriage is based on not only love and friendship and mutual respect, but on hard work and commitment and patience as well. Karen believed that too—we spoke about it numerous times—and for twenty-five years we were the envy of most of our friends and family, with an affection and devotion so obvious we were often teased for the way we adored each other.

I stop. I've been pushing uphill now for almost forty minutes straight, jamming the point of my sticks into the hard dust/dirt/stones among the rocks as I climb Maale Yamin almost as if I'm beating the earth, stabbing the mountain, taking my anger out with each sharp bang! of my boot on the path. It hurts, I'm mad, I've got all this energy, it feels good, great even just to bash something. But I'm exhausting myself. It's so hot, and my legs are really in pain. So I take a break, sitting on a large rock, halfway up this incline which seems to never end.

And something clicks. I can accept this physical pain. And if I can't enjoy it, revel in it, celebrate it—as my high school football coach taught us: I hurt therefore I am—I can at least acknowledge it, endure it . . . and then move beyond it. I can see the top of the hill, and I'm halfway there. At this point the pain is a given, a constant. Tolerating it, recognizing it's there, I can take steps, like this pause, to manage it and keep going.

Resting on the boulder, every muscle aching, a flash of awareness hits me. If that's true of the pain in my legs, how much more so the pain in my heart? I've realized I can't change this reality I'm living—just as I can't wish myself off the side of this mountain. The humility inherent in that recognition of my inability to change the fact that I'm now divorced leads me to an astonishing acceptance of that reality. Maybe it's obvious to some, but it's not to me. Why am I doing all this soul-searching? I seem to be desperately looking to understand what happened—but why? So I can learn to be a better husband or person? Not so much. It's so I can change something. How crazy is that? Like I can go back and do something different, prevent the divorce? Like I can not be on this rock? That's the acceptance—of the pain, of the mountain, of the situation—I need to get to. Then I can stop this constant obsession with what was.

It is what it is. Perhaps I could have/should have/would have done something different; but perhaps there's nothing I could have done, and this is the situation now. Live with it, and allow yourself to not only tolerate it, but to let it inform your next steps.

I could have chosen not to set out this morning; but I'm here on this mountainside and ahead of me is a hard climb; after that is a night-camp where water awaits me (supposedly) and where I can rest and ponder all I'm learning this day. Yes, my legs hurt, but rest and nourishment can and will alleviate most of the pain, and walking more carefully and slowly will help as well. Acceptance becomes key: this is my reality. I can persevere and find all the positives and beauty in it, or moan and complain and stew in my suffering. I choose to pursue the positive: "choose life," "ובחרת בחיים" I quote to myself, from the Torah. Take life as it comes, not passively but actively choosing to look on the bright side and to focus on the wonders and beauty, on the Trail and always.

Just as this thought comes to me, and I turn to put the snacks I've been munching back in the pack, I hear and then see a man bouncing his way down the hill toward me. Shouldering my pack, I notice as he approaches that he's about my age (the white beard kind of gives it away), and something about him tells me he's an Anglo, the term we use in Israel for any English-speaker—perhaps his hat, or shorts and shirt, or gait. We stop to chat as we come abreast; it turns out that Barry, a Conservative rabbi and former high-tech guy, is hiking the Shvil in segments over the course of the year. And he lived for some time in Portola Valley, literally my back yard growing up in Menlo Park! Not only that; he's a friend of my good friends Yossi and Susan—what a small small world. We take a photo, which he says he'll post on Facebook, and part ways—after he tells me it's quite a ways to the night camp overlooking the Machtesh HaKatan. *Hmmm—thanks. Stay positive. Keep your thoughts LIGHT. Accept this reality . . .*

Trudging along—with less stomping and more breaks than earlier in the day—the afternoon stretched out. Arriving at the spot Haim Berger told me the water would be waiting, I clambered up the side of a hill by the road, as instructed, near the signpost, behind the shrub, above the large triangle-shaped rock (like a kids' treasure hunt)—and found dozens of bottles. All empty. Maybe the empties near the road should have suggested some sort of a warning. I was so angry, and frustrated, and not a little frightened—I needed this water! Fortunately, there was decent reception as I switched on the phone, and calling him calmed me down; to his credit, he immediately said he'd bring water (a good hour's jeep trek for him each way), though not until later that night. Someone probably stole the water and drank it on the spot, and I was aggravated at the delay and at the feelings of despair the initial discovery aroused, but I scrambled back down the hill and started to make my way up to the night camp overlooking המכתש הקטן *Machtesh HaKatan*, the Small Crater, and Maale Eli, the Eli descent.

I had hopes—unusual for me, seeking my solitude—that there might be others there from whom I could take water, as I did from the students beneath the cliffs of Hod Akev the previous week. There were none; but I heard a car coming and went to flag it down. A Hertz rental, it drove right by, with the passengers literally looking right past me. They could not have "missed" me, standing not a meter from the roadside; they purposefully ignored me. I had to think for a moment—דן לכף זכות give people the benefit of the doubt—maybe I look like a hobo (shades of Cheryl Strayed!) or a terrorist? Or just like a dirty, desperate hiker? Either way, it really made me mad. I didn't care if they were tourists; you don't pass a person standing on the side of the road in the middle of nowhere who's trying to flag you down! What if I had an injured or sick friend or child a few meters away? What if I was dehydrated and desperate for water?

I didn't feel that distressed; but I was certainly concerned. It had been a hot day, I had drunk most of my water knowing I had Haim's six liters waiting for me, so didn't have much left for cooking or washing and definitely couldn't wait up for Haim to arrive late at night. It wasn't exactly a well-travelled road, and certainly not as the sun disappeared behind the hills. I looked up at the sky, wondering how long it would be until dark, hoping another car might pass. A balloon off in the distance floating high above Dimona made me wonder: could it see me? Is someone watching? I wanted to ask Mimi whether some intelligence branch monitored the photos/videos—presumably so, protecting Israel's only nuclear reactor some 20 kilometers to the northwest—and whether if they saw a hiker in distress they might do something about it. Silly, really, but it offered some form of comfort—like there was someone watching over me.

Having to climb up a hill behind the night camp to get reception to call Haim again added to my exasperation, and I somewhat angrily threw the tent up and tossed my stuff inside. Out at the road again, a car approached—I ran over and this time I literally stepped in front of it and waved my arms, rather than relying on the stand-on-the-side-to-flag-it-down more subtle approach. It was the same car from before, I realized as it slowed! I forced it to stop. Two German tourists, making their way back to the Dead Sea. I was lucky, as it was definitely the last car to pass before dark. They kindly gave me the last of their water, about half a liter bottle, and I was very grateful. With it, I made asparagus soup, and the hot soup along with the (delicious!) veggie salami from the Black Hebrew's store buoyed my spirits somewhat—though the wind rattling the tent tempered my happiness slightly (Video 5). (I had to open the tent flaps, having cooked inside the tent, against all the rules due to the danger of gas fumes; it was just too windy outside, and starting to spit a bit of rain.)

Writing in the tent, I reviewed the day and those feelings—of anger, of confusion and resentment and frustration, of sadness and regret, of conviction and positive energy and optimism—and after some silent meditation, came to that place I'd discovered a few times already on the Shvil—acquiescence. Acceptance. Acknowledgement. I explored all sorts of synonyms, and repeated them to myself.

It's over. This hard day is over. This period of my life is over. This marriage is over. It's over. Accept it.

I had a Snickers bar as comfort food, and a shot of whiskey, for even more comfort. Climbed out of the tent to brush my teeth and pee quickly, and went to sleep. It was such a long day. It was not yet 7 p.m.

7:32 a.m., sitting by the fire (too hot!), making coffee and oatmeal; it's Monday morning the first day of the Hebrew month of Adar—"משנכנס אדר מרבים בשמחה"—*"With the beginning of Adar, increase* simcha *(joy/happiness)!" Well, 12 hours in the tent, can't really say "sleeping" as much as constant tossing and turning. 12 hours in this tent, felt like I was suffocating, had to get out, so though it's cold out here it's still a relief of sorts. It rained last night—real rain, not the drizzle of yesterday—I should*

*have recorded it, having recorded the blustery wind and the claustrophobic mess
inside the tent. I'm certainly glad again to have schlepped the tent! Haim brought the
water about 11 p.m.—hearing him drive up, and his steps to the tent, I couldn't be
bothered in the midst of my half-consciousness to get up or even to call out—and he
left me a little surprise of a bag of peanuts as well. A peace offering? (A sin offering!)
Kind of sweet, but more important, I appreciate his professionalism and dedication,
considering the cost in time and effort to make the special trip out to resupply me.*

*It's a peculiar, overcast morning—cloudy and already getting warm. I wonder—
will it rain? I'm prepared to walk in a little rain, like the drizzle on that first day
out of Eilat, but can't say I'm looking forward to it. And not least as I just read this
is the "steepest" descent on the trail, Maale Eli (Eli's Ascent), oy. Note to myself for
next breakfast: make less coffee, and less oatmeal—shame to waste! I'm taking it a bit
easy this morning—not sure I really want to do Maale Eli but I figure, looking at the
maps and elevations, I guess I will, as the last desert "challenge" I'll face. I climb to
the top of the hill again to get reception and spend a good half hour making calls and
posting Facebook messages and sending texts and photos to the kids, and to my nieces
Gabs and Ariella who I miss a lot, and more. I send Tehila, my new daughter-in-law,
thanks for the use of her walking sticks. I look at the maps again . . . and finally get
going three hours after waking up, at 9:50.*

Too late! I still hadn't learned the lesson of previous days—and wouldn't for
another few—to check elevations as well as kilometers. What a day that was—
and what a night too. Maale Eli descent was indeed a challenge, made possible
and passable by strategically placed cables, ladders, railings and handholds (and
footholds) at various segments of the trail as it winds down the cliffs which make
up the crater's sides. Slow going, and not least due to the strange haze, which
meant also that I couldn't at all see any of the "beautiful" and "expansive" and
"stunning" views described in the Guide. But in a rather novel way it held a
beauty of its own, the *Machtesh* crater in the haze—like a mysterious kingdom
shrouded in the clouds, with the sun fighting (and failing) to get through. But it
was hot too—and getting hotter.

Toward the bottom of the descent into the crater, the going was still rough, so
a bit of singing made it easier—and again distracted me from the very real fear of
falling which accompanied each step. And the echo, once I was deep in the crater,
oh the echo! I sang and sang—at the top of my lungs. Every Simon and Garfunkel
song I knew (and I know many); James Taylor, Jim Croce, camp songs, every version of שיר המעלות *Shir HaMaalot*, the Song of Ascents psalm; all sorts of *Eretz
Yisrael* Land of Israel songs like I'd sung on the Carbolet; Fiddler on the Roof,
Sound of Music, Pirates of Penzance, even some West Side Story . . . and of course
"Zippidy Doo Dah" and "Oh What a Beautiful Morning," my morning standards.
Starting, as usual, with רבות מחשבות *Rabot Machshevot*, about how wondrous and
indecipherable are the thoughts of God, and the *Tefila* prayer songs, which accom-
panied me every day. But this time I sang at the top of my lungs, all alone in the

mist, surrounded by the walls of the crater which at times I couldn't even see the tops of in the haze, echoing all around me like the hills were answering my prayers. It was awesome, in so many senses of that word.

A few hours later, reaching the other end of the Small Crater—having wondered at the development of the amazing colors of the sand and earth at its floor, here dark brown, there rusty red, next to it mustard dirty yellow—I passed a few school groups coming the other way. The guide for one, on saying hello and hearing I was hiking the Shvil, took the opportunity to explain to his students in a few sentences what it is and how far I'd already come. It was sweet, and I allowed myself to feel a sense of pride as he gushed about the length and the difficulty. A few of the kids, old enough to be impressed but young enough not to be embarrassed about it, took photos—so I asked one of them to send a photo to Mimi for fun, and with a message that they'd seen me and I was all right. (It was a good idea, as it turned out there was no reception at the night camp that night. I had agreed to let Mimi know how and where I was every day, more in response to the anxiety and entreaties of my close friend Hadas than due to any concern of my kids. Our basic agreement was that while in the desert on my own, I'd send a text every evening, including plans for the next day. If I missed one day, no one was to worry. If I missed two, Hadas was allowed to call the police.)

Striding along the bottom of the crater, I thought I was making good time, while resting more responsibly, almost every hour, and with almost no calf pain (though with a growing discomfort in my left big toe).

I was wrong.

Alone again, on the huge, ugly, hazy, long, steep climb out of the crater, Maale Tzafit, I was sweating buckets. It was HOT. Wow. Finally at the top, after taking multiple rest stops as I struggled upwards and drinking most of my water, I checked my watch. 4 p.m.—OK, great, I figured I had an hour and a half or so of sun, about 6 kilometers to go, no problem!

Problem: I had more like 10 kilometers to go, much of which was steep inclines and declines. Looking at ELEVATION still wasn't my forte; and as I wrote in my journal that night, "And Lesson two (duh): GET on the TRAIL by 8 a.m. LATEST!"

With the haze cover, dusk basically started about 4 p.m. I wasn't too worried—realizing this, I knew it would be a little "dusky" earlier than usual, but still somewhat light until 5:30 or 6 p.m. Except that at 5:30, then 6, I was still walking—up a hill, down, across a hillside, down to a wadi, up a steep incline, down the side of a mountain to a creek-bed, up a path between and over huge boulders. It was truly a beautiful hike, and the fading light and haze played with shadows and the orange-rust colors of the hills, but I was rushing as time was so limited, and rushing meant concentrating extra hard so no step went awry. "You don't need a sprained ankle or worse," I kept telling myself. I put off turning my headlamp on for as long as possible, both to preserve battery and I suppose as a mechanism to make myself feel less foolish for miscalculating. I was debating whether to turn it on—walking in the semi-darkness had its own magic—when a bobcat crossed my path not four meters ahead of me. At least I think it was a bobcat: it was cat-like, twice the size of my Sam, not at all shaped like a fox or the jackals I'm familiar with near my home. (More about those soon.) We looked at each other for at least five long seconds; I could see his/her sillouette and it occurred to me he/she could see me better than I could it, for sure—and then we both continued on our way.

Occasionally I wouldn't see a Trail sign for ten, twenty, thirty, forty steps longer than was comfortable; at one point I stumbled and my pole smacked against the side of my head—that hurt! It was about then that I put the headlamp on, set on low, and navigated my way up slight inclines and flat patches as I lost and found the trail too many times to count. At no time was I really scared. I knew I was going in the right direction; the terrain was not too steep (yes, I checked the map carefully by this time); and I knew (I kept telling myself) I had all I needed to spend the night. So if I just got tired or fed up—I was certainly sweating a great deal and though not (yet) dehydrated was reaching the limit of my endurance—or if I did get truly lost, I felt confident I could just pitch my tent right there on a level patch of the Shvil. I could make my dinner, I had enough water for that and could replenish in the morning, and the trail would be clear in daylight. I was exercising, almost without knowing it, my newfound "acceptance" doctrine.

The darkness returned my thoughts to our marriage as I stumbled along the path. It wasn't all roses—Karen and I certainly had our dark times, whether emotional, financial, child-related or in terms of our relationship. We disagreed on very little, but when we did it was powerful; and those disagreements almost always related to aspects of child-raising. When to be more strict or lenient, whether to use incentives or consequences, when to use anger or affection, were some of our challenges. But those brief periods of darkness were short and fleeting, like the night. There had never been a point when these or other arguments brought us to reconsider our commitment to each other, and we always appreciated one another. So when she told me she wanted a divorce that night in the middle of Pesach, up in a beautiful B&B in Rosh Pina where we'd gone for Passover vacation with both sets of parents, children, and her brother and his family, I was absolutely shocked. I was gobsmacked, as my father-in-law Philip would say. I was torn in two, or in so many pieces I couldn't count them.

It's not hyperbole: I felt my heart was tearing, almost could hear the ripping. After asking the obvious "Why?" "What's happened?" I received an almost casual, if loving, "I just don't want to be married anymore" in reply. I left the room and the estate and wandered around the old city of Rosh Pina. I was torn, also, between my own pain and my understanding of hers; between my intense longing to remain together and my recognition that my love for her includes a commitment to her happiness. I kept thinking, if this is what she wants, if this is what will make her happy, how can I fight that? And what exactly am I fighting? What's happening here? Did Karen actually just tell me she wants a divorce?

I did feel even on that first night that there was more to it than the simplistic "I want out." And so at the time and since, though I insisted we get counselling, I chose to channel my love into understanding and even supporting her feelings, even while not agreeing with their basis, hoping that she'd discover other reasons for her unhappiness, or other solutions to her discontent.

My thoughts strayed as I wandered the streets of this quaint century-old town so full of history (Rosh Pina is one the very first "settlements" the Jews returning to our land built, over 100 years ago). As I returned to the room, around 2 a.m., it occurred to me that Karen and I had connected, originally, due to a happenstance meeting on Pesach; now we were discussing divorce, on Pesach. What a sad coincidence. That night and since, I've wondered what meaning this might have. Passover. Commemorating the Jews' delivery from slavery and exodus to freedom and journey to our Land. The first time the Torah uses the term *Am* "people" or "nation" to describe us, and the first step as a nation on our way to the Promised Land. I'd always felt that our meeting because of my chance encounter with that *Refusenik* in a Leningrad synagogue on Seder night was itself a miraculous and divine statement: our love and marriage and building a life in Israel was intricately tied up with the Jewish people's return to our ancestral homeland, then and now. The rabbi who spoke to us under our *Chuppah* marriage canopy, Mickey Rosen of blessed memory, moved me to tears when he humbled himself before us for our decision to make our lives in Israel. I've yet to figure out what significance there is in the timing of our separation, except the rather facile connection between our national liberty and Karen's desire for freedom, as it were.

It's really getting dark now. Should I continue on? Confidence is good; foolhardy risk-taking, less so. I suppose Hadas has a point: hiking alone has its risks. If I make camp here and now, I trade the comfort of a night camp (what comfort? Psychological; water availability; perhaps other campers; proximity to a road in this case) for the reduced risk of tripping and falling and breaking my leg and dying on hilltop by Roman ruins no one's ever heard of. It was nice to visit but I wouldn't want to be buried there. But seriously: think. It's dark but my light is good; it's rough terrain but pretty flat til the very end; I'm tired, which carries its own risks, but there isn't much further to go. I make my decision: I'll keep going, but if I find I've lost the trail once more, I'll make camp rather than retrace my steps and look for it.

And I'm so glad I carried on, because only about ten minutes later I find myself at the top of a rise and I can see the road—and headlights too, on it—about a half-kilometer away. Whoohoo! And I start singing—and then stop, when I see a campfire across the road, a few hundred meters ahead and to my left. Being crazy is one thing; proving it to complete strangers is quite another. I wind my way down—carefully, slowly, don't put too much weight on the sticks on the descent—and cross the road. Following Haim's directions, I put my pack down by the remains of a building in this sprawling Byzantine fortress (this is Metzad Tamar, the Tamar Fort), and start to search for the water drop. After the last few experiences, I don't even hesitate: at the first hint of confusion, I turn on the phone (reception!) and call Haim, and when he gives me different, more accurate directions, I find the water. I take one of the bottles and pour it all over my head, rinsing out my hair in a spasm of luxury.

My dinner is a great combination of corn soup, vegan sausage with mustard, quinoa AND noodles with Hawaij, oregano, garlic, salt and pepper, all from my neat little pill-box with separations, and then chamomile tea, topped off with a little Captain Jack Daniels. ("GREAT" is what I write in my journal.) I then climb into the tent with a feeling of accomplishment and a sense of purpose. I consider walking over to the group sitting (and singing, I hear faintly) around the campfire a few hundred meters to the north, but I'm beginning to reflect on the day and my thoughts during it, and decide instead to write a bit.

I've been thinking a great deal about what I'm learning already on this trek. About recognizing my place in the universe—and how insignificant, really, we all are. (Without self-deprecation.) About accepting the cards we're dealt (without dismissing the importance of our own decisions and actions). And from these two ideas another is emerging. I may be small; I may accept the challenges thrown at me. But my life is not only its ordeals; I have so much to be thankful for. I can "accept"—celebrate and embrace!— these cards I've been dealt as well. I am so grateful for all the incredible, wonderful, beautiful, wondrous gifts in my life, from my parents and children and friends (and marriage too) to this experience and Israel and all it's given me.

And I'm beginning to realize that the lessons of this physical and psychological, emotional and spiritual journey of mine not only can be applied to the challenges I'm facing in my life, but might also be helpful to others. There's so much wisdom out there—not mine, but which I can draw on and perhaps in a new and creative, original way combine with my experience on the Shvil into a fresh approach to overcoming personal hardship. Rambam, Rav Kook, Ramcha"l, Rav Soloveitchik, the Gemara; and also Gandhi, Frankl, Covey, Buscaglia, Sakharov, Sharansky . . . the list is endless. And we could even perhaps apply them to the challenges of this centuries-old conflict here in the Middle East. I have to think about this.

To sleep! It's 10:15 p.m., and that's so very late for me these days.

What happened the next day is difficult to relate. It was a definitely a breakthrough. It affected the rest of my time on the trek . . . and the rest of my life. If that sounds exaggerated, I make no apologies. It was clearly part of the process I'd been going through for months if not years, and was a direct result of my ruminations the previous evening while hiking and then that night while writing and falling asleep. All the insights about the marriage and divorce, acceptance and humility came together; and the ensuing gratitude hit me with full force that amazing day. And thank God, it has not left me since.

The day started out as mundanely as the days before it. Up at 6:15 a.m., a quicker breakdown of camp and earlier start to the day than the day prior, no campfire but a cooked breakfast of oatmeal and tea, and it still took an hour and a half to pack things up and get going. The walking was not that tough, as antici-pated; relatively flat as I wound my way north into the hills. Just before starting out, the group from the campfire wandered by on their way south, and I felt a pang of regret that I didn't join them the night before. A small group of late teens from Australia and the UK, they were still singing Beatles songs as they walked by and said good morning. As I wrote in my journal that night: "'You only regret what you don't do,' as Grandma Edie used to say. 'When faced with a choice to do or not to do something—always do it,' according to Mimi's friend Aya. ☺ "

I walked the entire morning without seeing a single soul. Crossing into the Judean Desert Nature Reserve I was a bit surprised. The sign welcoming the hiker was rather inexplicable; it's just not accurate. What nature? There is *nothing* there; just rocks and sand and dirt as far as the eye can see (or the foot can walk in a day). Up and down small rises and falls, on straight dirt roads and narrow trails, with a hot silver-blue shimmering sky, still somewhat hazy. A turn here and there, with trail signs occasionally pointing out the obvious, it is one great big nothing-ness. Nothing. Zero. Zilch.

How to describe this nothingness? If further south there were interesting rock formations, here there was only flatness. If elsewhere there were colors, here were only shades of gray and brown. Looking ahead the ground appeared dark gray; looking closer it was light brown sand/dirt covered by countless small black rocks, melding together into the distance in one seemingly solid sea of gray. If elsewhere there were shrubs and trees, plants and even occasional flowers, here there were none. If previously even in the desert there were birds and insects, ants and beetles and lizards, here there were none. Nothing. Silence. Even the wind had disappeared.

Judean Desert Crossroads

There, in the absence of anything—even the absence of sound, it seemed—I found peace. And meaning. And understanding. If above I sounded bombastic, this probably seems downright pretentious, but this was how I felt: I began to sense what it must have been like for the prophets of Israel, wandering these deserts, to discover and talk with God. In the silence and stillness there was something akin to that "still small voice" described in the Bible. And it spoke to me.

I don't mean I experienced a revelation, or talked with God. It was perhaps less dramatic than that, but extraordinarily vivid and moving all the same. Walking alone in this expanse of desert nothingness, there were no distractions, no interruptions, no stimuli to provoke observations or thoughts. It was as if I were alone in the universe; not just walking on my own on a trail in the desert, but like Antoine de Saint-Exupéry's *Little Prince*, all on my own in all of existence. It was just me and God, or me and the source of all existence. I felt connected to everything in the midst of nothing.

It's hard to put into words; it is the kind of sensation one strives for in the midst of a Zen sitting meditative session, in a very tangible way. It was an event that if not experienced cannot be understood or appreciated, and once undergone cannot be related in any meaningful fashion.

But I'm trying. I was so aware of so much as I walked through this expanse of desert rich in my people's history. King David escaped to here; too many prophets to count meditated here and communed with the Creator of the universe here. Jesus, a good and learned Jew, walked here. Here the children of Israel—my ancestors—passed when, as a family/clan, they wandered down to Egypt. Later, as a nation after receiving the Torah at Sinai and crossing over the Jordan River, they came through here to possess the Promised Land. In ways I can't explain and I still don't really understand, I suddenly felt a part of this wide swath of our people's saga in a way I hadn't felt in thirty years of living in Israel and visiting Jerusalem, Hebron, Jericho, Shechem, Tzippori, Katzrin, Masada, Megiddo, Shilo, and all the other religious and national archeological sites of the country.

It's not that a historical link with our people was new to me. One of the ways I explained to my grandmother my decision to move to Israel from the US at age 21 was through our own family's history. Our ancestors had left the Land of Israel at the Roman expulsion, followed a phenomenal path through Spain and Portugal, Holland and London to Montreal and New Amsterdam (New York) in the Americas as one of the first Jewish families to come to the New World, in 1690. I was merely closing the circle by returning to the land of our forefathers, I told her. And religiously the spiritual bond was also not new to me; I had been privileged to enjoy a number of powerful and uplifting encounters with prayer and song and fellowship over my years of exploration, not least as described earlier.

Yet some unique combination of history, geography, memory, inspiration, meditation, and the profound silence and nothingness surrounding me created a mystical and deep, inexplicable connection to my people, my land, my history, my humanity, my God.

Sitting on the edge of a forest, over two years later, writing these words, I still carry the experience with me. I can't overstate the power, the intensity, the impact of that day, that moment, and the clarity it brought. On the heels of all that came before it—my upbringing as a Jew in America, my exploration of various forms of religious expression in my youth, and my return in young adulthood to the normative foundations of our faith and practice; my decision, as part of this return, to take part in this experiment in sovereignty in our ancestral homeland which is this nation-state of the Jewish people, Israel; the festivals celebrating our freedom from Egypt and receipt of the Torah and delivery and protection in the desert, the holidays contemplating our purpose on this earth, the commemorations of our national tragedies, and the singing of praises marking our modern independence; the birth of my children as *Sabras*, native-born sons and daughters of the land and country; the meditation and prayer, the hikes throughout the country and of course this ongoing trek—I gained an enormous, and enormously profound, sense of self, of purpose, of anticipation . . . and of peace.

At one point, I stopped by a shrub for a break—and decided to pray. I'm not, I will admit even in this public forum, what's known as a "*matmid*," one who joins a minyan prayer group three times a day or even once a day, and I often don't get around to *davenning* (praying) the afternoon service, Mincha, most days. A philosophical and halachic discussion of my many transgressions, and those of others, and the balance between the ritual requirements of our tradition and the moral imperatives, let alone the interpretations through the ages of each, will have to await another time and another setting. But that day, I felt a deep need for my soul to sing, born of the meditative and contemplative nature of this seemingly never-ending trudge through the desert wilderness. I was alone but felt at one with all—all-one.

My *tefilot*, my prayers, began as always recognizing God as the God of Avraham, of Yitzhak, of Yaakov—and I knew, right then, that yes! They were here, or nearby anyway, in history and in my mind and in my heart, that we were together, with all the nation of Israel, with all humanity, struggling and accepting, in humility recognizing God as King, Helper, Savior, and Shield (מלך, עוזר, מושיע ומגן), the words of the opening paragraph of our daily prayers. With the traditional wording used by Jews for thousands of years, I expressed intense gratitude for the incomparable goodness shown us, for our lives which are in His hands. I voiced passionate appreciation for the miracles which are with us every day and for the wonders and kindnesses shown us every moment, evening, morning, and afternoon . . . (על . . . נודה לך . . . על חיינו המסורים בידיך . . . מודים אנחנו לך נסים שבכל יום עמנו ועל נפלאותיך וטובותיך שבכל עת—ערב ובוקר וצהריים).

When I sent a photo of me meditating on a mountain top the previous week to my great friend Moshe, an acclaimed psychoanalyst, he called my journey on

Shvil Yisrael "one long walking meditation." At this point it was clear he was right. Jewish meditation is meant to bring spirituality and meaning to the mundane world, rather than the otherworldly ecstasy often associated with meditative practices. And the result of my experience in this walking meditation in the Judean Desert was banal in the extreme: I wrote a song.

Give me a sunrise to start my day
Show me the path to send me on my way
Lend me a spring in my step, clean air in my lungs
That's how I'll know my day has begun

    Show me you love me
    Tell me in the blue sky
    Whisper it in the leaves on the trees and
    Breathe it in the flowers
    Shout it to me in the mountain streams
    Give the birds love songs to sing
    Clothe me in love
    Clothe me in sunshine and love

Give me the strength for every new step
Send a warm desert wind to dry my tears when I've wept
A bush with some shade for relief from the heat
An afternoon breeze at my back to take the weight off my feet

    Show me you love me . . .

Give me the wisdom to accept what I must
I'm grateful for your kindness, I take it on trust
I'm willing to forgive, I've got nothing to forget
My life is full of meaning, haven't begun to live yet!

    Show me you love me . . .

Give me a sunset to close my day
Send me a moonbeam to take me away
Give me love in my heart, love in my hand
Someone who loves me . . . someone who can

    Show me you love me . . .

I should clarify: I *rewrote* a song. The basis for it was written when I was 18, one summer at Skylake Yosemite Camp. Those summers were a formative part of my childhood and youth in California, where for nine years I was a camper, a counselor, and leader of a values-clarification group (in addition to driving a speedboat and being a water-ski instructor).

Then, the song was an unsophisticated attempt to express a wonderment of the natural beauty I saw at and around camp. Now it was a vehicle to articulate my sincere and multifaceted, deep-seated sense of gratitude and purpose borne of these recent experiences. The tune is upbeat and light, full of energy and hope.

Perhaps I'll record it one day and post it online for anyone interested to listen to. (Actually, I did record an informal version of the chorus, a few weeks later while hiking near Jerusalem, just for fun, and again up north. Listen here—if you're into self-punishment [Video 6].)

At base, it was a manifestation in song and words of all I couldn't really express fully, using a melody that reflects my heartfelt awe of nature and God (without a traditional definition of Him/Her) as well as my growing understanding of the centrality of humility, acceptance, and gratitude to my personal growth . . . with a hint of my thoughts about forgiveness and meaning as well. As I wrote later in my journal when recording the words of this new/old song (written in the new/old land): "On Tuesday, March 4, ב' אדר ב', the desert works its magic . . ."

I have to stop singing. Having worked out the words to my new/old song and fit them to the tune, adjusted for the years of wear and tear on my vocal chords, and having sung it over and over (and over again) to myself, loudly and quietly, while walking and while resting, I need to give it a break. So as I sit eating lunch under the first bush I've seen in over five hours, crouched over to catch some of the minimal shade offered, I write the words in my journal. I am ecstatic, though not in the spiritual sense (I think); just thrilled at the phenomenon. I haven't written a song for three decades, since before I was married. I really didn't think I had it in me anymore. And this is a good song, I can feel it. And a great one for me. Something has transpired; I can feel this too. Whatever transformation I was looking for out in the wilderness, whatever inner sense of destiny told me the desert was the place I could perhaps find the solace and strength, the courage and serenity I need to move on, I have found it. I am a changed person, as unabashed as that sounds.

As profound as this is, I abruptly feel lighter, almost playful. It is profoundly meaningful, deeply moving me to my core, though I can't seem to find the language to describe it even to myself as I think while I walk; yet I am unexpectedly feeling silly. I start to almost skip, light on my feet (or as light as I can be with this cursed pack on my back), swinging my poles and planting them like Fred Astaire places his black and white cane on the dance floor before swinging around it. It's a strange and glorious feeling, reminiscent of a few experiences I had at college in Berkeley. It's a sense of "the world is perfect, I can do anything, everything is all right, there are no limits." I remember that top-of-the-world feeling now; and I remember my decision one day when I was twenty to resist pursuing it through chemicals, and how much I missed it for a while. I've felt that sort of euphria only very fleetingly, occasionally, at peak moments since those years. It's really a wonderful "high," and I'm enjoying it tremendously as I bound along.

The intensity of the desert walking and communing with all-that-is has passed; I'm so happy to be back in the real world, such as my trudging-along-dirt-roads real world is, with only about five kilometers left to go to the road. I pass a group of trucks with workers laying huge water pipes. One driver asks what I'm doing; I stop and we chat for less than a minute, at the end of which he says, "20 kilometers in one day?

That's more than I'll walk in my life!" I laugh pretty hard, and am still chuckling as I walk on, and still more a few hundred meters on as I look back at the array of a dozen or so trucks, seeing the men standing around now talking, with some of them pointing and looking at me.

I make my way uneventfully to the road at Be'er Ef'e—discovering while there that apparently the map symbol of a blue circle with a dot in it refers to a seasonal spring, with water only in winter, and I make a mental note of that. I allow my frustration at wasting a half hour looking for the well to just dissipate as I wait for a car to come along. One eventually does, and it drops me at the entrance to Arad; walking to the Trail Angel I'd called the day before I realize two important things. First, this signifies the end of my time in the desert. Though Arad is very much a desert town, tomorrow I'll traverse the geographic boundary between the Negev/Judean Desert and the Hebron/Judean Hills. So it's not merely a transition now from desert to town, from solitude to civilization; it's a physical transition, geological, with new flora and fauna, climate and topography ahead of me. I'm excited, as I walk through the streets of this relatively successful "development town," even as I begin to regret the end of my wilderness sojourn.

And second, I realize I've added a full three kilometers to my day's hike by choosing an Angel in one of the neighborhoods farthest from the Shvil and the entrance to town. This, I didn't need.

As a first experience actually staying with a Trail Angel, meeting and staying with Arieh and Leah Schiff in Arad was a real marvel. Named for their son Ofer, who was killed in a tragic car accident in 1997, a Bedouin-style tent (*HaOhel shel Ofer*, Ofer's Tent) welcomes hikers with a dozen mattresses and blankets, an old fridge and kettle, and a wonderful shower/toilet bamboo hut right next to it. I

Arad Trail Angels' Bedouin Tent

was the only guest that afternoon, and enjoyed the quiet as I planned my next two days and made a few calls to finalize arrangements. The blankets and mattresses were a bit musty—but as I told myself at the time, I'd slept in much worse conditions in my 17 years of doing 35–40 days of IDF reserve duty as a combat medic in an artillery unit . . .

I enjoyed the (hot! Hot!) shower, hoping that neighbors couldn't see too well through the gaping holes in the bamboo, and used my hiker's towel for the first time, hoping it would dry by the morning. I really appreciated the soap by the sink which I washed my underwear and socks with. At about 7 p.m., just as I considered climbing on a mattress to read, write a bit in my journal, and get to sleep early, knowing I had a big and hot and dry day ahead of me . . . Leah popped her head out of the window of the house and said "We're going to help a friend bottle his wine—want to come?!"

"Are you serious?!?" I exclaimed. She obviously couldn't have known that I've made wine for almost twenty years. I produce around one or two hundred bottles a year, from grapes I grow in my garden and others I buy from vineyards across Israel. I'm no wine snob but I know and love the grape and its juice, and naturally couldn't resist the opportunity.

We drove together through the quiet streets of Arad to the industrial park on the edge of town, where a small group of men and women were operating a loud mobile bottling machine mounted in a trailer. Amidst the noise and bustle, I learned that Leah and Arieh's friend, Amir, is one of the owners of the relatively new Midbar (Desert) winery; after we helped put bottles in boxes (the filling, gassing, corking, and labeling were all handled by this miracle of modern technology, something I have to look into), we joined Amir at the winery's tasting room. Considering that it's next to a carpentry shop and across from a small food factory, near a somewhat noisy ironworks workshop, they've done a decent job making the small square space feel a bit like a real winery, complete with wooden bar, hanging glasses and vine-related artwork.

But what really captured my interest and fired my imagination was learning that some of the grapes had come from Nachal Tzin—the same Nachal Tzin, though a different part of it, I had walked along just a few days ago! And so, in keeping with the spirit of my trek—now that I'd committed to visiting any wineries I came across—I ordered a few bottles to be shipped home.

We returned to the house, and I to the tent; after planning, writing a bit, and a cup of hot herbal tea, I was asleep by 10 p.m.

The next morning, Wednesday, didn't start out too well: I was tired, after tossing and turning much of the night; hungry too. I bid farewell to Arieh and Leah, and he took a photo which he immediately printed out and pasted into his "Shvilistim" book, and I wrote a note next to my picture. I walked for a while (longer than had expected), and after finally catching a ride into the town center walked a bit further to find a place for breakfast . . . which turned out to be disappointing.

By this time I was hot and bothered—and really not looking forward to trudging first through this not-as-picturesque-as-I-originally-thought town and then across the barren brown baking hills which I could just about see in the distance through the haze. So I flagged down a cab and had him take me to the archeological site of biblical Arad. Leaving my backpack in the shade near the entrance—with a smile for the young woman at the reception office who tells me that as a Shvilist I can enter without charge—I started up the incline of Tel Arad.

I'm not sure what I'm looking at as I walk up the hill. What era are these remains from? There are walls and wells, walkways and buildings—it's just huge. I decide to go back and get a brochure; I always prefer to know a bit about the history of a place, and the dig here is surprisingly extensive. I had no idea how significant this site is—and as I learn more, I realize I had no idea either how impressive its saga.

As I walk around the uncovered lower city, I'm surprised to read that it dates back 5,000 years (!) to the early Bronze period. That's before even Avraham came to this land. And as this part of the site wasn't built over, it's in pristine condition (for a ruin). Here are the living quarters; here are the storerooms; I walk down to the deep well, peering into it and noting how smooth its sides, and the stairs winding down into it. At three or four meters in diameter, it's bigger than other ancient wells I've seen, and testifies to the major and thriving community which lived here. As do the big rooms of the "palace" near the top of the site.

As if I'm walking through a time-warp, I head up the path to the top of the Tel. Arad's king attacked the Children of Israel as Moshe led them toward the Promised Land, as described in the Hebrew Bible. After the Israelite victory the city was named "Chormah," or Destruction. Other remains, from a bit later, around 1000 BCE or the late Iron Age, testify to the importance of the city as a fortress guarding the southern and eastern edge of Judea.

Arriving at the upper city, I'm both incredibly moved, and distressed and confused, by the descriptions in the brochure and on various signs. I'm moved by the almost palpable presence I feel of those early Israelites—or Judeans/Jews I suppose, or Hebrews. (What did we call ourselves then? What should we call ourselves now? As a national group we are Israelites and Judeans/Jews/Hebrews, now Israelis and Jews. As a religious group we are Jews. What a confusion! Were they as confused back then . . . ?) This archeological site is almost alive, so well-preserved and well-presented it is. Here is a kitchen; here are living quarters; here is a defensive watch-post; here is a mikvah ritual bath, and another, and another. The mikvaot really make an impression on me: if there is one thing which makes a dig in the Land of Israel different than one anywhere else, it is this proof-positive—were any needed—of the very Jewishness/ Israeliness of a settlement. No other culture has such a construct, of ritual baths made in such a specific way, situated in private homes throughout a village.

But I am confused and troubled by one thing. There is a description of, and partial reconstruction of, an incense "altar," and references to a "mikdash" or sanctuary. Why? If these are Israelites/Judeans/Jews, what business do they have with setting up alternatives to the Temple in Jerusalem? This bothers me more than I really understand; it's as if I feel betrayed. And also: why on the western side of the settlement? Even in those times, in the kingdoms of Israel and Judea, we faced toward Jerusalem in prayer—so it should be on the northern side! I'm reading now about how during the reign of King Chizkiyahu (Hezekiah) or King Josiah the altars were taken down . . . phew. I guess this is one of the "high places" which the Bible describes in pejorative terms, where altars were established as alternatives to the central authority of the King and High Priest.

Why this upsets me is curious; but not enough to spoil my deep, almost mystical appreciation for the personal connection I feel with those who lived here. And now I'm reading about the unprecedented find of ostraca from the seventh century BCE, before the first destruction of Jerusalem (when Arad was also destroyed, about 580 BCE) referring to Arad as a "House of God" ("YKVK"). I so wish they hadn't removed all these finds and put them in the Israel Museum. Personally, I'd rather see them where they were discovered, where the full power of the connection between people, land, history and me in the here and now could be felt.

I shake off my disappointment, and focus on the story of this city's development, with its Citadel founded during King David and King Solomon's time. It was clearly used continually for thousands of years—and not only as a city and fortress but as a site for religious worship and pilgrimage—through Israelite, Babylonian, Persian, Maccabean, Roman and early Muslim times, as evidenced by the many ritual pottery shards found strewn all about. Some elements of the Roman fortress demonstrate how important the site was; looking out from the top, it's clear to me how this hill controls the trade routes (and military routes).

As I begin to walk back down, I stray from the path and wander across a field of small bushes and weeds. There are hundreds of large rock lizards basking in the hot and hazy sun, and I photograph a few. I come across a few of the famous black Irises of Arad, and photo them too, for Flo, my mother-in-law who is an avid flower collector and grower. I think I'll send her a few photos of the flowers I've taken, she'll like that (I think; I hope). And seeing a small shard of pottery, I pick it up. It's clearly a handle of a jug; can't imagine it has any religious significance. I ask a park ranger, and she gives me permission to keep it. Am I crazy? Am I going to now carry this piece of pottery the rest of the way across the country? I think I might . . .

And then it was time to move on. As I was leaving the park, I looked to my right, to the west, where the Shvil seemed to shimmer in the distance as it wound its way to the start of the climb up to Har Amasa at the eastern entrance to the Yatir forest. Then I glanced ahead, to the south, where I could just make out the buildings of the Yatir winery, about a kilometer and a half away. On to the trail? Or back the way I came, to this next winery? It wasn't even a rhetorical question.

I walked leisurely across to the winery—and I was so glad I did. Considering my general appearance, fit more for bumming cigarettes off strangers in a bus station than visiting one of Israel's most celebrated and successful wineries, I suppose it wasn't unreasonable for Etti, the business manager, to hesitate at first. But after a brief introduction, she happily took me for a private tour and tasting.

I heard about some interesting developments I wasn't aware of, and which fascinated me as a vintner. (Yes, that's the official term, even for someone like me who makes wine merely for fun.) They have the only hydraulic grape crusher in Israel, brand new when I visited, which is both much more gentle to the grapes as well as more efficient, and cleaner, than traditional rotor or electric crushers. And they have an amazing new "combo" steel vats, nicknamed a "cigariya" or cigarette, in which fermentation takes place on top and the settling and then aging on the wine on the bottom, obviating the need to transfer or "rack" the wine from one container to another.

Naturally my thoughts turned to the dream I've had for years of opening my own winery, and I asked Eran, the chief vintner at Yatir, about the cost and efficiency of these new contraptions. He humored me—what other word can I use, his winery produces 100,000 bottles a year, and I make 200 or so—and we talked a bit about developments in wine-making and the success of the Israeli wine industry. I said that it's extraordinarily exciting that we're re-discovering the beauty and meaning of Jewish wine-making in our land, an art going back at least 3,500 years, and he was a bit skeptical—till I pointed out that just up the road there is evidence of wine-making from the time of King David, at the Arad archeological site I had just visited. So near and yet so far; he wasn't even aware of the historical connection to our land and people that I felt so very powerfully. But he thanked me for pointing it out, and we agreed I'd host him soon at MediaCentral, the project I ran in Jerusalem providing services for the foreign press visiting the region.

As I walked the kilometer and more back up the road to the trail, the heat and the wine combined to make it impossible, or so I convinced myself, to do the rest of the ten or so kilometers up the mountain. I stood for a few minutes where the trail left the highway, until a young woman stopped to offer me a ride. Merav was her name—my older daughter's name, what fun—and she told me of her life setting up a new community in the hills of Hiran/Huran "to block the Bedouin takeover of all the land." We spent the twenty minutes or so winding up the mountain discussing the historical and political complexities of the country and the region; while she acknowledged the reasonableness of the Bedouin wishing to continue their nomadic lifestyle, I acknowledged the truth of her position that as they settle into semi-permanent encampments on public land, and then claim ownership based on the concept of squatters' rights and a non-provable "connection" to the land, they encroach on our more modern standards of land-use, zoning, property ownership and the like. We didn't really have time to explore the nuances, but the conversation both intrigued me and reminded me of my desire to connect with some of the Bedouin I see along the way. At that point, I started to think maybe I'd stay with one of the Bedouin Trail Angels, if I could.

All this, though, is forgotten as I leave the car and hike the three kilometers or so up to Har Amasa. I stop repeatedly to take photos. The geography is different—hills and mountains that are high but not steep, with terrain more dirt and rock than the sand and boulders I've been used to these last three weeks. The flora is startlingly different too: I photograph about twelve separate species of flowers in the space of ten minutes, just have to keep stopping as they are so beautiful, wild, natural, and welcome. I think again of Flo, and of my friend Moshe the gardener (and I think of Karen too, the green thumb of the two of us), and have them in mind as I take picture after picture.

I start to feel a bit sentimental—I miss the interactions I'd always taken for granted with Flo, and even more, with my father-in-law Philip, with whom I'm still incredibly close. I miss Moshe, our talks and our closeness, and the fact that he would revel in all these weird and wonderful flowers I can't name or identify but which are so full of colors it takes your breath away: blues and purples, pinks and yellows and greens and reds, stars and circles and ovals and even squares and triangles and more. Appreciation for all this beauty—and for the privilege of taking this trek, living this life, being here in Israel, just being—wells up inside me. I am so very grateful to be alive, to be here, to be me. I wish I could share this with Moshe. It's a bit strange, and wonderful, this new-found sense of gratitude. I've always been a positive thinker, looking for the best, celebrating the wonders of my life; but somehow now it's taken on a whole new meaning. Having accepted my situation, I feel like I've given myself a new lease on life.

As I walk on, the green of the hills—not green hills, so much as more green in the hills, breaking the monotony of the brown dirt and gray rock—strikes me also as somehow familiar. I can feel I'm getting closer to home, to the kind of terrain I'm used to. As I approach the fence around Har Amasa, this feeling grows; and of course the shifting geography reminds me of these internal transitions of mine.

Before going in, I stand with my back to the kibbutz and can see the dull brown hills leading down to Arad in the distance; there's a virtual line distinguishing the central Negev and the northern Negev. As I look out over the vista I can actually see where the shrubs and flowers start; even the cooler late-afternoon breeze at the top of the hill reminds me how much has changed. Visually and physically, I know it; internally, emotionally, I feel it too. I'm moving from acceptance to gratitude. I'm in a different place now.

Ain't that the truth. Talk about being in a different place: I could smell the marijuana as I walked through the paths, following the sign to the Shvilistim room at Har Amasa. A failed kibbutz, taken over by a young crowd of hippie types, it resembled more a transit camp for refugees than an Israeli agricultural settlement. Arriving at the room, I was a little annoyed: it was so filthy I seriously considered just camping outside on the lawn. Instead, I spent a good hour sweeping, wiping, mopping and otherwise cleaning up the room and bathroom (I couldn't even consider using the shower or toilet without doing so), and then settled in. I had no complaints thereafter; the water in the shower was hot, I cooked up the last of my quinoa and soup on the electric stove rings, and did a bit of laundry—which I then strung up over the stove rings to ensure the clothes would dry by morning (and to heat the room, as the evening was getting chilly). I walked around the *yishuv* for an hour or so, and discovered from one not-overly-friendly resident that there are about thirty families there. I enjoyed a few more whiffs of weed floating on the air, and after spending too much time on the cellphone, I turned in, as I knew I had a long 25 km day the next day. I slept decently, if a bit aware of various forms of wildlife creeping and crawling in and around the room. I was certainly glad to be up and out by 7 a.m. the next morning.

At this point, leaving Har Amasa behind, I feel good. I feel great, actually, and not least as I'm in a forest where, though the ground is still brown and dry, the trees surrounding me are green. There's no question, I am much more of a forest and hills person than a desert person. But clearly there's more to it than that. I was up early, got a good start, have had my coffee; it's still pleasantly warm, the trail is clear, and with its mild descent through Yatir Forest I feel like a million dollars! I stop for a break after about 45 minutes, filming a bit of of the walk and the vista. Realizing I have no video record of me, no "outside'-of-self view of what it looks like, my striding down the path, I set up the camera and walk through the frame, clicking my sticks and feeling clever and foolish at the same time. Although I dislike it when people check after every shot, in this case I take a look, just to make sure it's captured what I wanted—which it did, and in fact very well. I play the video over a few times (Video 7)—you can hear the wind, and the birds, and my steps and sticks, and I find it strangely moving and a bit humbling. Look at me! I'm walking the Trail! It's actually pretty impressive, looking at me from afar, with the pack and all.

I sound like a bit of a broken record (to myself): I am so very grateful for the privilege of this experience; for my life in all its aspects, for my parents and my kids, for my friends, for my Jewish and Israeli identity and love of hiking. Is it my ancestor's blood/tradition/values running through me, transmitted from my parents? Am I simply continuing their history of wanderlust, coming to America in the seventeenth century and then out West in 1865 or so? But I'm not merely a wandering Jew; I love the outdoors so much, something my great-grandfather Lucius Levy Solomons would have approved of, as the developer of the John Muir Trail in the Sierra Nevada mountains. I have always been happiest when I am outside, in some form of nature. It's in my blood. And so here I am, on a stunningly beautiful mountainside surrounded by trees and shrubs and flowers of various kinds and colors, a nature-loving Jew wandering my homeland . . . and I'm overcome with happiness.

OK. Time to move on.

Yatir forest is "a bit like a Swiss forest (not)," I wrote in my journal later, and walking through it was pleasant at first, but it became hotter and more difficult as the day wore on. I stopped too many times to enjoy the view, look at the flowers, take photos, rest etc. In the middle of the day, near the "Forester's Lodge," I ran into Laura, from Scotland, and she was, I must admit, exactly the kind of "wacko nut job" my son Netanel had warned me to steer clear of while on the Trail. She was coming the other way; or in fact not, as she had stopped and was struggling with her enormous backpack when I came upon her. (It was, I have to admit, like something out of *Wild*—which my brother Mark had sent me to read before I set out on my trek.) Out of politeness, I stopped to ask if I could help.

I listened with growing impatience to her plight. She flew in the previous day, had come directly to Yatir, I'm not sure why, and started hiking the trail going south into the desert with no background, no training, and no real familiarity with even the rudimentary aspects of map-reading let alone the crucial issues of water, shoes, weight, timing, pacing etc. Not that I was the world's expert; but even prior to starting out I had a glancing acquaintance with those fundamentals—not least as a former IDF medic, map and terrain enthusiast, weekend hiker and father who accompanied three children at least once a year each on an annual school overnight trip for over a decade. After 30 minutes, including a few evangelical religious references and a number of bizarre side comments relating to personal issues back in Scotland which I presume she'd prefer me not to repeat here (though her telling a perfect stranger on the trail might indicate a lack of concern for making them public), I said, perfectly truthfully, that I really had to get moving to keep to my schedule. I gave her my phone number in case she needed anything in an emergency, though I doubted I could do much, and suggested a few ideas for her hike and pack. After a photo, which I sent her by sms, we parted ways.

Nati was right.

I then took way too long a break at the Forester's lodge, including using the bathroom and maps in the Shvilistim room there, and briefly considered just staying rather than pushing on to Meitar for the night. I could have: the next day, Friday, I didn't have too far to hike, and would have just set out earlier Friday morning and arrived later in the day before Shabbat. Good thing I didn't.

The rest of the day was hot, and hazy, and much, much longer than anticipated. More, the trail included a number of rises over hills which, while noted in the Guide and maps, seemed higher and harder, longer and steeper, than they should have felt. I walked on . . . and on . . . and on. I took photos of various panoramas overlooking the flat plains of the northern Negev ahead of me, and of the Hebron hills to the right of me in the North. I shot a few videos of the vistas looking over at the biblical village of Yatir and at Hirbat Hiran, just two of the many ruins from over two thousand years ago which increase the feeling of my returning to the haunts of my forefathers. Running into a herd of sheep and rams and lambs, minded by their Bedouin Arab keepers, I marveled at how little has changed in two millennia or more—though I supposed David and Saul didn't have jeeps, nor little camp stoves on which to brew their coffee.

I thought of stopping to say hi and chat, but didn't want to be pushy or insensitive. Happily, one of the men called to me as I nodded in greeting, and asked if I wanted coffee. I stumbled over (had to leave the trail, and the terrain was more rocky than it seemed), threw my pack on the ground, and enjoyed some incredibly sweet, dark, thick coffee, while we traded "where from" stories. "Kol haKavod" they said—"good for you"; but they also asked "Why are you doing this?" and aside from a brief comment about connecting to the Land and enjoying the hiking, I didn't want to get into a political discussion. Their friendliness, and enthusiasm, in spite of their skepticism, was pleasing.

But it was getting late. The sun was low and shimmering in the haze ahead; I could see on the map that I still had at least five kilometers to go, plus another four to the Trail Angel in the community of Meitar whom I had spoken with last night. (I had almost given up after five "nos"; I still harbored the thought of camping out, just to avoid those last 4 kilometers. That became my plan as the sun set in front of me.)

"Trail Angels" is such a perfect term. An institution unique to Israel, these islands of refuge quite literally become saviors in time of need. I remember as if it was yesterday, the end of this seemingly never-ending day from the Yatir Forest to Meitar Forest.

It's a beautiful sunset, and this terrain is becoming increasingly familiar as I near the center of the country. But now, as the day comes to a close, I'm exhausted and a bit confused; through the hazy overcast I keep thinking I see the Meitar Forest ahead, where I'll find the night camp (and water)—but it keeps turning out that, no, this is just another hilltop with a few trees. Now I have to climb up it—again—and then down, and then up, and then . . . what happened to the gentle downhill slope I'd anticipated?

A little earlier, approaching the Bedouin and their flocks, I took a photo of the setting sun, casually appreciating the orange and brown hues through the clouds and mist. Now I'm beginning to worry. Not too much: I've been caught previously in the dark, and survived with my headlamp and a little cool-headed recalculation—and this isn't that bad, at least it's not the desert. But I see that it's a bit steeper on the next downhill segment than I realized; not good, in the dusk. Carefully, I stop singing to myself and just get on with it. I can see lights in the middle distance, and far way: that must be Meitar, or is it a Beduin village? Is that Beer Sheva over there? I'm not really worried, I'm enjoying myself. Just beginning to feel a slight unease. Not quite sure of the distance to go at this point.

Just as darkness closes in, I come to the bottom of the hill, and clearly this is the beginning of Meitar Forest. No problem—according to the map, I have only a little ways to go, up and over the hill in the middle of the forest, to the night camp. I'm thinking of the Trail Angels I'd been in touch with yesterday about staying, and I'm tired, and starting to feel like I can't be bothered to walk through the yishuv to get to their place, even for a bed and shower. In fact, I'm too tired to hike up this steep hill facing me, in the dark; I see a trail which, though longer, goes around the hill and ends up at the night camp. I think I'd rather stay on the relative flat; anyway, the faint moonlight out in the open is more welcoming than the dense tree-covered gloom of the forest.

So I start on the trail. Then I see a shortcut across a flat area, nearer the hill. Why should I follow this dirt road all the way around when I can cut at least 300–400 meters off the route? Halfway across, I realize my mistake: First, I'm trudging through a crop field dampened by a light rain earlier, sinking further into the shallow mud with every step. Second, I guess this is also a pasture, as the cow patties are becoming more frequent. Slogging through, my slow-going progress begins to depress me. I'm such an idiot. A little push up the hill and I'd have been there already; instead I'm getting more tired and cold by the minute, not to mention angry, and now I'm completely lost, can't figure out which of three trails ahead of me makes the most sense. Me and my brilliant ideas.

Here we go: I step quickly on to the middle trail, which seems logical as it goes into the edge of the forest but seems to keep on the flat, heading in the right direction ("right" if my map-reading skills haven't completely failed me). After about ten minutes, a little ways into the forest, I'm not at all sure, as I trudge along with trees on every side now blocking out most of what little light there is.

And then I see them. At first, it's just a feeling, and an uncertain hint—are those a pair of eyes to my left? Another? And ahead; and to the right? It becomes clear, a minute later. I'm surrounded by about twenty jackals—those rather small, coyote-like field animals I'm familiar with from the wild areas behind my home in Beit Shemesh. They're a nuisance there; sometimes they get into my yard and once chewed through my drip irrigation pipes. (I never could figure out why.) Here, I'm terrified. They're not so small! And though I know—I KNOW—they do not, and would not, I think, attack a human, it's more than a bit discomforting to be surrounded by something like 40 pairs eyes staring at me in the dark. Yes, I count them, as my headlamp is reflected when I turn this way and that. At least they're not doing their pack-like howling . . .

Of course, like it was scripted, as soon as I think that, they start wailing. When it happens at home (almost every night in the spring and summer), it's almost musical, and kind of fun—hey, we live near the wilderness! In the blackness of the woods now, at the end of such a long day, when I'm not only tired and aching but getting lonely again, it's pretty unnerving, and threatening. I turn my headlamp to full, which though it helps somewhat also makes the red dots of their eyes seem even more menacing. At this point I really don't have a choice: I can panic, and run, and risk falling down and hurting myself or getting further lost, or worse. Or I can take three deep breaths and accept that I'm in the middle of a pack of wild animals which aren't *a real danger to me, and acknowledge that I've made a mistake in navigation. But I can also recognize that I'm fairly near the camp site (and the village, and civilization) . . . and move on.*

Thankfully, I manage the latter. I keep walking at an even pace, singing Zippidy Do Dah pretty loudly. I figure the louder I am, the less assertive they'll be. About twenty minutes later, after passing out of the forest, I see the lights of the perimeter fence of the yishuv a few hundred meters away. Walking along what clearly is the dirt road encircling the forest which I had left an hour earlier for this "short cut," I come to a set of picnic tables and campfire circles—with a set of water faucets! No signage, but looking one last time at the map, I know this is the night camp, and I throw my pack down with a finality and resignation: I'm going to just pitch my tent, climb in, and go to sleep. It's about 7 p.m., and I've no energy for anything else. Tomorrow is Friday, and I'll be walking a short distance (a few hours' hike) to Sansana for Shabbat, and I know I'll get a shower and hot food and a bed . . . so I can give up on those for tonight.

I call the Trail Angel family out of a sense of politeness, and their college-age daughter Ronit answers. "Hi, thanks so much, I just arrived, am just going to pitch my tent and stay here, wanted only to let you know and say thanks again . . ." "Okay, 'sababa,' be well," she says, and that's that. (I'm showing my age, and sense of responsibility. I just think it's the polite thing to do, to call to cancel; wouldn't want them to wonder or worry.)

I start to take some things out of my pack, wash and refill my water bottles & Camelback, and begin to set up my tent. Within 60 seconds my phone rings. It's Esther, Ronit's mother. "Where are you? We're coming to get you!" "No, it's really okay," I reply; "I'm fine, just tired, going to hit the sack." "No way," she says, "I'm not leaving you to sleep alone in the forest, forget it!" She continues, "I'm a Polania [Jewish mother/yenta] and I don't care how old you are, I'm not letting you stay there. We're on our way!"

Like knights in shining armor, my angels from the small Negev community of Meitar came out on that cold and rainy night, and (having first gotten lost in the forest looking for me), picked me up and took me back to their home. There, a hot shower, cosy room, comfortable bed and home-cooked food made me (almost) forget the blustery trek I had just suffered through. I haven't described it yet in much detail: there's something exceedingly Israeli about this concept of Trail Angels, people who open their homes to Shvilistim, with no compensation whatsoever, and go to great lengths to help us out. Every Angel is different, and offers what they can, from a tent on the lawn and use of the bathroom, to a virtual bed & breakfast including sheets and towels, dinner and breakfast, gre and even food to restock, advice and a ride from/to the trailhead, and more. Trail Angels provide hikers on the Trail with not only a respite but a refuge of sorts, whether from the elements or from the loneliness, from the exertion and from the intensity.

Other treks do have something vaguely similar, like the Appalachian Trail's 3-sided huts providing free shelter along the way. The Pilgrims' Trail in Spain and France has organized B&Bs, and treks in Nepal and South America offer guides and hosts as well—all for payment. Only in Israel is there a list of people willing to house/host treckers at the last moment without consideration. I can only explain it in one way—which is how it feels. This is family. It's like hearing from a distant cousin—"Hey, I happen to be in town, could I crash by you tomorrow night perhaps?" And of course you say yes—"love to see you!" There were four times when I was told my hosts wouldn't be home until later—come in, the door's unlocked (twice, on kibbutzim) or the key's under the mat (twice, too)—and I had free run of the house/apartment, to shower, relax, snack, prepare for the next day, etc. It is a fascinating—and emotional, uplifting, wonderful—element of the Shvil, and of Israeli society. And like so much that is Israel, it is not well-known, and not appreciated sufficiently. Except by me—and of course other Shvilistim.

After Meitar—only the second night I'd spent at a private home of Trail Angels—I called my daughter Meira and told her "When I get home, the day after Pesach, I'm listing us as Trail Angels." Even though it means offering a ride from and back to the trail, as our home is some five kilometers from the trail depending on where you leave it, I just felt I had to. And since returning home, we've hosted dozens of Shvilistim—in groups and singly, older and younger, men and women, Israelis and foreigners, observant and less so. I love it, knowing as I do exactly what they need, ordering in pizza for fun, having a beer, leaving them alone to get organized, and having granola bars and quinoa and chocolate and nuts and herbs in the house for the them to take.

Esther and the rest of the family in Meitar were incredibly solicitous; their son drove me to the trailhead the next morning, after a scrumptious breakfast. Friday passed extremely pleasantly, a mild incline into the foothills of the Hebron/Jerusalem range, to a small and relatively new community called Sansana.

Along the way, a young man had pulled up alongside me as I walked on a stretch of the Trail adjacent to the road, and called out "Where are you for Shabbat?" When I said Sansana, he offered me a ride, which I politely declined, with a smile, as the leisurely walk, while quite warm, was so enjoyable (and I knew it wasn't far). I was pleasantly surprised when it turned out this guy—Tzur Sofer—was the son of the family who runs the Trail Angel hut at Sansana.

A few months earlier, my friends' daughter, Michal, had offered not only her help, as described earlier, in planning and packing, but a bit of authoritative advice as well. One of the things she absolutely insisted on was that I spend a Shabbat in Sansana. "Why?" I asked her, and with a smile she just said "Whatever you do, arrange your schedule so that you spend a Shabbat there!"

Intrigued, to say the least, I arrived at Sansana Friday afternoon, and was led by a boy of about ten along a dirt path out of the yishuv, it seemed. Or at least down a footpath which clearly led away from all the other buildings and homes (including caravans, or trailer-homes, which is where the Sofers live, in a "compound" near the entrance to the community). Imagine my surprise—and delight—when I'm led, down a small incline and over some rock-stairs, to a small building on the side of a hill overlooking the nearby forest and the plain below. With a deck supported by stilts, the "*bikta*" (cabin) stands on its own at the edge of the trees, set up by the family of a young Israeli named Yishai who loved to hike but who died tragically on a trek in South America. With a large room, modern shower and toilet, and a small kitchenette, it's more than any Shvilist could dream of. It's like a luxury "*tzimmer*" or B&B, but with a dozen mattresses piled in the corner instead of beds, and without the usual Jacuzzi (no complaints). It was certainly as spotlessly clean as any cabin for which you'd pay $150/night or more. It even has coffee and tea, and milk in the fridge . . . and a box of home-made cookies with a note saying "for you" and "Shabbat shalom." It was one of the Wow moments of the entire adventure.

Hanging washed laundry up to dry in the strong arid desert wind, I paused to look out from the expansive entrance balcony and experienced an incredible rush of gratitude: to the family of Yishai, for their generosity; to Yishai, for his intense love of the land and of hiking, as described in the plaque by the door; to the Sofer family, for the warmth of their welcome and their apparent efforts in the upkeep and maintenance of the hut; and of course to Michal, Aaron and Hadas's daughter, who had so very enigmatically but unrelentingly insisted that I not miss this remarkable place and experience.

Shabbat passed in utter tranquility, with a pleasant and relaxing combination of sincere prayer in the communal synagogue, somewhat raucous meals with my Angels, and a great deal of quiet time to rest, meditate, sing and just stare out over the trees from the balcony of the little house. It was a welcome return to "normality" for me, in one way, to pass a Shabbat in the bosom of a religiously-observant community so much like my own. On the other hand, it turned my thoughts repeatedly to the fact that I was not only very much alone there; I was alone in so many other ways as well.

The Sofer family were exceptional, in their energy and enthusiasm and in their indefatigable hospitality. I was, and remain, so very grateful to Tehila, Ohr, Tzur (from the car), Oron, Ro'i (who walked me to the cabin) and a sweet little girl whose name escapes me. After the Shabbat, I wrote in my journal about them, and about the Shabbat itself:

Journal Day 21—Saturday night March 8:
LOVELY, crazy, spirited, free-wheeling, hectic, loving, warm, fun, Torani, weird, exotic, exuberant, close, helpful, welcoming, warm, somewhat bizarre family—and I'm so appreciative of their hospitality and warmth.

As always—sometimes I get more lonely in the company of people than on my own. I thought I'd enjoy a "normal" shul/שבת [Shabbat] experience but it made me miss my shul [synagogue] and my friends and most of all my family. And my "family" will never be the same anyway; I don't have much of a family to go home to, as it were. Considering the divorce, Nati marrying, and Merav living in the States, our family of five is just a thing of the past. Gone. Finished. But I miss home anyway—and of course Mimi.

It was soon after I wrote this entry on Saturday night that Mimi in fact turned up, with her boyfriend Bini, for a visit and resupply. What a reunion! It had only been two weeks—"only"!—but given the emotions of the Shabbat I was so grateful to reconnect with Meira, for the reassurance that comes from the unconditional love of family in general, and from my youngest in particular. We'd already been through so much together. We had a brief but enjoyable visit, the three of us catching up on news and (mostly) their listening to a few of the stories of the Shvil.

I began to describe for them the incredible generosity of the Trail Angels I'd stayed at so far, and the unexpected beauty of the surroundings I'd passed through, as well as the feeling of accomplishment I'd begun to have and the deeply spiritual awakening I'd experienced in the desert those past three weeks. Trying to put into words some of my thoughts over that time, I found it difficult to actually verbalize them.

These interrelated themes of humility, acceptance and gratitude—on the hike and in my life—were hard to relay. Mimi and Bini were patient enough to listen, but it was clear I couldn't adequately express some of the ideas I'd been ruminating over—my sense of self, my recognition of the reality I and we live in, and my appreciation for all the incredible miracles in my life and in our family's life, let alone the magnificence and beauty of the natural world around us. Clearly I had more thinking to do, to bring some of these ideas together.

Mimi and Bini drove me (in the rain) to the small moshav of Lachish, skipping a small section of the Shvil; after they dropped me off I fell into a bit of a funk. My plan was to start the next day on the week's trek up to and then down from Jerusalem, which would circle my home town of Beit Shemesh while not actually entering it. "So close and yet so far" was to become the theme of that week. But that Saturday night it was still in the future. I enjoyed another night in a bed, courtesy of a lively and modest family in Lachish, yet another set of Trail Angels I couldn't have anticipated and wasn't to forget. The Fromm family, like most of those in this small cooperative settlement originally from Cochin, India, literally made their home my home. Their son gave up his bedroom for me, and I was more than a bit embarrassed. I explained that I was happy to sleep on the couch, or on a mattress, or in my tent on their lawn; but they insisted, and at ten past midnight on a Saturday night I couldn't be bothered to argue too strenuously.

As I settled in, still feeling a little blue, I surfed a bit online. I came across an amazing quote from Michael J. Fox (who of course has faced incredible health and life challenges), which virtually screamed at me from the screen.

Acceptance doesn't mean resignation; it means understanding that something is what it is and that there's got to be a way through it.

A way through it indeed; I was on my way through it all. This shored up my mood immeasurably; I posted an update on Facebook, and was asleep within ten minutes.

From my Facebook post on that Saturday night (March 8):

This was a week full of transitions, of different sorts. From the deep descents and ascents of the south to the more (relatively) gentle rolling hills of the center; from desert(s) to a savannah-like climate; from solitude to more social interaction; from desperation to hope. (Well, not really, but almost . . .) ☺ And in other ways, too.

A kind of routine developed, on these difficult mornings. I sing a lot—sometimes just 'cause I feel like it, often simply to pass the time, occasionally to distract the fear, and . . . also literally to hear myself sing—as the echo was tremendous! I now have a habit of starting the singing each morning with an old Camp Swig tune for the prayer ברוך שאמר—*Baruch She'Amar* . . . Imagine me singing at the top of my lungs as the echoes form a sort of "round' . . . Fortunately no one else is there to notice. The words mean a lot to me, and it becomes a form of תפילה *Tefila* [prayer] and meditation. (That and רבות מחשבות [*Rabot Machshevot*] are my kind of theme songs these days . . .)

In the bleakness of the rocky desert, looking for a song to sing, I recalled a song I'd written more than 30 years ago, and started singing it. But I couldn't remember the words—and that was so very frustrating. A few minutes of striding along, humming the tune, which is an incredibly uplifting, fun and hopeful melody, and my anger turned to inspiration: If I can't recall the lyrics . . . I can just write new ones! So over the next hour I did just that—and I think the new lyrics may even be better than the original. Certainly they're more powerful—and more relevant—than the musings of a 20-year-old. First time I've written a song in 29 years . . . This week the Shvil also became more social. For the first time I stayed at a few מלאכי השביל (Trail "Angels') and each is in their own way warm and giving, curious and sometimes envious, and often with their own story to tell. One hosts Shvilistim in a sort of Bedouin tent in memory of their son Ofer. And the little cabin I spent Shabbat in at the small community of Sansana is in memory of a young soldier, Yishai, who died on a trek

---

in South America. Both of course loved hiking in Israel, so what a fitting way to honor and preserve their memory. Hosted by the tireless Sofer family, I was immediately made to feel not only welcome but part of the clan—which was incredibly timely, under the circumstances, and really heart-warming. Transitions . . . Spending Shabbat with them, and in such a young and vibrant kehilla (including a new friend, Shai, who shared some of his fine single malts with me ☺), made me miss home and my family and friends. . . . But [had] a visit (& re-supply!) this evening by Mimi & Bini, and [am looking forward] to . . . continuing the journey . . . Shavua Tov

Chapter Four

TO/FROM JERUSALEM, CIRCUMNAVIGATING HOME: GRATITUDE

[Week Four]

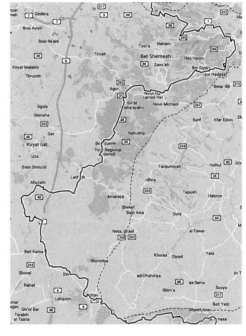

It was drizzling as I walked out of the house in Lachish, and I really wasn't sure what to do. As I neared the road, it started to rain harder, so I trotted over (imagine that, with my pack and all) to the gas station at the moshav's entrance and went into the little adjacent store. To my delight, I interrupted a general grumbling session among a half-dozen farmers, complaining it seems of everything from the weather to the cost of laborers and produce pricing. It turns out that one was—lo and behold—Mr. Fromm, in whose home I had slept but who (as a farmer) had been asleep when I arrived and left at sunrise long before I awoke. I happily accepted a free cup of hot, thick "mud" coffee ("קפה שחור, בוץ" "botz"), and asked the group whether they thought the rain would continue.

What a mistake! Instantly, each took out a mobile phone or tablet and called up his unique program purporting to predict exactly how many centimeters of rain would fall on exactly which parcels of land at exactly what time. All this information and no real understanding to be had, but I appreciated their attempts to help guide me. The only problem was: they each offered a different bit of advice. "Stay here all day!" "Leave now!" "Wait an hour." Very helpful.

Within a few minutes, the rain had diminished in its intensity, while the bickering among the farmers had increased in *its* intensity, and I took my leave.

As I returned to the Shvil, I realized I was passing Tel Lachish, an ancient fortress and settlement, one of the "bonfire" communication sites I'd read so much about in various day hikes in the area with the kids. These were hilltop beacon fires, lit to create smoke signals to relay news of invasion or other information, or to notify outlying communities of the new moon starting the new month. In the misty drizzle, I decided to climb it and learn more. As the sun breached the cloud cover, I found myself mesmerized by the vista. It was too overcast to see the other hilltops, nor could I see the coast. I knew that on a clear day one could; I was able at least to make out the hills of Hebron and Jerusalem in the distance to the east, and felt truly near the center of the country. More, or more personally, I felt looking north that I was heading home, a feeling which was to accompany me the entire week, and which would return only as I neared the journey's end five weeks later, when I came back to these foothills of Jerusalem.

But at that time, I was content to feel the closeness to my hometown of Beit Shemesh, the "House of the Sun," both geographically and historically. Reading a plaque near the site of the Tel Lachish stronghold, I was aware that this was one of a number of Tels in the area, many of which I'd be walking by or through in the coming days. All of these were populated by the Israelites at the time of King David and King Solomon—including those near Beit Shemesh. I was grateful I knew a little of the history; I lamented my lack of more detailed knowledge, and that I couldn't schlepp with me a history book or Hebrew Bible to which to refer. (I've wanted to take the official Israel tour guide course for years.)

In alternating periods of spotted sunlight and gentle rainfall I made my way from Lachish to Beit Guvrin, passing Tel Maresha, mentioned also in the Bible as one of the centers of commerce and defensive positions from the beginning of the Israeli national presence here. Today one of the small wineries in the region has taken the name. I was learning so much about this area, I found myself excited and embarrassed at the same time: having lived nearby for over two decades, how could it be that I'd never visited Tel Lachish, or Tel Maresha, or Tel Azeka, among others? Not to mention wineries I'd not heard of! I wrote later that week in my Saturday-night Facebook post:

> It's really a bit amazing—as an avid biker in the area over the last 20 years, and as a winemaker familiar with the two dozen or so wineries and their vineyards in these Judean hills, I thought I knew most of the hills and fields and vineyards around here. But no: Wow. I must have walked by or through or around at least 100 vineyards this past week, rolling through the hills and valleys between Lachish and Mesillat Tziyon, including some spectacular hillside כרמים vineyards in the Jerusalem hills.
>
> Cabernet, Petite Syrah, Carignan, Merlot, Shiraz, Pinot Noir, Chardonnay, and Petite Verdot—and those are only the ones I could identify (by signs

or asking; yes, I can pretty well distinguish them by taste or bouquet, but not by leaf or branch!) . . . And I won't go into the almost spiritual beauty of luscious rising and falling fields of green wheat stretching into the distance, watched over by ruins of biblical settlements in a panorama reminiscent, I'm sure, of how it was in those times as well . . .

Napa, Bordeaux, you have nothing on Ella, Adulam, Lachish, Eshtaol valleys.

From Arad to Lachish to Beit Guvrin I feel I've completed the transition from desert to hills, from brown to green, from emptiness to civilization; from isolation to community, and from foreignness to home. I'm beginning to feel a longing for home, as the terrain becomes so very familiar. I've walked and ridden these hills near Beit Guvrin a dozen times; I'm twenty minutes' drive from home! I'm lonely and excited, tired and energized simultaneously. I want to go home; I want to keep walking.

Not far from Beit Guvrin, four jeeps come up behind me, and I move to the side of the dirt road to let them pass. The first slows, then stops. Yes, "Shvil Yisrael," I say with a smile. They don't offer a ride (which shows they understand) but call out "Kol hakavod!" and drive on, as then do the other three. About an hour later, at the ruin of an old building near the main road I run into them again, where their group is hearing a description of the area and having a barbeque. I accept a cold drink, as well as the praise and applause following the guide's description of my trek so far. I listen for a few moments to his comments about the building and region's history; then move on.

I am not one to brag, nor to even really admit to my achievements, but I'm beginning to accept that what I'm doing is, in fact, a pretty nifty feat. Both in the abstract, and specifically "at my age," it's a real triumph—now that I'm almost halfway through, and as others continue to congratulate me, I'm starting to enjoy the feeling of accomplishment. That's the feeling I have as I stop at the gas station, and in celebration I treat myself to a diet Coke.

Arriving at Beit Guvrin—like Lachish, a modern settlement, a socialist kibbutz in fact, named after and adjacent to an ancient village/archeological site—a bit earlier than I had planned, even with the late start due to the rain, I wander into the excavations of the Roman arena and market stalls. Walking through the long stone corridors beneath the vaulted ceilings on top of which sit the spectators' bleachers, here too, I admonish myself: how come I've never stopped in here? Never taken family or visitors? It's just incredible, in the true meaning of the word: remarkable, and phenomenal, the way they've both uncovered and restored the remains of this historic landmark. And they present it, with signs and descriptions, so simply and clearly, it's fantastic. Life-size posters bring the scene to life, and the solidity and cleanliness of the stones and the dirt floor and pavement make it seem timeless. I'm so glad the Red Guide recommended taking the time to walk around. As one who has visited the Colloseum in Rome, I have to admit that, while smaller, this is more impressive. Here, I have the feeling that with a few animals, a few food vendors, a few gladiators and spectators it could all be functional; I feel the presence of real people and see how it all worked.

Satisfied, and noting the raindrops plonking on the stones and the gathering gray clouds, I know it's time to get over to the kibbutz itself. I follow the signs to the Mechina *(a pre-military prepatory program of learning, training and volunteering) which I'd been in touch with and whose counselor had said they'd have a bed for the night for me. Arriving just as the skies open up, I seem to have a guardian angel keeping me more or less dry! Gordy, a young man who just made* Aliya *("going up" or immigrating to Israel) from Chicago, meets me and two German tourists walking south on the Trail from Jerusalem to Arad, and leads us through the rain to the building. I feel a little strange, as I'm of course much older than the students; but less than I might, as I'm Israeli and a bit more "normal" than these two thirty-something Germans who strike me as almost drifters.*

Called Nachshon after the Israelite who was the first to jump in at the parting of the Red Sea, as an act of faith and leadership, this Mechina turned out to be a branch of the same Mechina my daughter Merav attended a few years ago. No coincidences! Made up of mixed boys and girls as well as observant and less-so, its focus is on leadership-training and volunteering. Many of the students were out on location this evening and night, doing their service work, so it was relatively quiet, and I enjoyed a hot shower (even though it brought back memories of my worst high school gym showers, let alone my most traumatic IDF reserve duty showers I wore my sandals throughout, needless to say.) But I was nevertheless grateful for the generosity involved.

I notice a sign in their makeshift lounge as I come out of the dorm area (I've been given a bed in a room with four others): "Who needs sleep? Sleep is for WIMPS!" What the . . . ? Now I'm worried—will I be able to sleep, or am I in for one of those nights that we fathers know occur but are loathe to admit to, where our kids party all night, getting into who knows what trouble? I look for Gordy but he's not around anymore. I'm considering pitching my tent on the lawn, even though I know the kibbutz doesn't allow it, because I can really use a decent night's sleep. Fortunately, one of the students comes in, and I ask him in a friendly manner what the sign means. "It's from an activity we had last week, don't worry" is his reply, and I'm somewhat mollified, even as a stereo is cranked up in another room and a bunch of laughing, yelling girls come through the door.

In the end, I sleep fine, if somewhat rough with the normal noise of sharing a room and a hall with young men. Breakfast that Monday morning with the group is a pleasure, not least watching as they take turns to cook and help clear up, cooperatively and in good humor. A few of us chat at the table about Israel, the Shvil, their choice to do a voluntary year of study and service prior to their mandatory three years (two for women) in the IDF. I'm so impressed with them all. The loyalty to and pride in their country, the principled decision and desire to help others, the interest in their Jewish and Israeli heritage and dedication to build the country all combine to instill in me a profound sense of confidence in our future. I look at them and see all my kids, all my

friends' kids and my kids' friends, and I stop the train of thought so as not to look like
a weirdo if I'd start tearing up.

I invite Gordy, and a few others, to come for Shabbat after Pesach, when I expect
to be back home; they wish me well and I'm on my way.

Except that as I approached the gas station near the trailhead, it started to
drizzle again. I checked the forecast—light rain, sunnier in the afternoon—and
decided to wait a bit before starting, and treated myself to a coffee and shakshuka
(another version of the Israeli fried-eggs-in-tomato-paste-and-vegetables breakfast
standard I enjoyed back in Sde Boker). By noon it was clearing—in fact it hadn't
actually rained much since I'd arrived at the gas station, defying the forecast—so I
started out. Forgetting to turn off my phone, I received a call from my good friend
Deborah, and we spoke at length as I hiked, about life and hardship and all the
things that happen to us which we have to accept out of a sense of humility, but
not hopelessness. It was good to talk a bit to someone who had accompanied me
throughout the period of the breakup, and someone who had experienced her own
disappointments and travails. It was almost symbolic of my nearing home to speak
with her as I walked toward Beit Shemesh, sort of like coming out of my (desert)
shell, as I hadn't spoken to any friends since setting out.

But I was glad, too, when the call ended, and I could return to my more
silent contemplation. If I felt connected to the desert wanderings of my people in
the previous weeks, here I felt connected to my own life and community, country
and people. I walked on the trail as it meandered parallel to Route 38, a road I'd
biked down countless times, an area I'd hiked with my children's class groups
more times than I can remember. I enjoyed walking this section tremendously,
as it brought back memories of my kids' class trips, crawling through Maccabean
(Greek)-era tunnels with flashlights, on our knees in the water, scared and exhilarated and almost ignorant of the historical significance. The spring wildflowers
were exquisite to look at, too; far too frequently I stopped to enjoy, to photograph,
and to ponder.

After a few hours I arrived at Mitzpeh Masua, a Jewish National Fund
(JNF) forest watchtower and picnic area. Setting up my coffee-making gear in
the forest next to it, I texted a few friends just in case they were in Beit Shemesh
(unlikely at 4 p.m., but who knows?) and invited them for coffee. Receiving no
replies, I sat on a picnic table and enjoyed a cup of herbal tea instead—I didn't
want the caffeine. Walking around the site, I was sorrowed by the fact that the
charming little restaurant located there for many years had been dismantled.
We had made Netanel's Bar Mitzvah party there, a unique event and one I
remain incredibly proud of, as it combined (even then) my love for nature and
for Israel and Judaism in one place and time and event. And then I started
thinking about how happy that time was.

I suppose it was the height of our innocence in a way. Before the kids
became teenagers but already old enough to both have a real relationship with

them and to be so very proud of them. Surrounded by family and old and new friends, somehow the Bar Mitzvah was a statement of arrival, of permanence, of moving from the stage of "young couple" or early family life into the more stable, established phase of middle age. Returning to the picnic table under the trees, I connected that time of great joy with my current pleasure in revisiting the site. Sitting there thinking of my friends, our shared celebrations, my family and all the rest, I remembered an incredibly powerful episode from my silent meditation retreat the previous year, when the entire structure of my life was coming crashing down.

On the Shabbat afternoon, there in Bat Ayin, I had walked across the valley to the nearby spring for a ritual dip. To be honest, it was as much an escape into nature, the dipping permitted on Shabbat only due to the ritual nature of the act, as it was a religious expression of devotion. But I needed it also as an act of cleansing, of purification, of transition, as over the course of that three day escape I had reached the beginning of the acceptance I've described earlier, and the immersion in the "living waters" of the spring/*mikvah* was part of my process. It was a powerful experience, one I hadn't anticipated (as is often the case, I guess, with enlightening mystical and spiritual events); I walked back feeling almost literally on top of the world. At one point on the path—sort of on top of the world, really, where the entire coastal plain is laid out before you, as you stand some 700 meters above sea level in the Jerusalem/Hebron hills looking west—I stopped to enjoy the view. I could see Beit Shemesh a ways below, and I was immediately and powerfully overcome with emotion.

I was overwhelmed with gratitude for all my family and friends there in Beit Shemesh, and for all that was beautiful in my life. I stood there, like an idiot, and started to thank them. Out loud. I listed my children, and my friends; my neighbors and members of my shul; my friends outside Beit Shemesh and those around the world too. I turned to my parents, and with tears streaming down my face thanked them for the years of love and support even when they opposed and resented my becoming more observant and moving to Israel. I ended by thanking Karen, yes Karen, for the wonderful and beautiful 28 years we had together, for the marvelous children we had and raised, for the outstanding communities we helped build in Givat Ze'ev and Beit Shemesh, for the outstanding partnership we created and continued during those years of struggling as an immigrant couple with no family in the country.

Having begun to accept her decision, and the fact that we were on the way to divorce, I started not only to recognize her right to make it, but to appreciate her contribution to my life as well.

These memories flooded me as I sat at Mitzpeh Massua, site of the incredible *simcha* (joy) of Netanel's coming-of-age celebration, so close to home and within sight of Bat Ayin where that experience took place. Almost a year later, I felt I had completed the process. I again experienced the deep and powerful gratitude for all the tremendous good and beauty in my life, physical and emotional, personal and national—this time with no melancholy or sadness, no hesitation or awkwardness.

Looking out toward the west, I could see the Mediterranean Sea in the distance. (I told Yaakov Saar, author of the Red Guide, he was wrong when he said that we wouldn't see a sea between viewing the Red Sea from the *Milchan* and approaching the Mediterranean in the north. Hah! Here it is, seen from right in the center of our country.) And I saw not only the sea. From this vantage point, you overlook 70 percent of Israel's population, and 90 percent of its industrial capacity, between Ashdod in the south and Haifa in the north. I was looking out over the biblical and modern Israel, the historical and the vibrant heart of my people and my country. So much to be grateful for!

Noting the sun making its way toward the sea, lower in the sky than I anticipated, I headed down the hill, bouncing and stumbling through the rocky hillside between the fir trees, as the day became mildly cooler. An hour or two later, with thoughts of thankfulness on my mind, I lurched up a small rise covered in brambles and crossed a road into the small settlement/village of Srigim and to my friend Arieh O'Sullivan's house to spend the night.

My phone battery died! I suppose I have to take fewer photos. No panic, it's a small yishuv; there can't be too many O'Sullivans here, and I more or less recall the directions Arieh sent in a text message earlier. Left here, right there, wait, back up . . . ah, here we are! I'm so proud of myself, my memory, my sense of direction! Okay, let's not get carried away. But I'm glad to arrive, it feels like it's been a long day, though I didn't really start walking until noon. Arieh's son Jordan greets me, and I shower and settle in until Arieh arrives. Though we're not close friends, there's a shared affection which grows as the evening goes by.

I tell him a bit about my situation and the trek; then the conversation takes an unexpected turn. It appears Arieh's wife left him just a few weeks ago, and we find ourselves comparing notes and commiserating. What a very strange coincidence; a very strange world. The circumstances are quite different, but the end result eerily similar. We talk while enjoying the delicious dinner he made—grilled salmon, bulgur wheat, and green beans, with excellent wine—and not surprisingly we find ourselves talking more about personal relationships than our usual talk-in-trade, international relations.

I share with him some of my thoughts about humility and acceptance and he responds positively, but it's a bit raw for him at this point and I don't want to wax too philosophical. It's actually so enjoyable that I almost forget I'm hiking the Shvil—it's like we just met up for fun and companionship. Then my close friend Aaron from Beit Shemesh joins us, coming after work on his way home (not quite), and we enjoy a bit more more wine and whiskey. Aaron and Arieh's shared passion for poker is more compelling a topic of conversation than Arieh's and my shared wifely predicament, and that's fine with me. An hour or so later, walking Aaron back to his car, I mention to him how much I've missed him and all our friends, telling him of the contradictory feelings at Sansana of enjoying the company and feeling all the more lonely for it. It's really good to see him, and I really appreciate his making the effort to come by. He's a good friend.

Up at 7 a.m. Tuesday morning, I'm driven by Arieh (in his Jeep, "General Lee," with his dog) to the edge of the yishuv, and he walks with me up a path to where it meets the Shvil. This has been the first time I've stayed with someone I know on the Trail, and I tell him how much I enjoyed it, and appreciated it. He reminds me that his son maintains "The Cave," a listed Trail Angel bivouac, and how happy he was to do it—and we both agree we look forward to getting together again after I complete the trek. I stride up the trail, the morning sun low and bright, a cool breeze taking the edge off the heat. The light is shimmering through the trees and making the purple and blue and pink wildflowers sparkle with their morning dew, and I feel just great. I take a photo or two, send one to the kids (for them to enjoy? to prompt a desire to join me perhaps?) and turn my phone off. I'm looking for quiet again, and I'm remembering the battery dying yesterday. I have 28 kilometers to go today, including some decent ascents, and I'm glad to be getting an early start.

Within half an hour or so I come to Tel Azeka. Once again I'm a bit nonplussed: I've lived not five minutes by car from here for over twenty years; I ride by this hill at least once every two weeks on my bike; how have I never been up here before? I'm already moved (and beginning to despair about ever finding a better word for that feeling) by the biblical verses etched in stone every ten steps or so as I begin to ascend to the top of the Tel. It feels surreal to be so very close to home; and more so, to be reading these phrases as I climb up, all from the Book of Shmuel/Samuel I: "And Shaul said to David: Go, and may God be with you." And then, "And David said to the Philistine, 'You come toward me with a sword and spear and javelin; but I come toward you in the name of the Lord of Hosts, God of the armies of Israel whom you have taunted.'" And the most poignant, for me: "And all this assembly should know that it is not by sword or spear that God will deliver, as the battle is to the Lord and He will give you into our hands."

Aside from the fact that this battle between David and Goliath, between the Israelites and the Philistines, took place in the valley below me, I'm stirred by the principles articulated so clearly in the Biblical text. I so believe in this concept, in this reality: it is all in God's hands, including our victories in war and the deliverances we've received, as well as all our personal successes. We go, and as God is with us, we triumph, and if so then only as the thing is according to his will.

This is not some evangelical homily or sermon; it's not a fundamentalist (Jewish or Christian or Muslim) abdication of responsibility for our behavior or dismissal of the importance of our own efforts. It's merely a recognition of the most basic truth of existence: We are not as in charge as we think; our conquests, personal, communal, and national, are the result of many factors including our labors but also primarily a combination of forces and circumstances beyond our control—and one central element of that is the hand of God. If one doesn't believe in God, one can consider that *as fate, or nature, or Karma, or the Force; whatever name we give it, it is a power beyond our own. For me, this is as real today in my life, in our lives, as it clearly was for David and Shaul. Standing at the top of Tel Azeka, from where I can see Tel Lachish (". . . We are watching for the fire signals of Lachish . . . because we cannot see Azeka," from the Lachish Letters ostraka), I feel so very connected to my people, to this Land, to our history, to our God, to my family, and to my town just over the next hill, in which real people live today in a modern incarnation of these cities of old.*

And now it's time to climb down the hill and keep moving.

The remainder of that Tuesday, so near to home it was eerie, was a combination of slow and pleasant walking, though with a great deal of uphill climbing as well. It included meeting a few girls doing their national service as educational tour guides and preparing to bring a group of pupils to the area; finding a strategically-placed water fountain, courtesy of Mekorot (Israel's national water company), for the explicit use of Shvilistim; and bemoaning the ugly encroachment of my town, Beit Shemesh into the verdant hills above Kibbutz Lamed Hey south of the city. (I took a photo of the building project scarring the hilltop just past a turn in the trail, with a trail marker in the foreground. I wanted to label it "the most beautiful view on the Shvil." A little sarcasm while the sun is high in the sky.)

I missed an incredible photo op: a small deer crossed the trail just 20 meters or so ahead of me, on the edge of a long field of bright green young winter wheat. I stopped, and as it moved on, another followed, and then another, and as I fumbled for my camera a total of six deer (צבי ארץ ישראלי *Tvi Eretz Yisraeli*) walked across my path. In the middle of it I just looked up and said quietly, "hello there," "nice to see you," and reveled in the encounter. And especially in knowing it never could have happened were I in a jeep, or even on my bike—just a 10-minute ride from my home.

I met some Bedouin grazing their sheep, chatted for a minute and ascertained they were soon to move down south as they do every year, and sent a photo of a cute set of lambs to my daughter Merav. And I really enjoyed hiking up the Roman steps, "Caesar's Way" as it's labelled, built over two thousand years ago to allow Roman battalions to bring supplies from the port at Ashkelon up to Jerusalem. These same Romans renamed Jerusalem "Aelia Capitolina" in an unsuccessful attempt to erase its Jewish nature after they conquered the city. Again, here was something I drove by for two decades and had never stopped to explore, and as with all the Roman ruins I visited I relished it, not only for the great historical and archeological interest but the fact that their attempt was so utterly unsuccessful. As Mark Twain said, where are they now? Yet here I was, walking by foot up to the holy city they tried to wrench from us. The holy city which even in its destruction remained central to our sense of self and destiny, the heart of our people and the capital of our nation. OUR "Capitolina"! I imagined myself trudging up the same steps a simple Roman soldier might have, with a heavy pack on his back full of arms or food, and thought to myself, in the here and now: "I'm here. You failed. Take THAT."

It wasn't perhaps the most generous concept, but it was genuine. And I was tired. And it looked like rain. At the top of the hill, I decided to leave the Trail as I had hiked this part before (with Michal and her parents, Aaron and Hadas, when Michal was doing the Shvil). I wanted to make my way to my next stop before nightfall and before it started to get wet. As it was, I just made it there, to my friend Ilan's home in the small town of Tzur Hadassah, as dusk fell and as the mist turned into rain. Along the way, a car whizzing by in the other direction honked to me; soon I received an excited text message from my friend and neighbor Esti, who had apparently recognized me schlepping along the side of the road and was the driver who honked as her kids had started yelling and whooping. Fun.

Aryeh on the Roman Road to Jerusalem

Ilan was welcoming and generous; again, in turning to an acquaintance not knowing how I'd be received, I was pleasantly surprised by the genuine warmth, interest and consideration shown me. Before bed, though, I had a fun, if a bit

Bedouin camp in Jerusalem Hills

incongruous, evening. Our town, Beit Shemesh, that House of the Rising Sun as I occasionally playfully refer to it, had a re-vote that day in our mayoral election (due to illegal shenanigans which no one apparently is being prosecuted for). I had been told by a number of people in no uncertain terms that if I didn't show up to vote and "our" candidate lost, I would lose their friendship and might well suffer even worse consequences. One friend told me, honestly, that he'd drive anywhere in the country to pick me up and return me to the Shvil, that's how important every vote was. As it turned out, I was just up the hill, and so arranged for my daughter Meira to come get me. We voted together (and met a few friends, mostly hers, but including the Michal I've mentioned a few times, who was particularly excited to see me in the midst of the trek, and I her), and then went to get a bite to eat.

Surreal is not the word. In all my travels abroad for work, when sitting in a plane alone I often look out the window and marvel at the towns and cities below, with all the traffic and movement. I am always taken aback by the fact that there are people down there, thousands and millions of people, going about their daily lives, in happiness and misery—and they have no idea of, and no interest in, my existence high above them. Here too I felt incredibly out of place, irrelevant, and disconnected. Here was a whole town going about their business, carrying on "normal" life, and not only couldn't I relate, they couldn't possibly understand what a different place I was in. I didn't even bother to try to understand, nor to explain. I had a few polite interactions, in line to vote and at the cafe; even Meira sensed my disconnect. We had a really nice supper, and then as we both needed to get an early start the next day, my friend Yaakov agreed to take me back up to Tzur Hadassah for the night.

So close and yet so far away. Meira dropped me at the top of our street, across from Yaakov's house. I was less than 50 METERS from my home. I was incredibly conflicted—I wanted so much to go home, and I wanted so much to get away. It was frustrating and exhilarating at the same time. The place I was in emotionally was so far from the place I was in physically; it was almost an out-of-body experience. I was so glad I had pre-arranged my ride with Yaakov, or I might have given in and just walked in the house. As I wrote later in my journal: "My house! My garden! (My bed!) My . . . But nope, got in Yaakov's car, he took me back up to Tzur Hadassah . . . and that was that."

That indeed was that; I climbed into bed and come morning, following a light breakfast with Ilan, headed out before 8 a.m. on Wednesday.

It starts to rain within about 30 seconds of my stepping out the door—a light drizzle, not worth stopping to put my coat on. Or maybe it is. Within five minutes, it gets a little wetter, and after crossing the road I pop into the gas station to get my bearings. I take out my rain gear—windbreaker, pack cover—and repack the backpack, adjusting a few things as the weight wasn't sitting comfortably anyway and I've got a serious hike ahead of me, down into Emek Refayim, up to the "Yad Kennedy" memorial, and on up and down and up and down to the outskirts of Jerusalem at

Hadassah hospital in Ein Kerem. I feel bad using the space back by the fridge in the little store, and explain what I'm doing to the two young people behind the counter. They look a bit confused—"Really? The whole country?"—and then smiling say it's no problem. I buy a coffee and a croissant, as a treat, and a candy bar—Snickers of course, memories of the Carbolet!—to assuage my guilt for messing up their floor and bothering the other customers.

Looking out the window, it seems the rain's letting up. Forecast is for "some showers, mostly cloudy," so I think I should risk it; I'm bored and feeling antsy here so let's just get going. I find my way down through the village of Mevo Betar, a small, quiet community with attractive stand-alone distinctive houses on the edge overlooking the forested hills, wow! I'd never been inside it though of course drove past it a thousand times (no exaggeration, if about twice a week for twenty years). At first I don't see the hole in the perimeter fence, and am angry that the Guide and maps point in this direction; now I'm curious and a bit cynical—what does this mean for the security in this community?!? (There was an incident only a few years back when two women hikers were attacked by terrorists. One died of her wounds, not at all far from here.) These are some of the things one thinks of when hiking here which I suppose don't occur to those on treks in Nepal or on the Pacific Crest Trail.

The beauty of the trees and mountains and the vista looking down Wadi Katlav and Nachal Refayim toward the coastal plain serves to distract me, and allows me to dismiss those somewhat morbid thoughts. (In fact, I have no real security concerns; I read earlier, and am confident in the fact, that there has never been a violent incident on Shvil Yisrael. Theft, yes, but never a murder or rape or mugging or even beating. Pfu pfu pfu I say to myself, to ward off the evil eye. As if . . .) I spend the next hour almost mesmerized by the hushed woods and hills of the northern Judean mountains.

It's just gorgeous! I love my life! Here I go, the final ascent to the holy city! I begin to play with the idea of breaking my schedule and walking around the Jerusalem Trail for a day or two; but realize that having lived and worked in or near the nation's capital for 30 years, there's not that much I haven't seen or visited. Also, I really do want to stay on schedule to get to Mesilat Tzion on time for the planned Shabbat b'Shetach *(Shabbat out in the wild) with Zvi.*

And then it starts to rain again. At first, it's light, and I stop under a tree for some Tefila—*yes, I had started out without saying my morning prayers, and said them while walking, as I did some days. Sue me, I think there are worse things I've done if I'm going to hell.*[7]

I sang a bit too, as I waited for the rain to abate. It didn't, really, but did let up a bit, and since I had my coat and pack cover, I just walked on. It was

---

7 Just to be clear, that was an attempt at humor as I talked to myself while walking. Judaism doesn't really have a concept of "hell" as normally understood in western society. And certainly, though there is a powerful understanding of reward and punishment related to our behavior, as expressed most clearly in the Sh'ma prayer, it is overlaid with all sorts of complex theological and philosophical layers elaborate upon by thousands of years of scholarship and commentary, well beyond the scope of this little reference.

spectacularly dazzling—the sun occasionally peeking through the trees, the leaves glistening all around me as they swayed in the slight breeze, the mist and gentle sprinkle of rain almost enveloping me with a sense of comfort, like a wet but welcome blanket. I wasn't cold; that is, I felt warm enough with the jacket on, but not so warm as to venture to jump in the springs I passed on the way. Arriving at Ein Kobi spring, I ventured down some steps in to a little cave to find shelter from the rain which had intensified (was this perhaps a mikvah? A bath of some kind? Or a store room?). Under the arched roof of stones in this damp little hall not quite tall enough to stand in and just wider than I can reach with both arms extended, I was glad to have the rest, and meditated for a bit while watching and listening to the light shower coming down just a few feet away.

My thoughts, following a peaceful 20 minutes or so, turned to how strong and cheerful I felt. How can I be so full of gratitude? I asked myself. What is it in me, or in us as humans, which can focus so successfully on the positive? As I suggested earlier, we have an incredible capacity to interpret things in so many ways, and to choose—often unconsciously, unperceptively, but choose we do—to see matters in a positive light. I know *I* do—choose, though most times without thinking—as I am an optimist by nature. But from where does that nature come? And perhaps more important (as I have less interest in psychology, biology, sociology or cultural anthropology than I used to, and more in the practical application of these meandering theories of mine), how can we cultivate that natural tendency, and encourage it, for our benefit?

The cup is often half full, but so many don't see it that way. I even like the idea that the cup is *completely* full: just half of it is air. Some cultures, some religions, some families and individuals focus on the negative, on criticism, on discipline. Others focus on a more affirmative approach—yes, always looking to improve ourselves, but from a constructive perspective. I learned at age twelve in seventh grade from Mrs. Jones, the principal at La Entrada Elementary School, in our *Who Am I?* class, that I Am Lovable And Capable. This message was relayed via the story of a boy who every morning put a sign around his neck reading "I.A.L.A.C.," which is torn apart by the events of the day (slow to rise/dress, missed bus, late for school, bullying, tripping, criticism, a bad grade, an impatient parent, a dismissive older sibling). Even though the sign is torn to shreds by the end of each day, it would reappear intact the next morning. This lesson—of the inherent potential of the individual, and the natural goodness of the world—has stayed with me throughout my life.

That one lesson took perhaps five minutes to tell and another thirty to discuss in class. I wonder if Mrs. Jones knows how instrumental that one parable has been in my life. (In fact I know she does, as I told her a few years later, when I was leading *Who Am I?* sessions at Skylake summer camp.) My "nature" was nurtured by that, and I've spent a lifetime believing in myself because of it. Another influential figure in my youth was known as *The Wombat* (nickname for a Skylake camp counsellor from Australia named Robert). Much of my love of life and adventure—and male sensitivity and respect for others—I learned in the same impressionable years from him. His cheery and can-do approach to every day contributed also to my lifelong commitment to staying positive, looking at the bright side of life. From Mrs. Jones and Wombat, I learned to focus on all the good around us. I know I've helped others take a similar approach, in small ways and large, over the years, passing on these lessons as I could. I am convinced that these values, along with the humility and acceptance I've (re)discovered on the Trail, is a key to prolonged happiness in life.

I started to wonder: How can such an outlook be harnessed in the wider sphere? Is there a way cultures can be encouraged—trained, if not coerced—to appreciate the manifest blessings they've been showered with and frame a worldview in positive, optimistic, confident terms? I had a few precedents to ponder, from America's "exceptionalism" to Herzl's and Zionism's and Israel's "If you will it, it is no dream"; and a few pithy aphorisms which came to mind, from Rebbe Nachman's "מצוה גדולה להיות בשמחה תמיד" (*Mitzvah Gedolah Lehiot B'Simcha Tamid*—"It's a great Mitzvah to be always happy"), which of course brought to mind Bobby McFarren's "Don't Worry, Be Happy," to Dale Carnegie's *How to Stop Worrying and Start Living*, among others.

My mind wandered to the traditional Jewish approach to celebrating a festival, or a wedding, whereby Jewish law demands simcha, joyfulness, at certain times even when it may be difficult or if you're not feeling like it. We sing "ושמחת בחגיך"—*V'samachta b'chagecha* "And you will be happy in/at your festivals"—and it is as much an exhortation as it is a description. We *must* feel happiness, not only pretend; we must feel joy as we celebrate, and there is joy in the very celebration. Harnessing these external calls for gladness, internalizing them, was Rebbe Nachman's theme.

With the rain letting up a bit, I threw my pack on to begin the descent down Nachal Kobi to Nachal Refayim as these ideas percolated. I remembered something Voltaire is believed to have said: "I have decided to be happy, because it is good for my health." Perhaps that's something a culture might adopt for its nation's health—ie. for their own good, no one else's. Walking down the steep path of the Avrom Silver Nature Path along Nachal Kobi, I wondered how such a sense of gratitude and optimism might be encouraged in various modern societies.

And then I slipped on the mud.

Geez Aryeh! Pay attention for crying out loud. Stop trying to save the world and focus on not breaking your neck. Wouldn't that be a riot: having survived Har Shlomo, *the* Carbolet, *the* Milchan, Maale Amram, Maale Eli, Maale Palmach, *even the sharp descent down* Tel Azeka, *without injury, you twist your ankle sliding down a muddy footpath, where five-year-olds skip happily on any given summer day. Not.*

I carefully pick my steps, using rocks and boulders for stability, on this not-well-tended part of the trail. (I think they presume no trekkers will descend here until the rain stops. Go figure.) Suddenly it occurs to me that this nature path must be named after my friend Shoel Silver's relative! Perhaps his grandfather even (I knew his father also, Nathan), or uncle. It's dedicated "by his wife and children"; so I take a photo standing in front of it and email him a message. Fun—connections. It's a different feeling than being in the desert; I've had my alone time, I'm getting more comfortable now with social interactions. Not a lot, but some. I take a great number of photos, as it's so charming, and the rain has petered out. Steps hewn in the rock or using stones and roots help navigate the harder sections, and there are rustic wooden benches placed in the shade every fifty or hundred meters or so on the steep descent, to rest and enjoy the view and contemplate life.

Tramping and slashing my way through the next section, it's even less well-tended than before, I've lost the trail a few times in the wild undergrowth. Swearing my way slipping and sliding down the hill, I finally arrive at the train tracks and, crossing underneath them, I find myself at the edge of a roaring, splashing Nachal Refayim stream. Wow! This is flow! I actually video it, as I've never seen a Jerusalem-area stream surging so impressively. I gingerly step my way across, stopping to splash some water on my face.

It's a long and slow hike up the mountain to near Yad Kennedy, another site I haven't been to in 30 years of living in and near Jerusalem; in fact it's somewhere I've always wanted to visit, as I'm so interested in Kennedy and his attitude toward Israel and the Jews. Maybe I'll have time, will try to fit it in. I stop for lunch in the shade and am SO THANKFUL to Ilan for the yellow cheese and whole wheat bread sandwich with mayo and paprika, basil and garlic he'd had me make this morning. I get up sooner than intended, hoping to be able to do the detour to Yad Kennedy; starting off again I find a slightly less severe incline to skirt around a small section of the Shvil which literally has you climbing hand-over-foot up a cliff for a dozen meters . . . and then BAM! There had been some light rain and mist on and off this last few minutes coming up the hill, but Boom! Thunder and lightning hits like they're right overhead and all around me. What, had I been asleep while awake? Where did this COME from?? Before I know it, it's coming down like a מבול Mabul—a flood of biblical proportions. There's no time even to run for cover; within seconds I am COMPLETELY soaked—trousers, boots, hat, everything. And then . . .

HAIL!??! Yes—hail! I photograph it on the ground; I have proof. Aaaaaarrgghhhhh! Seriously? SERIOUSLY?!!? This is March, middle of the month even, not November or December, January or February! This is Jerusalem, not the Hermon, or Moscow, or Oslo!

At this point I literally just shrug. I push through it—even given my earlier reflections on thinking positively, I can't say I do so with any great enthusiasm—and in fact end up on the wrong trail, have to retrace my steps (it's still raining, darn it), and end up finally on the Shvil HaMayanot, *the Trail of the Springs, as the hail and rain and drizzle tapers out.*

I had always wanted to "do" the Shvil HaMayanot, and had actually mentioned to the kids the idea of their perhaps meeting me to walk it with me (those who lived or worked in Jerusalem). Though they had work and couldn't join me, we had agreed to at least meet up that evening when I planned to stay at the Shvilistim cabin run by the staff at Hadassah hospital as Trail Angels. I walked on, and it was pleasant enough; "sloshed on" might be more accurate a description, as my boots were in fact quite wet. But it wasn't what I had planned: I took Bini's refrain seriously, and my intention all along was to jump in to every spring on the route, even though sometimes it wasn't possible. Where else but on the "Trail of Springs"? Oh well. I took a photo of one, me all wrapped up in a hooded jacket with a scarf and gloves (thanks Bini, the hat and neck scarf were yours in fact), and sent it to Bini and Mimi. "Should I jump in?" I asked? "Go for it!" Bini wrote back. Ha. "You first," I sent him. Right. Freezing, raining—not happening.

I made it to Hadassah just as the rain started teeming down again. Too cold to shower, I put on the only dry clothing I had, my light cotton trousers which doubled as cool pajamas, and laid all my clothes out to dry on the radiator, while stringing up other stuff and turning the cooking rings on high to add to the warmth. I put my sandals on to let my boots dry out. Standing there considering the events of the day, I had to laugh and did enjoy—decided to enjoy?—the various experiences I had just gone through.

And I was so very grateful for the people at Hadassah, offering me this refuge from the storm, literally, with beds and blankets (okay, hospital blankets, but who's complaining?). I spent a few hours reviewing maps and plans for the next few days. I couldn't find a place to stay the next night (nothing! No Angels available in any of the villages of the Jerusalem corridor! It's not that I resented it; nice enough for people to list themselves as angels. It's just that I wouldn't have expected to not find a *single* place available, even to pitch my tent on a kibbutz lawn). Then Netanel called; we were to have met up a bit later, he and Meira and me, at 7 p.m., and I planned to take them for a bite at the little café in the hospital complex right next to the Shvilistim cabin. We said he'd let me know when they're near.

Nati's message says they're in the parking lot and I should come out. "I'm confused—just park," I write him, "and come in, I want you to see the cabin!" He replies "No! Come out!" so I throw my hiking trousers back on and go out into the rain; can't find him—ah, he's parked by the stairs. But he's not parked; the engine's running. Meira comes toward me, and Nati gets out of the car; after a hug, Nati shows me a bandana and says, "Put this on," and then proceeds to put it on me himself, covering my eyes. "What's going on?" I ask. "Nu be'emet!" ("Come on, really!") They bundle me into the car—my car, I might note, but that's just fine—and we drive off.

As a good fan of James Bond and Sherlock Holmes, I try to get my bearings; a bump here, a turn there, I'm thinking they're taking me into a forest for a "poika," something I've Netanel discovered in the IDF but I've yet to experience. We arrive; no, we're backing up—this is in fact a steep incline. I hear cars passing; then voices.

Tehila, Netanel's wife, asks me to get out. (I should have guessed something was up when I saw Tehila was in the car; originally this was planned as a quick and informal get together and she probably wouldn't have missed an evening's studying for that. Or so I was thinking as we exited the car.) I still have the blindfold on; I've stopped asking questions. We're walking up stairs, and with the traffic noise (in the rain, did I mention the rain which hasn't stopped?) I at least know this isn't a forest.

"SURPRISE!!!" yell about a dozen voices as we walk into . . . a fancy restaurant in the Jerusalem neighborhood/artists village of Ein Kerem. As Nati removes the blindfold I see Aaron and Hadas and their youngest son Eitan, Michael and Deborah, Jeremy and Mandy and their youngest daughter Sivan! Along with Nati, Tehila, and Mimi (Bini's on his IDF base, couldn't get out), it's like a homecoming. It's not like family, it is family, these friends of mine. I'm just flabbergasted; so touched. I hide my tears—I've missed my friends and family so!

From my journal, written the next morning while waiting out the rain in the Hadassah Shvilistim cabin:

> **Journal Day 26—Thursday morning, March 13:**
> We had a great meal; I had RIBS, so naughty as a vegetarian, but it was a special occasion, and a Teperberg Meritage, deep purple-red and strong and fruity. It was a little surreal—that word again—to be in a fancy restaurant with friends in my hiking shirt and pants all caked with mud. Netanel did, I admit, suggest a few times that I take a shower but I didn't understand of course; no shave either. Just to see and be with them all was fantastic, uplifting, warmed the heart, lifted my spirits even w/the rain. Ended w/a toast on Michael's Jura—"To the best friends ever—and the best children/daughter-in-law ever."

On the way out, I told Hadas and Mike about being lonely while surrounded by people at Sansana the previous Shabbat. I don't know why, but it was important that my friends be aware of that loneliness even when with people. Perhaps I wanted to remind them I was not "where they're at." For them, this was a normal, fun, somewhat special night out. But for me it was a pleasurable but also painful reminder of who/what/where I was and what I was doing, at once truly enjoyable and extremely jarring. I loved the surprise; I hated to leave them all. But I wasn't ready, either, to return to them yet. What a rollercoaster that day and evening were. I wouldn't trade it for the world.

I woke a few times during the night to what sounded like a deluge; when I got up at 7 a.m., the torrent had not yet ceased. I *davened*; had tea and granola bars, coffee and halva (that great Israeli/Middle Eastern sesame-based sweet packed bar full of protein and carbohydrates). I looked at maps, called the kids, called Zvi, checked Facebook, and sent a few WhatsApp messages including thanks to all for last night. (Those who came, along with Zvi and two other friends, Yaakov and Shalva, who couldn't make the dinner, were all the members of a WhatsApp group Meira had set up to make Hadas, and to a certain extent Mandy and Deborah, a bit more comfortable with my hiking alone in the desert. Mimi sent along to them my updates.) As the storm continued outside, I made more tea; burnt some toast on the stove-top burners in the cabin, heated my boots under the radiator, wrote in my journal . . . and four hours later it still hadn't stopped pouring down.

Finally the rainstorm is slowing down. Should I start walking, and flag down a cab if I get caught? I've been calling again to find a place to stay for the night, with no luck, and getting more and more frustrated with every passing moment. At the end of my patience, I eventually call Meira.

"Look, Mimi," I say. "This is silly. You're thirty minutes away from here. Come pick me up and take me home. Like at any other Trail Angel, I'll stay the night, sleep like a mensch, have a good shower, do my laundry and you can take me back up to the Shvil in the morning." There's a pause on the end of the line. "אני לא מרשה," she says. "Ani lo marsh'a." "I don't allow it."

WHAAAA? I'm laughing and not; "What're you talking about?!" I call out to her. "Nope," she replies. "You said you don't want to come home; it's not good for you, it's an interruption, you really shouldn't . . ."

After a longer pause than is perhaps necessary, but which is indicative of my state of mind—I really really miss home, especially after last night, and I'm tired of hiking in the rain—I have to admit she's right. What a story I have now to tell: my 21-year-old daughter, living in my house, eating my food, driving my car, won't come 30 minutes away to pick me up and take me home. I love it!

But hah—I'll show HER. I'm ready to give up on Trail Angels and there's no way I'm going to camp out in this flood. I'm willing to give up on going home. I have many friends who live in Jerusalem, but I'd be embarrassed to ask them to stay, as I could just remain here at Hadassah another night. So that's OUT. And so is staying here—no WAY. I'm packed up and ready to move on; yesterday's surprise was tremendously exciting but I want to get going. This place is getting depressing, and not least as it's a bloody hospital, for all I appreciate their hospitality and the refuge it provided from the storm. So I make a call . . . and grab a cab. Driving down and up and over the Jerusalem hills west of the city, watching out the window splashed with the non-stop rain as we pass a number of points where the Trail crosses the road, I start to feel ever-so-slightly guilty for skipping another segment. The road is actually longer than the Shvil's route over the mountains; but just as I start to second-guess myself, we arrive at the Sunny Hills guest house at Kibbutz Shoresh. Hahaha! Take THAT, Mimi!

I discovered many disadvantages to hiking the Israel trail at 51, following a divorce. No friends would join me, for one—not a single friend or even family member hiked with me for a day, as I had anticipated and hoped they might.[8]

---

8 Except for the very last day of my trek, which was so very delightful; see below.

This is no complaint; all are busy with their own lives, and few have the sort of job (or family) which would allow them to simply take a day or even half a day off to wander down a forest or desert path just for fun. A number of times, some met me along the way, as I've described and will continue to mention; each visit was lovely and filled me with warmth and love. But unlike the younger crowd, I didn't have even occasional walking companions, save of course my recently found friend, Yaron, whom I met on the Shvil itself. We will return to him in a little while.

Another disadvantage was of course my physical state. Though in decent shape—and more so as the weeks (and miles) went by, naturally—I still felt the pain in my feet, calves, thighs, buttocks, lower back, upper back, shoulders, neck and arms (get the picture?). I was definitely more in pain than the young people I met on the Trail and since. An additional disadvantage at my age was the pressure of "normal" responsibilities, off the Trail, which I still bore (though I postponed or handled them only when pressed). My office and business required my attention periodically. My kids and parents needed input or guidance or updates occasionally. My community and friends and wider family, as well as various initiatives and projects I'm involved in—from sitting on a synagogue board to planning a US speaking tour after the trek, and more—all demanded a certain amount of responsiveness. Few 20-year-olds on the Shvil had any such cares.

And yet there were a number of recognizable advantages of my somewhat advanced age (if that's the right term) as a Shvilist. One was—as described adequately above, I think—a combination of calmness, and confidence, as well as heart-felt pleasure in all the little things along the way. Few younger people enjoy a flower, or a sunset, a vista or a conversation with a stranger just for the sheer pleasure of it, as I did and do. Meira once pointed this aspect of my personality out to me in a birthday card, and she was right; and it had deepened and widened over the past few decades. Many of the younger people I met on the trail were so intent on arriving at their destination for that day, counting the kilometers and the hours and the liters of water, already calculating the best time to leave in the morning to conquer the next hill, that they failed to really appreciate the wonder and beauty of the trail itself.

Another advantage, I must say, was the network of friends, acquaintances, colleagues and family I connected with along the way. It's true that it's a small country, and most Israelis are connected with less than the famous six degrees of separation, as noted above from my meeting a friend's kid's friend in the Ramon Crater. But most young Israelis hiking the Shvil (even with circles of friends from home, school, perhaps a *Mechina* or *Midrasha*, the IDF or *Sherut Leumi*/National Service or university) are still somewhat limited in both the geographical breadth and the depth of connection, which restricts somewhat their ability to call on friends and others for a place to stay. I was so very lucky; I've referred to a few already, but in the North as will be seen, I managed to stay more with friends and family than I did with officially-listed Trail Angels.

But the most distinct advantage in hiking the Shvil at 51, and the primary reason for this digression, was the tangible financial cushion which being older afforded me. I paid for Meira's gas and lodging to come visit me in the Ashram, as I did for Zvi's gas and hotel room at the Reef on the Shabbat before starting out. I could purchase some of the delicious wine I tasted and have it awaiting my arrival home as a special treat and reminder of the Shvil on Pesach and thereafter. I could pay for water drops in the desert without thinking twice, treat myself or a child or friend to a snack or dinner with no reluctance, take a taxi when desired so as not to get too wet . . . and I could reserve and enjoy a modest Kibbutz Guest House room in the midst of a torrential rain in the Jerusalem hills without a moment's hesitation. And I had a massage to top it off!

I went into some detail describing that day and the next in my journal, written after the weekend:

Journal Day 29—Sunday, March 16:
Thursday rained ALL day nonstop . . .

Thanks to all who didn't recommend a place and to the Angels who weren't available! LUXURY! Even in a Kibbutz guest house. Bath and then—massage! 45 minutes from a guy named Ezra, nice, what good decision, glad he was available when I called, what a brainwave. Then shower (twice in one day—whaa?!?). Then . . . 6 hours of TV from 5–11 p.m.! Kevin Kline and Kirsten Scott Thomas in *Life as a House*—great timing, about a divorced couple who get back together for/because of the kids, hah. Then *Godfather 3*—still a classic. Then Robin Williams in something also about marriage—what gives here? Ugh—but he's always great.

Then up Fri morning early and time enough to have another bath! Was raining so had to wait a bit; nice basket breakfast with fresh bread, hard-boiled egg, cheeses, jam—very Israeli, very homey, actually almost French come to think of it. Then DECIDED finally where to stay for Shabbat—YES, we'll do it in the WILD—having been hesitant for days; called Zvi to confirm. And decided too, it's now time to go even if there's a little drizzle. Set out about 10:45 a.m.

Absolutely beautiful, then even moving. Hiked down (w/some up) along the דרך הג׳יפים Jeep Route and Burma Road [dirt roads carved out of the mountain during Israel's war of independence in '47–'49 as an alternative to the blocked and much-attacked main Tel Aviv-Jerusalem highway via Shaar HaGai]. Lonely butterfly (no photo!); panoramic views of the highway and to the coastal plain w/clouds and some sun. At first bitingly cold. A photo I posted on FB in real-time with me all bundled up complaining of "arctic conditions" prompted response from Vivian [Canada's ambassador to Israel] chiding me for using the term! It got a bit warmer, though more rain was to come.

Har El/PALMACH memorial at 16 משלט [Hilltop Outpost 16] was

strangely inspiring & moving—more than a *thousand* Palmach members killed, listing all sorts of situations, not only during מלחמת העצמאות [the war of independence] + pre-war defense but in Iraq (Falujia!) and Europe and more. The loss of all these young people (men mostly) weighs heavily on me, and never fails to provoke my gratitude and commitment to remain and defend מדינת ישראל, ראשית צמיחת גאולתנו [*Medinat Yisrael* the State of Israel, *Reishit Tzmichat Geulatenu* the beginning of the flowering of our redemption (a phrase from the religious Zionist standard prayer for the State).]

I was, as noted in this journal entry, touched by the variety, not only the numbers, of those killed in defense of the Jewish people even before the establishment of the Jewish State. I was especially stirred by the mention of all the places outside the Land where those brave Palmach fighters fought for their people's freedom, lives and dignity. Natan Alterman, in the first years of the State, coined the term "silver platter" to describe the incredible cost, and value, of the lives of the fallen in our constant defensive military operations and wars, before and after independence. I felt very strongly that it's true, we were handed this country on a precious, beautiful silver platter. My mind was so distracted by these national memories that I had to constantly remind myself to pay attention and look where I was stepping as I spent the next three hours slowly climbing and tripping over the boulders and roots of the relatively mild but often difficult descent toward the coastal plain.

Having arranged with my friend Zvi to join me in the forest for Shabbat, I managed to get down the hill, past Shaar HaGai, to the small moshav of Mesilat Tzion with enough time to shower at the home of Yoav and Odella Cohen, friends of my friend Mandy, who had invited us for Shabbat dinner that night. Yoav drove me around (thanks!) to a good site to camp. It was a decent location, though perhaps not as deep into the forest as I might have favored. Still, it offered easy access for expected visitors as it was near Road 38, it had a few picnic tables, and it was close enough to the community for convenience (with a relatively smooth path through the woods for safe nighttime walking), so was perfect otherwise.

Zvi (Howard) went out of his way from Jerusalem to go by my house and bring various supplies Meira had put together or purchased, including my guitar, Shabbat clothes (and shoes!), a *Chumash* (Pentateuch, to read the Shabbat Torah portion from) and a larger *Siddur* prayer book. Plus a lot of very good wine and whiskey, cheeses and munchies and other food. They forgot the tent, so Bini drove out to drop it off—it was great being just 10 minutes up the road. And it was so good to see and get a hug from Bini.

All these comforts from home were so welcome—and especially the four-person tent and thick foam mattresses! As Shabbat came in, Zvi and I walked over to the synagogue in the moshav. He was saying Kaddish, the mourner's prayer, for his father's memorial day and so needed to pray with a minyan, a quorum of ten men. Like so many other aspects of this trek it was a welcome coincidence that he insisted on going, as otherwise I (lazy, complacent or just tired?) probably wouldn't have bothered. That would have been a shame; as their Shabbat תפילה prayer service was an experience not to miss. This community is made up mostly of immigrants and their children from Chochin, India (like the family I stayed with the previous week, in Lachish), and theirs is a unique service, with its own melodies, accents and traditions.

Dinner with Odie and Yoav (and their extended family) was very congenial; as I wrote in my journal, they are a "sweet & generous, warm & welcoming family." The delicious meal was dairy, rather than meat (which is more usual on a Friday night). Odie had explained to me they are חילוני, *chiloni*, or non-observant, and it intrigued me that they used that term, as they have a distinctive combination of practice and non-practice when it comes to their Judaism. No Kiddush, the traditional blessing over the wine inaugurating the Sabbath; no singing of Shalom Aleichem to welcome the Ministering Angels who, according to Jewish mysticism, accompany every Jew throughout Shabbat; no lighting of candles even (a custom observed by many non-Orthodox and non-practicing Jews around the world, including my mother and father and their mothers and fathers from time immemorial). Yet they do have a Friday night dinner; they attend an "egalitarian" shul where men and woman participate equally; they had a lively discussion at dinner on various philosophical topics including some related to that week's reading in the Torah; and Odie assured me the food was Kosher. I would not, in my vocabulary, define them as *chiloni* or "secular" as it's usually understood in the Israeli idiom, as they did.

After a delightful dinner Zvi and I made our way back to the campsite, made sure the food and stuff was well packed in my little tent, and climbed into the large tent we were sharing. Zvi's a good friend; actually a great friend, the best. A good definition of friendship: when one who dislikes the outdoors, and especially camping—hates it!—agrees to spend a Shabbat in the wilderness with his friend just to keep him company. Not to mention one who loves meat—and takes the *mitzvah* of having meat on Shabbat seriously—agreeing to have a dairy Shabbat.

But . . . Zvi snores. Then again, so do I. Or so I'm told. Not really—I just breathe heavily. Or that's my line. I manage to get a decent sleep; so does he, so no complaints on either side.

We actually manage to have a really nice Shabbat; when Zvi goes off to shul in the morning I clear up a bit (cats ripped a hole in the little tent and enjoyed a few burekas and Challah—and left a reminder of their presence!). I say/sing my Tefila in concert with the soft sound of the wind in the trees, and make Kiddush when Zvi comes back. We eat a terrific lunch—and agree that with smoked salmon, cream cheese, Challah, egg salad, tomatoes, who could possibly want more? Later we go for a long walk and talk through the forest, and I share with him some of the processes I've been going through and the transitions I've felt over the past four weeks. We're covering the personal and emotional stuff, and the physical and geographical and experiential; less so the intellectual, but that's fine and normal and very pleasant indeed. Not too heavy.

As the light fades toward the end of the day, we sit at the picnic table singing a bit and having Seudah Shlishit, the third Shabbat meal—Labane cheese with olive oil and Zatar, crackers, tuna salad and more, with a nice red wine of course. We can't see the page as it got darker, and don't know all the words by heart, so we sing the first verse of Yedid Nefesh over and over just to hear it and enjoy. When the stars come out we make Havdalah, the ceremony separating the holiness of Shabbat from the mundane week, with an Earl Grey teabag (as we have no other spices). This week has been a bit weird, this combination of home, friends, family, and familiar scenery in the midst of the trek, some bits of "normal" life but still on the Shvil. I thank Zvi again for joining me; glad he actually enjoyed it eventually. After Shabbat, as my good friend Aaron arrives, I light the campfire and Zvi says his goodbyes with a hug. It really was a lovely Shabbat.

With the close of Shabbat, the festival of Purim began, which is why Aaron came soon after dark. Purim is the celebration of the Jews' victorious defense against the genocide planned by the evil viceroy of Persia, Haman, around 350 BCE, and is a radically different holiday than any other on the Jewish calendar. Americans' tendency to compare it to Halloween is mistaken; the similarity begins and ends with costumes. Purim is a bit more like New Year's celebrations on January 1 combined with July 4th—carousing, eating, drinking and great fun, with the sense of deliverance one occasionally recalls on America's Independence Day. It's always been one of my favorite festivals (along with Succot, the Festival of Tabernacles, where we "camp out" for a week in the yard or on the roof balcony under branches in a "booth" of sorts), and definitely not just because drinking is involved. There's something about the free spirit of Purim, where anything in good taste goes, and people become playful and creative—especially with the costumes. I had been trying to figure out what I could do for it: since I was so near home, I considered just going to my synagogue Saturday night to hear *Megillat Esther* (the Scroll of Esther, the story of Purim) and then again in the morning, asking Mimi to pick me up and take me back. That would have been the easiest thing.

But it didn't appeal to me; I'd resisted returning home for a week now, with Mimi's help of course, and the "normalcy" of being with my community, however enjoyable, would be an interruption to the flow of the hike. So I asked a few friends whether they'd like to come by my campsite (or would be willing to come by actually)—and it turned into a wonderful, and wonderfully unique, holiday.

Aaron showed up in a toga to read the *Megilla* to me; I put on a fluffy blond wig and we sat on the bench of the picnic table near the fire and got started—but first had a nice Auchentoshen single malt Scotch whiskey to get us in the mood. (Auchentoshen, a delicious, smooth and light whiskey, is my favorite for Purim, not least as it sounds so much like a traditional Purim food called a "Hamantashen.") Fun and games aside, I have to admit it was one of the best, most meaningful, Megilla readings for me ever. Sitting next to Aaron as he read, I could hear every word (important!) and followed along in the scroll—and his handmade parchment was a work of art, a "Megillat HaMelech" as Aaron taught me ("The King's Scroll"), named not only for its beauty but because it is spaced such that every column starts with the word "מלך" "Melech" (King). This is also a nod to one of the classic understandings of God's role in the story of King Ahashverus, Queen Esther, Mordechai the Jew, and Haman the wicked vizier. Suffice to say we had a lot of fun—and of course I really treasured our time together, as I had with Zvi, and was so thankful to Aaron for schlepping out in the cold night.

Just as we finished—as we were pouring another dram, this time a Balvenie 12-year-old—my friends Jeremy and Mandy showed up unexpectedly, and their arrival was very welcome. I threw more wood on the fire, and poured another round (Mandy is Scottish, and while from Liverpool, Jeremy's an honorary Scot, more even than I am, so they are true partners-in-crime when it comes to single malt Scotch). We all sat around the campfire and talked for a bit.

When Aaron left, Mandy and Jeremy stayed, and the talk became serious. They wanted to know how I was *doing*; I was obliged to them for their concern, but I was more interested in hearing how *they* were doing. Their sweet, vivacious, beautiful daughter Nava had died in tragic car accident just three months earlier, only eight months after her wedding. In an upsetting course of events, I gave Karen the *get* divorce papers on the morning of Nava's funeral, rushing straight from the Rabbinical Court in Jerusalem down to the cemetery in Beit Shemesh. It was a painful set of memories for us all; of course more for them in many obvious and some less obvious ways.

Our families were exceedingly close; we have spent many Shabbat meals and festivals, including Pesach Seder, together. I feel particularly close to their three youngest children, and had been at the hospital with them, and Nava's husband Tal, a number of times the week after the accident before she passed away.

Sometimes people just click, it's not clear why and not easy to analyze (and why should we have to?), but we all did, from the start. Jeremy and Mandy had "been there" for me through the years Karen and I were separating and I tried to support them after Nava died, though there was really very little I or anyone could do to ease their pain. I felt a heaviness descend as we talked on. Had it really only been 10 weeks or so?

And yet they made a decision, for themselves, for Nava, for their other four children and for Tal, not to let Nava's accident dictate the course of their lives. In addition, for the family and more, as the people they are, they simply refused to give in to despondency. We spoke about my "moving on," about the divorce, about different ways of grieving, about Nava and about their other kids and how they were coping. We talked about how my kids are dealing with the divorce.

Somehow, it seems, talking about others coping with their suffering helps us to deal with our own, with no comparisons between them, and slowly the conversation became lighter.

When Jeremy and Mandy left, these thoughts occupied me as I cleared up. Their conscious choice to look forward, to be positively engaged in life rather than miserably focused on their loss, is inspiring. Like my penchant to allow my hope and enthusiasm for life overcome my grief. I remembered reading (was it tending to the fire which made me think of Indians?) how an effort was being made to draw Native American communities, and especially youth, out of a cycle of poverty and despondency—and how this initiative was based on Norman Vincent Peale's "power of positive thinking."

I started to put my guitar away, but I wasn't ready for sleep. As I got in my pajamas (another treat from home) I thought of how Mandy spoke of how thankful she is to God for all her children—including Nava—and I had agreed. However cliché it might be, we're of the same mind: our children are God's greatest gift to us.

It was getting late, but I still didn't want to sleep yet. Putting another log on the fire, I sat to play my guitar, the last of the treats from home. My guitar! A handmade Japanese S. Yaari dark red steel string acoustic beauty I bought when I was about 15. It felt so good in my hands. I finally had a chance to play, not just sing, the song I had resurrected and rewrote back in the Judean desert. Was that just a little over a week ago? Seriously? It felt like a different life; in a way, with all the transitions I'd been going through, my new sense of self, the social interactions I'd had since, the forest I was sitting in compared to the desert trek back then, it was a different life. I played the song over and over again, and again, improving a word here, a chord there—it's actually a really good tune. Then *The Boxer, Christopher Robin, Cats in the Cradle, Fire and Rain* . . . and to bed at 2 a.m.

I awoke Sunday morning before 7; had a great breakfast (including toast on the campfire!) after *Tefila*, proud of myself for remembering in it the special prayers for Purim. I partially broke camp and packed up, looked at maps to plan the rest of the day, and had a little Woodford Reserve (American) whiskey which Bini had brought—it was Purim, after all—as I waited for my friends Jay and Emmy to come to read the Megilla for me.

One is obligated to hear the Megilla twice on Purim, and I didn't want to burden Aaron with a second trip out. In any case I was more than happy to see Jay and Emmy, and would have greatly missed Jay's reading, as he reads every year in shul with various humorous trills and voices. Reading with him was just as perfect, if different, as with Aaron the previous night. Sitting next to him on the picnic table bench, as I did with Aaron, and being able to hear every syllable, every nuance (usually the reader is in the middle of the synagogue, and though one can of course hear, it's not the same as having him *next* to you), following along in his scroll, I had such כוונה *kavannah*, was able to concentrate so—even with Emmy shooing the cats away all around us—that it was a singular experience.

They sung a few of the Megilla's closing verses to a tune I didn't recognize, and afterwards they explained (after laughing at my ignorance). "קום והיתהלך בארץ (*Kum v'hithalech b'Aretz*—"Arise and walk through the Land") is a classic early Israeli folk song, based on a passage in the Torah commanding the Children of Israel to explore the Promised Land. The folk song speaks of grabbing your walking stick and pack and setting out to re-encounter the hills and valleys of the Land of Milk & Honey. And here I was. They gave me they lyrics on a piece of paper, which I carried in my front pocket for the remainder of the trek, and it became another theme song of the Trail for me. We had a l'chaim before they left, and I told them how much I appreciated their making the effort to come out, as Jay reads numerous times during the course of any Purim (for sick members of shul or others who can't make it out, as well as a second, or sometimes third, time at the synagogue itself for those who come late).

My friend and neighbor (and biking partner—sometimes) Yaakov came afterwards for a visit, which was really enjoyable, and of course another whiskey (see a pattern?). He was my savior: I charged both my phones in his car while we talked. Then my close friends Ken and Ruth, along with their daughter Adina and son Daniel, showed up—and the party really started. The Greens and Spiros had shared Purim Seudah, the feast of the day, for more years than I can count, with enough memories together to fill a book (though most of us would I'm sure prefer they not be published, as each year different members of the family embarrassed themselves in some way or other). It was a raucous and unbelievably fun meal. Bini and Mimi showed up halfway through, somewhat hungover from their Purim party the night before. We actually all didn't overdo it this year, which pleased Ruth no end. We all agreed, Seudah in the forest is the BEST and we must do it again next year!

And then it was time to go.

Most hikers on Shvil Yisrael go in one direction: North to South in the Autumn, and South to North in the Spring. I had decided much earlier in the trip, planning the schedule, to do something a little different. The seed was planted by a suggestion in the Red Guide. In this season, the author wrote, it's recommended to stop on arrival in Tel Aviv, take a bus to the North, and work your way south back to Tel Aviv in the center of the country. Hiking south from Kibbutz Dan on the border with Lebanon, the idea is not to miss the Spring flowers blooming in March/April up north.

I adopted the idea, but added my own twist. I had been a little worried about how I'd end my trek; arriving at the last point of the Shvil at Dan, I hoped to be met by as many of my friends and family to celebrate the accomplishment and to welcome me back to civilization . . . and to my (re-)new(ed) life. But my schedule called for me to arrive there so close to Passover that I realized it was unlikely anyone could or would drive four hours up north on a Friday before Pesach, and four hours back, just to greet me on my arrival there.[9]

The idea then crystalized around my desire to actually *walk* home, to literally end my hike by striding down my street into my house, so my homecoming would be just that: coming home, physically and not just metaphorically. I had discussed it with the kids and all agreed it made sense; whatever offense might have remained to some concept of purity of walking the Trail in only one direction was easily overcome by my family and friends' reaction—one of great relief it seems, aside from the logic (and symbolism) of the decision.

And so that Sunday Purim afternoon, after happy goodbyes all around, I found myself in my car, with my son Nati driving, heading north. Traffic and other events having delayed various arrivals throughout the day, our departure was much later than planned. Without stress, I had thought to just take a few busses, not least as Nati needed and wanted to be in Jerusalem that evening (Jerusalem celebrates Purim a day after the rest of the world). But he insisted on taking me part of the way, and we agreed we'd play it by ear, and he'd turn around when we got to a point where I could continue by bus and he could comfortably get back to Jerusalem before the festival started there. It was great to have a little time with him; we talked mostly of hiking issues, comparing notes a bit between my tribulations and his various marches/exercises in the IDF. I enjoyed the intimacy of the car journey and felt close to my first-born and only son, while as a (married already!) adult he selflessly helped me out, and commiserated with the hardships of the hike as well as more subtly with the lonliness and challenges of the wider situation.

After about two hours, I jumped out of the car—literally, to rush to catch the bus—in Afula, a small development town about halfway to the northern border, and we said goodbye by phone. I was on my own again. I wrote a funny Facebook post while on the bus to Kiryat Shmona, and made a few arrangements calls. Arriving in Israel's northernmost city (well, a small town, really, but in Israel everything's relative; a "city" is any locale with more than 20,000 residents), I grabbed a pizza. I explained somewhat tiredly to the men sitting around smoking what the Shvil is, and that yes, I was hiking it alone, yes at my age, and yes I do have a job . . . and then hopped in a taxi to Kibbutz Daphna, where I'd arranged to sleep at a Trail Angel. I had the passing thought while in the taxi that I should have taken a train, and found a horse to ride, to cover all the transportation possibilities in getting there. My host Tamar and her roommate had left a key out—that most amazing and most mundane of things, somewhat remarkable and quite heartwarming—and I showered and settled in on their futon. I was glad to be in the North; I was exhausted, more mentally than physically.

9　Most of my friends and family in Israel, though by no means all, are observant Jews, as am I, so not only do we not travel on Shabbat, we spend most of Friday or the eve of a festival like Pesach preparing. The unique and complicated, time-consuming preparations for Pesach and the special Seder meal mean most observant Jewish families devote weeks to preparation in the lead-up to the holiday. Hence my concern that no one could or would show up.

Though I was tired, my head was buzzing. Starting with these two young people who were willing to share the smallest apartment in the country (I'm sure of that, like a Japanese cube almost) with a perfect stranger, and then going through all those who had shown me kindness in previous weeks, and all the friends and family who'd been so caring over the past years, I practically couldn't bear how thankful I was. I lay in the darkness, almost reveling in my gratitude, at one with Mandy and Jeremy and so many others from whom I've learned the power of appreciation.

In that past week, my fourth on the Trail, I started to put the pieces of this theory of mine together in a more concerted fashion, following the transition from desert to forest. Remembering my emotional experience at the meditation retreat in Bat Ayin from the year before as I listed all those I was so grateful for in my life, I realized how crucial a sense of appreciation and gratitude is to move beyond our pain.

I've already mentioned the humility of Moshe, and its centrality to his being appointed by God to shepherd the Jewish nation on its march to independence. As noted, the humbleness Moshe demonstrated was partially based on an acknowledgment that God, and not I, controls what happens in this world. From that acceptance we come to an appreciation for the wonderful gifts we've been privileged to enjoy here on earth. Somehow, accepting our lot in life can lead to appreciating that lot; or put another way, recognizing that all comes from God opens our eyes to the gifts we're actually given. Even after a divorce.

The meditative practice I followed on the Shvil described in the Introduction, using one of the most mysterious of God's names when He revealed himself to Moshe: "אהיה אשר אהיה" *Eheye Asher Eheye* "I will be as I will be," brought these pieces together for me. Humbly accepting the twists and turns of my life, I was able to feel the most profound gratitude for all my blessings. This was expressed by concentrating, as explained earlier, on the מודה אני *Modeh Ani* "I am thankful" phrase. I used this meditation daily on the trek, and the combination is powerful.

As I lay on the futon, nearing sleep, contemplating these themes, something else came to me. What I realized was that appreciation isn't diminished by pain; in fact, the suffering can have the effect of increasing the gratitude. Can I say that Karen's leaving made me more grateful for our years of marital happiness, the building of our family and communities we lived in? As someone who always appreciated his blessings, I can't believe that's quite accurate. But it did intensify my gratitude. And once I had accepted my personal situation, and worked on remembering and appreciating all the incredible elements of our shared endeavor over the past almost thirty years, something new emerged. I started to be open to a sense of forgiveness.

On that first night in the North, this notion of forgiveness became the theme on the next stage of my trek on the Shvil.

Chapter Five

ALONG THE BORDER WITH LEBANON: FORGIVENESS

[Week Five]

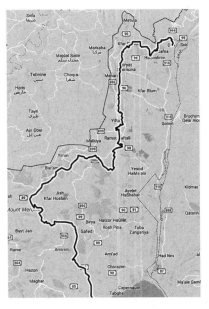

*W**ow. The difference up here on the northern border is not only noticeable; it's all-encompassing. The air. The weather. The packed earth. The view. The birds and flowers and trees and orchards are all unlike anything I've seen or felt so far on this trek. I'm walking through a patch of almond trees all in blossom (Yaakov Saar was right; would NOT want to have missed this). Beyond them the Hermon rises like a watchman, like a mother hippopotamus guarding her babies. I realize that's a rather unusual image but looking at the bumps on the Golan just below the Hermon and just above me here outside Kibbutz Snir, baby hippopotamuses come to mind. It's not like I've never been in the area; some of my favorite memories of family vacations were all around here: splashing at Banyas Spring, the source of the Jordan River; staying for Pesach in the snow at Neve Ativ at the foot of the Hermon; crashing after a hike with Netanel before he went into the IDF at the charming rustic cabins of Biktot B'Arafel in Nimrod; camping with Mike & Deb and Aaron & Hadas and their kids at Horshat Tal, including walking along Nachal Snir/Hatzbani river— which I'm about to walk along. And I've taken foreign journalists on field tours here more times than I can count.*

So no, there's nothing unfamiliar about the area to me. But jumping up from being in the Jerusalem area yesterday, with the memories of the desert so fresh in my mind, let alone the rain and hail in the rocky hills even more recent, I feel a strong sense of disorientation as I stride through the fields along the border with Lebanon.

I'm like Spock—"beam me up Scotty!"—I've been transported to another planet, and need to get my bearings.

That's actually easier than you think, when walking with a heavy pack on your back. You get a sense of the lie of the land as you struggle up a small rise; when you turn around to take a look at where you are or have been, you do so slowly, and that helps to orient you. Within about an hour, I'm much more comfortable—in my shoes, in the terrain, in my self. I'm here where I want to be: hiking the Shvil. And not only that: I'm really familiar with this part of the country. Especially since starting MediaCentral in 2006, a few months after the Second Lebanon War (and having spent much of that war on the border serving in the IDF Spokesman's unit), I've been here dozens of times—including many visits right there, over that field, at the small and neglected, somewhat dispirited Alawite village of Ghajar. I trudge through the fields just south of it, dodging cows (and bulls—oh my, what bulls!) and their leavings, making my way to the section of the Hatzbani/Snir on the Israeli side of the border.

And then I arrive at Nachal Snir/Hatzbani. Not yet at the national park nature reserve, but just east of it as the trail follows its meandering. Ghajar is just to my right, to the north, above the cliff carved into the hillside by millennia of snow melt flowing down from the mounts of Lebanon. The river (really, a stream) is running strong, overflowing its banks; the Shvil seems to go right in and through it. I stop, and look ahead—yes, I see a marker! The Trail doesn't just cross it; it continues back and forth through the water—and the water is so high it's not like there are rocks or banks to

Mt. Hermon from Kibbutz Dafna

walk on or hop to and from. I take my pack off and, laughing out loud, look at my special water-proof sandals hanging on the side—bought exactly for this moment.

Years ago, on a tiyul with Aaron and Hadas and our kids, we had done this hike, which includes walking through the water in various places. I had on a brand new pair of hiking boots from the States—these boots! I'm wearing them now!—and I didn't want them to get wet. So Aaron carried me on his back a few steps. We have a photo of it on the back of my front door. And now, arriving at Snir, lowering my pack, I pull the sandals off, hang my boots in their stead—and take a photo to send Aaron: at Snir without you, but I came prepared!

I enjoy every step. It's getting hot and the cool water is so refreshing. I keep the sandals on even as the trail continues on dry land, since I know what's in store. Coming into the reserve I don't even bother stopping at the bathroom or the little kiosk: I know exactly where I'm headed, and am looking forward to it. (And the picnic area is full of families with little kids, great fun but I'm not in the mood.) I do stop to take another photo, this at the trail signpost, and send a WhatsApp message to Aaron and Hadas and the kids, "Wish you were here." That doesn't slow my progress much. Within half an hour, sweaty but so very excited, I arrive at one of my favorite spots in the world, let alone in Israel and on the Shvil: a pool in the middle of the stream, about the size of a volleyball court, where the water flows in quickly enough to push you for a ride a few meters and then swirls around in a basin deep enough to dive in and swim. There are even a few little "seating" areas on each side, enabling you to rest and enjoy the coolness and the sound of the river.

I strip down—without hesitation or embarrassment, but with enough modesty to look around and listen carefully to ensure I'm alone for those few seconds that I'm unclothed but still out of the water—and dive in. Oh my God this feels SO GOOD! I feel euphoric; under the water, it's like a spiritual immersion—wish it was Friday, could consider this a mikvah dip—and floating a bit, as the stream carries me along, looking up at the trees in the dappled sun, I'm just rapturous. That's the word that comes to mind. Does life get ANY better than this? I can hear the birds chirping—different birds than in the South and though I can't identify any of them, I can distinguish that up here their song seems more melodious, more pleasant-sounding—and I just know they're singing for me, only for me. I get out, and keeping my shorts nearby for quick access, sit and dry naked in the sun. I have to admit to myself, maybe as I'm a true Californian, or free-thinker, or just a hippie, but nothing feels the same as swimming, and sunning, with nothing on. You'd think it's a minor issue, but the difference is palpable. Hah! "Palpable" indeed.

I see something out of the corner of my eye; it's the Shvil marker on a stone, which I'm always of course looking out for, but this one is faced in the opposite direction to the one I'm walking, so I hadn't seen it before. The mottled sun seems to highlight it; and I notice that one of my favorite flowers, a white Rakefet (a Cyclamen—I look it up on my phone, was always curious but never knew the English term), is growing out of a crevice in the rock right under and in front of the marker. I jump up—it's just too good to miss—and go photograph it, from a few angles (taking my shorts with me just in case).

I return to my rock; slide into the water again, swim around a bit and "wash" my hair, float more, this time listing to the rush of the water as my head dips in and out; climb out and sit in the sun; jump in again, and sit in the crevice which I'd like to think was put there just for this purpose, nature's friendship-offering to hikers and swimmers. A memory comes to me of Netanel, about age 12 or so, leaping in and splashing around, swishing down the "rapids," and my taking Meira in, age 7, and Merav, age 10, holding one in each arm, swishing them back and forth . . . and I'm so full of love for them, and for my life . . . and for Karen. It's an enigmatic set of emotions: I am so very happy right now, elated and euphoric even, sitting here in the cool water with my head and shoulders in the warm sun, hiking the Shvil, My Shvil Yisrael; life is wonderful, as Jason Mraz says and I sing so often, truly amazing. And I am feeling strong and up, looking and moving forward.

And yet I am so perplexed and sad at the turns my life has taken. I love my kids so; and to be honest, I love our family as a unit. That's hardly unexpected, and I am (still? Yes, still) dazed and a bit flabbergasted by what's happened. I'm not only still shaken up but also a bit scared—what will this mean to us all? Our family dynamics have been inalterably transformed. I'm still incredibly close to the kids; closer in fact than I have ever been, partly a result of events, partly just due to their continuing to grow up. But I realize, sitting here in the water, we will never again have the sort of family outings I always presumed to be part of our future, stretching into infinity.

I hold on to this image for a minute: years of togetherness and love stretching into the future, visiting this pool with my kids' children, with Karen and me as grandparents growing old together, watching them fool around in the water, laughing and splashing . . . and then, with a long sigh, I let it go.

I don't know if it's the past few weeks or my train of thought over the past few hours, but I presently become conscious of a simple reality: I forgive her. I forgive her the pain and the betrayal; I forgive her the lack of commitment and unwillingness to try harder; I forgive her the independence and conviction which brought her to the decision. I forgive her for not loving me enough to make it work; I forgive her for not caring enough about my hurt, or the kids, or her or my parents, to stay. I forgive her for not being me. I forgive her for being human.

And—yes, I'm crying now, but with all the water around I don't care, as if I'd care anyway—I realize something more profound, more powerful even: I forgive her beyond all the above. I forgive her for doing what was right for her, leaving aside any need to refer to how I feel about it or how I interpret it or how it hurt me or how I think she could have done things differently. It's a different, completely new, much deeper level of forgiveness than I even thought I was reaching for. It's not intellectual, or rational—my usual starting and ending point, as my friend and analytical guide Moshe would attest to. It's emotional and almost spiritual; in this quasi-meditative state I'm in, sitting in the water, my love for Karen is so deep and complete that I forgive her completely, accept her completely, and can honestly say I harbor no more resentment or anger toward her.

At which point I shake my head rather violently and half dive, half slip into the water, and pushing off from the rock, glide underwater until I can't breathe anymore, and burst up into the sunshine, with a loud laugh. I feel terrific; lighter; free. I'm ready to move on—literally, and figuratively—even if this is just the beginning of the process.

The rest of the way to Kfar Giladi, my stop for the night, was rather uneventful. I suppose, compared to that seminal experience at the pool, anything short of being attacked by Hezbollah terrorists or a rampaging bull would have been an anticlimax. (Hezbollah flags can be seen flying from rooftops in the villages a few hundred meters across the border so the former was perhaps more likely than the latter, though I was close enough to the cows and bulls to feel the second threat more immediately.) I climbed up the hill toward the kibbutz and enjoyed "sneaking" in through the back entrance, taking photos of the sweetly-cute-but-still-cooped-up calves in the enclosures I passed. I found my way to the center, where I bought a bit of cheese (and a small thing of mustard) and fresh rolls, and sat outside at a little table in the shade to eat while I waited for the Trail Angel to come meet me.

Ruti came, as she promised, and she told me as we walked that she's giving me the "nicer" lodgings because I'm a Shvilist, and the other to someone who's "just a tourist." (This is known as *protexia* in Hebrew, a very Israeli phenomenon of having a connection and leveraging it to one's advantage). I may not have asked for it, but I did appreciate the gesture, and I told her so. It was an apartment—a whole apartment, furnished and with pillows and blankets too!—which I also didn't expect, and that put me in a good mood; I knew I had a strenuous day planned for the next day (and was emotionally if not physically exhausted), and was looking forward to a good night's sleep.

Boiling up the eggs I had bought (keeping kosher, boiling is about all you can do if you're not sure of the pots and pans), I indulged in a delectable supper of soft-boiled eggs and toast, quinoa and tomatoes, cheese and tea, and settled in for the night. I thought to play a bit of guitar, as I had brought a small guitar purchased specially for the trek, and was keen to make use of it. (Mimi had brought it to me on Sunday. It is only 2 kilos or so in weight, less than the amount of water I ceased having to lug around now that I was in the North and not the desert; I carried it strapped to the outside of the pack.) Or I thought to plan the next day's route, or read the book I had taken from Meira's supply box, or make some calls, or to do one of the other nighttime activities I had intended to accomplish. Instead, I finished all the Balvenie I had packed, and half the Auchentoshen left over from the previous day's Purim celebrations, which I had brought along for the fun of it. As I wrote in my journal, I drank "first, to 'lighten the load' (weight), but then after hearing an Adele song just got MAUDLIN."

I had just that day, sitting at the small table near the grass outside the kibbutz makolet little store, started to listen to music on my iPhone. Both as there was a noisy group of teens nearby which I didn't feel like hearing, and as I knew that I could recharge at night, and I suppose also as a result of coming a bit out of the in-the-desert/nature thing, I was more inclined to "plug in and tune out." So in the apartment, as I prepared supper, I had put music on, with the "shuffle" function active. Big mistake.

"Silly, stupid, regressive, self-indulgent self-pity" is how I put it in my journal a few days later. "Got over it & went to sleep. (Mimi texted 'you okay?' at about 1 a.m. . . . so sweet. Said 'now I am' . . .)." And that was about it. I must have sent a WhatsApp message to her in the midst of my melancholy—a great advertisement for "don't drink and text" advice—and I did appreciate her checking in that late. I remember feeling foolish and juvenile even as I drank more; yes, I'd been sad, but I thought I'd gotten over it, moved beyond it, had a great day and a great revelation. I was embarrassed at my weakness; but I was also aware—not completely sloshed—of my need for release, or at least a desire to let go, to forget about all the seriousness and heavy stuff. So I let myself—and woke up feeling refreshed and raring to go, even if I had to spend an extra half hour in the morning getting things together and planning the day. I was ready to get back to some serious hiking.

Tuesday is a long and hard day—more climbing, more heat than I'd anticipated—but really fun nonetheless. The perspective over the Hula valley from the reaches of the Naftali mountain range is impressive—and not least when you reflect that we drained all this which was once a big swamp. I can see as far as Mt. Bental on the Golan; I can see where the Hula nature reserve is slowing bringing back the water, and the millions of migrating birds, far below. And of course my pace is so different than any other experience I've had in this area I've visited often, it feels like another whole country.

I feel different, too. It seems these last few days were cathartic in a real way—both the pool yesterday at Snir and last night—and my reflections on the first pioneers as I started out today at the monument to Yosef Trumpeldor, hero of the earliest Zionist defensive struggles, are surprisingly light and cheery.

I was clearly in a bit of a happier mood; I even took a video of myself walking along above the Hula Valley (Video 8). That week was a more social time, certainly. I stayed with my friends Cheli and Moshe—children of friends, but friends still—in Hatzor, and played with their older daughter Roni. I spoke at some length with them, as well as with others I happened to meet, including a few lovely, idealistic, fun and excitable teens making their way north near Ramot Naftali who insisted on walking with me in the opposite direction for a few minutes. I had a number of fun discussions and with the drivers of the various rides I'd caught ("tramps," as hitch-hiking is known in Israel), including Shafrir, Meir, and Avraham, all local moshav farmers. Interesting how it was the locals, and left-wing old-fashioned Labor Zionists at that, who both picked me up and who were most intrigued—and enthusiastic—about my escapades. Then, Wednesday morning, one of those drivers triggered a delightful (and delicious) start to my day.

It's not only the terrain and weather, flowers and trees, and my mental state which is undergoing the transformation: it's my attitude as well—I'm really having fun! I mean—I was enjoying the trek from day one, but now it's mostly fun, as opposed to occasionally or "also" fun. The heaviness has left me; what remains is almost pure enjoyment. Even when I'm tired and fed up, like now, as I flag down my third "tramp" of the day, in the heat, wondering whether I'll ever get to the trailhead. . . . But yes! A small, old, muddy truck is pulling over and I climb in, bustling my pack into the back seat, full of appreciation. The somewhat laconic driver, Avraham, about 65 or so with a bushy gray beard, prominent gray and white eyebrows, and calloused, muscular hands on the steering wheel, says he's only going as far as the Dalton industrial park—and I abruptly have an inspiration! Dalton! One of my favorite wineries! I sneak a quick look at the map, and my watch, and yes—I have time for a bite and a brief tasting, why not?

It's about a kilometer walking from where Avraham drops me off—but I'm happy to walk it, it reduces my guilt feelings for taking tramps and for what-I'm-about-to-do. Arriving at the entrance to the industrial area, I see and remember also the charming restaurant/café at the Adir Winery, a smaller outfit than Dalton but one with just as good wine, and walk over to it.

What a morning! Scrumptious "Israeli" breakfast of eggs, fresh breads, assortment of cheeses, olive spread, and dried tomato spread and Labane with Zatar and olive oil, coffee and juice and jams and more, but here augmented by a selection of three Adir wines to taste. Hearing of my own wine-making as well as my Shvil endeavor, the owner comes over to chat and then asks me to taste their very special Rose Port, which is phenomenal. I order a few bottles to be delivered to Meira (surprise), take a few photos and a few last sips to savor . . . and walk out the front door ready to face the day. As I wrote in my journal the next day—"Adir! Indeed!" [The Hebrew word "adir" means "mighty" and "glorious" and in slang, "terrific."]

Seeking a ride to where the Trail crosses the road, I have some good luck, quickly catching one ride part of the way and another almost immediately also. The second is from a local wine-grower, and the grapes here in the upper Galilee are some of the country's best, so I take his number for later this year, perhaps to get some Petit Verdot from him. I reach the Alma bridge trailhead by 10:30 a.m., well within the parameters I'd set for myself for today.

Back on the Trail—and so happy to be so. What I wasn't expecting, though, was how beautiful the day is; every step is a pleasure, every vista enchanting, every bird soaring above a call to freedom, every breeze a gentle caress, every turn a sweet surprise. I'm taking many more photographs than I've done previously (and of course I've taken quite a few as it is). Is it objectively more pretty, or is my perception of the beauty around me affected by my having forgiven Karen, having forgiven God, having forgiven myself, having forgiven my kids and my parents and former colleagues and bosses and neighbors and I don't know who else?

I spent the day—Wednesday, my third full day in the North—ruminating on this theme. Why is forgiveness such a central motif in human interactions, in love and in war and peace, in human behavior? I recalled talking with Meira once about forgiving others for unkind remarks, about how *we* control our feelings, not they. That we have the power to forgive, and to forget, even while we learn from any particular episode—a key element in the Jewish concept of repentence (*Tshuva*). My mind wandered to the Reconstruction in the US following the Civil War, and to all we'd been taught in school in the US about the greatness of Abraham Lincoln—which was not only his freeing of the slaves, but his dedication to reconciliation and unity. (I remember learning about his statement that if he could keep the Union together by not freeing the slaves, he would—a moral dilemma and clash of values and priorities which garnered intense debate among us 16-year-old moral authorities in tenth-grade AS History with Mr. Weaver.) And I thought of the Ireland situation, and Jewish/German relations, and of course to the more recent processes in South Africa. Asking for forgiveness is key, and perhaps more importantly, forgiving as well.

Here I was, about as close to the border with Lebanon as you can be and not be shot at, strolling along Nachal Dishon (yes, even with my backpack, I felt like I was out for a stroll, it was such a lovely day and the inclines and descents were so very gentle, I was swinging my poles more like a walking stick), and thinking about forgiveness. I wondered, what made the Christians of southern Lebanon see themselves as allies of the otherwise-hated (Jewish) Israelis? What made even (some) Muslim Lebanese more inclined to discuss or even work toward coexistence than many other Muslims and Arabs in the region? I'm not sure they possess deeper levels of humility or acceptance or gratitude; I do think, in some ways, there is a greater sense of forgiveness.

With those thoughts in mind, I walked for hours through green and brown canyons and hills, trying to capture soaring hawks on video (and failing, and then giving up and just enjoying watching). The morning, and early afternoon, passed quietly and mostly alone; while I played guitar sitting on a rock in the shade at the bend of a dry river bed in Nachal Dishon, a large group of senior citizens trudged by, some of them smiling, one or two stopping to chat for a minute. Then it was quiet again. I sang a lot; loudly, while walking, including my "Clothe me in love" new anthem. It was marvelous. I felt the positive vibes pulsing through me; I was full of humility, acceptance, gratitude, and now forgiveness, and it affected everything: my pain was reduced, the heat felt less oppressive; the hills seemed more gentle, the breeze more of a caress.

I walked on and on, the path became more of a dirt jeep track, I crossed a road and continued to climb—not too steep, but tiring nonetheless. At the peak of the heat of the day, around 2 p.m. or so while walking along the dirt road following the route of Nachal Dishon, I was passed by a jeep full of five "Breslover" Hassidim, a sect of strictly Orthodox Jews known for their spiritual (and spirited) dancing and singing. Soon enough I came through the trees and across the stream into a clearing, and saw their jeep parked by something I couldn't really identify. I kept walking, as I wasn't in the mood for company, and then turned back—what was that blue thing?

On a raised platform, bordered on all sides by a rusty fence, was a tomb of some sort, painted in that sky blue reminiscent of Santorini and other Greek islands. It was weird; I was just curious enough to want to look, but not enough to take my pack off. The Hassidim were a few paces away; standing with my back to them, I read the little plaque with the name ישעיהו בן אמוץ—Yeshayahu ben Amotz. I was confused: I didn't recognize the name. Who was this? Why the tomb; why here; why the fence and attraction for these others?

It turns out I had stumbled upon the grave of the prophet Isaiah—at least according to tradition. Yes: Isaiah of the "lion shall lie down with the lamb" prophesy; only one of the most important, most famous, most profound and most optimistic, future-oriented prophets of Israel. Isaiah's exhortations to morality and ethical behavior continue to inspire millions of Jews and Christians (and others) today, including the famous "swords to plowshares" message embedded in the stone at the entrance to United Nations Headquarters in NY.

What? I couldn't believe this was his final resting place; I tried to understand how it could be possible that I'd never heard of, or been to, this place, nestled so gently by a murmuring stream just beneath the wooded hills of the Baram Heights forest. I took my pack off, and resting it against a tree asked the group whether this was really Isaiah's tomb, and what else they could tell me about it. They were neither knowledgeable about the history nor very interested in the historicity—they accepted as a given that if tradition said this was Isaiah's tomb, there wasn't anything further to ask or know. I was a bit skeptical; but still, I used the opportunity to meditate quietly at the tomb about the long path of history of the Jewish nation, and Isaiah's role in it, as advisor to kings and prophet to our people. I knew very little of his life's story; I have since discovered much, and not least that it is considered unlikely that this was indeed his final resting place. But it was still inspiring.

And then I was brought a bit down to earth from my spiritual high.

As I come down from the raised platform on which the gravestone rests—a sort of round-top elongated cover like a sarcophagus—I struggle to get my pack on, and one of the black-kippa'd, white-shirted Hassidim helps me to balance it and supports it while I pull my arms through. Nice. He offers me a drink, and though I had water I can see they have a cooler which is dripping with condensation, too tempting to even consider refusing. I accept, and boy does that taste and feel great—cold cold water in a plastic cup. We chat a bit; they aren't aware of the Shvil, and are genuinely intrigued—not least as they're certainly among those who love the Land and they really enjoy their brief excursions around it. So that's kinda cool—we share a connection beyond the clear differences between us.

Then they ask where I'm staying tonight, and I tell them a little story about how Michal Friedman had insisted I MUST stay at the Kibbutz Baram Shvilistim room (like she did about Sansana, but keeping the details a big secret) . . . and this one fellow, a kid really, pipes up with "אתה יודע ששם אין בכלל שומרי מצוות—ממש טרייף!". *("You know that there aren't any mitzvah-observant people there; really treif [not-kosher]!") "What does that matter?!?" I say in surprise. "They're Jews!"*

I shrug and let it go at that, stifling my disbelief at his attitude. To their credit, his companions don't agree with him, but neither do they argue. I'm not in the mood to get into it and so, thanking them for the water, turn and walk on. Rounding the corner after the gravesite, I start to think to myself about all the ways I could have and should have *responded.*

מה?! הם מקיימים מצות יישוב הארץ. הם מקיימים את מצות הגנת הארץ ויושביה! והם קמיימים את המצוות התלויות
באָרץ—כי מוכרים את תבואתה!"

"What?! The Jews in that Kibbutz may be 'secular' but they're fulfilling the commandment of settling the land. They're keeping the commandment to protect the land and its inhabitants! They're observing the agricultural land-related commandments—since they sell its produce into the Israeli market!"

ואתה? אתה עובר על המצוות ה-'לא תעשה' של
הוצאת שם רע ולשון הרע ודיבה "

"And YOU? You're violating the prohibitions against slander and gossip and making someone look bad . . ."

I stop for a moment: is it worth my turning around? It's only been a minute or so since I left them, I've walked maybe 100 meters. I should go back; it's my duty to engage him. Argh—I really can't be bothered. And with those strange connections our mind makes, I'm already forgiving him. It's so beautiful, this land; he doesn't know any better. I bet my initial reaction already shook him out of his complacency, and I have a hunch his friends, a bit older and wiser, will help him to understand why his casual judgement was out of line. And If I've forgiven him, I don't have the motivation really to confront him.

And this takes me back to my theme for the day, all this forgiveness. I slow down my walk to a snail's pace, remembering, remembering. Not that it's specifically related to this incident, but I'm putting the pieces together, and I realize that this new-found willingness to forgive, like my sense of gratitude, comes from one of the incredibly powerful experiences I had at Bat Ayin.

On that three-day silent meditation retreat, there was a point when I found myself alone on the small balcony outside the main room, in the late afternoon on Shabbat. It was a few hours before the end of the Sabbath, our third and final day. The covered porch was a square about 3 meters or 12 feet across; earlier I'd seen a few people doing slow walks around its periphery, in a circle/square pattern of sorts, which hadn't really appealed to me. I'm more of an open-space person (duh) and preferred to do my slow-walking meditation on the paths through the hills or the dirt road alongside the house or in the small grassy area out back. At that point in the afternoon, conscious that this was to be our last meditative walk before Shabbat and the retreat concluded, I thought to go on to the balcony just to look at the view, in order to decide where to go for my last brief slow walk.

And then a strange thing happened. As I rose and approached the open sliding door to the balcony, I caught a glance of the opposing hillside in the distance through the trees. I could just about see the spring across the wadi, in which I had dipped on Friday in preparation for Shabbat—and something inside grabbed me. I resolved to dip again in its cleansing waters while it was still Shabbat (an ancient mystical tradition, related to the waters of Eden and the womb, which I described earlier). But at that moment, standing at the threshold of the balcony, looking across the valley, I couldn't move. I couldn't step through and onto the porch. For some reason, or no reason at all, I was frozen in place, quite literally.

Without thinking, somehow I knew that this would be the site of my last slow-walking meditation before Shabbat went out. I had to cross this threshold; I had to get to the edge of the balcony. I HAD to.

Those four steps were the hardest in my life.

I wasn't yet thinking of anything spiritual or deep, in the practice I'd started the day before and described earlier here. No; at that juncture, my focus was entirely on stepping through the doorway. I lifted my right leg to cross the threshold, and as I did, something held me back. Some deep reticence to head in that direction restrained me from picking up my right foot, and once I did it took all I had to bring it forward and put it down on the other side of the transom. But I did it, and then brought my left foot through as well. Standing with two feet on the other side, having passed across the doorsill, I took three deep breaths, and sighed. I had progressed, and overcome that initial reticence. It felt good, though was only that pleasant feeling of settling in to your chair at the beginning of a college exam, having all your pens or paper or calculator with you, still knowing the test is yet to come. But I was there, and ready.

Why this happened I cannot explain. But something drew me to the spring; I felt that if I could only reach the balcony railing, it would be symbolic of my walking to the spring itself. And then the spring itself, which the day before had been icy, frighteningly cold, would welcome me differently; would welcome a different me. I knew this in such a deep way; I had no idea what I was doing.

With an acute sense of humility, I stood there with my back to the portal; I was alone; I stared through the trees at the spring. This was the spring which the day before, Friday, had taken my breath away—physically, not metaphorically. When I slipped into the water I thought I was drowning, I couldn't breathe it was so cold. As a native Northern Californian Pacific Ocean swimmer and life guard, that had never happened to me, ever. I wondered whether I was having a heart attack; I jumped out so quickly I startled a few other men standing nearby. Standing the next day, Shabbat, on that porch, the spring seemed to beckon me, and I focused all my energy and all my thought on these waters of creation. As I lifted my left leg, in the slow slow arc of bringing it forward, I repeated that phrasing described above—אהיה אשר אהיה *Eheye Asher Eheye I Am That/As I Am*—and a profound sense of acceptance descended on me. It is what it is; this is my lot; it took about ten whole seconds for that second step.

I waited, thinking nothing other than that, balanced with my right foot behind, left foot forward, alone on the balcony, alone in the world, taking the world as it is. Slowly, painfully even, like my foot weighed a ton, I lifted my back foot and brought it forward. מודה אני *Modeh Ani—I am grateful*—and I was crying already, the tears streaming down my face, full to burst with an appreciation to God for everything in my life, including this experience. By the time my foot came down, I had to steady myself for a second with my hand on the wall of the house. I was crying loudly, but I didn't care if any of the others in the room behind and next to me noticed; in fact I didn't even know they were there. I wasn't aware of anything: the room itself, our teacher, the other participants, nothing existed aside from me. I was just full of gratitude.

I had one last step to go. The railing was ahead of me. I knew I could do it; it was the hardest step I've ever taken. I was thinking so many things and nothing at the same time. I paused, and breathed deeply, and looked out over the valley as the leaves glittered and tossed in the wind, blocking and revealing my view of the spring, aware and not aware of the birds singing and sound of the breeze. "I am coming," I remember saying to myself, calling to the spring; "I can do this." I was at this point sobbing, rooted in place with my right foot forward, a little less than a meter from the end of the balcony. I couldn't reach out to touch the railing; I needed to take that last step to do so. I didn't want to move; I couldn't bear to take that action which by raising my left leg, lifting up my knee, arcing my foot and bringing it to rest in front of me as my body weight shifts from back to front, from past to future, from then to now, would symbolize moving on; arriving; living. I didn't want to; I knew I had to. And in a crash of understanding, I realized—not decided, not concluded, but discovered—forgiveness. I began to forgive Karen.

When my hand touched the railing, I was crying and laughing, breathing and holding my breath, coughing and sighing and swallowing all at the same time. It had taken a full twenty minutes to cross the balcony. Those four steps on that porch—through the threshold and up to the railing—changed my life. And the most profound element was my recognition that indeed I could forgive her. I was ready to move on; and when I did, twenty minutes later, arrive at the spring, before I went in to the (same, freezing) water, I already was sure what to expect: while still cold, it was refreshing and not at all threatening; the previous day's suffocation and panic were replaced with a wondrous feeling of rebirth, regeneration, excitement, fulfillment and optimism. Because I was full of gratitude, and ready to begin to forgive.

As I walk along Nachal Dishon, I'm aware of how my Monday's experience in the water of Nachal Snir/Hatzbani was a direct continuation, a fulfillment or completion, of that turning point on the balcony at Bat Ayin amost a year earlier. I'm walking slowly as I mull this all over; but it's hot, it's beautiful, it's late, and this is all way too serious. And—what's this? A little pool under a waterfall appears to me as if by magic. Spending the past hour or more re-living the mikvah/spring episodes at the meditation retreat, it strikes me as appropriate and even serendipitous to stumble on a spring now. And of course I remember my promise to Bini (and disappointment on שביל המעינות *the Trail of Springs in Jerusalem as the rain and hail fell), not to mention the heat and tiredness. So I dump my pack at the foot of a massive but low tree with smooth branches the size of my calves extending in every direction, and begin to strip my clothes off.*

According to my map it's called *Ein Aravot*, the Spring of the Willows, and it's about as close to a private paradise as I was to find on the Trail. What fantastic and fun memories of reading to my children (and in my own childhood) that old classic *Wind in the Willows*! I could hear the water trickling down the mountainside through a riot of green, yellow, and brown vines and reeds even before I saw it. At the base of a small cliff I found a small pool; two in fact, but the smaller and shallower one nearer the hillside, while prettier perhaps, isn't deep enough to go in. The larger pool—about 2 meters in diameter, looked to be about a meter in depth. And so clear and cool and inviting it was like it was put there—just a kilometer or two from my destination, Kibbutz Baram—just for me. Just for this hot day, just to match my train of thought, and to relieve me of the burdens of all this somber thinking.

In my underwear, I couldn't resist taking a dozen photographs before getting in, from various angles, trying to capture it all. The combination of colors in the sunlight, the trickling/falling water over the rocks from a height of about ten meters, the pools and trees was stunning. It was impossible—impossible!—to get the picture right. So frustrating! But that's the difference between hearing about the Shvil and hiking the Shvil—to capture the essence of the splendor of the place. Even the video I shot didn't come close; I gave up and elected to simply enjoy the moment, timeless as it was, solitary as it was, perfect as it was.

I looked around quickly, and tilted my head (yes, I actually cocked my head to the side to listen more carefully) just to check I couldn't hear anyone approaching, and then quickly stepped out of my underwear and threw it over a branch of the tree a few meters from the larger pool, and was immediately in the water. OH MY GOD. I think kids don't appreciate the power of the expressions we use today. "OMG" seems so facile, so casual, so shallow. Oh! FEEL this! God, Creator of the universe, how awesome is this world you've created; and you are

MY God, we are connected, this is here for me and I am here for you! That's how I felt at that moment. I'm sure my kids, and all kids, and perhaps us adults too, aren't usually thinking along those lines when we use those three letters OMG on Facebook or WhatsApp, but it was almost the only expression fitting the occasion and sensation.

That's the sort of exhilaration you feel, the real high you get, when sliding into a cool (okay—pretty darn COLD) natural pool in a forest on a hot day after hiking for a dozen miles or so. I dunked a few times. It wasn't Friday or Shabbat, but it was a regenerating and rebirthing mikvah dip in the purifying waters of Eden in any case. I felt a resurgence of energy pulsing through me, a love for all things, a sense of acceptance and gratitude and forgiveness all together. I really, really didn't want to leave.

But the water was cold indeed, and after about five minutes (a long time when you're on your own), I was ready to get out. But I wasn't ready to just move on; and I needed/wanted to "air-dry" in any case. I was pretty near the road—in fact I could hear, and vaguely see through the trees, cars swooshing by above me, about fifty meters up a small rise—so I wasn't about to just hang around naked. On the other hand it felt so good that I wanted to drag it out a bit. So I dried myself a little with my (not so clean but who cares) shirt and put my underwear back on, but that's all. I then detached my guitar from the pack, and stood there (took a selfie and sent it to Bini and my other kids), and started to play.

It was a great end to a great day. What day which starts with breakfast at Adir Winery, continues through an invigorating walk through forest and hill while contemplating the great questions of life, and ends in a natural spring pool with a warm wind bending the tall evergreens, could not be great? I could not even *imagine* how much better it was going to get.

Walking, then trudging, and eventually struggling up the hill toward Kibbutz Baram I start to wonder, as I get nearer the entrance gate, just what awaits me. Michal was explicit: you MUST stay at Baram! In the end, it worked perfectly into my schedule from Alma en route to Mt. Meron and Tzfat (Safed), so I didn't have to artificially wedge it in; but I'm curious why she was so adamant. I call Yehuda, the kibbutz member in charge of their Shvilistim room, and get directions. Meeting him there, he unlocks to the door and leads me in to what an only be described as the Waldorf Astoria of Trail Angels.

It's not fancy—on the Shvil you don't need fancy—but OMG (yes, again—I even end up writing that in my journal) it is real oasis on the Trail. The first thing I see as we enter, looking through a doorway into a kitchen, is a set of deep shelves, full of provisions. But Yehuda leads me through the entry/dining area into a bedroom, complete not only with four beds with pillows (pillows!) and sheets (!) and blankets, but a desk (with paper and pens and pencils and maps) and a stereo. Yehuda says there's only one other person who's called in, and sure enough a few minutes after we arrive, a young man named Evyatar comes in. We agree he'll take the other room;

if any women come, he'll move over to my room (he too is observant, or it seems so, wearing a kippa like mine).

It's not quite a Tzimmer bed & breakfast inn—it's still a Kibbutz, and one of the Kibbutz' older housing buildings at that—and the beds are shallow mattresses on wooden planks, but for me it's the height of luxury. Walking into the shower room, I see PILES of large fluffy TOWELS, on a shelf across from the showers! I haven't used a towel in weeks. I can't even remember when I last used a large bath towel—but I'm certain it was at the hotel in Eilat. Where's Eilat? When was Eilat? A world away and a lifetime ago.

And then I see shampoo. And conditioner. And body wash. And body lotion. And sun screen too. And none of it the cheapest stuff either. No WAY! I seriously cannot believe this. I know, anyone who's stayed in a decent hotel in the last generation expects these as a matter of course—myself included—but seriously? In a little Kibbutz apartment nestled among the trees on a mountain top a kilometer from the Lebanon border? I'm a little nonplussed—but only for a moment, and with a great big grin turn on the hot hot strong stream of water and take one of the most luxuriant, satisfying, cleansing and restorative showers I've ever had.

The piece de resistance—hah, isn't that the truth, I can remember my high-school French and that's really what it is, the main course!—is the kitchen. After a bit of time getting organized, I'm hungry and go into the kitchen. What I saw from the door as we came in earlier turns out to be even more impressive than I grasped: As you walk in, in front of you are five shelves FULL of every imaginable non-perishable foodstuff—and a sign saying "Eat/make what you'd like, and take with you what you want and need—we'll replenish the stocks daily." Seriously. All sorts of noodles; canned tuna and vegetable spread and pickles and olives; humus and techina mix, soup powder, crackers; grains and rice and legumes and seeds and nuts galore; and an abundant assortment of munchies, cookies and packaged cakes.

"Abundance" is a word whose true meaning I learned from Karen and her mother. Our goal at a Shabbat or Festival meal is for our guests to feel שפע "shefa," the feeling of plenty which fills your heart and soul with a sense of overflowing bounty. This kitchen is that, and more—since no one on the Kibbutz was going to enjoy this bounty with us! I set about making dinner, and Evyatar joined me in the kitchen. Together we "kashered" two pots[10] and put together a feast worthy of the name.

Evyatar, 19, from an observant family in the center of the country, is being drafted into the IDF in two weeks. He is two or three days away from finishing the Shvil (moving much faster than I have or could), heading north from here in the morning. At nineteen he is younger than most Shvilistim I've met or am familiar with, as most do the Trail after serving, not before. He's full of energy, perhaps even

---

10   Food is termed "kosher" or "non-kosher" either in itself or in its preparation; cooking and eating must be done with kosher pots and pans and utensils. The process of preparing the utensils/pots is called, in the Hebrew-English of Orthodox Judaism, "kashering".

a little manic. I don't try to analyze what his issues are, what's driving him; we share a meal, a passion for the Land of Israel and its people and state, and leave it at that. It's amusing, rewarding, revealing, intriguing and in the end simply pleasurable that we two, separated by everything—age, upbringing, native language, culture, all the rest—are in fact brothers in spirit, though he is younger than my youngest child.

After dinner, attempting to adjust the radiator heater on the wall, I manage to break the control handle, spraying boiling hot water all over the room and my stuff. While I (more or less successfully) manage to stop the eruption with the palm of my hand, and to (more or less continuously) hold the flood back, Evyatar calls Yehuda and begs him to come back urgently; he does, with another fellow from the Kibbutz and they/we spend another ten minutes trying to find the spigot outside. Eventually it's found, the water is turned off, the handle fixed, my possessions laid out all over the room to dry, I've chosen a different (dry) bed, and crisis is averted. Or concluded, more accurately. Something had to come to shatter the perfection.

Yehuda explains that he manages the Shvilistim room unassisted, with a (rather generous) budget from the Kibbutz which he had to argue for over the course of years. As a Kibbutz, with their economies of scale and purchasing power, it's feasible for them to stock the place so generously. Still, I can't compliment him enough, and through him the Kibbutz, for the effort and resources expended to create such a haven for the hiker. I'm now really not happy that I didn't go back and tell that Hassid off for his casual comment about this "non-observant" Kibbutz having no value or worth or, worse, being off-limits for a religiously-observant person like myself. I hope I meet him again; I'll tell him how "Hachnasat Orachim," hospitality to guests/strangers, the

View from window of Kibbutz Baram Shvilistim room

great and grand mitzvah of our father Avraham, is taken to a copious extreme by this "non-religious" Kibbutz.

I go to sleep, tired but so very filled with food, warmth, caring, achievement and satisfaction.

Thursday dawns bright and cheery. My tefila prayers come naturally as I stand at the window and am inspired by the vista: rolling hills of dark green trees spread out before me in all directions; the green and white leaves of what I think is a birch tree sparkling just below. Evyatar was up and out quickly; I took a photo of him as he walked off, impressive young man, and wished him luck. I made an extravagant breakfast of eggs, toast, cheeses, jam, juice and coffee and, after washing my dishes and leaving a note of thanks, somewhat reluctantly put on my gear. It's a paradox: the more generous, hospitable, a Trail Angel is, the more you just want to stay and be pampered. Yet the stronger the feeling of gratefulness, the more you feel both energized and motivated to move on. It's almost an obligation to do so out of appreciation for their kindness. They've not hosted you because you're family or friends; they've gone out of their way to spoil you precisely to support your next stage of the journey! You feel like you owe it to them to get moving.

My phone rang, and it was his luck that I'd not yet turned it off: Evyatar had left his (other) phone on his bed. I was basically ready to leave, so I found it and set off down the hill. It was such a glorious morning—oh, what a beautiful morning indeed!—so I sang and sang as I walked down the road to the point where the Trail crossed under Israel's northern highway.

My mood was buoyant, for so many reasons. The first and most obvious explanation was the countryside. The winding road down from the Kibbutz through the forest reminded me of all the bike rides and hikes and drives I took as a kid growing up in northern California. I could almost see my dad striding ahead of me, as he always used to do, with a walking stick sometimes and a funky hat on his head. He loves to talk about his grandfather, Theodore Solomons, initiator of the Sierra's John Muir Trail as I described earlier. The trees and hills really did look and feel and even smell like those of the Coastal Range west of Menlo Park, where I grew up; Woodside, Portola Valley, SandHill Road and Laguna Honda were like my backyard. I had explored those hills and lanes in my most formative years: by foot; on my bike; on horseback (the memories of riding up to Windy Hill together with my first girlfriend, Nina, started to come back to me); later on my moped and then Vespa motor scooter and eventually (at 14, sorry Mom and Dad) by car. I felt like I was there again, and enjoyed the sensation.

Evyatar was waiting for me at the bottom. We took a last photo where the trail post indicated our direction: he to the North, I to the South, and that made the small re-connection fun; we quite literally headed off in opposite directions, and even waved to each other after a few hundred meters before he disappeared around a bend. Funny, how these brief associations added so much to the enjoyment of the trek.

People ask me sometimes what was my favorite part of the Shvil. I always preface any response with a disclaimer that every day, every segment, every aspect was simply incredible, and that I'm afraid to pinpoint even a few highlights as it seems to diminish the splendor and magnificence of all the others. And I choose those words carefully; it was, and is, truly magnificent, in all its aspects and diverse variety. Yet highlights there were, and favorites there are, and I would be remiss in not noting that when I consent to reply, my answer is: That day hiking up Nachal Dishon and Nachal Tzivon from Baram via Mt. Neria to Mt. Meron. Maybe it was the associations with my hikes in California with my family, my Skylake friends and colleagues, my youth groups and school groups and synagogue groups, and just with friends. Or maybe it was the greenness of the surroundings, which for whatever geological or historical reason was so much richer than anything I'd seen in the preceding days. Maybe it was the phenomenal, absolute, overpoweringly uplifting silence. Whatever it was, that day stands out as one of the most memorable in the trek.

The second aspect making that day so very special was the quiet. It was palpable, and palpably different than the silence of the desert. It was a moving, changing, whispering, buzzing, chirping, flowing silence. I stopped counting the different types of birdsong I could hear after reaching a dozen or so; in a meditative sort of way I knew they were there, I was there, they weren't singing for me but they were singing with me, I didn't disturb them nor they of course me. I sang—how I sang!—for hours. (I actually recorded myself singing *HaAretz HaZot*, for Philip and Flo—my "Outlaws" now, yet for whom I retained, and retain, an abiding love and admiration, affection and appreciation —but no one else will ever hear that recording. Never. Unless they sell it. Which they won't, as they still love me. I hope.)

I walked along ridges of green wild grasses with trees dotting their tops, and along expanses of flowering fields surrounded by tall evergreens and short round oaks, with the Dishon stream running through them cutting a blue/green/black ribbon dotted by white Egrets on the bank. If I came too close, the Egrets would rise up, circle around ever higher, and then settle back down where they were. I climbed up the Tzivon dry creek bed, scrambling among the brambles, muttering to myself "why don't they clear this off?" I had expected the day to be easier; but even the heat and slope, rocks and trees and vines combined couldn't put a dent in my mood.

A third facet which made that morning glorious, not just beautiful, was that I was heading south, and I really felt I was making my way home. I had circumnavigated Beit Shemesh, not stepping foot in my house, preventing myself from being tempted by always focusing on the Trail and my commitment to see it through. Now I was focused *davka* on doing just that: I was walking home! I knew I was not like David Grossman's heroine in his recent book *To the Ends of the Land*, running away from her pain. Whatever running away I had perhaps done, now I was returning to my point of departure, reconciling with my pain, heading back to where I belong, to real life. And that felt good, and strong. I felt a bit like a horse, who, when his head is turned toward home, instinctively picks up his pace.

A fourth aspect of that extraordinary day was being, once again, all alone. And the aloneness was welcome, and welcoming. I was happy with myself, and happy to be with myself. I continued to sing as I came into a clearing at the crest of the stream bed, and then went silent as I saw a number of huge butterflies, white and gray with patterns and yellow and green and light blue, all seeming to dance and play with each other as a sign of welcome to a hot and bothered but happy and smiling hiker. The quiet again was comforting; as I walked, I was at peace, and looking forward in every way.

Lastly, I used the term "buoyant" above as that most accurately describes my frame of mind that morning. I felt like a burden had been lifted, as I had crossed a new threshold—that of real forgiveness. In the desert, I experienced the liberating effect of humility and acceptance and my optimism had returned to me. That was intensified by the gratitude which circumnavigating Beit Shemesh had reinforced. But this week, that appreciation led to the ability to forgive. Truly forgive. And reaching that level of absolute forgiveness was simply redemptive. It went well beyond, and deeper, and was more powerfully absolute than the initial forgiveness I found that day in those four steps on the balcony at Bat Ayin. This feeling of deliverance was the primary source for the incredible lightness of being I experienced while walking and singing and climbing and swimming through those spectacular green mountains of the upper Galil.

Crossing the northern highway where it meets the Trail near Kibbutz Sasa, I could have jumped in a car and gotten a ride home, I felt so light and "complete." But of course no, I wanted to finish the journey.

Sasa! Oy the memories, of the Second Lebanon War. Here I am, feeling "at peace"; the last time I was here it was hardly peaceful. I was serving in the IDF Spokesperson's Unit during Israel's Operation Change of Direction in response to Hezbollah's continuing deadly terror attacks. I wonder—how far up the road is that room we stayed in? Can I walk it? Would it still be available to crash in? I still can't believe the conditions we put up with, Michael, Marcus, David, Dan, Doron and all the rest of us. A bunch of 40+ year olds sleeping on mattresses and kids' cots, then and even more today successful bankers, NGO heads, film writers, authors, an ambassador even. I'd actually like to go back there, to enjoy the peace and tranquility of this idyllic spot. Maybe one day I'll come up here on vacation. But not now; checking the map, I see it's a few kilometers away, and I've arranged to be picked up by my cousin Chagit in a few hours. At least I can stop here at the side of the road for a rest in the shade by a little creek.

As I sit on a small boulder and listen to the trickle of this cheerful stream, my thoughts turn not surprisingly back to my new favorite subject of forgiveness. I now realize: I've come far, but I'm only halfway there. I've forgiven Karen—a while ago and now more recently—in many ways, for many things. But I am not done yet; with all my intellectualizing, something seems to be missing. I know I have more work to do: and listening to the birdsong all around me, what better place and time than now? So I take off my pack, pull out my burner and pot, and make a cup of herbal tea.

*My cup in hand, I walk slowly through the trees. Forgiveness, mercy (Gods and people's), compassion and reconciliation are constant themes in Jewish prayer and tradition, from the Golden Calf through modern times. Something comes to me; I begin meditate on the phrase "*סלחתי כדבריך*" Salachti k'dvarecha, "I have forgiven according to your words," which has a central place in our prayers on before and on Yom Kippur, the Day of Atonement (from* Bamidbar, *or* Numbers, *14:20). Or maybe that's not the right translation. The Hebrew is complex; it could be "as per your sayings" or "ideas" or "doings." I'm aware that I'm thinking in English; it occurs to me I could translate it as "I have forgiven according to your* things." *Meaning: according to the things you have done, the things you are, the content or essence of you, I forgive. Meaning: I forgive all the things you have done, and I forgive all the ways you are and have behaved, whether I understand them or not, whether I agree with them or not. Wow—did I read this somewhere? Is there a source in Jewish tradition which could corroborate this translation? I know my Hebrew pretty well; it's not a farfetched approach, even if it's not the normative interpretation.*

"But forget whether it's a conventional reading of the text!" I say to myself. This idea fills me with wonder, and with a poetic meaning; an almost revelatory awe. I have forgiven Karen intellectually; I have found or concocted all sorts of explanations for her actions. But I have not forgiven her completely; I have not truly forgiven ALL her actions, nor have I done so with my HEART rather than my head, even at the pool a few days ago. I must forgive her כדבריך—*k'dvarecha—within the context of all the myriad things which made her who she is and caused her to act as she did; and I must do so with all my being, not only cerebrally.*

I'm walking in circles; and thinking in circles too. The day is hot, but the tall pine trees provide ample shade; I'm stepping around small rocks and treading a pattern now in the green & yellow tall grass. I can do this. I wander a bit further, toward a small hillock beyond the trees. I'm meditating and not; thinking and not. I'm walking and climbing and standing and turning; looking all around and seeing very little. I am doing this. I am full of love: I feel all the love of my children and my family and my friends and all the strangers-who-are-friends I've met on the Trail (and throughout my life). And, also, I feel a fullness of love within me, bursting to escape, to be felt, to be expressed, to be given.

And then all these thoughts of love bring me to a pinnacle of understanding. From this feeling of love inside me, I start to meditate on the second paragraph of the

Sh'ma, Judaism's primary statement of identity and the foremost expression of the
love *between the Jewish nation and the Divine.*

וְאָהַבְתָּ אֵת ה' אֱלֹהֶיךָ בְּכָל לְבָבְךָ וּבְכָל נַפְשְׁךָ וּבְכָל מְאֹדֶךָ. וְהָיוּ הַדְּבָרִים הָאֵלֶּה אֲשֶׁר אָנֹכִי
מְצַוְּךָ הַיּוֹם עַל לְבָבֶךָ . . .

"And you shall love the Lord your God with all your heart and all your soul and
*all your might. And these words [*דברים*] . . . shall be in/on your heart . . ." (*D'varim/
Deuteronomy 6:5)

What an incredible connection: the "words" (d'varim) must be in your heart;
the same Hebrew term for word/thing *used above. All these words/things/actions, all*
these THINGS *which I'm forgiving—it must be from the heart, in the heart, of the*
heart. Love God with all your heart; God forgives according to your words/actions/
things; you can forgive according to her actions/things, out of love with all your heart.
This I understand. I get it. I truly, clearly, deeply, intellectually and emotionally and
psychologically, forgive her.

It is done.

By the time I reached the slopes of Mt. Neria at the approaches of Mt. Meron,
after another hour or two of hiking along winding paths through woods of pine
and birch, I reckoned that I had solved not only my personal problems but all the
problems of the world. And that was a good thing: Mt. Meron is one of Judaism's
spiritual meccas, where Yochanan Ben Zakkai, the rabbi considered the founder
of Jewish mysticism, the *Kabbalah*, is buried. And perfecting the world, removing the "*klippot*" or external layers hiding inner truths, is one of the essential elements of the *Kabbalah*. Though I'm no scholar of these sacred traditions, I knew
enough to appreciate the powerful, subliminal connection between my personal
struggles and those of the Jewish people and of all peoples. So the ascent up Har
Neria and Har Meron were faster and lighter, smoother and more graceful than
they might have been, in the heat of mid-afternoon: I almost felt myself being
pulled up, lifted and buoyed by the waves of inspiration and illumination my
thoughts brought on.

Mulling over these reflections on love and forgiveness, I take a break for lunch at
the top of Har Neria; I so appreciate the bread and cheese and tomatoes from Baram!
Christoff, a young man from Poland, joins me for a few minutes and we chat briefly
about his interest in Israel and Jews. The lookout is impressive; you can see far into
Lebanon from it. I'm moved by a plaque dedicated to the son of neighbors from when
we lived in Givat Ze'ev, Uriel Peretz, who fell in the (First) Lebanon War in 1998.
I've heard his mother speak movingly about her loss—of two sons in fact. Her second,
Eliraz, died in 2010 in Gaza. And then her husband died as well, seemingly from
a broken heart. She is inspiring in her devotion to Israel, our people and nation.
Reading the few lines in the memorial plaque I turn somewhat melancholy, enjoying
the haunting beauty of the area but remaining acutely aware of how much blood has
been spilled over the past century in reclaiming it. Here in the North the heartache is
so real. Yet at the same time I recognize, looking out over the rolling hills all around

and not for the first time, how much room there is for us all, if only we could find a way to live in peace with each other.

Arriving at the top of Har Meron, I come across a large and boisterous gang of teenagers, boys and girls, singing and running and making noise; Arab-Israelis, normal kids, having a fun day out. I sort of wonder why their school took them here, as opposed to other hilltops in the area, but presume the reason was no more complicated than that Har Meron is the highest lookout point in the region, without reference to the historical or religious significance of the site to the Jewish people. Nodding and smiling, I walk through them and around them, past the crown of the mountain, to rest in the shade on a picnic table next to the parking lot. My cousin Chagit and I arranged earlier for her to meet me, and I know she's on her way, so with more than a half-hour to kill I take out my little guitar and start to play a bit.

Soon, a small group of seven or eight of the teens approaches me; it appears they're waiting for their bus, are somewhat bored, and seem a bit intrigued by this gray-haired guy in shorts and a backpack picking away and singing quietly. Coincidence or not, I happen to be playing Simon & Garfunkel's "Feeling Groovy," and one of them recognizes it (with a holler!) and starts to sing along—much louder than I've been playing. I don't mind. Soon we're singing a few S&G tunes, ending with "The Boxer" which even the kids who didn't know the song join in, on the "Lai la lai" chorus of course. Music, a common language between Israeli and Arab, between Jew and Arab/Muslim/Christian, between old and young, between American and Middle Eastern . . .

Afterwards, one of the boys asks for the guitar, and plucks a bit without any real direction (or training) as we banter. Lots of laughter accompanies our various questions/answers; it turns out the kids are from a small village called Alut in the southern part of the Galilee, near Nazareth, out for their annual school trip. I'm quite intrigued by the variation in their command of Hebrew; it reminds me of my mother's experience teaching English as a second language to Hispanics in California—some are fully fluent, others speak haltingly. But all are friendly (and excited as only young teenagers can be); all are completely unfamiliar with the Israel Trail and fascinated by the idea and by my story. In answering their incredulity—"but why?!"—regarding the idea of someone wanting to walk the entire length of the country, I take a minute to explain the connection between Am Yisrael *the* People *of Israel,* Torat Yisrael *the* Torah *or* Religion *of Israel,* Eretz Yisrael *the* Land *of Israel, and* Medinat Yisrael *the* State *of Israel.*

They have never heard of all these connections.

This got me thinking, as the kids climbed on their bus and waved to me as they drove away, and as I sat and strummed quietly once again while waiting for Chagit. When those of us involved in promoting and defending Israel talk about the misinformation so prevalent in public discourse throughout the world at the highest political echelons, and among leaders of the world's churches, academics and the general public, we often forget two fundamental things. First, much of the hostility against Israel comes from ignorance rather than anti-Semitic Jew-hatred or animosity toward the Jewish State. And second, much of this lack of knowledge begins here in Israel. This is true among many Jews, let alone Arabs, Muslims, Christians, and others here in the Holy Land.

Many—most?—leaders and people view Judaism as a religion. It is seen as a faith community and system of beliefs and practices no different than Christianity, Islam, Buddhism and the like. Even many who consider themselves "pro-Israel," who support Israel's right to exist as a Jewish state and her right to defend herself against those who attack her and her citizens, are often acutely uncomfortable with the idea of a democracy giving priority to one *religion* over another. Moreover, those who are ambivalent, or hostile to Israel, would seem to have justice on their side: If, as demonstrated by those Arab Muslim kids on Har Meron, one views the "Jewish" state as a theological construct, religious in nature, and if one views those "of the Jewish religion" who came here in the past century as Europeans without any link to this land, then by definition they can be seen as interlopers, colonists, and "occupiers."

Yet the truth—objective, historical, legal truth, with no political agenda—is quite different. The people of Israel were sovereign in this land thousands of years prior to the Greeks, Romans, Byzantines, Persians, Arabs, Turks and others who have resided or governed here. No other national or even ethnic group has been sovereign here, as their homeland. Ever. Jews are the indigenous people of the land, with a direct, historical, and continual connection to it—even a linguistic connection, between *"Jew"* and *Ju*dea, between *"Am* (People of) *Yisrael"* and *"Eretz* (Land of) *Yisrael."* That the Jews are a distinct national ethnic group was acknowledged by the international community a hundred years ago, in every discussion of the nation's return to its land and in the many instruments of international law which led to the founding of Israel as the modern nation-state of the Jewish people. The Children and Nation of Israel re-established our sovereignty in our ancestral homeland, where our forefathers and prophets walked and reigned and lived and died, and where we have had a continuous presence for 3,500 years: the State of Israel.

In other words, the state of the Jews is not a "Jewish" state in a religious sense. In fact, anthropologists and sociologists have argued for years whether to describe the Jews as a "civilization" like that of the Japanese and Chinese, or to subsume Judaism under "Western civilization" (or to see the Jewish civilization as the precursor to Western civilization). But this esoteric academic debate serves to powerfully demonstrate the complexity of Jewish identity, well beyond any simplistic religious definition. The Children of Abraham, Isaac and Jacob/Israel became a clan, then a tribe, and then a nation in its exodus from Egypt and entry into the Promised Land, some 3,500 years ago. Zionism is, by definition, the national liberation movement of that Jewish people. And the Arab-Israel conflict stems from the violent rejection of these facts by Arab and Muslim leaders.

When this history, this reality, is understood, much of the hostility toward Israel dissipates. Legitimate policy debate continues—including discussions of whether Israel should or should not withdraw from the territories of Judea and Samaria (the "west bank" of the Jordan river). Israel gained possession of this heartland of the Jewish people in a defensive war in 1967, and asserts claims to it from the original Mandate given to Great Britain by the League of Nations to re-establish the Jewish homeland almost a hundred years ago. Reasonable people can and do disagree about whose claim is stronger—the Arab residents of the territories, known over recent years as "Palestinians," or the Jews (the original "Palestinians" of 100 years ago). And reasonable people can argue also about how to manage historical and legal issues with justice and morality, let alone geography and politics (including where the eastern 70 percent of mandatory "Palestine," now known as Jordan, fits in, with its population which is 80 percent "Palestinian').

In fact, the pros and cons of any given Israeli policy, from its defensive military operations to the building of Jewish communities in Judea and Samaria, can be intelligently debated. But ambivalence toward Israel's very legitimacy, not to mention the vicious opposition to Israel's founding and continued existence, is based on ignorance of this historical reality at best, and at worst on an educational and cultural milieu which distorts it, primarily in the Arab and Muslim worlds but in the West as well.

I began to think, not for the first time, that the acceptance on a national level must be related to this reality. And a forgiveness for perceived or actual injuries—something I spent some time thinking about while walking near the border with Lebanon—cannot possibly be achieved if there is no understanding of the sources of the connection between the Jewish nation and its land.

My brief exchange with that small group of Arab Israeli teens made me both disheartened and hopeful. Dismayed, because I knew that such unawareness permeates Arab-Israeli, mostly Muslim, society—and this is true even in the situation where Israel itself supervises the education system and curriculum these students learn in! These youths were so oblivious to the Jews with whom they share this small country. How can we hope to build peaceful relations internally, let alone with our neighbors, if there is such ignorance?

But I was encouraged too, because I could see how fascinated these kids were by this new information, how eager to learn more, and how intelligent their questions were. These young people, having grown up in a free society in Israel's robust democracy, approached me with no reluctance; they were open to learning new information and willing to process the ideas and challenges it raised. I hoped that with their eyes being opened to these facts, they began then and there to develop a more informed and nuanced approach to understanding the complexity of our situation in Israel. And that, I thought as I played Simon and Garfunkel's "Sound of Silence" quietly to myself, is central to reaching an accommodation based on these themes of humility, acceptance, gratitude, and forgiveness I was developing on the trek.

As these thoughts were percolating in my head, Chagit drove into the parking lot; I jumped up and ran to greet her like the long-lost relative she actually was. It was so sweet of her—driving almost an hour from home just to pick me up, drive back to her home, give me dinner (kosher, with some effort and improvisation), wash my clothes and all the rest. Chagit is my only relative in Israel, my second-cousin-once-removed (her grandmother and my great-grandmother were sisters, in Hungary). Though she is completely secular in outlook and practice, Chagit and I had become closer over the past decade or two.

As we drove to her home and ate supper, we spoke of many things, including comparing notes on our incomparable experiences: her continued mourning over the loss of her husband Yoav less than a year previously, and my continued mourning over the loss of my marriage. She powerfully reinforced for me the importance, and relevance, of the ideas I'd been thinking of those past few weeks, as I shared them with her. She, too, had reached a level of acceptance, based on a profound sense of humility, though she doesn't necessarily define it as such, and certainly not with any religious or even spiritual overtones regarding God as Creator and the like. And she, too, expressed a deep gratitude for the years she had with Yoav, for their children and grandchildren, and even for the extension of time with him beyond that which the doctors had estimated. Chagit has little to forgive, and no real address to complain to other than a nebulous "fate," as it were; but she herself came to a form of forgiveness in her acceptance of Yoav's death as a part of the life she built, and spoke clearly of not having any regrets.

Later that evening, in the quiet of her guest room, I spent a good two hours laying out the framework for my final three weeks on the Shvil. I compiled a few to-do lists, called Meira and Zvi, did some bank stuff via my phone (celebrating the technology which enables us to be "connected" even if we're disconnected from everything normal), and fell into bed exhausted, knowing that the next day would be hard but fun, hiking down Har Maron and then up to the holy city of Tzfat to spend Shabbat with my friends Avraham and Ruth. It was indeed, and incredibly uplifting and enjoyable to boot.

The sun is still relatively low in the East, having risen a few hours ago from behind the Golan Heights which I can still see in the distance through the haze as I bounce down the eastern slopes of Har Meron toward Nachal Meron. I just can't believe my luck. I want to sing! I want to dance, I want to call someone, I want to meditate, I want to celebrate and ululate and undulate! I'm feeling the effects of eating too much of Chagit's homemade whole wheat bread this morning (Yoav's recipe and specialty, actually). So I'm taking it slowly; I supposed "bouncing" is a bit of hyperbole. It's a bit harder than I had thought it would be (and what are these uphill parts? We're supposed to be heading down *the mountain), but I'm so enjoying it.*

I stop about halfway down and take out my guitar. Remarkably, I'm singing about the Messiah while on the slopes of Har Meron, looking at the holy city of Tzfat across the hills and valleys, in the lead-up to Shabbat. In fact, it's downright extraordinary; reminds me of my days as a student, taking my guitar on a Friday afternoon up to the crest of Windy Hill above my home in Menlo Park or riding to a hilltop outside of London on my motorcycle, to welcome Shabbat in my own distinctive fashion. It's uplifting, a bit weird perhaps . . . and simply wonderful.

I'm singing Shabbat songs—including L'cha Dodi, Come Greet the [Sabbath] Bride, the mystical poem and song sung around the world to welcome Shabbat written by Rabbi Isaac Luria right here in Tzfat in the fifteenth-century—and then all my usual standards . . . but now it's time to get moving. Shabbat is coming!

At the foot of Mt. Meron, I took a break to eat and drink and rest, at a table in the shade of tall evergreens near the entrance to Moshav Meron. It was quiet; a family with three small kids picnics nearby, the children running around a little bit too much for my taste, so I reached a quick decision. I had planned to hitch a ride up to Tzfat from the moshav, and had allowed myself to both take it slow down the hill and to play guitar for a bit longer than might have been prudent. But at that point, seeing Tzfat up ahead through the trees—about five kilometers, perhaps, as the crow flies—and looking down the valley covered in pink and purple blossoms and sixteen (or so) different shades of green, I just decided to go for it: I'd hike up to Tzfat! (First *down* to Nachal Amud, and then *up* Nachal Shechvi)!

"How hard can it be?!?" I asked myself; and I wanted to dip in a spring or pond before Shabbat in any case if I could. A fitting, if somewhat clichéd,

Aryeh on Mt. Meron with Tzfat in the background

preparation for a mystical Shabbat in mystical Tzfat. I figured I could make it before the onset of the Sabbath ... but knowing Ruth and Avraham, I felt comfortable risking being a bit late even, since they are some of the most relaxed, accepting, and generous people on the planet.

And oh, it was worth it. From the moment I set out, passing the largest, most striking pink-and-violet-blossoms tree and traipsing through a long and narrow wadi full of fallen and decaying logs by the stream, I was enthralled. What a way to bring in Shabbat! I wound my way down (and a bit up) to Ein Yakim spring, where I jumped in the water in my underwear since I wasn't alone, almost but not quite a full pre-Shabbat mikvah dip (which must be unclothed) but so glad I did it. The water was crisp and clear and cool, and deliciously invigorating, physically and emotionally and spiritually.

The path then continued on down, past other springs including a few you can't even see from the trail but you can hear the young people laughing and splashing in through the trees. (I wanted to stop and slide in to each one; couldn't afford the time.) I strode on, noting in my mind the location and surroundings, promising myself to return one day to enjoy them properly. I found myself literally walking through a tunnel, a sort of vine-and-tree parapet which continued for about fifty meters. This, and a number of stunning wildflowers, made this extra effort that much more worthwhile; I stopped to take photos so often I ended up talking firmly out loud to convince myself to stop it and keep going.

I sang most of the way that day; sometimes softly to myself, sometimes loudly enough to startle a bird or two. At one point I spied a hawk circling above. Standing very still, I watched as it circled, slowly, lower and lower, approaching and then soaring away from the face of the cliff, and then disappeared off to the South. Not certain why, but this moved me: the sense of purpose, of dedication, in nature's combining function and aesthetics, in the quiet of a Friday afternoon, as the sun glinted off the tips of its brown wings.

I reached Nachal Shechvi and its pools (not enough water to be worth going in) at 3:30 p.m. With Shabbat coming in about 5:30 p.m., and not sure how long it would take to climb up to Tzfat from the stream bed, nor how difficult the ascent would be, I just started up the trail along Nachal Shechvi which takes you to the western edge of the city. And I noticed something: after all my steep climbs in the South, I didn't find it all that difficult, sort of like the previous days' climbs up Har Neria and Har Meron, Nachal Dishon and Nachal Tziv'on. That's pretty funny, I thought as I reached the top: 700-meter descent, then 400-meter ascent, about an 18-kilometer hike on a Friday—no problem!

At the top, I caught a ride with my friend Zvi, who'd come out to find me (having come up to spend Shabbat with us—obviously he hadn't had enough of my company the week before). I enjoyed the respite while we drove through the narrow one-way cobblestone streets of Tzfat's old city; I reached Avraham and Rutie's at 4:30 p.m., well before Shabbat.

Shabbat was a pleasure; Avraham and Rutie were, as ever, the warm and welcoming hosts I had come to know over the years we lived near each other in Beit Shemesh, and the mystical ambience of Tzfat on Shabbat was palpable. On Shabbat morning, I left shul in the middle of the service, feeling a bit out of place and pining for the peace and tranquility of the desert, or the Ashram, or at least the forest of the previous week. Wandering the streets of the old city, I bathed in the sights and sounds—and smells!—of a traditional Tzfat Shabbat. Singing wafted through the air from synagogues representing all the children of Israel, Yemenite and Moroccan and Ashkenazic and Hassidic, sometimes along the same alley. Even without the quiet, and with the cacophony of eccentric people and over-crowded streets and synagogues, I made an effort to enjoy, and succeeded in feeling the spirit of the place.

I walked through the old city for about an hour, not wanting to return to the somewhat stuffy shul, hoping and assuming Avraham and Zvi wouldn't be worried as to where I was. (They weren't.) At one point I came across a small plaza, bathed in sunlight, where a few groups were milling about or walking through. I had to stop my singing; I had been warbling a few prayer-songs as I wandered the ancient alleys in my *Tallit* prayer shawl—and I very slightly resented their presence and its intrusion into my reverie. This was MY Shabbat, MY city, MY movie I was starring in! But just as those thoughts came into my mind—and just as I realized how silly, immature, unfair, and selfish they were, too—something else struck me.

I became aware how special, and beautiful, the scene I was witnessing was. I so wished I could have photographed it. (Photography is prohibited on Shabbat.) At a single moment, un-choreographed (except from Above), there were four different, even "opposing," groups of people in that little square. About eight Christian tourists in bright hats, led by a guide, looked up at an old terracotta shingled roof (I wondered what significance that building has, though never discovered); three Arab Muslim men waited for something under an awning; two bearded, hatted Hassidim with five small children hurried diagonally from one corner to the other, rushing home from shul perhaps; and two Israeli secular teens sat in the shade of a corner, by an arched entrance to another alley, looking at their phones.

It was the sort of sight that one takes for granted once you've lived in Israel for a few decades, and that telescopes, in a split second, so much of what is unique and wonderful about this country. In a moment of extreme clarity, as my eyes took in the tableau I not only instantly forgave the "interruption" of my singing; I reminded myself how that very forgiveness I'd been contemplating all week was essential for my own well-being—not to mention my enjoyment of Shabbat. And, as important, how much that forgiveness rests on an acceptance of all these others, who have every much right to be in, and enjoy, that little square as I do. It's THEIR city, THEIR Shabbat, THEIR movie as much as it is mine; and that very acceptance rests itself on the humility I'd been considering a few weeks previously. All this came to me in less time than it takes to write it; I spent the next ten minutes smiling as I walked back to join my friends at shul, full of the gratitude which comes from appreciating the world around me, not to mention the simple but plain messages God sometimes sends us.

We walked home from shul leisurely, for lunch and a rest, and then the third meal. I took the seat looking out the picture window to the West as the sun set behind Har Meron, where I had descended—and played guitar!—just the previous day. By Shabbat's end I was rested and full; Rutie and Avraham (aka "King of Soups") had fed us until we were close to bursting. I was ready to get back to the Shvil.

My Facebook post that Motzei Shabbat (Saturday night, March 22) summarizes surprisingly well how I felt as I walked these northern reaches of the country:

Starting to hike south Monday (mostly west in fact, but whatever) I noticed a few things. The scenery is radically different of course—bright shades of green in the trees and fields and mountains all around, streams with strikingly clear (and cold!) water flowing strongly, a riot of different colored flowers (which if you'd like to see photos, go to [my former mother-in-law] Flo's wall where I've been posting a few, as she's my gardening and flower guru), and orchards and vineyards and terraces galore. Slight change from the Judean desert.

But I've noticed also that I am walking faster and further with less difficulty: is it that I'm in better shape? Or is it because the weather is milder? Or the ascents and descents less steep? (Not the latter; yesterday I descended 750 meters & climbed up 400, over about 21 km, in less time & effort than similar hikes took me in the South.) Possibly all. But there's more. I have the growing feeling that I'm nearly done; that I've achieved what I've set out to do; that I'm walking home. And this seems to make the pack lighter (it isn't), the distances shorter (not). I guess I'm beginning to feel "lighter" in some way.

Yet, also, being in the North has introduced an element of pathos into this whole business. I am now walking the paths described in David Grossman's powerful book אישה בורחת מבשורה [Isha borachat m'besora—Lit. "A woman runs from a message" but titled in English To the Ends of the Land] and I keep asking myself—am I running away from something too? Am I in denial, like Ora in Grossman's dramatic but tender take on loss and escape and confusion? (An intensely riveting story if you haven't read it—and one quintessentially Israeli.) I've more or less decided not; I'm not her, this isn't that; but the congruency still strikes me as somehow poignant.

So the week was a combination of phenomenal scenery—the Hermon and Hula Valley, the hills of Lebanon & the Upper Galil, Snir & Dishon & Tzivyon & Meron & Amud streams, Meron & Neria & Naphtali & other mountains—and not a few ups and downs of a more personal nature . . . but on the whole extremely positive and wonderfully enjoyable. I walked through a few places I'd been before (like Nachal Snir, but this time no Aaron to carry me!) and many I'd seen from a distance or driven past but never really appreciated. Walking through (and sometimes sleeping in) some of Israel's and Zionism's pioneering settlements—like Dafna, Kfar Giladi and Ramot Naftali, kibbutz Baram and others, is strangely comforting, and inspiring. The hidden dark green and mustard brown valleys of Nachal Dishon and the trickling brooks surrounded by purple and pink and red and yellow and orange and magenta flowers in Nachal Tzivyon are so incredibly, stunningly beautiful it makes you want to cry. I didn't; but it does.

Chapter Six

NORTHERN TRANQUILITY: MORE GRATITUDE, AND MORE HISTORY

[Week Six]

Sunday, March 23, dawned hot and dry. After prayers overlooking Har Meron and the mountains I was about to descend, and a quick breakfast with Avraham and Rutie and Zvi, I literally walked out the door and back to the Trail. That was a good feeling, just setting out from where I'd slept, rather than being driven to a trailhead; I liked this aspect of continuing on the Shvil, like the first weeks down South. I stumbled down the steep eastern slope of the city, right through the ancient cemetery of Tzfat.

I stopped for a moment, doing a bit of a double-take, at the tomb of Channah. Yes, *that* Channah, of the Chanukah story, with her seven sons, all of whom according to tradition defied the Greek tyrant Antiochus and were murdered for their unwillingness to violate Jewish law. Once again, I was taken aback at the casual way we/I take the things we're used to in stride. Though I was aware of the questionable historical accuracy of this being their actual burial place, I was still moved, as I was when I stumbled on the prophet Isaiah's tomb the previous week. Our history, my history, is all around us when we walk this Land. Our land. Not in a possessive or exclusive way; we share it, after all, with Arabs and Druze, Muslims and Christians, Melkites and Karaites and Samaritans and Circassians and many others. It's the connection: History here is not *his* story, it is *our* story, my story.

I noticed a small distance away the graves of Rav Yosef Caro and Rabbi Isaac Luria, two of the most important thinkers and spiritual leaders in Jewish history, the former a great halakhist whose decisions still today form the basis of Jewish law and practice, the latter perhaps the greatest mystic and conveyer of the Kabbalah (and composer of the Shabbat hymn mentioned earlier). I was a bit thrown, standing there in my shorts and sunglasses with my backpack on and itching to get down to the Shvil, thinking, "Why didn't we come here on Shabbat, just two minutes away from the Zimbergs' apartment?!?" I did not want to be so disrespectful as just to traipse through the cemetery and be on my way. So I paused for a moment, but then, content in my knowledge that both they and the others buried there would delight in my love of this land and people, our history and tradition which so inspired the trek, I walked on.

I felt connected—to my people, my past, my homeland . . . and my future, and our future. On a much more mundane level, though, I was a bit confused regarding my more immediate future. Not sure exactly where the cemetery road connected to the lane heading down to the trailhead, and it already being hot, I trudged through an industrial area and, impatient in the end, flagged down a passing car as I left the factories behind and headed down a slight incline toward the trees and fields in the distance. What luck! The fellow wasn't only heading to the trailhead; it turns out there's a ma'ayan (spring) right there. My destination for the day's hike was the Kinneret (Sea of Galiliee), some 20 kilometers south. Who was I to refuse his suggestion to take a quick, refreshing dip prior to starting the descent into Nachal Amud, the long, steep, deep canyon that would lead me there? Bini would have liked the guy.

A well-constructed modern enhancement to an ancient spring, Ein Koves consists of a shallow square of water built with light-colored Jerusalem stone, a few water channels, and an arched roof covering a deeper recessed pool. I not only jumped in; I filled up my water bottles and Camelback with the crystal clear, incredibly cold, fresh spring water, replacing the (not bad, but still) tap water. Drying in the sun, I relaxed and chatted with the three men who had come for their morning dip, including the fellow who gave me a ride, a pleasant, simple, sweet thirty-something Yemenite Jew with a scrappy beard and *peyot* (side curls). They had never heard of Shvil Yisrael and were fascinated; I invited them to join me for the day, but the driver said he had to get to work, at a local factory we had passed driving down the slope.

I basked not only in the warmth of the sun but in the warmth of an overpowering sense of contentment and gratitude. "Who is as lucky as I am?" I thought to myself. And then I said it out loud, to the guys there, who looked at me a bit strangely, I have to admit. So I explained a little about my trek and why I felt so lucky; and they looked at me even more strangely. "You should be a Bratslaver!" one said (ie. a follower of Rebbe Nachman of Bratslav). I laughed and said, "מצווה גדולה להיות בשמחה תמיד"—"It's a great thing, a commandment even, to always be happy/joyous"—perhaps the most famous saying of Rebbe Nachman, who was a disciple of the Baal Shem Tov and a founder of one of the most famous Hassidic sects in Judaism. Put another way, in my lexicon, we are commanded to rejoice in God's world constantly, to be not only satisfied but fulfilled with our lot, and to celebrate all the gifts God has given us in this world and in our lives. Which, it's true, I have to say, I do try to do. It's one of the 613 commandments I try my best to fulfill, and one of the easiest, usually, though one of the hardest, too, at times.

There's no question it's becoming easier to regain that sense of happiness as I learn the lessons of the Shvil, I think to myself as I dry off and pack up. Somewhat reluctantly, I head out across a field of weeds and small fruit trees, along an indistinct trail toward what looks like an abyss ahead: the descent into Nachal Amud. I'm humming my mini-mantra to myself—"רבות מחשבות בלב איש, עצת ה׳ היא תקום"—*"Many thoughts/plans take form in the heart of man; God's guidance/plan is what will take form." Earlier in this trek, that refrain held such a melancholy connotation—man plans, God laughs, etc.—and it was a plaint, an expression of grief and anger and resignation. And then it took on a different meaning when I learned acceptance, where the laughter was comforting, and healing. And now, it's shifted again, becoming a celebration and an expression of wonder: man is laughing at the wonder of God's plans, and in a way I'm laughing with God.*

Instead of seeing this verse from Mishlei (Proverbs) as an expression of frustration, or desperation, or lack of control, I feel it is much more a feeling of incredulity and delight and even tenderness. It's an intimacy born of great pain, and distance, and then closeness, showing God's love for us. As I approach the edge of the cliff I feel so grateful and happy that I'm bouncing down the path—and if God is looking, he's definitely laughing at me now, since my pack is about to pull me over the brink. Seriously! Skipping and dancing on a rocky trail with fifty pounds on your back isn't something I recommend unless you're filming slapstick or looking to make a fool of yourself.

I am so GRATEFUL! Who has this sort of life, this kind of opportunity, to explore, to wander, to dream, to meet people, to go on or rest or stay or move as the mood hits us? What wealth I possess, what privilege, what a miracle my life is. I am more than halfway through this adventure, I feel the pull of home and the prospect of moving on with my life, and I am so thankful I can almost feel the tears coming.

Or it might have been the sweat already getting into my eyes; the day had become hot. The map, and description in the Red Guide, were pretty clear—it's a steep descent, and then a relatively mild continuation down to the Kinneret. I enjoyed and photographed the view down the valley, impressive not only for the steep lines of the "V" created by both sides, but for the deep shades of green vegetation and trees, the bright blue of the sky in contrast—and the complete lack of any indication where a trail could possibly find its way down the cliff side. I wondered whether I'd mis-read the map, and checked, and re-checked, stopping every few minutes to recalibrate, and even to check my phone app "עמוד ענן" (*Amud Anan*—"Pillar of Cloud"—named after God's miraculous protective and guiding cloud). Only in Israel can you imagine having a hiking app called that. The app is a terrific resource showing trails, ma'ayanot (springs), streams, and sites, which I'd just discovered and started to use. Sure enough, I was on the right path. If you can call it a path—mountain-goat trail (or suicide walk) might be more appropriate.

Slipping, stepping carefully, holding on to branches or boulders, leaning in to the mountain-side, I managed to make my way down, and as the cliff turned into more of a steep slope and the path into a more recognizable trail through brambles and bushes, I relaxed for the first time in over an hour. I wasn't even aware, really, how tense I'd been on the way down. I hadn't really had that sort of stressful, anxious, challenging section since—well, since the Carbolet. At least now the rest of the day would be less difficult. Or so I thought.

"The Red Guide strikes again," I wrote in my journal later. There was no mention of the steep, cliff-hugging ascents (and descents), the rock climbing with iron railings and handholds to keep you from falling down thirty-meter drops, or the 8-inch-wide trails (20 centimeters) along the side of the valley walls. It was like Maale Palmach or Har Shlomo and Har Yehoram near Eilat all over again— just with green leaves/grasses and weeds brushing against my face or catching on the backpack to make it even more challenging. It was a significantly more difficult day than I had expected.

I began to feel a bit depressed, with the combination of the difficulty, the heat, the length of the day and, it seems, the prospect of another three weeks on the trail. Meira had said to me, "Only three weeks to go" on the phone the night before, but I started the day thinking, "Do I want three weeks more of this?"

Walking alone these past weeks, making conversation with hosts, feeling dirty and tired all the time, miserable much of the time with occasional peaks of joy and satisfaction, had gotten me down. An SMS exchange with Karen on

Nachal Amud cliffside

a mundane topic didn't help—not least when she asked, "How's it going?" and I started to obsess how to reply. "What do you care?" and "I still miss you" and "I don't want to be here and to be doing this alone" were among the responses I considered. I settled on "Okay, am getting there," which worked, with a few hidden meanings.

And then I walked straight into a cow.

Or, almost. Coming around a bend on a medium-steep decline, surrounded by shrubs and low trees, weeds and wild grasses, I came upon a huge cow, coming straight toward me, slowly, about three meters away, looking right at me, chewing. With another two close behind her/him/it.

Cow in Nachal Amud

"What are you doing here?" I'm thinking to myself, and then say out loud. "How'd you get on this cliff? And what're you doing on my trail?!" More importantly, "Why are you here? What are you looking for?!?" She's probably thinking the same thing. The problem is, the path is really narrow and the bushes all around kind of make it hard to move aside. At first, I'm pretty relaxed, saying to myself, "Okay: animal psychology." Eye contact; confidence; show who's boss, like with the horses I used to care for as a kid. Take a quick photo. But then I'm thinking, well, they're like 10 times my size and weight—maybe I should be the one to step aside. And who knows if my "confident" stare/stance might not be interpreted by their cow-brain as a threat?

So I move two steps up the steep hill/cliff, into the brambles my size; at nearly the same time she/they bolted down an unseen mini-"trail." The way they clamber through the brush, pushing aside or crushing underfoot everything in their way—including bushes twice my size and tree branches—makes be realize how smart I really am. Not sure they'd even notice if they stampeded right over me. Watching them go, I see there's another path—too narrow for me, how do THEY get through it?!?—through the trees. I'm glad for the encounter and (truthfully) glad it's over. But it makes me smile. I'm not completely alone on this mountain after all.

A short while later, I found myself pulling on a metal railing as I climb up the face of cliff, then down, at the bottom of a ravine. A sign appeared out of the blue: Danger! Cliff Edge! Which is somewhat humorous, since I'd been walking along a cliff's edge for a few minutes already, reminding me of Bill Crosby's famous routine from my childhood, "You've just hit a bump!" I took a selfie with a bit of a wry grimace, since I wasn't in the mood for cliff-grabbing, and I hadn't anticipated desert-cliff-type struggles here in the beautiful North. I thought I'd send the photo to the Nature Authority.

I struggled down over a few boulders, thinking to rest a bit in the shade of a tree growing out of the dry creek bed, and found myself teetering on the verge of a rather sharp, sloping piece of granite. Losing my balance, I tried to right myself with one of my walking sticks, which slipped. Falling about two meters down, I twisted to the right and put my arm out to stop my fall. As I tumbled, I remember thinking "That's hilarious, you're going to break your arm in a river bed, instead of on the Carbolet or something."

Among the lessons learned on the Shvil, that day I understood how *not* to fall. Most of us trained in various physical pursuits already know not to fall on your hands; to roll with impact, to use the judo-like principles of allowing the force of the fall to be managed in a way which can be less injurious than a direct impact. I knew this, but had I practiced it, perhaps I could have avoided what happened. Such things should be part of the preparation for such a trek. And I had already considered that with a pack on, the best tactic is to maneuver yourself to fall on your pack, so its bulk absorbs the impact and breaks your fall. So much for the theory. The weight of the pack pulled me down fast, there was no time to think and I reacted instinctively, reaching out with my right arm to break the fall with my forearm. Landing, I tried to roll to the right, but the pack itself just stopped me right there. I lay for a few seconds—probably about a minute or two—staring up at the trees, allowing the dust to settle, breathing . . . and performing what we're taught as IDF medics to do on arriving at an injury scene, a mental and physical "Baga'ch" or "B'dikat Guf Chafuza" (Quick Body Check), to ascertain if and where I was wounded.

I had badly banged my elbow and it really hurt; within a few minutes it was swelling, the arm red with angry scrapes, and started to throb. Thankfully, it wasn't broken; none of the other three signs of a break (deep bruising, severe pain and an unnatural bone angle) were evident, though the pain was intense and there was indeed some bruising. I felt sheepish; the only other injury, if it can even be called that, I suffered was a bang/bend of my finger trying to photograph a flower for Flo back at Lachish, and here I'd lost my balance on a rock in a creek-bed. I'm glad I don't have more interesting injury stories to tell.

Within a few minutes, I was having difficulty moving my arm. Though the pain had subsided somewhat, the throbbing continued. I sat for a good 30 minutes, washing/splashing the arm/elbow with cold water and gently massaging it, and passed the time making up all sorts of scenarios where an injury would seem cool and courageous and a few days or weeks recovery at home both credible and reasonable. At least I was in the shade of the trees and foliage at the bottom of the ravine; it wasn't cool exactly, but there was a slight breeze and I was protected from the sun.

It didn't help my mood much. If before falling I was somewhat quiet and down, the pain only increased my melancholy. Getting up, I simply trudged on, holding both walking sticks in my left hand, with limited movement in my right arm, which still seriously hurt. As I wrote in my journal, "So literally from 8:30 a.m. until 4:30 p.m. I walked silently—first time, really. No singing, no talking to myself, nothing. That itself was an experience, if not the most pleasant . . ."

Yet as I look back on it, the experience was edifying. With the light-hearted confidence and enjoyment of that morning, I had felt such deep appreciation. But that gratitude was then submerged under the loneliness and heat, difficulty and then pain of the day as it wore on. Though sometimes it would well up inside me and just burst forth, often it took energy and concentration to bring such appreciation and positive energy to light. On that day, I couldn't be *bothered* to perk myself up; I was *tired of making the mental and emotional effort.*

Where had I heard these refrains before? I realized those were Karen's words; that had been Karen's approach to the marriage, or to ending the marriage. I had resented it so, seen it as such a betrayal of not only me but of the marriage itself. I told her that if *we* don't make the effort to work at a relationship, it's doomed. In Nachal Amud, in the silence of the canyon, the power of that truism hit me when applied to our own internal "work": if I don't do the work, how can I expect to become or remain happy? That day taught me such an important lesson, even though it was one learned in the breach: By *not* making the effort to pull myself out of the silent, angry and depressing place I had descended to, I learned how important it is to make that effort. For all the humility, acceptance, gratitude and forgiveness we might find or create, if we don't constantly nurture and reinforce it, we lose it.

How can we continually maintain and fortify these themes in our lives? I found at least part of the answer on the side of a cliff there in Nachal Amud, an hour or so after starting out again after my fall.

As the incident described in the prelude relates, I literally hit a turning point. I won't repeat the description of finding myself at the end of a non-trail, on the side of the cliff, scared to go forward or move back; you're welcome to re-read those opening paragraphs now. The change in my mindset is what's significant: on the edge of that rock wall, I did the work, and made the effort. I focused my thoughts and emotions on an acceptance of the situation and on my ability—and the imperative—to overcome the challenge presented.

In a way, all the themes of the trip came together in that place to enable me to move forward (or backward a few steps, in this case, before continuing on). Humility and acceptance allowed me to have perspective; gratitude played a part both in my appreciation for the beauty in the midst of the difficulty and in my thankfulness for Crum's approach (those three breaths) and my own ability to take charge and work out a solution. Even forgiveness played a role, as I was forced to (or chose to) forgive myself for missing the markings on the cliffside, and to forgive nature for creating such difficulty (and the Shvil planners for their lack of clarity and, perhaps, wisdom).

Moreover, as also related in the opening paragraphs, I had a goal. A simple one: find the trail again. And a larger one: finish that day's hike. My more expansive goal of healing personally and moving on with my life, we'll address in coming chapters. But that moment where I'd lost my way on the edge of the cliff was one of the transformative episodes on the Shvil. Through sheer willpower, with tremendous internal effort, I overcame the fear and hesitation, and assertively found my way and moved on. I might not have been able to articulate it as such at the time, but it seems that was the point when my thinking began to approach clarity. It became evident to me how much of our suffering—and therefore how many of our mistakes, whether in private decisions or public policy—is based on our mental state, our perceptions of reality, our attitude, rather than on any real situation or challenge we face. It's literally all in your mind, and the power of positive thinking, whether articulated by Norman Vincent Peale, Napoleon Hill, Dale Carnegie or Stephen Covey, is one of the keys. I rediscovered that, on the flank of that canyon.

We can strengthen and consolidate all these elements—acceptance, gratitude, forgiveness, etc.—by our own determined strength of mind. I remembered, as I clambered up the side of that cliff in Nachal Amud, holding on to the metal rings in the rock, a wonderful turn of phrase from the description of the Children of Israel's initial foray into the Land of Israel. In the book of *BaMidbar*, Numbers, the Hebrew Bible describes how Moshe sent Yehoshua (Joshua) and Calev (Caleb) along with another ten emissaries to scout out the Land, prior to entering it. On the return of the twelve scouts, some reported that the inhabitants were huge, and conquering the Land was impossible. Calev argued forcefully that God's plans were feasible, saying כי יכול נוכל לה—We are well able to overcome. The source of the famous slogan of the American civil rights movement, "We shall overcome," this had always been a significant illustration for me of the power of our mindset, as individuals and as a people.

And so, forgiving myself for screwing up (again), I continued on my way, scrambling over a grassy incline. Fortunately, the remainder of the descent to the Kinneret was mild, if long and hot. It included a few pleasant incidents which did much to improve my disposition.

First, about an hour down the path, I came upon a massive highway expansion project. The Route 85 construction site was huge, and necessitated the boring of a special tunnel for Nachal Amud to flow through—and walking down the 100-meter or so length of the passage, I had to step over a special high-tech sonar mechanism of some kind which, according to the worker tending to it, measured seismic activity. Whether natural, or resulting from the digging going on all around (or the vehicular traffic just above), wasn't clear to me—but standing watching the gyro spin I regained the respect I've always held for engineering types. As a social science and humanities kind of guy, I don't understand how a bridge or building stays up or how an engine translates combustion into kinetic energy to move a car or how a plane doesn't fall from the sky. I get that it works, can comprehend some of the basics (I took Physics 10—"Physics for Poets"—at Berkeley), but I couldn't possibly explain how it works to my child. Marveling at this gigantic enterprise was actually a pleasure.

Like so many features of the trek, there was something refreshingly beautiful in having a different perspective on things I'd only seen before from the window of a car whizzing by. Seeing roadworks as you drive (or sit in traffic more likely) is either something to ignore or be irritated by. At a walking pace, it takes on not only greater significance, but becomes something to delight in.

And then I met the manager of the construction site. It was this unique—and uniquely Israeli—conversation that bolstered my mood.

Emerging from the tunnel, I see a hand-printed sign pointing to a detour—for Shvil Yisrael hikers. I almost trip down about a hundred steps, mostly dirt buttressed with wood timbers laid across. At the bottom I come upon a pickup truck stopped at the side of the dirt road on which a series of huge trucks ramble with rocks and stones and dirt. I so appreciate the stairs carved into the hillside—and the evident care with which they've been placed there—that I approach the driver and say good morning, and ask him whether they had been built especially for Shvilistim. With an Arab accent (we're speaking Hebrew of course), he says yes—and then launches into a glowing description of how important it is to him, individually, and to his company, to enable the continued use of the Trail, as well as the creation of an additional crossing I haven't seen, for animals, as they build the highway above.

We chat for a few minutes about the Shvil, with which he's clearly familiar, and about the beauty of the land and the importance of preserving it. We exchange thoughts on the imperative of retaining and strengthening our connection to the land, each of us using the inclusive pronouns of "we," "us," "our" to refer to our personal/familial/tribal/national link to this land. It is absolutely clear from everything in this conversation, not least our facial and body language, that we are of one mind. In spite of the fact that we refer to separate national and cultural, even spiritual cores of identity, it's clear we both recognize this, accept it, and even celebrate it. We share a love for this land, a connection to it and a willingness to share it with each other as well. All this within the space of five minutes of conversation.

What a miracle, I'm thinking to myself even as we talk, to be able to have this exchange. I'm so very aware of how strange this will sound to anyone whose knowledge of Israel comes only from the media and is focused only on "the conflict." As the discussion nears its natural conclusion, he offers the use of the site's "office" area, a shipping container a few hundred meters away, where there's water and a place to sit. I can't help thinking not only how wonderful, but how casual and "normal" this is. It's the way it should be, and I'm practically writing a few sentences in my head about this interaction for my next talk about those unknown sides of Israel with which so few people are familiar.

An Arab Muslim construction manager giving me the same heartfelt "kol haka-vod!" send-off—"good for you!"—which I'd received numerous times, including from the Jewish guys this morning at the spring near Tzfat, and those Beduoin Arabs in the Negev. It just fills me with wonder, and gratitude, and forgiveness, and humility. And hope for the future. I'm thinking all these things as I bang my bag down next to the picnic table at the site's office caravan, and the water I'm splashing on my face feels unusually cool and refreshing. After the somewhat heavy and gloomy start to the day, I'm feeling more upbeat now. And the throbbing in my arm has subsided a bit, so the pain is bearable. I enjoy a break under the ramshackle canopy of this lean-to sitting at a falling-apart picnic table, even if it's not exactly my preferred nature-spot for a rest.

Since it was well past noon, I had to keep moving, to get to the Kinneret by nightfall. The path led through a sort of meadow, and I was bathed in gentle sunlight filtered through dark green leaves of small trees, while surrounded by tall grasses with small wildflowers of various shades of pink, lavender, yellow, and blue. In the near distance were the hills of the continuation of Nachal Amud (and its ravine). Brown-streaked rocks and low blue-green bushes glittered in the bright light; above me were three hawks hunting high in the sky; close by, bees and flies and a hummingbird or two flittered in between the weeds and grass. I stopped to take a photo, though not for the first time asking myself how anyone can possibly appreciate how the combination of all this, and the silence envelop-ing it, is so incredibly moving, and uplifting.

I walked on. The silence was now comforting, the walk enjoyable and not too difficult. There were so many cows I stopped counting after another dozen or so. Cresting a small rise, I stopped short to stare at the carcass of a dead cow. Its bones were visible but it clearly hadn't been dead for long; it was pretty much intact, includ-ing part of its skin. "*Ikchsa*" as we say in Hebrew—yuck. I thought of the cow block-ing the path earlier—"Well, that'll show you"—and that led to all sorts of rumina-tions on mortality and the "cycle of life." The mood I was in made it less profound and more superficial than my usual musings; the tranquility of the surroundings and my upbeat temperament from the construction site just couldn't be squashed.

An hour later, I rounded a bend and saw from afar the "pillar" for which the canyon and creek is named (Nachal Amud means Pillar Stream). Taking out my camera I tried to frame the photo with the sides of the valley, trees, and the Shvil in the picture, with the haze from the Kinneret in the distance and the pillar in the foreground, and just as I pressed the button someone wandered into the frame.

I cursed to myself. Continuing down the path a few steps, I saw it was a woman—a young woman at that, with short hair (hence the tardy gender identifi-cation)—and then another came around a turn in the trail, about 30 meters or so behind her. The second hiker caught my attention as she was incredibly small; then the first hiker approached me and began to apologize for walking into my photo.

"Sorry for ruining your picture!" this slight young woman says to me in Hebrew. "Don't be silly," I reply. "It's nice to have a human being in a photo occasionally.

*You made it nicer!" We start the usual quick exchange—Are you hiking the Shvil?
Where'd you start today and where are you heading? Where're you from?—and as
we chat, the other catches up . . . and looks at me kind of funny. Just as an initial
recognition is dawning on me, though I can't place it or her, this petite girl says, "I
know you! You're Meira's father! You came to visit us at Ein HaNatziv, and I came
to you for Shabbat!" I can't believe it—that's just too funny. Nava is her name—of
course I recognized her, just didn't know from where. It turns out she and her friend
Yoella are indeed hiking the Shvil, or parts of it, and she knew I was also, and had
wondered—and spoken apparently with Meira about—whether she'd run into me.
It's a little weird, but entirely natural and enjoyable, to have the immediate affinity
one has with any Shvilist augmented by meeting someone you know, not to mention
of course the connection with Meira.*

*We put our packs down and exchange a few anecdotes and catch up a bit, but we're
both pretty anxious to get moving, as the late afternoon sun begins to fall behind the cliffs
above us. I'm a little concerned about these two young women walking up and through
the construction site at dusk, being a father of girls, and knowing what construction
workers can be like (even with the friendly experience I had earlier today with the site
manager, and with apologies to normal and well-adjusted men working on building
sites). For a moment I toy with suggesting we just make camp together. We have enough
water, here on the Shvil, since we're both about an hour and a half from our destinations
and sunset is in an hour. But that strikes me as a suggestion that might be a little inap-
propriate. Some old guy talking about setting up tents and spending the night with two
girls my daughter's age—maybe that's weird too—or just too weird.*

*All this goes through my mind as we're comparing notes on the path and where to
stay and water sources and the like. I allow myself to offer a gentle word of caution to
them about the construction site—"as a father"—so they'll consider one of their possible
overnight opportunities prior to reaching it, or just be more aware than usual. As a man,
I'm even perturbed that I have to mention the conceivable danger—Why is this part of
our world? I ask myself—but as a dad just have to. They're pretty confident and it's a
nice exchange; we finish by trading suggestions for the coming days. It's revealing, and
enriching, to recognize that though we are indeed of different generations, on the Shvil
we are literally all equals, facing similar challenges and enjoying similar experiences.*

*Nava and I pose for a photo, which she promises to WhatsApp to Meira; we
have a hug and wish each other "B'hatzlacha" ("success") and I head south as they
head north. That was fun; I feel rejuvenated, though at the same time the alone-ness
starts to reassert itself; I decide I'll call Mimi this evening. All in all it was a fun and
heartening encounter.*

It's rather strange, writing this after the fact, how almost every moment,
every experience, each step it seems, is pregnant with memories and anecdotes
and often meaning. I could write reams about the last hour or two on that day,
the views and the anticipation of reaching the Kinneret, the pain in my elbow
and arm from the fall (and of course the usual pain in my shoulder and neck

and legs and feet), the flowers and (more! Many more!) cows and hawks and swifts, the shadows getting longer and my strides becoming longer too as my steps became quicker, and my marveling at the way the hills and trees turned from light and dark green to brown and even slightly blue as darkness fell. But that should suffice. Walking the last kilometer or so as darkness fell with my head-lamp on to ensure I didn't stumble over agricultural equipment or into a shallow pool in a recreation area, about two hours after saying goodbye to Nava and Yoella I arrived at the little market "pundak" little store at Kibbutz Migdal right across the road from the Kinneret.

The nice fellow behind the counter, named Alon—who repeatedly couldn't believe I was hiking the Shvil alone and all at once, nor that I had hiked with the pack he saw on my back (and the guitar) from Tzfat that day—sold me a phone charger to replace the one I had left at Avraham and Rutie's that morning. He said I could sleep on the beach across the way, "no problem." I bought some supplies and set out, in the dark with no real ambient light—there was no moon out—and found myself on the water's edge with nowhere really to make camp.

"No problem" in Hebrew really means "good luck, you're screwed . . ." or so it seemed. I decided to walk along the water's edge; perhaps Alon was referring to a spot more conducive to setting up camp than this muddy, weedy, mosquito-filled swamp-like lake-side garbage dump. In the dark. With my headlamp on. Tired, worn out, in pain all over. Not a happy camper.

But camp I did, in the end, but not there. I walked another kilometer along the lakeside to the original site I'd been thinking about earlier, an (almost) organized campground where for 40 shekels I earned the right to set my tent up under strong lights which would burn all night, enjoy a cold shower, and share in the music, smoke and banter of large groups of local Arabs out celebrating on a Sunday evening overlooking the water. I didn't complain. Much.

As I wrote in my journal later, I actually slept okay, all things considered. Monday morning after packing up, a quick cup of coffee, and thanks to the Arab proprietor/manager, I was ready to go. (I commented to the owner about the cold water, to which he replied with a slight chuckle and a nonchalant "ah, yes." That reminded me of the bed-and-breakfast matron in the movie Groundhog Day, one of my favorites of all time.)

As I walked toward the shore I had a great view of the water through the brushes near the shore. I decided it was a good place—and time—to say my morning prayers. Donning my Tallit and Tefillin, I offered the tefilot with all the humility, acceptance, gratitude and forgiveness I had been pondering the previous few weeks. It's not difficult to see why so many generations have drawn inspiration from the Sea of Galilee, the Kinneret: it has a quiet strength to it. A depth, if one can say that, which is impressive but at the same time comforting in its size and silence, its majesty and peacefulness. It was a good davenning, and ended with a fishing boat coming into view, which of course I photographed.

And then, with the waterfowl on the banks and trees and the brushes in the water, I finally got underway. The Shvil calls for a challenging climb up the Arbel cliffside, and continuing on over and down through the town of Tiberius on the lake's edge. I had hiked the Arbel at least twice before (on my children's class trips) and had no interest in doing it then, let alone with a backpack like mine. Discovering what's called the "סובב כנרת" (Sovev Kinneret "Circling the Kinneret") trail, I figured I'd walk the ten or so kilometers along the shore of the lake to Tiberius in a couple of hours and then join up with the Shvil to get to Yavniel, a small village where my friends Sam and Chana Veffer had offered to put me up as my trail angels for that Monday night.

Yes. After the relatively difficult hikes on Thursday, Friday and Sunday, and with the continuing pain in my arm, I decided to "take it easy."

Hah. Note the quotes in that remark.

I highly recommend the Kinneret Trail—it could be a great day's outing for an adventurous family without too many small children. Bring lots of water . . . and a swimsuit. And shoes for walking in water. Up to your waist.

The first hour was a pleasure; what a great decision I'd made. Eventually, after about two or three kilometers, I found myself at an established beach and recreation area, which though it wasn't officially open yet allowed me to set up a little (little? Huge!) breakfast feast on a picnic table. I sat for well over an hour, cooled by a nice breeze in the overcast heat, catching up with the writing in my journal as I hadn't written since Thursday March 22 (at Chagit's). And as I wrote then, at 10:40 a.m. on Monday morning the 24th of March, "Time to continue on the סובב כנרת trail to Tiberius. I think I can handle 5-10 kilometers today . . . it'll be a manageable + pleasurable leisure stroll—with only a liter of water to weigh me down (so 'only' 20 kilos or so . . .). ☺"

My next entry in my journal tells the story of my jungle-like adventure where over the next five hours I almost called the rescue services for the second time on this hike (finding myself surrounded on all sides by tropical jungle foliage with seemingly no escape, scared to death there was a poisonous snake under foot half the time), trudged through the shallows (and not so shallow waters) at the lake's edge, climbed, clambered, ducked, sinked, and jumped over various things like I was on an obstacle course . . . and discovered a few wonderful hidden treasures along the way:

Journal Day 37—Monday afternoon March 24:
Filthy! ☺ Wow—so that wasn't quite the "relaxing" "stroll" planned . . .
From מגדל Migdal beach walked on the סובב כנרת Sovev Kinneret trail to עין רקת Raket Spring—lovely spring & old (how old?) pool . . . and then continued along the trail, over rocks and through/next to orchards + trees—came to a מקורות Mekorot [water] pumping station, right after/ next to what was an amazing רחבה [clearing] (apparently used for מקורות

events?) with stairs down to the water. Having wimped out re: diving/ going in so far, that was it: stripped down, dove in—great! Decided to stay for a bit (to dry off!) hoping no one else would be doing the Trail . . . it was great. Meditated (naked) sitting on a rock overlooking the כנרת. Photo even! ☺

Then continued on—another מעיין + pool—נווה קוג'אן Neve Kojan— and stumbled on . . . a German couple, Marvin and Magdalena, camping out. (So many places you discover by walking!). Then continued and soon (1) lost the trail markings + (2) got confounded and "trapped" in the reeds and hedges, trees + vines + mud/slime/creeks/trickles . . . ?

Go back? Or go on? Ended up thrashing my way through with my sticks—bamboo, reeds, palm trees, vines of various sorts—mud in boots, on legs/arms/knees, pack keeps getting caught on branches + vines (darn guitar!) . . . even at one point lay down backwards on a row of vines/ branches + rolled over it w/the pack pressing it down—and made it out!! Success!

Bushwhacking . . . ☺

Then . . . next obstacle: some sort of baptismal church/holy site (very nicely done up mind you) with a square pool + water pouring into the כנרת Kinneret—[trail] sign says "straight" as it were so . . . up on the wall, holding on to the fence posts—wish had photo! Then . . . water! Put on sandals—take pack off again to help 3 guys on a boat to take water samples from the flow from the wall (!)—then walk through the shallows following the purple Kinneret Trail markings.

Fish! Then OMG! HUGE fish (photo)—like a foot & a half long (30 cms). Then—what!!? One about half a METER at least—probably more like 70 cm long! Catfish apparently . . . says דתי (religiously observant) fisherman I spoke to [later].

The remainder of that day was less eventful. I treated myself to a slap-up meal at a restaurant on the water's edge in Tiberius, having found my way there as the trail markings appeared and disappeared continuously, including leading me through various lakeside event halls and via streets at the northern entrance to the town, via the Scottish Church. I can't really believe they let me sit down considering how disheveled I looked. Even as a most-of-the-time vegetarian, I felt there was something poetic (or barbaric, depending on your perspective) in eating a delicious Gray Mullet ("Buri" in Hebrew) grilled to perfection, caught that very morning while I was plodding my way through the water. Accompanied by a 2009 Golan Mt. Hermon Red (and looking across the water at those very Golan Heights), it was a feast of celebration and release, accomplishment and gratitude for having made it through the day.

That last may sound bombastic, but I was near panic, twice, and I freely admit it, without embarrassment. A day previously, coincidentally, a man had been bitten by a snake, and died, on the southern edge of the Kinneret. I had heard about it when I was at the store the previous night—it hadn't made a huge impression on me at the time. So it wasn't only my consternation at not being able to find the trail, any trail; and it wasn't even the rising anxiety when I found myself literally encircled by foliage, not being able to at all even identify from where I'd come. With a strong sense of direction, I did know I could (probably) make my way back to find a trail, keeping the water on one side of me, if I couldn't push on, and would eventually find a path to the West and into a farm or other mark of civilization. I wasn't even too confident of that; but it was mostly the fear of a snake which really did me in, and it took all my concentration, will-power and energy to just force myself to move on.

I reasoned—reasonably, I felt—that (1) I had good, sturdy shoes, such that were a snake to bite me on my foot, the shoe might absorb the bite (and venom); (2) just because there was one snake-bite occurrence on the Kinneret didn't necessarily mean there'd be another; (3) I'm a medic and would know what to do if that probability calculation was wrong; and (4) my phone was charged and I could call for help quickly enough to save my life. The contrary facts were known to me: A snake could and probably would bite me on my leg or arm; statistical probabilities don't work that way; though trained to treat oneself, being a medic hardly counts if you're losing consciousness quickly after a snake bite; and phone reception was (as I saw) iffy at best and nonexistent most of the time there. I just pushed them deep enough down in my consciousness that I could ignore them. I suppose I subconsciously understood those facts, and the panic I felt rising a number of times was my mind's way of insisting that I not disregard what I knew I knew.

All this led inexorably to the real sense of achievement, even triumph, I felt on emerging from the jungle-like forest, to the special repast, and to eventually treating myself also to a taxi to take me to the little town of Yavniel. There, my friends Shmuel (Sam) and Chana surprised me by offering me not a bed in their home but a room in their Tzimmer, a fancy bed-and-breakfast room with a huge and comfy bed, coffee and tea maker, desk, and all the accoutrement. And it included an amazing, enormous JACCUZZI just made for a hiker to soak in after a long and arduous day on the Trail. Villa Ramona is what they call it, and to me it was paradise.

The bath did wonders for my aching body, and especially my elbow and arm. Following it, I could raise the arm above shoulder-height again, and by the next morning could bend the elbow enough to adjust the straps of my pack without great pain. Over a delicious pizza dinner from a local hole-in-the-wall joint, Shmuel and I enjoyed re-connecting after years of no real contact, and I really liked the go-with-the-flow approach to their move up there that he and Chana described. I crawled happily, exhaustedly into bed before 10:30 at night and was instantly asleep.

Tuesday morning dawned a bit overcast and not too hot; I was in such luxurious settings and such a comfortable bed I really didn't want to get up. But get up I did, and to help me get started, Shmuel drove me halfway up the very steep hill above the community. After thanking him profusely (and Chana, not least for the delicious-looking peanut butter and jelly sandwiches safely tucked in my pack for later) I started to trudge up the sharp incline past the local cemetery and water reservoir.

I stopped to take in the view beneath me: rolling hills full of fields of wheat and barley and orchards and rows of various vegetables brandishing their early spring growth in multiple shades of greens and reds and oranges. In the middle distance, a ridge with vineyards and fields and two other villages; behind and beneath that, the Kinneret shimmering in the haze. And rising above and behind the lake, the Golan Heights, spanning most of the horizon, gray and indistinct but formidable nonetheless as they dominate the eastern skyline.

Here I am, looking out over this pastoral scene, and I'm thinking: this is basically the view of the original pioneers who came to the Galil 100 years ago or more. They looked out over this expanse—Yavniel is located in a wide and shallow valley west of the Kinneret—and I can almost hear them saying, "Yes, this is a goodly land, a land of blessing and bounty." I'm saying this to myself, and wondering what language they might have said it in. German or Polish or Yiddish or Hungarian, those first immigrants who picked up the gauntlet and came to work the land and build a new kind of society came from central and eastern Europe; most of the communities I can see from here were settled by these idealistic early Zionists. And they just wanted to find some peace.

Wow. The peace and tranquility they eventually attained—and that I'm enjoying now, and just did in Yavniel—came at such a price. If only they were allowed then—if only we were allowed now—to focus on the planting and building, the farms and services, tourism and art, which are the pursuits also today of our modern pioneers living here. If only . . . what a world this would be, and what an amazing place this could have been even a hundred years ago.

With those thoughts in mind, I walk on.

That day, Tuesday, March 25, was a lovely but uneventful 7-hours plus of walking through the greenery of the lower Galilee. In truth, though the hiking itself may not have been noteworthy, as a Jew walking the Land of Israel with the history of our people foremost in my mind, it was anything but.

A Jew. I refer to our national identity, a "people" or "nation" as God referred to us for the first time in the Exodus from Egypt some 3500 years ago. At one point I read in the Red Guide that I was looking across at Mt. Gilboa. This is the Har Gilboa mentioned in the Bible, where Devorah and Barak defeated Sisera; this is the area where King Shaul failed God and consulted witches and the like.

I was walking in the footstep of my ancestors, and it's all so casual, listed as if this is of no more significance than a local supplies store or an idle mention of a tourist site marker. What is amazing about living in Israel—and about walking the Israel Trail—is that you come across, quite literally, reminders and pointers to the history of our people in even the most mundane situations. For me, the Trail encompassed three and a half thousand years of our national existence, from my time in the desert like the wanderings of the children of Israel to the days described here. I was walking the hills where Barak led the Israelite armies (and where different Baraks, including our recent prime minister and former Chief of Staff of the IDF Ehud Barak, also walked, among others). The knowledge of that history, and the connection it reinforced for me with my people, with the nation of Israel, has remained with me ever since, and strengthened my commitment to Zionism—a term I am proud to burnish and that I believe must be reclaimed, not least in political and academic circles.

As an American, I am extremely proud of my country, and as I mentioned in the introduction, my family has a phenomenal history in the United States. We Americans view history through the lens of centuries: first there were native Americans, then colonists from Europe, and then independence. Eight generations ago, my grandparents were a part of the founding of the US. We Jews look through the lens of millennia, starting with Abraham some 160 generations ago, or *four thousand years* ago. We were a civilization in our Land, living sovereign there off and on for over a millennia until the Romans expelled us. Our society, with its links between God, faith, Land and people, incorporated ethnic, cultural, religious, spiritual and ethical elements—and still does. And this is my family.

It is true: we are not the only people to have touched this land. Canaanite and Jebusite, Hittite and Roman and Babylonian, Assyrian and Greek and Persian, Turkish and British, Christian, Muslim and Arab—all these and others have also touched this land. They lived in them or ruled them, cared for them or abused them (and the inhabitants), bartered and traded them, dreamed of them, killed for and in them and been killed in them, loved them and rejected them, and ignored them or despoiled them.

Objective scholars of archeology and anthropology, history and law and political science, confirm that the Jews—not the religious faith of Judaism, but as a nationality—are the indigenous people of this land. (This is not a political statement: recognition of this verifiable, factual historical reality does not dictate any political agenda regarding our present-day situation. In fact, various political parties in Israel, and politicians around the world, promote numerous "solutions" to the Arab-Israel conflict which point in diametrically opposite directions, while acknowledging this fact of history. Jews are the only still-existing people with an undeniable historical, linguistic, cultural, political, national connection to this Land—irrespective of one-sided politicized UNESCO votes.[11])

Seen in this light, Zionism is the political movement asserting the right of the Jews to return to their ancestral homeland, joining those who remained throughout history. Israel is the embodiment of that goal. Zionism is "nothing more or less than the national liberation movement of the Jewish people," as a leader of the Left-wing Labor party, Abba Eben, once said. It is the modern expression of the Jews' age-old yearning to return to our land, since the expulsion of most of us by the Romans some two thousand years ago.

Thinking along these lines as I cross the Galiliee in the afternoon fading light is incredibly poignant. These concepts aren't new to me, of course; I lecture on these topics around the world. But knowing the facts of history, and feeling them in your bones as you walk, are two different things. Passing a small farm with a few cows in a paddock, it occurs to me: it's like the difference between thinking how their milk tastes, or how your favorite food tastes . . . and actually tasting it. I know our history; hiking by the sites where our story unfolded, I can taste it.

It's amazing what a person can get used to, and what we take for granted. Living in Israel, we're constantly living our history. Walking on a path which may actually have been trod by King Shaul, or Sisera, or Rabbi Akiva, or Jesus, or David Ben Gurion for that matter, is a heady business. And it gets you thinking. Sometimes I have to pinch myself when wandering around Jerusalem between meetings, passing by the Old City walls, seeing the Temple Mount or Mt. Zion from afar. It's easy to forget sometimes what those walls mean.

And if sometimes we forget, it is sad but perhaps not surprising that the rest of the world has forgotten too. Israel—the nation-state of the Jewish people, with its Jewish cultural and religious identity and symbols also—is such a multi-faceted society that sometimes in our internal (and external) debates we lose sight of the depth of our distinctiveness. We are unique in the annals of human civilization: In our continual connection, unceasing and uninterrupted, with our Land. In our combination of national identity and religious faith and belief system. And in our moral contribution to humanity. The Chinese may be able to lay claim to some aspects of the first two components, but as acknowledged by cultural anthropologists, no other people or nation (or religion) possess such the mixture.

This doesn't make us any better (or worse) than any other civilization or community or ethnic grouping. But remembering who we are, where we come from and that

---

11   If a Canaanite or Hittite, Jebusite or Philistine tribe were to appear miraculously from some cave, we'd have a discussion regarding whose land this is; but whatever credence one wishes to lend to a "Palestinian" Arab claim to national identity or a right to independence, the recent nature of that identity is indisputable. This, despite Yasser Arafat's and others' attempts to suggest they descend from the Canaanites. They do not. Most come from Egypt, Yemen, Syria or the like, only a few generations ago. Those with longer family history in the land are mostly descended from Jews forcibly converted hundreds of years ago, according to DNA and other research.

now we've come back, is what gives us our strength. When we take this to heart, it provides the basis of our commitment to both build our national homeland and to defend ourselves. It is the foundation of our dedication to the prophetic ideal of making the world a better place, as well as our devotion to our biblical and traditional values of the dignity of mankind, equality, justice, and truth.

Wow. It's amazing the thoughts that emerge when walking in the footsteps of one's kings and prophets.

It was thinking like this that brought me to the end of that day, where beneath Mt. Tabor I was picked up by my cousin Chagit. Again, she took great care of me and drove me back in the morning (and took me to the top of Mt. Tabor so I didn't have to climb up! Cheat . . .). We took a quick walk around the church and monastery atop the rather unusual, upside-down-bell-shaped mountain, accompanied by a few dozen mostly Christian tour groups. I enjoyed the relative serenity of the meditative ambience (quiet is encouraged and the gardens well-tended). We spoke of Devorah and Barak and King Shaul and marveled at the views, which were clear and just gorgeous.

After a half hour or so, Chagit left to tend to her life, and I traipsed down the steep northern side of Mt. Tabor. When I ran in to a large group of rowdy schoolchildren, I was pleasantly surprised when one of their teachers stopped me and, shushing them, asked whether I was hiking the Shvil. When I said yes, he turned and asked the kids whether they'd ever heard of it; one or two had, but most not. He then asked me to describe it, and share an anecdote or two; when I did, I was very pleasantly surprised by the interest, the quiet and the politeness of the group of 9–10 year olds. I encouraged them all to consider hiking the Shvil one day, exhorting them to love and learn and connect with our country and our land.

The Zionist and Jewish national musings of the day before accompanied me also through Wednesday and Thursday of that week, March 26 and 27, as I rambled through the hills of the Galil and through Jewish history. From Tabor I entered a picturesque Arab village, where a small hand-painted plaque with "Welcome to Shibli" greets visitors on the lamppost just above the painted Shvil markings. In the five minutes it took to traverse the tiny village I was greeted a dozen times with waves, smiles, "Shalom!" and even one "Kol HaKavod" ("Good for you"). The Jewish history I had been contemplating is replete with interaction with non-Jews, whether as neighbors, conquerors, or subjects, and I felt a swell of pride as my thoughts turned to the miracle—for it was and is a miracle—that in spite of the animosity against us permeating Arab and Muslim societies all around us, here in Israel we've managed to retain our commitment to our very Jewish values of tolerance and coexistence, and created an oasis of accord, where at least some of the Muslim Arab and most of the Christian Arab citizens of Israel share in those values.

Of course our society isn't perfect—which is?—but I allowed myself to enjoy that proud moment, as one who has had to argue and defend Israel on college campuses and in the media. The truth is that although Arab-Israeli leaders are vociferous in their public condemnation of Israeli policies and Jewish-Israeli society's shortcomings, many Arab-Israeli citizens are equally persistent in their expressions of admiration and appreciation for the democratic nature of that society—in which they can participate fully.

This became something of a theme for those days, and the coming week, as the Galil is the part of Israel where there is the most interaction and neighborly coexistence between Arab Muslim/Christian Israelis and Jewish Israelis. And it provoked a few new trains of thought, about humilty, acceptance, appreciation, and forgiveness. Most Arabs in Israel have accepted the historical and legal validity of the Jews' return to our land and the justice of the international community's support of it. They appreciate the benefits of living in the vibrant and unique democracy that the Jews created in Israel. (That is, until recent trends by radical Islamic and nationalist Arab leaders in Israel turned back to inculcating hatred and intolerance in their society. But that's a theme for another time). And they have "forgiven" the Jews for returning, and creating our state, it seems. This is not condescension; it was and is my perception of the reality among the majority of Arab Israelis in my over thirty years of interactions with them, validated by my experience on the Trail.

Here I was, walking with a rather large blue-and-white Israeli flag on my back through a Muslim Arab village, and being greeted not just pleasantly but enthusiastically by the residents. I meandered through the streets with no fear, no anxiety, whether for my personal safety or of provoking or getting involved in any political argument. It was a great feeling—and to be honest, one I hadn't expected. (Knowing something is not the same as tasting it.)

Continuing through the forest of Beit Keshet, I lost the trail on the climb up to Nazareth—and actually was grateful for the midday break afforded by my confusion. I sat on a breezy hillside in the shade of the trees, looking back and forth between the map and the terrain in front of me, just above Nachal Barak Ben Avinoam, a stream named for Devorah's general, Barak. Nazareth was behind me (Christian historically, now majority-Muslim); an Arab Christian village in front of me, and the Jewish town of Upper Nazareth just above me. In the distance I could see hang-gliders flying in the rising heat above Har Tabor. Sitting there in between Christian and Muslim and Jewish towns, I could see the small Muslim Arab village of Daburiyya—Muslim now but prior to Saladin a Christian hamlet and before that the biblical Israelite town of Daberath. This triggered a wave of thoughts. Whatever the history—and of course it's a violent one, from Greek to Roman, Arab and Muslim to Turkish and British—today we are witness to an incredible demonstration of the power of goodwill, the force of an ideology which stresses and teaches acceptance, cooperation and coexistence.

Karen had made a sweet, emotional film a few years earlier about four students at the Jerusalem high school for science and art—two Jews and two Arabs—which made this point much more personal. Israel has succeeded—in a way no other western country, Christian or secular, and certainly no Arab or Muslim nation, has—in developing a truly egalitarian, inclusive and open society. We are justifiably proud of our country in which minorities, whether national, religious, ideological, gender or orientation, are respected and feel included.[12] I began to wonder, looking for positive directions for my thoughts, what our region might look like if the rulers and people of Syria, or Egypt, or Jordan or Iraq or Saudi Arabia, let alone Iran or Turkey (or the Arab ethnic grouping known today as "Palestinian') would pursue a similar ambition.

I let those notions percolate as I decided I had enough rambling thoughts; it was time to let my legs do the rambling, as the sun was well past its highest point, and I still had a ways to go. Though I had been in touch with a hostel in Upper Nazareth, I really wasn't in the mood for institutional lodging, and I elected to push on to see if I could make it before nightfall to the forest near Tzipori. Finding my way up the hill, down the cliff, through the brambles and then an orchard, I finally rejoined the Trail and trudged my way up a steep incline.

Abruptly, I found myself on a street on the western and northern outskirts of the town of Natzrat Ilit (Upper Nazareth)! So very strange: an hour ago I was lost, uncertain even whether I'd find my way to the Trail, let alone to civilization; now I was angry and disappointed to find myself stumbling along a sidewalk, trying not to step in various leavings of dogs and who-knows-what,

---

12 This is not the place for a nuanced discussion of the complexities and shortcomings of Israeli society. Suffice to say here that (1) all democracies strive for equality and (2) none have achieved it yet, including Israel. The above does not suggest there are no criticisms to be made of Israeli society or its political leadership—Jewish and Arab. Rather—reflecting the themes of the trek—it recognizes with humility, acceptance and gratitude, the facts on the ground, which can be simplified regarding this topic in just a few sentences. Just as blacks or Hispanics in America, or Turks in Germany or Pakistanis in Britain or Algerians and other Arab or Muslim immigrants in France, are in some ways still discriminated against in those societies, so too do Arabs suffer from certain forms of discrimination in Israeli society. Yet there are black and Hispanic representatives in Congress or business leaders and academics in American society; and there Arab Muslims and Christians in Israel's Knesset and judiciary, universities and companies. And Israel's record in many ways is better—statistically and historically—on issues of inclusiveness than many European nations and American states—whether regarding Arabs or gays, women or Christians or illegal migrants. Stores and hospitals, movie theaters and factories, parks and playgrounds are full of people from all walks of life, a multicultural menagerie which should be celebrated by democrats (liberal and conservative) across America and Europe. The growing radicalization and violence of the Muslim community in Israel is worrying; it has provoked concern and fear among Israel's Christians and Jews, Druze and even other Muslims, and has led to a recent upswing in prejudicial attitudes and incidents of hostility and discrimination against Muslims. The Israeli government is counteracting these developments with educational and cultural programs in keeping with our society's dedication to our liberal principles.

nodding at Russian immigrant women and playful children who clearly thought I was either an alien or a joke, or more likely an alien joke or a joke of an alien.

Reinforced in my determination to escape the company of strangers and the trappings of modernity and technology (a Luddite in my soul, as you may have noticed), I didn't even look for a makolet or a water fountain; I was glad—glad!—when the marking called for a right turn down a steep embankment, full of junk and weeds, leading away from the street. Saying goodbye to what I'm sure is a lovely little town with nice people, I made my way into and through the small village of Mash'ad—another Arab Muslim community. It gave me such pleasure to note in passing the Kupat Cholim government health clinic, with signs in Hebrew and Arabic, as well as a community center, town hall, bank, and stores, all with Arabic and Hebrew in their displays (and many with English too, that international language of business—and marketing).

Passing a makolet, I realize this is a great opportunity to practice what I preach, and to get a feel for the local scene and mood. Also it may be my last prospect of buying some supplies—having remembered I'm low on almost everything, in spite of Chagit's generosity.

The young woman at the counter is not only pleasant and helpful, in decent Hebrew after I say hi in Arabic, but seems amused as I look at the ingredients on some unfamiliar products. I'm in an Arab store, in a Muslim Arab Israeli village, so am enjoying looking at the different sorts of things I don't usually come across: imports from Jordan, vegetables and spices I use infrequently or never, cookies and drinks brands I don't recognize. I decide to get some Arabic coffee (really it's Turkish, or called Turkish, but you get the point). The young lady becomes animated on hearing that I'm hiking the Shvil. She's heard of it, but not a lot, and didn't realize it goes the entire length of the country. Apparently she's aware there are people who hike through with some frequency, but assumed they were day-hikers from Nazareth Illit or tourists on a few days' outing. Describing the Trail, I offer a few sentences about our (shared) connection to our (shared) land, and how wonderful and important it is to appreciate it and all our blessings, not least when facing, or after facing, personal challenges like divorce or the like. (I've kind of got the spiel down to a minute, it flows out like a nice light wine, with just enough emotion to be real but not too much to make people uncomfortable.)

In Hebrew, it sounds less stilted, more personal I think. Words like ארצנו המשותפת "Artzeni Hameshutefet resonate more fully than their English equivalent, "our shared land." Perhaps "our land which is shared" is more accurate, and also reflects the subtle meaning of a common bond which is intuitive in the Hebrew. The "our" possessive is an integral part of the word "Land," and communicates the Land's importance in our self-identity and even soul. A Jew in his ancestral homeland, and an Arab with roots there for at least a few generations, can both understand and celebrate that connectedness. The fact that linguistically, culturally, religiously we can share the concept enables us to share the feeling and (perhaps, on one level, at times, with specific individuals) share the land itself. Or so it feels, as I hearken back to my conversation beneath Highway 85 with that construction site manager.

We finish the conversation and the transaction and I turn to leave. She, like so many other non-Jewish Israelis, says "Kol HaKavod!" Is it my imagination that she seems wistful, as if she wishes she could escape whatever drudgery she experiences at the store? When she says "B'hatzlacha" ("Good luck") I do sense she is sincere. She could have just said "You're welcome" to my "Thank you." And as I sneak a look back when I step out the door, adjusting the pack, I see she's still looking after me. Could be just bored—there are no other customers—but perhaps I've helped to give her a positive view of "the Israeli" and "the Jew." I hope so.

A few steps along the street and I see two kids about age 8 playing on the back of a long flat-bed hauler. Before I know it they call out "Shalom! Shalom!" and are waving at me. As I pass, I smile and wave back. Then a smaller child calls down from his perch at a window "Shalom!" Yes, it excites me and delights me. I know I shouldn't make such a fuss out of it but I remind myself I'm wearing an Israeli flag and so their exuberance can't be mistaken for ignorance of my identity. I allow myself to smile, in small celebration of the little victories of Israeli society, as the children on the truck reach out to slap hands with me as I pass.

Then, rounding a corner in the middle of the village, I get a double whammy. First, ahead of me is the central mosque, a small domed building with a low tower, surrounded by a rock wall and trees. And I see the Israel Trail marking, painted right on the stone wall of the mosque compound! I stop to take a photo. I know, and I chide myself: how many photos can I take of the bloody trail sign?!!? But it just thrills me, this mundane reality that appeals so strongly to me: it's just there, unremarkable, natural, fitting. The Israel Trail goes through Arab villages as it does Jewish villages, without controversy or comment. Just as it should. And that makes be proud, and happy, and thoughtful.

Mash'ad village mosque wall with Israel Trail marking

Just as I'm pondering this small victory in our search for normalcy in this country, I hear the scuffling of shoes to my right and, glancing over, I find three boys aged about ten playing basketball in their driveway. While I nod and smile at them, I begin to pivot to head on my way. Taking the ball, one raises it in a threatening gesture, as if to throw it at me. At first I'm confused—it happens so fast. Does he mean

to toss the ball to me? No: he does it again, one of those acts we all do as kids, pretend-
ing to throw a ball at someone, hard, pantomiming a menacing throw and stopping
it with the other hand at the last second.

I look at this kid and just say, "Lamah?" (Why?) And, deciding quickly this isn't
the time or place to try to educate an Arab Muslim Israeli child in theories of coexistence
or even manners, I turn and walk away—but not without a huge smile, a wave, and a
"Shalom! Lehitra'ot! Yom Na'im . . ." ("Hi/Bye! See ya! Have a nice day . . .") I know
it'll make no difference, but that's me, I can't change myself, I like my upbeat nature
and I refuse to let some kid's aggressive tendencies have the last word in this exchange.

Though of course, this incident sours my mood somewhat. I tell myself this kid
was showing off for his friends, as far as I know he didn't have a clue who I am, Jew
or Arab, Muslim or Christian—I'm just some old guy passing by and he was joshing,
poking fun, being provocative. But I'm not convinced; something about his expression
revealed a real antagonism and dislike. Although I've been enjoying the coexistence
so far, here is a reality check: perhaps all is not well. It is entirely possible that this
child has been inculcated with hostility and anger, resentment and opposition toward
Jewish Israelis and perhaps all outsiders.

That experience—and seeing a few teens a few minutes later, as I near the out-
skirts of the town—makes me just a teeny bit more wary, more careful, than I was
earlier. So instead of making camp on the verge of the forest, at the edge of town—my
original intent, as dusk is falling—I follow the trail markings deeper into the woods.
Early on, I see a few fire circles among the trees, with a few beer bottles and cans scat-
tered about. Sherlock I'm not, but I figure this may be where local teenagers come
in the evening to hang out, and so I decide to keep walking—just to be prudent.
Eventually I find a small clearing on the side of the dirt road, about thirty minutes
down a slight gradient, surrounded by densely planted firs. Throwing my pack down,
I begin to make camp.

There are a few photographs from the Shvil which have (for me) become
iconic. One is that Shvil marker on the wall below the mosque. Despite the incident with the kid with the ball, that picture and what it represents still gives me
pleasure. Another is the next morning's photo from outside my tent.

I went to sleep early, after writing in my journal and calling my kids, and
playing a bit of guitar—קום והתהלך בארץ (Arise and walk the land) to raise my
spirits a little. I slept decently on a bed of pine needles, appreciating the early
night and the decision to sleep rough as well as the sweet tea I made to take into
the tent. Sometime after sunrise I awoke to various shuffling sounds. Steps and
cracks, murmurs and grunts, sounds like leaves and branches brushing against
each other and like the crackling of kindling snapping. Loud. And sometimes
REALLY LOUD . . . and NEAR. My initial and immediate thought was "Oh
no! I started a forest fire with my campfire from last night!" But as soon as the
thought came to me I dismissed it—both as I knew I had extinguished my

fire, and as I could tell that was NOT the sound, or combination of sounds, I was hearing.

Moreover, I sensed movement. I felt the ground tremble, if ever so slightly. Hmmm: I could feel the vibrations as I sat up. Gingerly, I unzipped the tent flap, wary what I might face. I was almost prepared—almost—to see a cow standing not more than a meter from my tent, looking at me absent-mindedly while she munched a leaf and then walked on. And another beyond her, three meters away. And another—this bigger even—a step to the side. And as I looked around, I counted a dozen or so within a radius of about five meters, all around the tent. Without thinking, I said, "Boker Tov" ("Good morning") and the nearest one shuffled rather quickly through the small trees to the right, making a bit of noise in the sticks and rocks under foot (hoof).

I thought to moo—something I've been known to do from a car as we pass cows in fields at the side of roads—and quickly (wisely?) thought better of the idea. Who knows what these animals might think I'm saying to them? And I thought to stand up, and that too was rejected immediately. Some of the nearest were calves—not infants but yearlings (or that's what we used to call the horses at that age), and I really wasn't sure whether the mother cows would take kindly to what might be seen as a threatening move on my part. It was clear they were moving through; equally clear they weren't going to trample me or my tent or even my fire circle and the box I'd set up as a sort of table next to it. They were rather politely, if insistently, just making their way through. So I remained where I was, kneeling at the entrance to my tent, waiting not so patiently (since I needed to relieve myself, as one does in the morning on waking).

Hence the photos of cows surrounding and walking past my tent, and calves, and me in the middle. It was a bit frightening—not nearly as terrifying as looking down some of those cliffs I'd climbed up or down or across, but

Cows around Aryeh's tent in Tzipori Forest

scary nonetheless— since these animals are behemoths! And especially up close, and especially when you're on your knees—but I just breathed deeply and tried to enjoy the experience, knowing I'd have a great time talking about it soon enough. After a few minutes passed, I stood up, and saw a young man in the distance, clearly the caretaker of the cows. Calling to him, "Are these yours?" I was pleased to hear his response that yes, he was looking after them; yes, I was on the Trail path; yes, they were finished and not returning (that day); and no, I hadn't bothered them. (I kind of knew that; didn't seem like much, except perhaps the butcher's knife, could bother those monsters.)

It was a great way to start a great day.

It was a brief and pleasant hike of only a few hours to the entrance of the Tzipori national park, an archeological site I had last visited some thirty or so years previously with Karen and her parents, Philip and Flo. The Red Guide recommends taking a detour to visit Tzipori, and I had already decided to do so, knowing also that it was a relatively short distance to my next planned camping area, the "Solelim" forest. Tzipori was well worth the three hours or more I wandered around it. It is a magnificent site with remains from various ancient Jewish, Roman, Byzantine, Arab, Crusader, and Ottoman periods. Walking around and through it is like walking through history itself: tripping over the ruts in the main road made by ox carts, you feel as if you are right there on market day, can almost smell the animals and spices and see the colorful cloths and vegetables on offer. And I'm not much of a romantic.

I admired the care taken to excavate, clean, preserve, and exhibit the remains of a synagogue from over 1,500 years ago. I sat on a stone wall, allowing myself to imagine Rabbi Yehuda HaNasi, redactor of the *Mishna*, Judaism's earliest codification of law and lore after the Hebrew Bible, walking through the village, teaching and learning and deciding on issues of Jewish practice. Evidently, I read, this little area was home to some 30,000 people in the first five centuries of the Common Era, a multi-national and multi-cultural assortment of Jews and Romans, pagans and early Christians and others, living peacefully together in harmony. "That's interesting . . ." I thought to myself, "maybe there's a lesson to be found here."

The ruins are incredibly well-preserved, and I learned that this is primarily due to the decision by the town leaders not to participate in the Jewish Great Revolt of the year 66 of the Common Era against their Roman overlords. I was— again, and not for the first nor last time—quite moved when I stumbled upon *mikvaot* and the occasional *gat* (wine pressing circle and basin), testimony if any were needed to the Jewish presence and observance there thousands of years ago. Apparently, Yehuda HaNasi was not there alone; the entire Sanhedrin, the council of leading scholars that led the Jewish community in the times of the Holy Temple in Jerusalem, and for a while after the fall of the Temple, relocated there after the destruction of Jerusalem and prior to their settling in Tiberius. All this I discovered while wandering the passages of the lower city and then climbing up to the top of the hill, past the ancient Roman amphitheater seating some 4,500 spectators, remarkably still intact enough for me to stand on the "stage" and sing, pretending to be a centurion back from some feat of physical prowess. (Like hiking a thousand kilometers with a 25-kilo pack on my back. Have I mentioned that 50-pound backpack?)

At the top of the hill I find a "villa," built around the time of the destruction of the Temple. Housing one of the most famous mosaics in Israel—the "Mona Lisa of the Galilee"—it's not only impressive but fun and uplifting too. I love the depictions of Dionysis enjoying his wine, with Pan and Hercules and others. It seems not too much has changed in the Galil after all these years, with the incredible and ever-increasing number of new wineries (and even whisky distilleries) in the area and throughout Israel. I sit gazing at the fine and detailed mosaic of the young woman, perhaps Venus though no one knows for sure, and am just fascinated. Unlike the paintings in museums I'm used to, or even medieval woodwork, meant to hang on a wall and enjoyed by sight alone, these mosaics were built into the floors and seen/used every day. I can't help wondering what it must have been like for some Roman governor or even emperor to sit there and drink or eat or cavort with this beautiful, inscrutable face looking at you (glancing off to her left, actually, away from you). The detail, the colors, the artistry, are truly breathtaking. And perhaps inexplicably, I find the whole thing almost as moving as the mikvaot *earlier.*

And then, before leaving the park to continue on the Shvil, I wander around excavations of what was clearly a Jewish neighborhood, replete with a mikva in each and every house. I keep thinking and saying to myself, "Wow." Just wow. What other civilization has so distinctive an architectural quirk that makes it possible to clearly identify the occupants of a dwelling two thousand years after its destruction? These mikvahs speak to me: Jews were here; Jews prospered here; and Jews maintained their unique traditions and practices here, those same traditions we observe today. This is my people; these are my villages and my houses and my history.

When I go to the mikvah as I do every year on the eve of Yom Kippur and sometimes on *erev Shabbat*, Friday afternoon, in preparation for Shabbat—whether in a building or at a natural spring/*ma'ayan* or in the sea—I now think of those Jews who did the same thousands of years ago, freely and naturally in the land of their forefathers. It is a tangible, literally immersive and powerful link to everything Jewish/Israelite/Israeli. As I wrote that next Saturday night on Facebook: "My people prayed here; my ancestors farmed here; my family struggled here: these hills and valleys echo with the voices and tears, battles and songs and footsteps of the Jewish people, Am Yisrael, the house of Jacob/Israel. My people. Our people."

With only a tang of melancholy, I recalled fondly my visit to Tzipori with Philip and Flo, thinking how they'd so enjoy a return visit. I knew Philip, in particular, would be as moved as I was by the sense of continuity; I promised myself

I'd bring the Outlaws to visit the next time they were in Israel. Unfortunately, it was not to be: my beloved father-in-law, really another dad to me, passed away during the writing of this book. He was a sweet, gentle soul; I loved him dearly. He was one of the formative influences on my return to Jewish observance, my understanding of Jewish peoplehood, and my love for Israel and our people. He used to say that Jews making *Aliya* to Israel is "the correct and historically inevitable thing." That phrase, and the concept behind it, has informed my identity for well over thirty years.

That concept was, in fact, one of the ideas percolating in my subconscious as I walked around Tzipori. With a profound sense of history, and a certain lightness in my step from the marvelous feeling of serenity given me by the tour in Tzipori and the flow of thoughts resulting from it, I stepped through the northern gate and started down the path toward the northern reaches of the forest. I was glad I stopped; I was glad also to be moving on.

I scampered down an embankment, past the tomb of Rabbi Yehuda HaNasi, the compiler of the Mishna mentioned above—and I can't believe I just casually meandered by it. (That's like, say, walking by the Jefferson Memorial in Washington DC, for Americans, and not stopping. But even more.) Such is the reality of living in—and walking in—Israel. Passing a 2,000-year-old burial site of one of the founders of your nation and one of the most profound thinkers, scholars, and leaders of your people (and of humanity) . . . raising your eyebrows, and moving on.

I found myself panting as I trudged up a rather steep dirt road into the eastern part of Tzipori Forest, and was tickled and relieved when a truck pulled up beside me and the driver—Michael—offered me a lift. By then I was happy to accept. The funny part came when, as I responded to his question regarding what I was doing, and then why I was doing it, he just cut me off and said, "ניקוי ראש!" (*Nikui Rosh*—"Clearing your head!" or, literally, "cleansing the head"). As I wrote in my journal later, it was a great way to concisely describe the what and why without going into detail, and I decided to adopt it in circumstances when I didn't feel like having to explain all the history, divorce, etc.

A few hours (and a few winepresses and ancient structures beside the path) later, I found myself striding over the crest of a small tree-covered hill—and realized it was time to find a place to camp, as I didn't want to continue on to end up too close to the highway. I came upon a lovely clearing, with a view toward the setting sun over a lake (which turned out to be a reservoir when I looked more carefully the following morning, but who cares?), and set up my tent, hung up my shirt and socks to air out, and started to gather wood for a fire.

I had such a glorious evening that night. Finally made the noodles I'd been carrying since Tzfat on Sunday; had lots of tea (three different kinds! And with sugar too!), roasted marshmallows, and ate a bit of one of my chocolate power bar treats (which are more punishment than treat). Taking out the guitar, with a view of the southern night sky unimpeded by trees, I played and played, all the old favorites and some of the newer ones I'd learned or written recently. I sang softly a few of my own songs, including a ballad I wrote years ago about a mermaid's lost but remembered love; one about non-conformity and loving life called *Fairground*; and the new *Clothe Me in Love* I'd (re)written in the desert. I sang the only Hebrew song I'd ever written, for the first time in years, certainly since Karen had said she wanted to leave. Composed as Karen and I had first started to date seriously (and I realized I wanted to spend the rest of my life not only with her but in Israel and being religiously observant), it's about love and uncertainty about the future and how we rely on God's guidance and can be confident about what's in store. It starts simply: "Give me your hand, we'll walk together; there'll be time to do whatever we might want . . ."

The words of the chorus are:

אפילו אם אנחנו לא יודעים את הסוף
.לא נוכל להצליח לבד
באיזה דרך אשר נבחר
.ה' ישמרינו

Even though we don't know how it'll end
We can't succeed on our own.
Whatever path we choose
HaShem [God] will guard over us and protect us.

The singing wasn't forlorn or disheartening—the song actually has an uplifting and a fun, upbeat chorus. I played it a few times, slowly at first, and then picking up speed, as if to ease into it, allowing myself to enjoy, regret, accept, forgive, and enjoy again. Then "Bojangles" and "Christopher Robin" (for Merav, again), softly, and "Feeling Groovy." And then I started belting out "The Boxer" and kept that up for a while, "Lai la lai," hoping no one was going to come by and be startled.

Sleep was a bit hard—perhaps as my mind kept going in circles as I pondered our national history and current travails and my personal history (and recent travails). I was missing the kids and missing Karen but not really and not wanting to; missing Philip certainly and missing my friends and wider family. But I was also feeling surprisingly peaceful and happy. So maybe it was the sticks and rocks under my pad under the tent. I hadn't been too careful clearing the area out before assembling the bloody thing. I stayed in the sleeping bag for a long time the next morning; it was Friday and I was pretty close to my Shabbat destination. I took my sweet time getting up and packing up. It was noon by the time I had *davened*, made oatmeal and coffee, written a bit, looked at maps for the next week and made a few calls.

A fun thing about hiking the Shvil: sometimes people honk their horn, or wave from a passing car (or train), with a recognition that you're on the Trail. Maybe it's the flag, or the pack. When I was standing at the highway junction called "Tzomet HaMovil" near Moshav Alon HaGalil, so many cars honked for me it was almost embarrassing. But it definitely lifted my spirits. My friend Jacob, with whom I'd arranged to spend Shabbat (he and his wife, Haviva, were to be my Trail Angels), called to say he'd be a while before picking me up. Seeing a small placard, I wandered over and up a small incline (it's amazing what a few honks and a sign can do to inspire; I wouldn't have otherwise agreed to hike any further than necessary with my shoulders and knees hurting and tired from a sleepless night) . . . and discovered the Yiftah'el winery.

In a small and quite picturesque wooden building—an authentic historic Appalachian log cabin from the nineteenth century—shipped (it turns out) from America, I found wine and honey and an assortment of other local products, and enjoyed an hour of tasting and stories from Tzvika the owner. We laughed over the fact that I was hiking the Israel Trail and not the Appalachian Trail, and he explained how Allen Redli, a resident of the Moshav Alon Hagalil, brought the cabin to Israel, and how it stood vacant for a long while until being turned into the winery's visitor center. The wine was decent, but I bought honey as a gift, since Jacob had just recently opened his own winery, Jezreel Valley, which I already knew was producing fine wines of its own. Soon after, Jacob picked me up with two of his children and we made our way to their home in Kibbutz Hanaton.

Shabbat passed very pleasantly; and like each Shabbat on the Shvil, it was different. Which isn't to say it could compare, in its *differentness*, with the Desert Ashram or the Black Hebrews, but it wasn't a "standard" Shabbat in any way, either. If Sansana was traditional and young and vibrant, and Tzfat was social and full of history, Shabbat at Kibbutz Hanaton was inspiring in still other ways. I found it fascinating to observe, and participate in, this experiment in "post-denominational" Judaism. Established by a group affiliated with the "*Masorti*" (Conservative) stream of Judaism, the community made me feel comfortable and challenged at the same time, with their (bold? tangled?) intriguing combination of traditional observance and individualistic freedoms.

To wit: as a group they decided to close off the inner road of the central area of the Kibbutz for Shabbat—both to honor Shabbat itself and respect those who observe the normative proscription against driving on the Sabbath—yet the vast majority of the residents, parking their cars just outside the gate, use their cars. Similarly, the Kibbutz central synagogue uses a normative prayer structure with the *siddur Rinat Yisrael* (an "Orthodox" prayer book), yet is "egalitarian" both by including women in every part of the service and by changing a number of phrases to be gender neutral. Some of the families are more observant in a traditional manner, some are less—though it seems most fall on the latter side of the scale. From my perspective as a modern Orthodox visitor (if I must be placed in a box), the community reminded me of some Conservative shuls I've visited and spoken in over the past few decades.

I was both encouraged and unsettled by what I observed. I was moved by the attempt to make Jewish thought and practice relevant to today's society, within the confines—as broadly defined—of normative Jewish law. I was impressed by the earnest approach to spirituality in the *Tefilot* prayer services and in the discussions we had over Shabbat. But without being judgmental, it was impossible not to notice the discrepancy between the ideology as expressed in the brochure describing the community, and the reality of the behavior of many in the village. Some of the basics of Jewish practice were not observed, from Kashrut to Shabbat.

Haviva, my friend and host, is a unique character in this unique community. She is the first-ever Orthodox-ordained female rabbi and educator. Though no longer Orthodox, she became the first woman officially responsible for the running of a Mikvah in Israel, recognized by the (Orthodox, government-run monopoly) ministry of religious affairs. What she has done with this Mikvah in this remote village in Israel's rural north is extraordinary, a revolution in Israeli society, where religious duty becomes spiritual awakening, and where government bureaucracy becomes an uplifting service-oriented encounter. As a life-long advocate of women's equality and of their inclusion in religious life, I was thrilled to hear about and see Haviva's creation of a welcoming, inspirational, meaningful and rewarding Mikvah experience (which, for the record, is provided to male and female converts as well as to brides before their wedding and women every month).

I was so pleased to learn about Haviva's work; but I remained mildly troubled to discover how non-observant so many in the community were. The Shabbat I spent at Hanaton made me grateful for my life's experiences and community; it motivated me to continue to take my own spirituality seriously and look for greater meaning and depth in my own observance. And it reminded me how important the actual practice is: that it's not enough to know the long history of our religious experience and revel in that history and its wonders, we have to persevere in our own observance. Or it is lost.

One of the more amusing moments of the day occurred at lunch, when Haviva suddenly remembered the film about Mikvah, טהרה (*Tahara*—"Purity"), in which Karen and I were featured. (The ritual bath itself is used, as noted, for all kinds of spiritual purification. It is most associated with the marking of the end of the physical separation between husband and wife mandated in the Torah during the woman's monthly period.) The movie didn't present the institution of Mikvah in a very positive light, but Karen and I "starred" as a young couple who clearly respected the tradition, valued its more agreeable and meaningful aspects, and exhibited great affection for each other in the process. Realizing I was the guy in the movie, Haviva sort of blurted out "Wow—it's so weird that now you're divorced!" Her girls were more put out by that than I was; one turned on her and said "Mom! I can't believe you just said that!"

I had to admit to myself, as I rested later, that it was indeed jarring. Not her saying so, but the juxtaposition of that portrait of a loving couple (struggling to find ways to carry out and make relevant a cherished but challenging fixture of our faith) and my current reality of the dissolution of what was a beautiful marriage (full of explorations of just those sorts of spiritual and practical issues). I didn't dwell on it much—how far I'd come!—but the image stayed with me for days, and thoughts of Mikvah accompanied me as I made my way on the following days to my first view of the Mediterranean, that largest and deepest of Mikvahs.

It was a tranquil Shabbat, full of reflections on history; so it was a fitting end of that week. Jacob—whom I know from business and Jewish activism connections going back years—and Haviva—whose book *Life on the Fringes* about Jewish women's place in our society was one of the early catalysts for my own thinking—were marvelous hosts. Being with their family and friends was a real pleasure. I wrote in my journal later, "The Ner David household is a wonderful, vibrant, exuberant, wild, messy, fun, lively, crazy balagan—and great to be a part of."

They had asked me if I was willing to speak with a group on Shabbat afternoon about my experiences thus far on the Shvil and—though I had nothing prepared really—I agreed without too much hesitation. I was somewhat eager to try out some of these theories of mine, the lessons learned which I've been describing in this writing. I wanted to see what kind of interest my mental meanderings might generate; already, Jacob and Haviva were intrigued enough by what I shared with them at Friday night dinner to suggest the idea of a gathering, which was encouraging.

We called it "Tales from the Trail." In an informal setting, on Haviva and Jacob's balcony with about fifteen friends, I offered a few of the observations already described—the importance of humility, and acceptance, gratitude and forgiveness—each introduced by a particular memory from the Trail. It was fun; but much more importantly, it was exhilarating to feel the keen interest of everyone there. The comments and questions came quickly, and stimulated further thought and discussion.

One of the most frequent questions which came up—then, and again and again ever since—was "What was your favorite part/experience/day/place?" That afternoon, I came out spontaneously with the answer I've used ever since. I simply can't answer that question. It's like asking me as a father, "Which is your favorite child?" Or even more similarly, "What was your favorite part of being a dad?" Every day on the Shvil had peak moments; each and every day (till then, and in all) was incredible, and special, and wondrous, and spectacular. I said I can point to some amazing highlights—Har Shlomo, the Carbolet, Yatir Forest, the fields around Beit Shemesh; Nachal Snir and of course Baram Forest, as noted earlier, and even just a few days previously at Tzippori (and its forests!)—but "favorites"? Impossible.

Sitting and talking this all out was a challenge in a number of ways. How can you concisely condense weeks of experiences, thoughts, and ideas into a few sentences? How can I truly relate the power and poignancy of the trek without seeming either silly or pompous—and with the right balance of hiking detail and abstract philosophizing? And all this without boring the group to tears, or seeming to condescend to people who've gone through their own life challenges, learned their own lessons, and have as much to teach me as I may have to share with them?

I think I succeeded, though perhaps not as well as I might have liked. Fortunately, not only was it an informal group, it was a supportive and friendly crowd, interested and encouraging, and I think we all enjoyed the two hours spent sharing stories (theirs as much as mine) and sipping Jacob's delightful Jezreel Valley wine. (Aside from inducing me to think more seriously about writing this book, that Shabbat with Jacob reawakened my dream of opening my own winery.)

On *Motzei Shabbat*, Saturday evening, I accompanied Haviva and Jacob to a social and cultural evening in the Kibbutz library with an author who brings an unusual twist to his writing: an Israeli, living in New York, who writes in Hebrew. As my Facebook post later implied (below) I found it a bit disconcerting, and I wasn't and still am not convinced of the validity or necessity (or advisability) of such an endeavor. But I certainly appreciated the intellectual discussion provoked by his remarks and in a certain way was thankful it took a bit of the attention off me and my story, and allowed me to think of things other than myself, my problems, my learnings. And I was impressed by the very Israeli, and very Jewish, event, a throwback to the early Jewish pioneers (I thought) from Europe who'd sit around in "parlors" pursuing intellectual dialogue until late at night, just for the sake of it.

From my Facebook post on that Saturday night (March 29):

Six weeks . . . & counting.

At this point I really am counting. Counting the number of people who have been so very wonderfully generous and welcoming to me on the trail. Counting the number of times I've asked myself "what are you doing?" Counting the kilometers I've walked; and definitely counting the kilometers I've left to go. And in the simple sense of the phrase, counting the days till I can walk in the door and say "I'm home."

The North—the upper Galil and moving into the lower Galil, has been as promised: green, lush, verdant . . . tho also chilly, a bit rainy, and with far fewer people on the trail than I anticipated. Sleeping in my tent on 7° nights made me appreciate all the more the hot showers, comfortable beds, and most importantly warm hospitality of the friends I stayed with this past week.

Don't know how I would have made it through the week without my cousin Chagit; Chana N Shmuel Veffer who not only opened their home to me but spoiled me with an incredible stay in their beautiful Tzimmer Villa Ramona—which I can highly recommend to anyone looking for a special getaway in near the Kinneret; and Haviva and Jacob Ner-David who hosted me for Shabbat, and introduced me to all sorts of inspiring aspects of their life in Kibbutz Hanaton, a new experience in label-free Jewish life (replete with multi-nusached tefila, user-friendly mikvah, a vibrant Jewish cultural life . . . and an excellent winery, Jezreel). ☺

Truth is, I found it difficult to start the week; after a richly spiritual Shabbat in Tzfat I wasn't sure I shouldn't just remain for a few days and do some learning; then the hike down to Nachal Amud and then the cliffs—and the heat—took a lot out of me. I suffered my first real injury of the trip—lost my balance, stumbled off a low ridge and stopped my fall with my arm and elbow. Swelled up a bit, hurt like hell, couldn't lift my arm to my nose or pull my pack strips . . . and the day was much longer than expected. I spent the entire day in silence.

By Monday and my intemperate, spontaneous, almost whimsical jaunt through the shallows and hidden wonders of the shores of the Kinneret, I was back on form. Helped somewhat by the grand "Bouri" fish meal which I treated myself to in celebration of my victorious arrival in Tiberius. ☺ And the jacuzzi in the Tzimmer that evening went a long way to healing my arm and elbow too.

Tzipori is such a powerful example of what makes this trek so different from, say, the Appalachian trail or Nepal, Machu Picchu or the Pacific Crest Trail: This almost emotional, certainly spiritual and psychological, even metaphysical connection to the land I'm walking.

My people prayed here; my ancestors farmed here; my family struggled here: these hills and valleys echo with the voices and tears, battles and songs and footsteps of the Jewish people, Am Yisrael, the house of Jacob/Israel. My people. Our people.

On Friday after hiking casually right past a 2000-year old huge gat (stone wine press), I discovered a new winery, Yiftah'el, in Alon Hagalil, learned from Zvika of his family's generations of farming the area, and tasted his unusual wines (and honeys)—making that the seventh so far. (The others:

Rujum, Midbar, Yatir, Adir, Dalton, and Jezreel.) Talk about connecting past and present. ☺

Tonight, the week ended in a fascinating cultural evening, a discussion and reading by the author Reuven Namdar, an Israeli who lives in NY but writes in Hebrew—a new genre almost—about and from his new book, הבית אשר נחרב (The Ruined House). Fascinating, confusing, intellectual and extremely enjoyable talk, including a debate over whether a Hebrew culture is possible distinct from Israeli, and separate from Jewish. With wine and cheese, it was a great start to the week . . .

Shavua Tov—and see u on the trail . . .

Chapter Seven

THE GALIL & THE SEA:
ENDLESS POSSIBILITIES

[Week Seven]

*A*nd we're off again, Sunday, March 30, *not too early in the morning, climbing out of the Valley of Beit Netofa and heading up and over to the Jezreel Valley; the plan is to wind up at the western foot of the Carmel mountain range before dark. Jacob offers to drive me back to the trailhead, which I appreciate; but he's a bit late for a meeting, so drops me near Alon HaGalil, and I see a sign for a "Field Center" nearby. For some reason, I've developed a fixation on getting electrolytes, and presume they'll have some, so though it's about a kilometer out of my way and up a hill, I figure what the heck, it's Sunday morning and the day shouldn't be too difficult.*

Arriving at the Center, I find it's closed but then see two guys milling about; in fact it looks like they're breaking camp. I wander over, and as we start chatting I learn that Itai and Orr, young men doing the Shvil just after their IDF service, slept under the cover of the Center's patio last night. I don't have the heart to tell them of my bed and the hospitality I received from my Trail Angels Haviva and Jacob and the community at Hanaton. When the Center opens, I buy way more water tablets and protein bars than I need and begin to put my bag on. At that point Itai suggests we walk together, and rather casually I just say "sure!" and we set out down the hill on a path to the Shvil.

It starts to drizzle about ten minutes later. Funny but we hadn't even spoken about the weather, though I have my windbreaker on. We walk on and Itai and I argue politics a bit, nothing too serious; it's nice to have some company. To think this

204

is only the second time in the entire trek I've walked any length of time with someone else is a little overwhelming; I don't dwell on it. We do allow some distance between us occasionally, which I welcome; a little singing, a few photos, getting into the rhythm of the clacking of the walking sticks and I'm in my element, even with Orr and Itai a few dozen meters ahead.

At one point the rain starts to fall with a bit more force; I suggest we take cover under the fir trees in the forest lining our path, across from a small dwelling. It's not quite a house, but more than a shack. Itai and I return to our discussion of the Jewish roots of the land and the toleration we have for others inhabiting it. A few minutes into this discussion, a kid looks out, and then waves, from the back door of the shack. It seems this is a small Bedouin encampment, semi-permanent, and aside from smiling and waving to the child, the scene fits right in to our discussion of who the indigenous people are here. Itai acknowledges (he has little choice) that the Bedouin are nomadic in nature and came to this area only in the past hundred years or so; and that most other Muslim and Christian Arabs resident here came, similarly, in the past century, most particularly when Jews began to rebuild the economy and created jobs for laborers. Which isn't to say they have no rights; the opposite, as I chide Itai, they have all the fundamental human and civil, political and social rights as anyone in any free country like Israel. National rights, on the other hand, devolve from national identity, history, geography, demographics, international law, etc. He's quiet for a minute.

It's funny how these conversations, so serious in their content and intent, retain a kind of informality when you're sitting under a tree in the rain or walking along the Trail. And for me there's something incredibly casual, and pleasurable, in having such a conversation without the usual elements of my more formal lectures on college campuses and in communities around the world. There's no time limit, no structured "Q&A" session, and no feeling that if I miss out a particular point or argument, the audience will leave confused or angry. Here, we have all day, and though we may have different perspectives there is a mutual interest in real dialogue, unlike so often today in public discourse, unfortunately. I feel this, and enjoy it.

Itai, actually (with Orr's encouragement), starts to really get into it, and asks me for more background. When the rain stops, we continue our conversation while we walk. I spend a few minutes outlining the development of the Jewish people's identity as a nation, from Avraham's family to clan to tribe to becoming an "Am," a people, in the Exodus from Egypt (the first time the Bible refers to the Children of Israel as a "people"). I bring a few examples to prove how our connection to the land has continued these past 3,500 years, uninterrupted, including a significant and undisputed unique physical presence on the land (in Jerusalem, Tiberius, Tzfat, Tzippori, and the like). Of course we discuss the spiritual and religious, cultural and linguistic connection between the People of Israel (Am Yisrael) and the Land of Israel (Eretz Yisrael), including our prayers and songs of longing for Jerusalem and Zion over the centuries. I'm a little emotional as I walk along this trail, including through the Arab village of

Ka'Biyya, down the Tzippori stream, through the very Galil which was the center of Jewish life after the destruction of Jerusalem two thousand years ago.

Itai's a good listener; it's sometimes a wonder to me how little Israeli-born Jews actually know of our own history. A bit tired of talking, though, I'm glad when we arrive midday at the "תחנת הנזירים" (Tachanat HaNazirim—"Hermit's Station") just in time for a break. This is a bit more modern history, a flour mill from the Ottoman period, now being restored in the Kishon River reclamation project. We make a picnic lunch by the shallow circular pools and are joined by a large number of very friendly goats (!) making their way through and beyond the stream.

The three of us continue for a few hours of pleasant walking and only a bit more talking; toward the end of the day, as we near Kfar Hassidim, we discuss plans, exchange numbers, and tentatively set to meet the next day on the Carmel mountain range. They have friends nearby; I've arranged to stay at the Trail Angel in a kibbutz at the bottom of the hill, in spite of a few strange things I'd heard. I can't be bothered to change my plans. What can possibly go wrong? I ask myself.

It became something of a truism in my time on the Shvil that my optimistic and positive attitude was only sometimes justified by circumstances. Other times, I found myself angry or frustrated—or at least amused—at my own ignorance or stupidity. Such was the case with this Trail Angel. As I wrote in my journal, "Can't say I wasn't warned."

He was a nice enough young fellow, if a bit talkative; but over the course of a few hours that evening, and then the next morning, it was clear this young man had a few screws missing. Brash, loud, opinionated, ill-mannered, pushy, ill-informed, and oblivious to even the most obvious social cues I could come up with to attempt to communicate with him, he was nevertheless generous enough to offer a mattress, towel, coffee and tea, and shower, and I wasn't about to complain—not then, and not now. About 26, he was a secular kibbutznik, seemingly trying to become observant, but basing his observance on his own ideas and experimentation rather than on any form of normative (or even non-normative!) Jewish practice or traditions. Clearly, he had some behavioral/social "issues" (as my psychoanalyst friend Moshe would put it) but still—as I wrote in my journal—this was all part of the "experience" on the Trail.

I bought some cheese and a Kadesh Barnea Cabernet '10, very nice indeed, which I shared with my young host. We talked some religion, some politics, and turned in about 10 p.m., for which I was grateful. In the morning, after clearing up my stuff and setting the living room back in order (I had slept on the fold-out sofa in his small one-bedroom kibbutz apartment), I started to *daven* and he came in and, putting on his own *Tefillin*, started to pray alongside me. That was fine—even normal, in many situations—until he started to sway back and forth with increasing speed and intensity, and then raised his voice when saying the (usually quiet) blessings preceding the Sh'ma. I was mildly amused—but could see why those girls might have been a bit frightened by his behavior.

Still, I appreciated his hosting me, and after breakfast I thanked him and made my way through the kibbutz to the gate in the fence at the back, below the cliff-like face of the eastern portion of the Carmel. I stopped in the shade to fill my water bottle before the climb, and took a moment to look up the Kibbutz history on my phone. I'd just enjoyed the hospitality of one of Israel's largest, oldest and most successful kibbutzim, a stronghold of the pre-State Haganah defense force and a pioneer in business and education. Not as moving as visiting Ben Gurion's grave in Sde Boker, it's true, but it was yet another plank in this ongoing sense of history, ancient and modern, which accompanied me on the trek and informed my understanding of my people and our place here.

The climb up the Carmel was hard, and hot—but as I wrote later in my journal:

> "Eh . . . Small potatoes! ☺ Even my complaint about having to go up Har Shokef instead of just coming down the Carmel was pretty much in jest— it was all a piece of cake when compared with the others. Funny how perspective does change things . . .

In the end, I didn't reconnect with Orr and Itai, and that was okay; I was glad for the solitude of the day, having spent a very social Shabbat, and then Sunday all day walking with the two of them (and then Sunday evening and Monday morning with my talkative and somewhat demanding kibbutz Trail Angel). I had one fun social interaction midday, after walking through Daliat HaCarmel. A large Druze village, it's known for its special ethnic food and hospitality, and for the offer its mayor made of free accommodation to (mostly Jewish) residents of the South fleeing incessant rocket attacks by Hamas in Gaza. At the entrance to the forest descent on the edge of the village, I ran into a school group on its annual outing—and who called out my name but none other than Dror Sofer, the young man whose family had hosted me for that lovely Shabbat in Sansana, just over three weeks ago. A few hugs, a bit of catching up, it was like a reunion of old friends; and sweet how he had to tell all his buddies about me and the Shvil and how I'm a real "*gever*" ("the man" in loose translation).

After descending into a sort of hidden valley, and then ascending the further ridge, being on my own was especially welcome as I crested a hill on the western reaches of the Carmel, and breaking out into the open saw the Mediterranean Sea through the haze in the late afternoon sun.

I've always loved the sea. From as young as I can remember, I have fond memories of lying on the sand and staring at the waves, or listening to them as I drift in and out of sleep on family trips. It didn't matter if it was the Atlantic beaches of Rehobeth and Pompono Beach or the Pacific beaches of Pescadero and Pomponio, Santa Cruz and San Francisco Ocean Beach, or especially Stinson, north of the SF. Growing up in the Bay Area and studying at UC Berkeley made the ocean a significant part of my life.

Over the past thirty years living in Israel, I've taken my kids, and relatives, and gone with friends and family to probably every beach in the country, including in or near Ashkelon, Nitzanim, Ashdod, Palmachim, Rishon L'Tziyon, Bat Yam, Tel Aviv, North Tel Aviv, Herzliya, Netanya, Michmoret, Caesarea, Dor, Nachsholim, HaBonim, Haifa, Akko, Nahariya, Achziv, Shavei Tziyon, Rosh Hanikra and of course various beachfronts in and all around Eilat. I have camped, swam, played, dug, run, drank, smoked, partied, been sick, celebrated, grieved, argued, danced, sang, meditated and slept on more beaches than I can possibly count or remember—and have loved every minute of it. Every year I go with my friend Yaakov to a Mediterranean beach on erev Yom Kippur, the eve of the Jewish Day of Atonement, to sit quietly and contemplate life and to dip in the rejuvenating waters of the sea. מים חיים—*Mayim Chaim*—"Waters of Life" is how our tradition refers to the *mikvah,* which is any natural body of water, and which serves as a metaphor for our Torah.

Since that day on the Carmel, I have thought a great deal about the sea. There is something about the sea which speaks to us, which implies limitless expanse. But not only of nature. It suggests an endless capacity of our humanity: to think, to believe, to live, to love. Neuroscientists have a phrase for what the ocean does for us; they call it "blue space." Apparently, the positive ions in the water reduce stress; the open air and horizon boosts creativity, and the safe space and hypnotic repetition of sounds can ease depression. Researchers at Stanford suggest that the awe we feel at the sea can affect how we feel about ourselves, and perhaps even alter our perception of time. As Michael Merzenich, professor emeritus of neuroscience at UC San Francisco, puts it, "The smooth surface of the ocean rarely surprises. . . . When it's landmark-free, it's naturally calming . . . much like closing your eyes." Like many others, I return to the sea often for an injection of this awareness of the endless possibilities in our life, for a recharging of my spiritual and emotional batteries.

Now I understand a bit better why. When I crested that hill and suddenly saw the sea spread out before me, I started yelling, whooping and hollering. "Wow! Wowwwww! Woo hoooo!!!" I started singing "Here comes the sun . . . and I say, it's all right . . . !" And I began to cry, as I was singing "Little darling, it's been a long cold lonely winter," though even then I was laughing and yelling and dancing (a bit, I still had the pack on).

Afterwards, when I calmed down and began to descend the mountain, I thought about the intense emotion I had just experienced. An awareness came to me as I blundered my way down the slopes of the Carmel, no longer crying but still somewhat pensive. I sensed that there's a lesson to be learned from the infinite potential of the sea. I started thinking about our human limitations and whether *we too* have some unlimited capacities. But beyond these lofty musings,

I simply had a sense of my "having arrived." In a strange way, I felt that I was coming home, even with two weeks left on the Shvil and the fact that my home town of Beit Shemesh is nowhere near the sea. On seeing the vast expanse of water—and this from a vantage point high above, with the sun straight ahead and almost at my level—I felt as if I'd reached my destination.

And in a way, I had. If Beit Shemesh was my home territory, and Jerusalem the spiritual core of my Zionist "return" to the land (and the center of my work life and social life), the coast of Israel was and is very much a source of my emotional connection to Israel. I often used to cry—and still do—on seeing the coast come into view from the plane on a return flight home. Though in the previous two weeks, as mentioned, I had the growing feeling that I was heading home, that day I felt it even stronger. Looking at the sea, I understood that my journey was at the same time, ending . . . and beginning. Like the never-ending sea with its indeterminate horizon, my future was unwritten, open, endless and undetermined.

Those thoughts, of potentials and possibilities, accompanied me as I found the path and made my way to the spot where I was to join up with Netanel, who was coming to meet me for a visit. I had planned to picnic there, and to camp in the forest; but it was chilly and I decided I'd prefer treating Nati (and myself) to a decent meal. We could drive to Zichron Yaakov, a small picturesque town on the lower southern aspect of the Carmel ridge and one with stirring Zionist history, and I could stay at the organized campground nearby.

When Netanel arrived, we sat and talked briefly as I reorganized my pack, and then set off down the mountain in the car to find the campground. By the time we reached Zichron (about 45 minutes later) it was pretty dark. In the rolling hills and flatlands east of the town, we drove up and down a few dirt roads and through a few vineyards; and then we gave up. I can't really say we gave it the old college try; we made a minimal effort but our hearts weren't really in it. Given the past few hours' emotional and physical exertion, I was in the mood for *pinuk* as we call it in Hebrew, a treat of sorts. Earlier, I had called Trish, the owner of a *Tzimmer* in Zichron and a friend of a friend, just to check if she had anything available. Once it was clear Nati and I were ready to stop looking for the campsite, I called her back and booked the room. That lifted my spirits, though being with Netanel had by then gone a long way to achieving that.

We parked and walked up the picturesque central street of Zichron, one of the first "settlements" of the Jewish return to the Land over a century ago. It brought back good memories (and some not-so-good, also) from various family outings over the years as well as visits Karen and I made there on our own. Soon we found a kosher restaurant called Limma, which looked not only good but like good fun, given Netanel's trip to South America after his IDF service and his fondness for such food and ambiance. He had a hamburger, I had fish and chips, and we talked. As I wrote later in my journal:

And really good talk too—perhaps the first time, or so it felt, that we had really related to the divorce, and to feelings. Not too lengthy or heavy but felt good to have some of the stuff acknowledged. He said "you didn't deserve this" or something along those lines (when I had said something like "I can't believe this has happened to me" . . .) Anyway—we did have a fun time, and he got home quickly & safely. I am grateful for the love and support, and whether the visit was really just for "fun" or a way of expressing his support, I so much appreciate it.

The original plan was for Netanel to come with some friends and do a "poika" cookout at the Carmel night camp. In the end, I was glad his friends couldn't make it that night. There is something about eating at a restaurant—and especially one which makes you feel comfortable, whether fancy or regular—which seems to open us up to the sort of informal, intimate interaction hard to achieve when at home. I know I felt open to it that evening, as did my son. We talked at length about his plans for after finishing law school and about his and Tehila's first year of marriage, as well as about my next steps—and we shared a rather nonchalant laugh about those endless possibilities I'd been contemplating that afternoon. How many 50-year-olds literally can start their life over if they want to? (Not that I had wanted to; I would have been happy to have nothing changed. But given the circumstances . . .)

It was interesting—fascinating in fact—to recognize that in many ways we were going through similar experiences in spite of our generational distance. He was considering options following the completion of his degree and I had considered/decided to leave my job at MediaCentral; he and Tehila thought about living abroad at some point (having spent a few months studying in London already) and I pondered taking a job elsewhere (having been flown abroad for a job interview a few months previously); and on other fronts as well.

When he dropped me at Trish's B&B, I was sad to see him go. We had always been close, but our closeness was as much a product of our being the two men in the family, and sharing pretty similar values and intellectual ideas, as it was borne of any sharing of inner thoughts and feelings. It was delightful to spend time just connecting—and that connection was such an important reinforcement for me as I looked to finish the hike. Truthfully, carrying his letter to me from the first day of the trek was symbolic of the bond we shared, and I felt his support throughout. The visit just made it tangible again, like his driving me up north two weeks previously; though I didn't want to say goodbye, the fact that we scheduled for him and "the boys" to come do a *poika* the following week made it much easier.

For whatever reason, I slept fitfully that Monday night. (So much for the advantage of a nice bed, could have camped and slept as poorly, for 500 shekels less!) I calmed myself with my daily meditation and *Tefila*, and soon was happy to be up and out. Once again, the fun of walking out of the house, striding a few minutes through the outskirts of town, and finding myself on the Shvil was a charming aspect of the trek. Just outside of Zichron, as I walked south to meet up with the Trail, I had to walk through the gorgeous gardens of Ramat HaNadiv, the national park which is both the resting place of, and the main memorial to, Baron Edmond Rothschild and his wife Emily. Laid out in the manner of the grounds of an English stately home, but with a distinct Mediterranean feel, Ramat HaNadiv is both beautiful and educational. I have tender memories of wandering its paths, once with my parents-in-law, once with my brother- and sister-in-law, at other times with other members of Karen's wider family whose British nature makes the experience all the more enjoyable.

I have memories of Karen, and of our kids and our wider family, almost everywhere I go. It's funny how my associations with certain places have changed over time; even over the course of this trek, I find myself recalling earlier visits even while building new memories. I think that's one of the reasons I cried when viewing the sea; Karen and I had a great love for the Carmel Spa just over the next hill, and spent hours looking at that view. Meandering in the shade now, I pay special attention to the displays and descriptions of local and regional vegetation and the names of wild herbs and flowers, something I had done with Philip not so long ago and many of which I've of course seen over the past few weeks of walking the land. The old meets the new; the new replaces, or augments the old.

Tearing myself away from the park's neatly trimmed hedges and manicured lawns (and my memories), I rejoin the Shvil just outside the parking lot, and in a few minutes find myself on the edge of these southern reaches of the Carmel range, with a large stone arch ahead of me. I'm curious—it looks newly restored, but old. There's no sign or marker indicating anything of significance, but I stop for a few minutes to explore. It ends up being a real pleasure: I'm walking through what turns out to be the remains of a Byzantine estate built on the remains of a Roman fortress built on the remains of a Jewish/Israelite community from the Second Temple period! And of course, here's mikvah so clearly and carefully built into the basement of a Jewish house, with steps descending and with what was obviously a bath near it for preparation.

Funny, that. I was just visiting the amazing mivkah in Hanaton and talking with Haviva about the modern relevance of the institution! And the day before I wandered around the ancient mikvaot in Zippori. The mikvah so directly connects me to my heritage, my land, my people and our history—as do the wine crushing floor and the olive oil press here, on the other side of the estate. It never ceases to amaze me, how casually one comes across these historical remnants, reminders of conquerors come and gone and of course of our ancient and recent connection to our land. This site—with the Shvil running right through the middle of it—would be a noteworthy find and tourist attraction in any other country; here, having been excavated and documented, with a few signs to note pertinent details, it sits quietly, with no road even running near it to afford easy access. Just the sort of discovery I relish.

Putting my pack down, I climb up on a wall to just sit and enjoy, and take more photos, including of the sea in the distance. Whoever owned this place, in Israelite or Byzantine times, was my kind of person! They must have enjoyed watching the sunsets with a glass of wine just as I do on my balcony in Beit Shemesh. I start to imagine finding a way to build my winery right here, adding a bed & breakfast tzimmer and a nice restaurant too, just to carry on the historical tradition. Slipping down, I slowly walk across, and back and forth, the smooth surface of the grape crushing floor, noting the drainage indentation where the sweet, pungent, dark purple juice would have flowed down into the rectangular bath-like tub cut into the rock just below it . . .

But then it was time to move on, and I let those daydreams accompany me for a few minutes until I reached the end of the trail at the top of a rocky, windswept cliff. I wasn't familiar with this lower extension of the Carmel range—basically its southern tip—and I loved being able to literally look down, as if from a low cloud, on the fields and highway below, across the coastal highway to the beach and sea. In the distance, the outline of an Arab village was silhouetted against the sky and sea behind it. A train came by just as I was standing there, next to the cliff beneath me, and I decided there could be no better place to stop for lunch.

Somehow, once again, I found myself in an idyllic spot, alone, marveling at the combination of nature and human construction, flora and stone, sky and sea and countryside, history and modernity, all coming together in the most mundane and casual fashion. Literally high above it all, with my feet swinging in the air, I chewed my cheese sandwich and drank my cold water, hot from the walk and cool from the breeze. When I finished, I took the descent slowly. Another train came by while I was right by the tracks, and the engineer sounded the whistle for me; I waved, and then again as passengers waved back. That was fun.

I was soon distracted by a fork in the trail with no clear sign which way to go. I chose the left (correct) path, and wandered through a lovely little moshav . . . with an aqueduct running right through it. Yes—I discovered, looking in the Guide—this was *that* aqueduct, built by the Romans over 2000 years ago and still standing. And here I was walking alongside it, in the little village of Beit Chananya, where it basically was just a curiosity, like an old fence by a former horse corral might be in Woodside, California near where I grew up. I saw above me that some teenagers (presumably) had left a few plastic chairs at one point on the top of the aqueduct, a sort of hang-out spot I suppose. So casual; so natural; so incongruous; so amazing.

From there, under the highway and along a small road, I found myself in the center of Jisr az-Zarka, a picturesque if poor Arab town right next to the Tanninim Stream ("Alligator Stream," in Hebrew; the "Blue River" in Arabic, for which the village is named). One of Israel's poorest towns, settled by a Bedouin tribe in the early twentieth century, it was "protected" by its Jewish neighbors in the War of Independence due to the good relations between them. I was comfortable following the trail markings down its main street, and stopped at a kiosk for a strong coffee and chatted for a minute with a few men from the neighborhood, who described their interest in turning the village into a tourist site. I could see the stream from where we stood, and told them I thought it was a great idea. The sun was getting low in the sky, it was romantic and peaceful and enchanting; it reminded me of a little village in Greece I had stumbled upon, in the Peloponnese, thirty years previously, and I told them that too.

The Shvil led straight to the edge of the stream, past some rowdy kids playing soccer who called out "Shalom!" There, the National Parks Authority and the town council had partnered to create a charming promenade along the riverside, which reinforced my confidence in the place's tourism potential, as well as my sense of comfort, as a Jew and hiker and Israeli, in the very real coexistence it represented.

And then there I was, climbing up a ten-meter-high dune, the wind rushing into my face, arriving at the sea. I stood with my arms outstretched as it blew all around me and whistled in my ears, calling/singing/yelling "Whoohoo!" over and over. I looked up and down the beach and felt yet again, as I had the day before on the Carmel when first sighting the sea, this sense of having arrived. Somewhere, so to speak. I'd never even been to this particular beach, just north of the ancient and modern port town of Caesarea, but I felt very much at home. I knew I didn't have much time, as the sun continued its decent and I wanted to get to Caesarea before dark, but I needed to document this, to celebrate. So I bounded back down the dune to the stream, took out the camera, and retraced my steps up to the crown of the little hill, taking a video of the ascent and arrival,

Tanninim River and Jisr az-Zarka village

along with a few photos (Video 9). I almost lost my hat in the process, the wind was so violent.

I started to sing Naomi Shemer's famous song *"Halicha l'Kisarya"* (Walking to Caesarea), of course at the top of my voice:

אלי, אלי

שלא ייגמר לעולם

החול והים

רשרוש של המים

ברק השמיים

תפילת האדם . . .

Oh Lord my God
I pray that these things never end
The sand and the sea
The rush of the waters
The crash of the heavens
The prayer of humanity . . .

Aside from my hat, I almost lost my voice, I was singing so loud and so long, combining in my one voice the melody, the harmony, the accompaniment.

I sang it in Hebrew and in English as I walked along the shore, finding a few fishing boats moored just a few feet into the water on what was clearly an ancient stone pier. I balanced my pack on a large boulder and sat down to add the guitar into the mix, playing for more than ten minutes. And then, however rousing and fun that was, it had to come to an end and I continued on south toward Caesarea.

As I set off, two Arab Muslim women came along the shore beside me, and we walked abreast for a few hundred meters, after nodding pleasantly and smiling to each other. When they said "Shalom," I asked them where they were from, and as expected they said the nearby village of Jisr. We had a brief conversation about the difficulty of walking on the sand—especially with a pack (their comment, not mine). One might say it was unremarkable; but in these days of frequent conflict and expressions of animosity, I found it promising that we could converse blithely and without effort even as unspoken currents of "this land is my land" might pulse just under the surface.

I thought to myself: How many times have I driven by this small Arab town and seen, perhaps even enjoyed looking at, its minaret? Wondered what town it was, and where its people came from; maybe even how long it's been there and what its relations are with the nearby Jewish towns? It's quaint indeed from afar—I loved the colors and shapes silhouetted against the afternoon sky and the sea from the cliff earlier—but who really notices it? That's what makes this trek so marvelous. Walking through it, just the pace awakens one to all sorts of realities you just miss otherwise; it's so different even than biking, let alone driving.

I noticed the distinctive architecture, so unlike that of the moshav I had just walked through. The economic distress of the village was clear, but the number of building projects I saw indicated some steps were being taken to alleviate it. I heard the laughter of the children at play, and noticed a combination of pleasure and boredom, satisfaction and frustration on the faces of the men I spoke with at the kiosk. And I felt, rather than heard, the contentment of the two women walking near me and then in front of me (as I slowed down to take a photo), on their companionable exercise walk in their hijab and chador on the beach.

I stood, as they continued on, and watched the boats in the little harbor sway in the light swells of the outgoing tide. I walked slowly, and kept my eye on them; their rhythm, the smooth, soft cadence of the sea, kept time with my pace. Or I guess I kept time with its measure. Walking—how magnificent, how extraordinary and memorable these moments were.

And then.

Coming into Caesarea was both an enjoyable and painful episode. On the one hand, I know it so well: our oldest friends as a couple had been the rabbi and rebbetzin there for some 13 years, Dov and Freda. We spent countless wonderful Shabbatot and Chagim and other times with them, and made a number of dear friends in the community in the process, and I just love the place. On the other hand—or on that same hand, in fact—these were memories of a distinctly married/family nature, and this was the first time in years I'd set foot in Caesarea on my own. This realization came crashing down on me as I saw the Roman aqueduct coming closer. I had planned and executed the most unique and exquisite (if I may say so) surprise 50th birthday party ever, for Karen, on the very beach I was walking along. This was painful; at that moment, I was there very much alone. Such magnificent times; such amazing memories; such fleeting pleasure, it seemed to me as I stood there.

Yes, I shed a few more tears, I'm not embarrassed to admit, as I walked under the arches on the exact spot we had stashed the firewood for that party only a few years previously. I did what I suppose was expected, however cliché: took my pack off, paced back and forth over the sand where the tables were laden with fine wines and exquisite cheeses. I stood just where we had sat around the campfire sharing stories about Karen—the kids, friends old and new, even her cousin (almost sister) who had conspired with me to fly in and surprise Karen. I leaned against the arch, and then sat down, sighing.

I didn't cry any more that day, but I did reflect on the certainties and uncertainties of this life, and in particular on that brilliant and terrible Yiddish phrase, "Man plans, God laughs," which I've had reason to refer to already. On the one hand, I was still astonished at the turn of events in my life, saddened and pained as I reviewed the previous few years which brought me to that point. Yet sitting under the arch of that 2000-year-old aqueduct—two thousand years!—I was also incredibly grateful for all the blessings of my life, and not least the wonderful years of marriage I did have. It was somehow comforting to have the reminder of the grand sweep of history above and surrounding me.

Resting there, I recalled giving a "Welcome to Israel" talk right on that spot as well, years ago, to a group from America who came straight from their arrival at the airport. (I call it *3,500 Years of History in 35 Minutes.*) "It's so important to understand and internalize, as you wander and wonder at the modern state of Israel, the wider perspective and the long stretch of the history of the Jewish people on this Land," I told them. "You cannot fathom what Israel is all about today, in all its complexities, without appreciating the historical context of this indigenous people returning to our ancestral homeland." I quoted Mark Twain to them, about the Romans and others holding their torch high for a time but now having vanished, as the Jew saw them all fade. Sitting with my back to the arches, I took comfort from that, in my own little world focused on the here and now, in the same way I wanted these American visitors to see the current unrest and animosity toward the state of the Jews: as only one small element in a much broader universe. I wasn't denying my suffering or my challenges, personally; I took solace in knowing how resilient I can be, just as my people was and is.

Wow—I said to myself, hoisting my pack on my back—you are so full of yourself. Cut the hyperbole! But I was loving it, and really relishing the turn to the positive and the return to my optimistic thoughts of the day before, about potential. Like the sea stretched out before me like a never-ending blanket of water, my life was full of endless possibilities. And here I was, in the final stretch of this mammoth undertaking to walk the Land. I was but ten minutes away from the real luxury of my friends Arnold and Judy's home in Caesarea, a hot shower and good company and soft bed awaiting me. I was ready to accept, with humility, how my plans, like so many Jews before me and since, had God laughing. I was grateful for the kindnesses of so many, and full of forgiveness. I was both living in the moment—thank you Jason Mraz—and focused on the future.

It seems to me, as I'm walking up the quiet, broad streets of Caesarea, marveling at the size and variety of the stunning houses here, that most of us aren't willing to allow ourselves to consider, let alone explore, the possibilities available to us. I remember discussing this one Shabbat, regarding the number of Jews who chose not *to leave Egypt at the time of the Exodus. And about the "multitude" of non-Israelites who chose to accompany the Jews out. And how, during the Second Temple period, when the prophets Ezra and Nechemia led our people back to our ancestral homeland, they were followed by only about ten percent of the nation of Israel at the time. 90 percent stayed behind! They couldn't see the possibilities inherent in the return of the Jews to their land. Their myopic outlook, like that of those who chose to remain in Egypt (or for that matter, in Germany in the early 1930s), blinded them to the opportunities right in front of their eyes.*

Not only am I so grateful for all I've been given, I'm thinking as I approach Judy and Arnold's home; I'm grateful for the attitude instilled in me by my parents, and my teachers, and my community and country, that nothing can prevent us from pursuing our dreams. That we all have skills and talents to develop and share; that any kid can become president of the United States, as it were. Herzl said "If you will it, it is no dream" in reference to the re-establishment of a Jewish commonwealth in our ancient land. I find it so very funny—as in ironic, fantastic—that here I am walking through one of the most wealthy, thriving communities in the modern state of the Jewish nation . . . and it's called Caesarea. It's named after the harbor town created at the time of that Roman tyrant, Julius Caesar, and to honor him. Caesar did great things but, as Twain said, he has faded away, as has the empire he built. And here we are. And here I am. What a lucky person I am to be living in this time. Not only am I able to participate in the pursuit of our national dream, this return to Jewish sovereignty in the Land of Israel after two millennia of dispersal; I also have the opportunity to try to fulfill whatever personal ambitions I have as well. What a terrific demonstration of the power of pursuing our dreams.

Hah—there I go again, waxing poetic. I think my main ambition right now is a decent shower and an early night. Here I am indeed: at Arnold and Judy's.

They were so warm and welcoming, I felt like a long-lost brother or cousin coming home. Arnold and Judy have a way about them which makes even strangers feel embraced, and I was no stranger either to them or their home. After showering and a quick hello, we were off to the shul for a Rosh Chodesh barbeque (the celebration of the new month). It was a bit more social than I might have been looking for, but enjoyable nonetheless. I had the pleasure of meeting the new rabbi, Rav Tzvi Elon, who was more than politely interested in hearing about the Shvil. He is also more than a little similar to their former rabbi, my close friend Dov, in demeanor and in appearance, which was amusing and even endearing.

Of course, staying with friends is different than being hosted by Trail Angels, as I had already learned. Both experiences are great; but very unalike. In the latter situation, one makes polite conversation, if warranted/invited; sometimes a real connection is made (as it was with the Sofer family in Sansana, for instance), but usually even if there is a warmth evinced from both sides, the association is fleeting. With friends, there is both greater intensity, and greater investment of time and emotional energy—not least in my situation, where "catching up" often involved lengthy discussion of the divorce in addition to news of the kids, as well as of course my friends' news. This was unquestionably welcome; it was wonderful, and important, for me to reconnect with each of these friends. And it was also somewhat exhausting, and I never really learned how to allow for it in my schedule, or compensate for it in my planning.

In this case, rather than making preparations for the next day or winding down with a little guitar or reading, I joined Arnold and Judy in front of the television for a few hours (!)—something I couldn't actually remember doing for years, just hanging out and watching TV. They were watching a series called "Suits," a program I was unfamiliar with but which was great fun to see with them and laugh at together. It seemed so very normal, over a glass or two of very nice wine. I avoided the temptation to slip into melancholy ("This is what normal people do; why is/has been my life so intense; see how happily married they are . . .") both by remembering this is their second marriage ("Hah!—and look how happy they are!") and by focusing on my maps and plans for the next few days, in between scenes.

The next morning, Wednesday, I wanted to get out on the early side. Though as the crow flies the distance to my next night's lodging in Beit Yanai, on the coast as well, is only a few kilometers, for a number of reasons the Shvil turns inland, and I had a full day's walk ahead of me. I took a few minutes for a deliberate, meditative walk in Judy and Arnold's charming garden, barefoot and with measured steps and deep breathing, which helped to restore balance and infuse me with energy. It turned out to be one of the best days on the trek, in spite of the fact (or because of it? I just don't know) that some of it had me meandering through urban streets and walking alongside the freeway. And it included a long-awaited reunion with my new Shvil-friend, Yaron, whom I'd last seen in his yellow van in the Negev desert, that Sunday morning on the road outside the Ashram, just under six weeks earlier.

On the way out of Caesarea, I find myself walking along the road by the Roman port and amphitheater. Oh! The memories, especially of all the Shlomo Artzi concerts I've been to here, bittersweet at the extreme. He was/is not only my favorite of performers (Israel's Bruce Springsteen, I like to say), but having introduced Karen to his music he became "ours" in a manner of speaking. okay—let's keep moving, we used up this week's allotment of reminiscing, let alone historical philosophizing, already. A nod to the historical importance of the site; have to take a photo of this ancient synagogue mosaic I haven't seen previously; now let's move on.

The Trail is a bit frustrating. At a glance at the map last night I saw how—due to power plant and a navy base on the coast which you can't walk through, as well as the attraction of the Hadera forest and Alexander River—the Shvil goes back and forth, east and west and south and even a bit north, winding its way back and around to the sea, then inland again, then back. I keep debating whether to just cut away from the Shvil and walk down the coast from after the power plant . . . but I can't really consider that. I have a lovely treat in store for myself!

So I keep on—and the frustration builds somewhat as I reach the highway at the Caesarea interchange. I'm disappointed to be walking alongside the highway—Road 2, Israel's first highway, the coastal road linking Tel Aviv and Haifa. Quite literally alongside it—the Shvil markings are on the ugly low steel traffic barriers off the shoulder of the road. I can't hear myself think; definitely can't hear myself sing; it's unsightly and noisy and I can smell the exhaust—seriously?!? What were they thinking? But as I stop for a minute to adjust my bag and the water tube, I realize: this too is Israel. This Trail is meant to explore all of Israel; when I give that "Welcome to Israel" talk, I always take a minute at the end to refer to the modern "history," the current period, in all its miraculous spectacle. Freeways; traffic; the wealth and relative luxury of a society overflowing with private cars and industry, representing a thriving middle class and upwardly mobile population. I start to look at the cars whizzing by—and though they're moving fast, I start to really see the people in them. Men and women, dark and light, young and old, Jewish, Bedouin, Druze, Christian, Arab, Ethiopian, Asian, you name it—it's a mosaic! Sparkling new Audis and decrepit old trucks, moving vans and sports cars and SUVs and weary family wagons—it's a moving-picture of Israeli society in true color, real life, right in front of me. Fascinating, wonderful, uplifting, and just plain cool.

Very few gaze back of course—drivers concentrate on the road, and even passengers are speeding by too quickly even to register. But a number show a quick sign of recognition—"Hey! There's a hiker! Neat!" is what it seems to me their instant wide smile says—and that's fun too. I begin to feel a bit foolish, standing there staring at the traffic; and a bit irresponsible, as someone might either stop thinking I need help or, worse, have an accident because of the distraction I've caused. So I walk on, still enjoying this new view into the Israel of today: fast-moving, always stuff happening, full of people going places, like any other modern culture, just as Herzl wanted.

Soon, after an enjoyable interlude of nature where the Shvil turns west along Hadera Stream, I come to a charming sight, a graceful white pedestrian bridge with spans reminding me of a small Golden Gate, though with wood and bright steel, and happily cross over the river into a park with a few grassy knolls and benches. From there, heading south on a long, straight, boring, hot stretch of virtually unused road, I consider flagging down the one passing car, but am too late. I end up in a northern residential neighborhood of Givat Olga, west of Hadera and the highway. Though I don't relish the idea of walking through a city, I don't really mind, with my new-found acceptance. (And thanks again, Bill Bryson, as I'm reminded of that passage where you observe that the cities and towns along the Appalachian Trail are part of the experience too.) I take special note of the urban development, and particularly enjoy the Trail marker painted on a large round sewage cover, in a small field behind a low-income housing project abutting the highway. The Trail has returned to the freeway, and I've had pretty much enough of the traffic and noise, which has lost its appeal. So for the first time on the Shvil, I plug in my earphones and turn on my phone. I know I'll have electricity tonight to recharge, and what the hell, I feel I've done enough meditating and contemplating for a lifetime, let's listen to that group Netanel loaded a while back.

What's their name? I find it: Kings of Leon. Never heard of them, but if Nati recommends 'em, I'm game to try; in any case, happy to have both a distraction and something new. It's a whole new experience—now I'm walking in time to the music, and somewhat unexpectedly I begin to understand why people in gyms or exercise groups work out to music! It's a real motivating influence; a bit artificial to me, as I'm so used to setting a pace for myself, whether with music in my head (or out loud) or just with an internal rhythm pattern, but I like it and it works. And I really like these guys; their music has a power to it, their lyrics some real meaning—and not least as I start to listen more carefully and they're singing about getting "Closer," "Wait for me," being "Somebody," "It don't matter to me" and then (the best!) the "Comeback Story." So the Kings of Leon accompany me through the streets and neighborhoods of Hadera, along the highway, up and over the overpass and past an incongruous field full of cows on the other side of the freeway, past the train station and into the Hadera forest.

The woods are such a relief, in so many ways—the shade, the availability of water, the flat expanse of greens and browns, not to mention the QUIET—and I'm exulting in every step. I wonder how many people from other parts of the country even know about this oasis of tranquility in the middle of Hadera. Finishing all three albums of Kings of Leon (thanks again, Nati), I decide to continue this new tradition of music-on-the-trail, looking for something to soothe my now-aching muscles as I pick up the pace.

I just noticed the time; having set the forest as a tentative rendezvous spot last night by text messages, I realize I'm supposed to meet Yaron in less than an hour, and still have a good five kilometers to go. In that time I traverse the tallest Eucalyptus trees I've ever seen, planted 100 years ago to drain the swamps it seems, just like up in the Hula Valley. And I traverse also the whole spectrum of emotions as I listen to the music on my iPhone which is, unintentionally but naturally, full of memories. I tear up listening to Adele, which evokes those days in Rosh Pina when Karen announced her intention to get a divorce; then again with the soundtrack of Once, singing loudly "Leave!" from Once and going back to Adele with "Take it all," coming full circle with tears while belting out "Don't you remember?" But even so, it's as if I'm allow-ing, or even encouraging, this melancholy: the tears are real, but aren't as heavy as before. I feel like I'm saying goodbye to all that, almost having a last fling of sorts, as I move on from the sorrow and pain. I'm not smiling exactly, through the tears; but I'm aware of a lightness surrounding the sadness.

I finish off with a medley from Loggins and Mesina and soon I'm striding ahead brightly to "Danny's Song" and "Your Mama Don't Dance." I send Yaron a text pin-pointing where I think we'll end up meeting; he confirms he's about the same distance away. I'm not sure why, but I'm full of energy now, walking almost as if I have no pack on, swinging my poles as if they're walking sticks and I'm some Englishman out for a country stroll. Forty delightful minutes later, I come across the perfect place to meet: a picnic area beneath the trees, with tables and even water. I don't bother messaging Yaron; there's no way we could have missed each other (if we both were on the right trail, and I'm sure I am—here's the sign, on a tree right here before the tables).

After throwing my pack down on a bench and splashing water on my face, I set about boiling water for coffee and placing literally all the food I'm carrying on the table. This is going to be the picnic of all picnics on the Shvil; it's the reunion of the Fellowship of the Trail, the Two Walkers. I'm not sure if we're Rangers like Aragorn or Elves like Legolas and Elrond or Hobbits like Frodo and Sam . . . but do know I'm looking very much forward to seeing him. I think we're hobbits, I decide.

I lay out the cheese, bread, Labane, crackers, cookies, munchies, and the rest of the stuff I bought a few hours ago at the little store at the gas station near the Caesarea interchange, listening to Kings of Leon singing "This could be the end." Once Yaron texts me he's near, I look up every few seconds or so—my camera's ready, I want to capture his arrival—and sure enough, there he is! I see him coming over a rise a few hundred meters down the dirt road, and casually stroll to where the trees meet the path; first I take a video of him striding toward me, his smile as wide as mine. Then I take a few photos, including in the frame the Shvil markings on the tree. "Welcome to Aryeh's Hadera Rest Stop!" I call as he nears; he bounds up, big hug. Pointing to the water faucet a few paces away, I tell him I'm making coffee and lunch is ready . . .

It was a real treat; and it all went way too fast. In fact, that's one of the first things we talked about: how we were both nearing the end of our trek, and it seemed (now that most of the suffering was over) the time had gone by so incredibly quickly. As described earlier, though our personal journeys were very different, we shared enough that we had a real bond, a common language, not only about the hike itself but certainly that also. We compared notes, and laughed a lot about the various exploits we'd had since we parted that Sunday morning. "Was that really only about six weeks ago?" It passed so fast, but to us both, we agreed, it seemed like a lifetime ago.

What is it about friendships—about love between two human beings—that sometimes is ignited by the simplest of events? It's not that a secular Israeli-born Jew and an observant American-born Jew in Israel can't find common ground; it happens all the time, especially to those of us who are open to it. But it usually takes work. Yaron and I fell into step that first morning, walking toward Timna, with a comfort borne of, I suppose, a combination of curiosity and loneliness, but mostly (for me) an immediate awareness of the intelligence, and kindness, and interest Yaron exhibited, and the swift recognition of the shared challenges we faced.

I guess he felt the same. Our talks that first day, and then over the course of the intense ten-hour trek up the *Milchan* and over to Shacharut, created an attachment as powerful as that between friends of a decade. It reminds me of the intensity of summer-camp relationships: within days of the round-the-clock interaction with bunkmates (and later when on staff, with other counsellors), you feel as if you've known someone forever. On the other hand, it reminds me somewhat of those deep conversations you sometimes have on an airplane with the complete stranger sitting next to you: with nothing to prove, no history, and no future connection to be wary of, we open ourselves up in ways we might not otherwise.

To a certain extent, my relationship with Yaron was a combination of both. We'd just met, and in those first days it was very much like the friendly person on the plane, where with a connection once made pleasantly we may have just said to ourselves "why not? What's to lose here?" Then, in occasional calls and messages since, we subtly acknowledged a shared desire to continue the friendship—like camp friends or airplane seatmates who reconnect afterwards. The uncertainties of our situations created a brotherhood of sorts where we shared with each other, and *only* with each other, something unique. Others may go through divorce, or career re-alignment, or hike the Shvil; none would combine them as and when and how we did. *That* was what makes our friendship exceptional.

We all have friends with shared experiences as well as shared beliefs or values. Of course family ties are by definition made up of just that stuff. Living together, travelling together, facing hardship together, celebrating together, creates bonds which (usually) can't be broken. That was of course one of my most powerful arguments to Karen why not to so casually decide on divorce, or so I thought. No one else could ever share the years we had together, the raising of our kids, dealing with families, building communities, creating lasting friendships—and didn't those shared experiences and values mean something? I felt so; in my understanding and definition of marriage they mean as much as romantic love. But I digress.

Having history in common cements relationships. I have friends from UC Berkeley and our fraternity, Sigma Alpha Mu, where I spent most of my college years and served in various positions. I have friends who, like me, became more active in their Jewish observance, having grown up in Reform Jewish families. And I have friends who, like me, grew up in America and moved to Israel. But I have only one friend in the world, Robert Koltai, who shares with me all three of these features. I have friends I studied with in the Reform rabbinical school, Hebrew Union College in Jerusalem; I have friends as above who have become more observant; I have friends who I've shared apartments with. But I have only one friend in the world, Mordechai Kraft, who shares all three. (Funny enough, Rob and Mordechai know each other, learned together in the same Yeshiva, completely unbeknownst to me for years. Go figure.)

So it was with Yaron and me: a bond unique to the two of us. We spent about a couple of hours together that Wednesday in Hadera Forest, talking about the vicissitudes of our lives and sharing—really, genuinely revealing to each other—our anxieties toward the future, our exhilaration on nearing completion of the trek, our hopes about our next steps. And we talked at length also about the possibilities open to us, not surprisingly. For Yaron, that meant pondering not only new job opportunities but whole new professional directions, perhaps even moving his family to another part of the country. For me, that meant not only thinking about finding another life's partner but, like Yaron, contemplating a move to a new community, as well as all the prospects I'd been considering regarding my career: stepping aside as director of MediaCentral, pursuing a new initiative to reassert the legitimacy of Israel and Zionism, opening a winery, returning to the business world, and all the rest.

After about two hours—which of course passed far too quickly—we both realized we had to get moving, if we didn't want to end up walking in the dark. (Which we both did, in the end.) As casually as we met, we parted, with a hug and a wave, both lighter on our feet for the encounter, with promises not only to be in touch but to let each other know when we neared completion of the trek, hoping we might be able to greet each other then.

With my head full of this talk of "possibilities," I spent the next few hours trudging up and down small sand dunes, which Yaron had warned me about, slowing things down considerably. I had fun walking along the railroad tracks for a good hour, with trains rumbling by every ten minutes or so, waving every time one passed. As I approached the turn into the woods of Alexander River national park, I welcomed the beauty and coolness of the emerald- and bronze- and vanilla-colored trees, so vibrant and alive in the early Spring. Coming to the water at the riverside—wow!—I dove in to the splendor of yet another spot I'd never been to before. (I didn't actually dive in; wanted to, but wasn't sure it's permitted, and also wasn't sure of the time remaining ahead of me until sunset, the sun being already low beyond the trees as I headed west along the river toward the sea.)

I got lost—happily so, knowing the general direction—among the sand and leaves and rocks and trees, and ended up in a lovely picnic area with numerous tables, water fountains and even small wheelchair-accessible decks jutting out over the river. Smiling at a small child and his parents as I ducked my head under a water faucet, I continued at a good pace along the water's edge. I took photos periodically of the changing hues of deep greens and blues and yellows as the sun sank lower on the horizon, repeatedly noticing the differences when you face one way—upstream—and the other, downstream. It was like two separate rivers, two different worlds—such a lesson in perspective, yet again.

A few teens stopped to chat while I rested by the riverside. As I wrote in my journal, it's interesting how many Israeli kids know and respect the Shvil— "כל הכבוד!" and "בהצלחה!" repeated often, *Kol Hakavod*—Good for you!" and "*B'Hatzlacha*—Good luck!." Nice. Choosing a light and melodious Sade album to accompany me, I continued along the river. I climbed up a hill to look at and walk around a small ruin, apparently a not-so-old building used by Ottoman customs officers. I enjoyed a small thrill of both noting how the river mouth was used as a locus of trade, knowing how the Ottoman empire vanished as did the Roman and others, and then reading about the "illegal" immigration ships which unloaded their Jewish refugees against the wishes and (illegal) regulations of the British. The first of these, the ship Velos, broke the British blockade right there at Beit Yannai beach.

I arrive, soon enough, at the beach, continuing the singing I had started earlier, unplugged at this point and loving the sounds of the birds and the wind in the trees, and now the waves on the beach. Crossing underneath the highway and coming up to the beach, I'm rewarded by not only an impressive pink and orange sunset but a few hang-gliders as well. Amazing, and inspiring, the way they just float, catching thermals—fantastic, the "possibilities" they latch on to!

I call my Trail Angels and am (pleasantly) surprised when their daughter offers to come pick me up. Agreeing happily, I retrace my steps to the road where I cross the highway, and soon enough, as darkness falls, she pulls up—so sweet to come get me. Little did I know that Calanit is herself hiking the Shvil as well! She tells me she's at home due to a painful foot blister, intending to return in a few days—and this is the first time her family has hosted Shvilistim, with three others already at the house. Calanit knew exactly the disappointment, bordering on despair, to have arrived at the beach, at the end of a 20-kilometer day including traipsing through sand for over an hour, only to discover it's another 2 kilometers to the house. I am, of course, the anomaly. I'm an older guy with a story rather than a run-of-the-mill it's-the-thing-to-do post-army type. She enjoys getting the initial details from me as we drive to her village of Havatzelet HaSharon; on arrival I take my turn in the shower after Einat, Yaella and Meira, the other three (yes, young) trekkers before me.

Rachel and Gady, Calanit's parents, are not only friendly and generous hosts; they are perfect examples of that cliché about strangers only being friends you haven't met yet. We have supper, chat for a long while, very enjoyable; then Gady and I play guitar together, a delightful surprise. Finding even more in common, we finish the good bottle of wine he had opened with dinner, graduate to a decent single malt, and turn in, they to prepare to take their son Yuval, a champion fencer, to the European youth finals in Bulgaria tomorrow, me to plan out my route and schedule.

In the morning, after barefoot תפילה *Tefila* prayer and meditation on the grass in their garden overlooking the beach and sea, I decided to do something I hadn't ever done before. With enough time and a short day ahead of me, having arranged to spend the night with friends in Netanya, only about 12 kilometers away, I left my pack at Gady and Rachel's, and walked up the beach to where I left the Trail at Beit Yanai. Without being sure why—except that since arriving at the coast I hadn't really taken time to actually enjoy it—I just felt like taking my time. Finding a café right on the beach, I grabbed a chair on the sand, ordered an espresso, and pretended I was just hanging out; not a Shvilist for the moment, just someone delighting in the seaside and sunshine. Soon enough, though, I'd had enough; I was itching to return to the Shvil. Retracing my steps, lightly, I grabbed my pack, said goodbye, and was back on the Trail. And so glad to be, too. As I wrote much later, looking back at that point in the trek, in my journal: "Walking the beach down to Netanya (and on from there Fri & Sun & Mon) was really special. Each moment pretty & perfect & different—rocks & sand & pebbles & boulders & cliffs & wood & shells & birds & weeds & trees & brush & jelly fish & more birds . . ."

Having sat at the café on Beit Yanai beach earlier, I decide to repeat the pleasure, at Neorim beach before arriving at Netanya, in order to write. From there, I climbed up the incline into Netanya, following the trail markers, losing them, finding them again, strange to be doing so in a bustling city on a cliff overlooking the sea. I put it this way in the journal: "Walking into and through Netanya was weird: first time I'd been in a city since Arad. Heard more Russian than Hebrew!"

Here I was, like those youthful tourists I sometimes smile at making their way to/from Jerusalem's Central Bus Station and the hostels in the city center near my office, lugging a huge backpack through the middle of a lively metropolis. Okay, Netanya's not London, but it's one of Israel's bigger cities, and more important, has a thriving business and tourist section right there on the bluff above the beach—through which the Trail threads without a qualm. I did enjoy the experience, however incongruous. And more, the feeling was building how near home I was getting. I used to work in Netanya—a 50-minute drive from my home in Beit Shemesh! This was, familiar territory. In fact I walked right by a hotel where family from abroad had stayed while we—the "poor Israeli relatives" as it were—stayed across the street at *that* hotel, a dive really, and crossed the street to eat dinner with the family. Some memories we don't need to be reminded of.

And then I chided myself for complaining about staying in the wrong hotel. *Here* was the Park Hotel, where the Seder massacre suicide bombing was carried out in 2002, one of the most horrific terror attacks in Israel's history, with 30 civilians celebrating Passover Seder murdered and 140 injured. It lead to Operation Defensive Shield, Israel's major incursion into the territories allotted to the Palestinian Authority under the Oslo accords, following years of terror bombings across the country. This particularly gruesome attack had galvanized the people and government to understand that no one—NO ONE—is going to protect our citizens or prevent terror attacks other than our own forces.

Without spending too much time on maudlin thoughts of terror and war, I began to mull over the various sites I'd passed, whether locations of terror attacks, or memorials to terror victims or to fallen soldiers and others, and realized how our little country is literally dotted with these sites. There is something so very upsetting about the loss of lives so unnecessarily (war being unnecessary in essence, except when in defense, of course). Yet there is something so very inspiring, both in the heroism of our defenders and in the unity generated in our society at times of national danger.

In a very tangible way, there is a real awareness here in Israel of the fragility of everyday life, and therefore its value; and we recognize also the importance of remaining vigilant and on guard against attack. This awareness hasn't been really appreciated by most Americans or Europeans since WWII, though in recent years unfortunately it's beginning to return to consciousness due to the growing scourge of terror there as well. I felt it there in Netanya, a city which has suffered many assaults on its residents, but has remained resilient, and in fact has flourished, in the face of the onslaught. I wasn't sure why this comforted me, but I had an inkling it has something to do with our sense of purpose in being here.

I didn't mind this train of thought; but I didn't really want to dwell on it. I thought again of Alterman's "silver platter," as I had at the Palmach memorial in the Jerusalem hills, and gave heartfelt thanks for all the sacrifices made so I could be there, at that time, wandering through Netanya, this oasis on the eastern coast of the Mediterranean. With all the motivation in the world to turn my thoughts in more upbeat directions, I enjoyed and celebrated the dazzling, colorful flowers all over the houses and sidewalks. On the southern edge of town, I found a Kosher café on the promenade at the top of the cliffs, high above the waves, and sat on the wooden deck with a Stella beer and pretzels to read and write and pass the time until David and Amanda, old friends from Beit Shemesh who had moved to Netanya a few years previously, finished their pre-Pesach shopping and I could walk the last thirty minutes to their house. After meditating on the cliff's edge with a magnificent sunset behind deep gray and blue/purple clouds above the dark blue-green sea, I made my way there.

David and Amanda were—as always—wonderful hosts, and very interested in my Shvil stories. But more, we had a great deal of catching up to do, about the kids, theirs and mine, and the community, as well as politics and philosophy to discuss. It was great to see them as well as their son Avichai, who was a close friend of Meira's in earlier years. Amanda showed me a photo of a friend of theirs, on Facebook, as a potential match for me; I told her it was a bit early for that, with a wan smile, as I was aware that this was the next stage I had to accept, even embrace, in my personal journey. They were sweet, and supportive; and, knowing that the next two nights I'd be out in my tent, I took special pleasure in the shower, bed, towels, sheets and everything else which is part and parcel of a "normal home"—so foreign to me, in a way, by then. And did some laundry too.

I didn't need an alarm Friday morning: David's dogs provided that service. I knew it was a relatively short hike to where I planned to camp for Shabbat, but

Aryeh walking on the beach south of Netanya, photo taken by David

wasn't sure how long it would take to shop and settle in and "make Shabbos" as we say, so wanted to get on the way. Needing to walk the dogs, David offered to walk with me a bit, and I welcomed the gesture and the company. He hiked with me for some 3 kilometers, including through an exquisite cliff top with small yellow and white flowers, the famous "Iris reserve." Descending with the dogs to the beach, David accompanied me a bit further; at one point he wanted to try the back-pack, but after about thirty seconds (and David is a big guy, a good head taller than I am, at least, and stout) he said "Wow—this is heavy!" and handed it back with a groan. I think I pulled a muscle helping him take it off. We parted with a smile and a handshake—and then a hug, unusual for him as a Brit, and all the more appreciated for that.

I wrote afterward in my journal, "Finding the חוף השרון [Sharon Beach] was like seeing an old, familiar face." Considering how much I love the beach, and camping on the beach in particular, I was excited as I hadn't been since perhaps that first morning of the hike, spending my last Shabbat on the Shvil here. I set up my tent near the cliff—not so close to the cliff that I was worried about falling rocks but far enough away from the water that I didn't fear the tide either—and threw all my stuff in it. I asked a young couple sitting nearby to watch the tent and went off to find *Challot* (Shabbat loaves) and food for Shabbat.

Without the pack, and after a short half-day of hiking, I couldn't complain about the schlepp out to the road—but then was frustrated not to find a single supermarket or store. Wandering around the strip mall, I had a (delicious) falafel for a late lunch, and in the end walked out to the little convenience store at the gas station near the highway, where I found and bought a few pre-prepared sandwiches, some munchies, and—most important of course—wine, and started to head back. I stopped at a (kosher!) kiosk where a Druze woman in traditional garb was making one of my favorite Mediterranean foods, *Laffa*, a huge and extremely thin crepe-like pita baked on a meter-wide domed iron pan over an open wood fire, served with *Labane* (sour cream cheese), *Zatar* and olive oil. It's about as authentic as one can get in this region. She was so sweet: when I explained to her I'd be keeping it aside to eat later and the next day for Shabbat, she wrapped it all up, separately, with extra olive oil and Zatar in containers. It may not have been traditional Shabbat Challah, but the pizza-sized large flat *Laffa* bread certainly qualified as *Lechem Mishne*—the mandatory two whole loaves reminiscent of the two portions of Manna given to the Children of Israel in the desert on a Friday to cover their needs over Shabbat. It was perfect—more so than finding fresh *Challot* in a bakery ever would have been.

Returning to the beach, I enjoyed a leisurely swim including a quick naked "mikvah-dip," achieved by removing my swimsuit while in the water, dunking three times, and then putting it back on, all while ensuring nobody is near enough or even sees from the shore—a skill developed over years of going to the sea on erev Yom Kippur with Yaakov as described earlier. After rinsing off with the fresh water of the shower pipe near the path up the cliff, I was ready to prepare for Shabbat (and there wasn't much to prepare); as the sun descended lower in the western sky, I took out the guitar and strolled over to a set of large rocks at the edge of the sea, to pass the last few minutes before Shabbat actually commenced.

I sat with my feet in the water, dressed (as it were) for Shabbat with the trouser extensions zipped on to my shorts, my relatively clean "Not 2 Young 2 Walk the Shvil" T-shirt, and my white *kippa*, made for me by my Meira and worn on every Shabbat since she gave it to me (and every Shabbat on the Shvil of course). I played and sang and played more, a kind of pre-Shabbat welcome of the Sabbath Queen, as the beach emptied of visitors and the sunset began to turn the sky every shade of orange and red, purple, and gold imaginable.

Just as I was ready to wrap up—perhaps ten minutes before the actual onset of Shabbat, as the sun became a round, bright yellow-orange fiery eye right above the edge of the water—a couple approached, walking their dog along the water's edge. Smiling, the woman asked, "What are you playing?" and I told her—it just happened to be the song I sang on reaching the beach three days earlier, *"Halicha l'Kisarya,"* "Walking to Caesarea," about the sand and the sea, as I described above. They started to sing with me! At first I was embarrassed but then it was just fun, and we sang the whole thing through twice, with me adding harmonies on the second go-round. Smiling still, they said, "Shabbat shalom," and turned to continue on their way. I was left with Naomi Shemer's refrain: "Oh God, that these things never end—the sand and the sea, the rush of the water, the crash of the heavens and the prayer of man."

What a way to welcome Shabbat haMalka, the Sabbath Queen. I couldn't top that, so just stopped, and, putting the guitar in the tent, took a few last-minutes photos (when else does one have the chance to capture that ephemeral moment just before the mundane day turns into the holy evening? It's not at all the same as an ordinary sunset the other six days of the week . . .).

And then it was Shabbat. After extended prayers, including singing every part one can, I sang *Shalom Aleichem*, the traditional Shabbat-table introduction to the meal welcoming the Shabbat angels. Alone on the beach, I sang it at the top of my lungs, repeating it with all the four or five melodies I loved to sing with the kids, with a small sliver of moon and a few stars providing just enough light to see the pages. I gave each of my children the traditional blessing, with my eyes closed, as I do every Friday night, whether they are with me or not, this time a bit slower than usual, especially the last phrase ". . . and give you peace." I focused on the needs of each of my children for physical, psychological, emotional comfort, wholeness, serenity and stability. After making Kiddush, sanctifying the Shabbat with a very nice "Har" Cabernet Sauvignon from Tabor Winery, I ate a sandwich and then a candy bar for desert, and was as satisfied as with any "normal" Shabbat feast. I said the blessings after the meal with extra *kavana*, extra focus and feeling, with all their references to our Land and the connection between the Land, the food and our people.

I took a short walk; it was only about 8 p.m. or so—and found only a few fisherman, half a kilometer or so down the beach, along with a small group of teens gathered around a fire. Chatting with a few of them, I was intrigued by the innocence—perhaps illusory but still—of this group of young Israelis who, rather than clubbing in Herzliya or doing drugs in a forest, chose to spend a Friday night full of camaraderie around a campfire. Returning to my tent, I fell onto my sleeping bag and was quickly asleep, glad for the mattresses I had found on the beach and dragged over to my spot (and placed under the tent as they were, shall we say, not as clean as one might want to put into a tent).

In the morning my תפילות *Tefilot* prayers were some of the longest, and most meaningful, ever, with so much singing it took well over an hour. Morning Kiddush was cake and the last of the whisky—great timing. Shabbat was just perfect, as I wrote in my journal.

> Read and dozed; ate and drank; walked twice, swam once with swimsuit—beach was packed! Crowded, really. Families, couples, groups of young people. It is eye-opening, as I wrote the kids—us people who keep Shabbat have no idea what others do on Shabbat. (Even when we stay at a hotel it's not the same understanding.) There was so much going on: swimmers, surfers, wind-surfers, kite-surfers, hang-gliders, sail boats, yachts, motor boats, jet skies and of course just lots of people on the beach with rackets and bbqs & beer and music and all the rest. (One group played trance music all afternoon—I ended up singing סעודה שלישית songs in tempo . . .)

By late afternoon I began to feel a bit down. This was perhaps natural, inevitable even; since Karen had moved out, it was an expected aspect of my Shabbat, though it had become less intense over the past few weeks. The sunset, the songs, the incredible beauty, this last Shabbat on the Shvil, everything that led up to it and all which was part of it and now of me combined to bring on a few tears. But I made it through, without too much effort. I turned my attention to observing the juxtaposition of the diminishing light of dusk and the decreasing numbers of people on the beach.

As the sun set, as if on cue, families packed up their blankets and balls, teens rolled up their towels and finished a last few bashes of "matkot" (that only-in-Israel paddle/ball game with no score and no teams), and the shore quieted. Within about 20 minutes I was virtually alone. I sat on a rock about halfway between the cliff and the water's edge and contemplated the coming days, looking forward very much to seeing a few friends I had tentative plans to see and stay with. I was especially excited to be seeing Netanel and the gang who were supposed to meet me midweek out camping somewhere. But I was very much aware also that this was all coming to an end. And more: that within a week I was set to arrive home and start my life, or restart my life, or whatever life I was supposed to create now for myself. I made a promise to myself, then and there, to focus on the possibilities—all those amazing possibilities I knew were ahead of me, and available to me, and waiting for me.

Listening to the soft lap of the surf as the tide came in and the sun sank into the sea, I thought of the vespers I attended once in a monastery, the slow mantra of the waves reminiscent of the monks' gentle humming. For whatever reason (who can explain the links our brain makes?) this brought to mind the haunting tune of *Kol Nidre*, the initial prayer chanted at the beginning of Yom Kippur. Forgiveness. Acceptance. Humility. Gratitude. It's all there in the Day of Atonement's liturgy, and though I don't know it by heart, the themes came to me in waves of thought as I watched the water slide up and back from the shore. And it occurred to me: in forgiving Karen, I had taken the last step toward freedom. Laying down that weight, that burden, is what had allowed me to be open to all the possibilities before me. Until that moment, I hadn't made that connection.

With the end of Shabbat, at stars-out, I made Havdalah, separating between Shabbat and the rest of the week. I really concentrated on the meaning and the significance of the blessings in the prayers. There is such a difference between the holy and the profane, between light and darkness, between the seventh day and the six days of creative work/activity—just as there is a difference between sadness and joy, despair and hope, an end and a beginning. I was ready to dedicate myself to the positive sides of all this, and the many opportunities open to me as I moved into the next stage of my personal journey.

Tent on Sharon Beach

Dragging over a few pallets of wood I had seen on one of my walks earlier, I wanted to bring some real light into the darkness of that night, and warmth as well. Lighting the fire, I learned an important lesson: once lit, fire cannot be contained in one corner of a pallet! Duh. So much for my Boy Scouts Campfire Merit Badge earned 40 years previously. Soon I had a bonfire the likes of which one doesn't usually see; I had to sit some five meters away from it for over an hour. But making quinoa and soup and tea I enjoyed a pleasant meal, and then played guitar all alone on the beach until turning in about 10 p.m.

Pre-Shabbat song on HaSharon Beach

It was indeed a perfect Shabbat, and perfect as my last Shabbat on the Shvil. Like all the others, it was different, special, uplifting, restful, meditative, thought-provoking, and enjoyable. Unlike all the others, it was entirely alone, and that was a fitting cap to these past weeks, months, and years.

Chapter Eight

HEADING HOME:
MEANING AND PURPOSE

[Week Eight]

I certainly slept well that last Motzei Shabbat Saturday night on the beach; and with no telephone reception, I didn't even bother to try to contact the kids or the friends I expected to see the next day.

I was ready for a terrific day, when at about 7 a.m., sort of half-asleep in the tent which was warming up as the sun came over the top of the cliff, I was woken with a shout—"Allo! Allo?!!?"—from outside my tent.

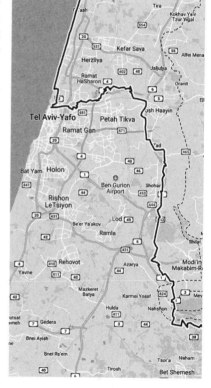

"מה אתה עושה כאן?!!?" ("What are you doing here?")

"אסור לך להיות פה!" ("It's forbidden for you to be here!")

"תתקפל ותצא—בעוד עשר דקות אתה לא כאן!" ("Break camp and get out—you'd better not be here in 10 minutes!")

I said, "Okay"—and he called out "מה "או-קיי"? זה לא " או-קיי"! וגם אסור מדורה" ("Whatdya mean 'Okay'? It's not 'Okay'! And a bonfire isn't allowed either . . .")

Fine, I said to myself—so sue me. I got up, washed, *davened*/prayed, made oatmeal and coffee (on my stove so as not to break the rules any further). I could see the guy sitting in his truck a few hundred meters up the beach as I started to pack—I took a photo of it for fun. Then at 9 a.m. or so he drove by again, stopping about ten meters away, between me and the water . . . and started to yell at me, literally spitting with anger: "Chutzpah!" I guess he was upset that his instructions hadn't been followed. He took photos of me—what, does the Park Service now use face-recognition technology to identify trespassers, find them on Facebook and send them tickets? I suppose it's possible, since a great deal of that sort of software has been developed here in Israel—and I took a few photos of him in reply, for good measure. Yes, chutzpah indeed; I called out "Sorry, I didn't know, I'm going, I'm going . . ." though it didn't help much. I was packing up anyway, suppose he could see that, and he soon drove off to leave me to it.

The hike down the coast to Herzliya was glorious. I ignored the Shvil's unnecessary (in my view) detour inland. According to the Red Guide the route was adjusted due to concerns of rock falls from the cliffs, and I reasoned that (1) walking along the water line is far enough from the cliff for safety; (2) the likelihood of an incident in this dry season was low; and (3) if I weren't hiking the Trail but rather just visiting for fun I would definitely continue on the beach. Possibilities, possibilities, I was thinking—and happy to literally pursue my own path. The walk was slow, relaxed, and really different: the seashore was rocky, narrow and challenging, and a breeze blew in off the water to alleviate some of the heat. At one point I scrambled across a kilometer or so of enormous flat rocks, some above, some just washed over by the water. Singing almost all the way (was that the coffee, or just me, I wondered?), sometimes to the large white water fowl standing on the rocks or flying over the water, it was a magnificent few hours.

And then I unexpectedly found myself in paradise.

The beach below Tel Arshaf, or Appolonia, just north of Herzliya, is one of the hidden jewels on the Shvil. (When I posted a note on Facebook at the end of the week, I refused to reveal the location. I'm hoping you'll keep it as our little secret.)

A stunning white-and-gray egret flies over a boulder right in front of me; as I pass it, I glance down from the bird to look at the water. Wait. I see the water! I mean: I really SEE the water. It's not the usual eastern Mediterranean—nice enough as always. It's a sparkling coastal vision out of some Caribbean tourist marketing brochure, or one of those James Bond movies I loved so much as a kid. The water is so very clear I can see the ridges of the sand—white sand! Like the Bahamas!—and a school of some fifty small fish moving together about three meters from the water line. It's aqua green and light blue, and darker blue a few meters out. There's a small swell and little lake-like waves maybe ten centimeters high. Ahead of me are more boulders and rocks and the cliff jutting a bit out into the water, with boulders at its base, so I can't see the continuation of the coast.

"Seriously?" I say out loud to myself. Where the heck am I? What is this place? I don't even hesitate: throwing my pack down I take a quick look around—nope, no one anywhere near, I even look up at the top of the cliff—and tear off my clothes. I just toss them on my bag and the rock next to it, very unlike me, not even caring when my underwear falls into the sand, and crash my way into the water. I'm hooting and whooping and diving down and jumping up, and loving every minute of it. It's hot;

and the sea is so cool. And the water is crystal clear. There's really no choice in the matter. I'm so excited to be in the water, I feel like a five-year-old; I just swim around for a while, out and back, side to side. I float around on my back and think of all I've been through and all I've been feeling and what it all means and where I'm heading now—physically, heading home, and otherwise, heading who-knows-where. I do some quasi-meditation in the water, staring up at the sky, closing my eyes, breathing deep, repeating אהיה אשר אהיה Eheye Asher Eheye, I am/will be what/who/that I am, and מודה אני Modeh Ani. I am so very grateful. . . . Occasionally I stand in the water up to my chest and looking out for anyone coming by. But there's nobody. No one. How come this place isn't crawling with people?!?

Eventually I come out of the water, calling on whatever modesty I have left by looking carefully all around and running over to cover myself with my shirt. I take a photo and then, of course, a video (Video 10).

It turns out that was my last swim in the sea on the trek, and it was delightful. And as with so many other aspects of the Shvil, I wished that I had someone to share it with. In my journal, later, I wrote,

> Yes, Karen would have loved it. In a normal world, in an alternate perfect universe, she'd have been with me or I'd have called her up to tell her about it or I'd have brought her there another time. In this world . . . I WhatsApped the kids a photo and a video . . .

As before, I notice that these sobering and somewhat melancholy thoughts don't overwhelm me anymore. Shrugging and accepting and in fact happy to

Paradise under Tel Arshaf

share the experience with the kids, I climbed over the boulders and around the point of the cliff, finding a mostly hidden path (that's why there was nobody else there, clearly—the rocks are a bit uninviting) and behold! found myself on the northernmost tip of the Herzliya beach. Fascinating: right ahead of me were a dozen or so groups/families/individuals laying on towels or sitting on chairs, not more than a few hundred meters from this little piece of heaven I had stumbled upon, with apparently no idea that close by was a private paradise just waiting for them to discover it.

From there, it was a matter of a few minutes till I reached the the ramp by the Sharon hotel. ("Yes, Aryeh, this is the same walkway you and Karen came down that time you came to this beach—so WHAT," I said to myself.) Within moments, my friend Jeremy swung by and picked me up outside the hotel—for a fleeting instant I thought to go in and price a room—and we went to lunch.

It was so very incongruous—and so very pleasant—to "do lunch" in Herzliya, Jeremy in his casual work clothes, taking a break from his high-tech job, me in my shorts and T-shirt. We could have done this any day over the past decade plus of our friendship, in the midst of a day of meetings I had in the area; but we hadn't. It was so kind of him to take the extra time and to drive me there and back (he treated me as well). We spoke of nothing of significance—though as I mentioned earlier, with the loss of his daughter a few months previously and my divorce the same day as her funeral, a certain somberness could be felt. We both, having acknowledged the continuing pain, focused on my tales of the Shvil. I couldn't help but be aware that my pain had lessened as result of the trek; that the experience had indeed done its work and I was beginning to focus on the future, in a way no parent a few raw months after the loss of a child could. I felt somewhat guilty in this, but could do nothing—and say nothing—to alleviate either my discomfort or of course Jeremy's pain.

Jeremy was (as he had been over the entire period of the separation and divorce), quietly and strongly positive about my future. He always was one to throw in "you'll be fine" at an opportune moment, or "there are great things still in store for you." Both he and Mandy were sympathetic to my pain and continually upbeat when we spoke, even in the midst of their own terrible sadness and suffering. They took a decision, as I've mentioned, to look forward and live their life. Not without reference to Navah's death of course but perhaps as a reaffirmation of her life, and in acknowledgement that without question she would have wanted them to live and grow and enjoy life, with her own tremendous love of life.

So it was natural for Jeremy to return to that theme as we finished lunch, when I spoke a bit about the transformative nature of the trek, and how the Shvil had, in fact, worked its wonders. I talked briefly about my goals for the coming year, both personal and professional, looking forward to pursing them and slightly trepidations at the prospect of reentering "real life." Jeremy sympathized with that. I imagine he had an idea what that is like; after all, he was forced to rise from Shiva, the traditional Jewish mourning period, and re-engage with the world.

In a way, it was a fitting beginning to this week of re-emergence, on my way back into "normal" life, having a lunch with a close friend in the middle of the work day. We said goodbye with a hug outside my Trail Angel's home, in one of Israel's most exclusive neighborhoods: the "Official Residence" of the ambassador of Canada to Israel.

My friend Vivian, the ambassador, had thrown out the idea one day a few months previously, saying, "I can be your Trail Angel!"—and I thought she was joking. But when the time came, she was as good as her word, in spite of her crazy schedule. It was a bit bizarre, certainly, for a backpacker to show up at the guard booth outside an ambassadorial residence and to say, "Hi! The Ambassador said to let me in, I'm staying here . . ." Maybe that's why it took a few hours for the security personnel (Israeli) to confirm my story with the embassy staff (not Israeli) and eventually the ambassador herself (who had been in a meeting and was not at all happy at my being delayed, as instructions had indeed been left). I didn't complain; after the initial backs and forth, the security guard had let me in to the grounds, and I enjoyed a lovely few hours sitting by the pool, swimming, reading, writing a bit, charging my phone, and making plans for the next few days.

All Shvilistim should be privileged to have such experiences. It was like staying in a deluxe hotel, in a guest suite to rival the best resort in the world. And I already mentioned the pool. Rough life, indeed, this trek of mine. After a long and vigorous shower, I settled in and made final arrangements for Monday. When Viv arrived, I jokingly welcomed her home, and we went to dinner at a fancy pub-style restaurant right on the beach. It not being kosher, I had a huge and delectable salad, sushi, and a fantastic Mojito. Though we did talk about personal issues, she having also been divorced and very interested in the Shvil as well, our conversation naturally turned to the situation in the region. Having met Viv years before through a mutual friend, I had provided a bit of input to her initial understanding of things Israeli and Middle Eastern when she wrote a column in a Canadian newspaper. In her current role, it was natural for most of our time to be focused on current events. I enjoyed both being brought up to date from her perspective and sharing with her a few of the new ideas I developed on the Shvil and their implications for our situation in the region.

I got as far as throwing out some thoughts about all the potential alternatives for resolving the Arab-Israel conflict I'd been contemplating, and then it was time to call it a night. As I fell asleep, I let the thoughts percolate, and then let them go, as I enjoyed the luxury of the Official Residence's incredible king-size bed and down comforter.

Monday morning I was glad to begin the day with a quiet walking meditation on the grass alongside the broad shaded patio by the pool. Viv had to get to an early engagement and so after saying thank you and goodbye, I enjoyed a quick breakfast alone on the patio, finished my laundry and packing and was on my way before 9 a.m. I had been in touch with Netanel to make tentative arrangements for the evening with his friends, and with my friend Tally about perhaps meeting up in TA—though looking at the map and length of the day's hike, I wasn't at all sure how it would end up.

It's funny to think of this as a "hike," I'm saying to myself as I shuffle along the tree-lined streets of up-scale Herzliya toward the sea. Without the pack, I could be out for a morning stroll. And in fact, I realize that however far I get today, it's all flat, and pleasant. I want to get out of the cosmopolitan, urban expanse of this central coast area. Keep going!

Meeting up with the Trail, I'm amused to find the markings on all sorts of mundane, almost hidden spots: on lampposts, sign poles, on low retaining walls, even on stores, houses, malls and the like. It feels weird to be walking along the Herzliya Marina (schlepping my backpack) where there are both buses running and most probably a friend or two inside shopping or eating. I feel out of place and alone.

That sensation is only exacerbated when, upon reaching the end of the marina, I find myself walking onto the beach south of Herzliya. This is one of my favorite beaches in all of Israel. Why didn't I notice this when looking at the map? I'm not sure; unconscious denial? This is where Karen and I came late at night once after a movie; where we met Dov and Freda "halfway" once with guitar and wine in tow; where I came once on my own, in hard times, and played and sang late into the night. Memories come, and cannot be denied.

"Warning! Warning!" I send in a text message to the kids on WhatsApp; I'm acutely aware how easy it would be to fall into a maudlin, self-pitying state. But I manage to stomp and sing my way through. Making new memories to replace the old, or at least to augment and contain them; just as I've done at Ramat HaNadiv in Zichron, at Caesarea or the Mitzpeh, the Reef in Eilat or others. I am encircling the old memories with new experiences, enveloping the old within the new. And I'm constantly aware of, and thinking about, my next steps. My next steps today, and next week; next year and the next decade(s). Alone but no longer lonely, I am looking forward.

Striding ahead along the beach, not thirty minutes later, I arrive at Tel Baruch, the northernmost beach of Tel Aviv. It's interesting, and heartening, to walk along a spanking new Tayelet (promenade); lovely landscaping, play areas for children, along a winding path with Shvil markings posted periodically—sometimes even on the trash receptacles. Passing Tel Baruch, with its past reputation as the main hang-out for prostitutes in Tel Aviv, I recall Herzl's wish for the nation-state of the Jews to be a "normal" country. A country where the burglars, swindlers, liars, thieves are Jews . . . and the prostitutes are too. I don't exactly agree that we should aspire to such "normality," any more than we should aspire to other aspects of modernity seen now as "normal" (such as dysfunctional families, cultural trends toward materialism, dishonest politicians, or violence in society). But of course I do share their desire that the Jewish State not be seen as, or treated as, different from any other nation state.

Which provokes more thinking, about our purpose as a country: just what we are doing here, anyway? As I approach the Tel Aviv port, passing by the small Sde Dov domestic airstrip, where planes take off about every ten minutes, I sit on a bench and take some photos of the planes. I'm trying to catch them just right as they glint in the sun, the blue Star of David bright on the tail of the El Al ones. And this seems to me to fit right in with my contemplations.

Our national air carrier is unique, and not only in that it provides the best security in the industry (of necessity). It also doesn't fly on Shabbat or Jewish holidays (and loses money thereby). And it offers the widest selection of kosher food (vegetarian; vegan; lacto-vegetarian; Glatt [extra-kosher]; gluten-free, and more) as well as space and time for a minyan (the three-times-a-day prayer groups of the Orthodox and other observant communities, on the planes and in departure halls). Not to mention the "Shalom Aleichem" song played on landing in the Holy Land, and wishes of "Shabbat Shalom" when disembarking on a Friday (or Thursday, too). Sitting on the wooden deck of the new boardwalk which spans the mouth of the Yarkon River, I was thinking of this, and other examples of the incredible privilege I have in being able to take part in this miraculous experiment in Jewish sovereignty after two thousand years of (mostly) diaspora existence.

I'm not romanticizing it, but Israel's Jewish identity is one of the most powerful, and most special, elements of the Zionist endeavor. There are challenging issues in Israeli society, from women's equality, freedom of (and from) religion, tolerance and coexistence, democracy and the rule of law. But none negate the extraordinary nature of our society and its culture of creative energy. And the thriving metropolis I was gazing at across the river called Tel Aviv represents that vibe.

And that too was interesting to me: Usually when I wax poetic about Israel, my focus and thoughts are on Jerusalem, the holy city of Zion and the font of Zion-ism; Or on the Galil or Golan with its Jewish history and natural beauty. Or on my hometown of Beit Shemesh, which hosts a diverse population of observant and traditional, secular and strictly-Orthodox (Haredi), Israeli-born (Sabra) and immigrant, black and brown and white and other Jews from America, Russia, Britain, Ethiopia, India, Yemen, Morocco, Egypt, Syria, France, Australia, South Africa, Ukraine, Romania, and almost every other country imaginable. And that's just one town in Israel with under a hundred thousand residents.

But that day, sitting looking at the high-rises of Tel Aviv and enjoying one small aspect of the modernity and cultural wealth of this vibrant city, at the refurbished port area now turned into a cultural hub, I saw the town in a whole new light. Having worked at a number of Tel Aviv high-tech companies, it's not that I wasn't aware of the city's strengths and features. But for whatever reason I had never taken to the place. I don't like big cities, and though it's small in comparison, Tel Aviv is basically Israel's New York. It calls itself The Big Orange (a riff on Israel's original iconic export, Jaffa oranges, and on New York's nickname), and also likes to use "The city that never sleeps" as a slogan.) I have enjoyed occasional visits, with visiting journalists or politicians and with family and friends. I've been to its museums, beaches, hotels, theaters; and to the refurbished early-Zionist neighborhoods, the Old Train Station near Yaffa and the historic German colony of Sarona in the city center. But until that day, I didn't really see Tel Aviv as part of the nationally or religiously significant locales of the Jews' return to their land. Rather, it seemed to me to be separate from all that.

Sitting there watching the planes take off, I realized how myopic I had been—not unusual for many religiously-motivated immigrants, for whom Jerusalem really is the focus of the Zionist dream. And understandably so, as it is toward Jerusalem we've prayed for thousands of years; it is of Jerusalem—"Zion"—that we have sung and dreamed of; it is Jerusalem which is mentioned at the end of every Passover Seder night and Yom Kippur day of fasting—"Next Year in Jerusalem!" But myopic it had been, and I chided myself for not internalizing the teachings of Rav (Rabbi) Kook, whom I had admired from my first stirrings of interest in more traditional Judaism. In his approach, the return to our Land and the building of our nation by non-observant Jews carries an inherent significance, and holiness.

Rav Kook writes, in his *Igrot HaRe'iyah* (1907):

> The fundamental moral force hidden in [the Zionist movement] . . . is its motto, "the entire nation." This nationalism proclaims . . . that it seeks to redeem the entire Jewish people. It does not concern itself with individuals or parties or sectors . . . And with this perspective, it reaches out to the Land of Israel and the love of Zion with a remarkable bravery and courage.

Later, in *Orot HaTechiyah* (1918), Rav Kook insists that "one may find in every Jew . . . precious gems of good deeds and positive traits. Certainly the Land of Israel helps elevate and sanctify them." Rav Kook saw the spark of holiness, of purity and greatness, in every Jew, whatever their level of observance, and I had always adopted and pursued a similar ideology. But my attitude toward the metropolis of Tel Aviv had been affected by my general distaste for big, secular cities. Then, on that bench watching the planes and the shoppers and the soaring office towers, I felt a surge of affection, and respect, for all the amazing achievements of the people and companies and organizations in Tel Aviv (meaning, really, all the enterprises and activities of Israel's modern society). The purpose of the Jews' return to Zion was not merely the re-establishment of our sovereignty in our ancestral homeland. The aim was—and continues to be—to be a "light unto the nations" as the prophet puts it (Isaiah 49:6), to make the world a better place. Tel Aviv represents the center of high-tech innovation in medicine, security and so many other fields with which Israel contributes to the advancement of society, and Tel Aviv is the base from which organizations provide clean water and food technology to Africa and send emergency rescue teams around the world.

And at that point, I realized how my mental meanderings about our national purpose, and meaning, were even more relevant, and more meaningful, than I had understood until then. And the same is true for me, personally. This journey, my journey, on my Shvil Yisrael, my Israel Trail, had so many purposes and goals rolled up in one trek. There were the obvious Trail-related goals: to see the country, to hike in nature, to learn more about my people and the Land, to enjoy the challenge. And there were the equally obvious emotional goals: to clear my head, as the fellow in Sollelim Forest so rightly put it. To take a break, to put the divorce behind me and reflect on my situation and on the potential future directions I might pursue.

These basic goals translated into various more specific aims: to hike alone, to camp out, to sometimes meet people, to stay with Trail Angels and friends, to meditate frequently, to disconnect from Facebook and email and even the phone. These broke down in the even more mundane objectives of any individual day: where to start and which route to take, where to stop for rest or coffee or lunch or sleep, how to make it over a particularly difficult passage. Even where to place my foot for each particular step, not least when the terrain was rocky or steep, slippery or hard to see.

Last, there were the more ephemeral goals, some of which I had set for myself, others which developed in the course of the hike. Naturally, these started with the very personal and emotional contemplation of future relationships. Was I ready, or interested even, in seeking a new partner in life? Not at the outset of the trek; but my personal journey on the Trail reflected my internal journey bringing me back to an appreciation of myself and my needs, my desires, and my capacity to love and give and nurture. And that most primary of goals—to find a soul mate to spend the rest of my life with, to grow with and to grow old with, to love and be loved by—surfaced in that last week. It appeared in a way I hadn't expected, as I walked along the Yarkon river in Tel Aviv, turning to the East, quite literally heading home.

Passing a tree stump with a planter on top overflowing with red, violet and yellow flowers glistening in the sun, boasting the three colors of the Shvil markings on its side—dusty rust/orange, blue, and white—I saw two birds perched on the edge. I remember looking at the pair of birds and thinking to myself: I will love again. I will *fall in love* again. I didn't know if these were the kind of bird which mates for life or picks a new mate each year. It didn't matter. Seeing them together, a couple, I realized that yes, this is a possibility I'm now open to. It had only been a few months since the divorce, but it was two years since Karen announced her intention to leave, and almost a year since the beginning of my acceptance of the situation at the retreat in Bat Ayin after Netanel's wedding. It was not only a possibility. I was recognizing a new lesson: love will not be a *possibility*. It will be my *goal*.

I almost called the kids right then and there, wanting to share my excitement. I didn't; all things considered, I had gone through a great deal to reach this point, and they didn't go through it with me. I wasn't sure how they would feel about my new-found goal. But my thoughts were coming fast. I was not only being open to possibilities; I made a choice and was going to *realize* those possibilities. I was elated, and I felt a renewed sense of purpose. I felt light-hearted; I started walking faster, as if hurrying toward my new goal.

Soon I had to slow myself down, or I'd arrive much too early to meet Tally. I started to walk more deliberately, with lengthier strides, but my mind was rushing ahead. How good it was to feel alive, in this so-alive city with boats on the river, joggers on the path ahead and behind and passing me, lovers and workers and teenagers walking and running and playing all around, in this well-planned, clean and impressive urban park; it made me think of a long, thin version of Central Park ("Hah! My own NY reference"). I was already thinking of other goals for myself.

Love certainly was my first goal, but it was only *one* of many things on my mind as I walked in the midday sunshine and smiled and nodded, even waved, at the various strangers/lovers/joggers passing me on the path beside the river. *Who am I?* I kept asked myself.

My sense of self was established, or rather solidified in a fashion, in seventh grade at La Entrada Elementary school in Menlo Park, California. There, the principle Mrs. Jones led a class simply and appropriately called "Who Am I?" as I've mentioned. In one session among many similar, she asked each of us to stand up and answer that question in various ways. She literally challenged us, over and over again, "Who are you?" "Who are YOU?" "Yes, but Who ARE you?" "Who ELSE are you?" She demanded we—at age 12!—look carefully at the different layers and facets of our identity, and I remember saying, "I am Eric"; "I am a person"; "I am a son"; "I am a brother"; "I am a singer"; "I am a pupil."

And in later years a thinker, a lover, a Jew, a human being, an American, a friend, a camper, a counsellor, an Israeli, a student, a pray-er, a writer, a speaker, a colleague, and then of course a husband, a father, an executive and all the rest. As I walked along the water of the Yarkon river that day, I thought of Mrs. Jones and her 1970s values-clarification exercises. I led similar sessions as an activity at Skylake for a few years, and in the ensuing years for various different groups, and I've always enjoyed exploring all the different "me's" which are Aryeh.

I began to set goals as I walked past the spanking new state-of-the-art sport facility on the Yarkon River, where I discovered a rowing club to rival those on the James River in Boston. First and foremost was thinking of my children. I felt I owed so much to them, for their support over the past few years. I also felt that I failed them in many ways, though I was confident I had not been a bad father. I had been a good father; in fact an excellent father, in the most important ways: I provided for them, both material and spiritual and emotional sustenance. I loved them unconditionally, and supported them in their development, including when they took paths I didn't agree with 100 percent. I hugged them often, cried with them, laughed with them, took them on outings, shared with them my love of and commitment to Judaism and Zionism, our people and our land, as well as the American and western and Jewish values I'd been raised on and discovered in young adulthood. I embraced their friends (even those I liked less) and I celebrated and participated in their interests. But knew that I had also made many mistakes.

I had sometimes been strict when I could have been lenient; I was controlling when I should have let go; I was calm when I should have been adamant and loud when I should have been quiet. I was very focused on giving them support and admiration, instilling in them a sense they could do anything; I was less focused on setting and enforcing limits and disciplining misbehavior; I was lenient when I should have been strict. I could have, and should have, been more aware of the challenges they faced with Karen, and more helpful in resolving the conflicts these created. Instead I hid behind both my love for each of them—which somewhat colored my understanding—and my general optimism that all would turn out okay. And allowing my very Californian *laissez faire* approach to life to inform also my parenting style was, in retrospect, not as helpful as I might have thought at the time. My kids were now grown—my youngest, Meira, just out of the army; my oldest, Netanel, married and finishing law school; my middle, Meravi, living in the US searching for her independence and her identity—and yet I felt I still had much to improve upon. I set specific targets for myself: to be more supportive, financially and otherwise; to be even more attentive; to help them navigate the travails of early adulthood, college, marriage, and the like, let alone the challenges this divorce business had placed before us all. This, my second goal in life, would be perhaps the easiest and most natural.

From there my thoughts moved immediately to work. Having been involved in so many different pursuits over the past 30 years, I both had many options open to me and no single direction to help focus or motivate my next steps. But over the past few weeks (months, actually, and years, but definitely while hiking the Trail) I had, as noted, already reached the conclusion that the time had come to move on from MediaCentral. That goal, at least was clear; what was not, was in which direction I wanted to move and on what I wished to focus. I began to make a mental list of my general areas of interest and expertise, and it was at that point I walked right by the Eretz Yisrael Yaffa ("Beautiful Land of Israel") center and restaurant, which helped me concentrate my thoughts even more. I had spent many lunches and meetings there, in my time at various high-tech companies in the North Tel Aviv area, which made me think about a possible return to the technology world. It was a possibility—and I was open to possibilities!—but it was not, I could tell immediately, a goal I would set for myself.

I was definitely interested in returning to the business sector—but only in a way which would allow me to dedicate my efforts to affecting lives, and not only to increasing shareholder value. I had recently helped my friend Yosef Abramowitz set up his company providing solar electricity for developing African countries. Yossi is Israel's solar energy pioneer and my inspiration and partner in a number of endeavors over the years, and wandering around the exhibits at the center, focused as it is on Israel's environment and ecology, it was only natural to think in terms of turning my informal assistance to Yossi into a more formal position. I could help him expand the company and bring clean and inexpensive energy to societies most in need. That became my third, tangible objective.

As I walked east under the highway and into Tel Aviv's Yarkon Park, I returned to my musings on Rav Kook and the contributions of all Israelis to our society, and to the betterment of humanity. I knew I couldn't ignore my love of Zionism and my desire to promote Israel. This is my personal and professional passion: I am committed to promoting Israel, and its legitimacy, on the world's stage. Yet MediaCentral, which helps the world's press to report accurately from this region, was, after ten years, too narrowly focused for me. I still believed in the importance of the wider goal, ensuring that Israel and the reality on the ground is understood. But I felt that the broader picture has been lost, and needs to be reaffirmed. The true history, culture and society of Israel, the very concept of Israel as the nation-state of the Jewish people, not simply a religious but a national construct, has been lost among the claims and counter-claims of various parties.

I had been involved in leading a new initiative, reasserting the very legitimacy of Israel as the ancestral home of the Jewish people in political circles, academia, churches, trade unions, and also the media, over the past year or so. And as I walked alongside the pastoral scene of elderly men fishing in the Yarkon while their children and grandchildren played in or near the water, I committed myself anew to pursuing this passion, and to turning the initiative into a tangible channel of activism on behalf of Israel. I made the connection explicit, in my mind: Just as other countries and peoples have the right and pleasure of the "pursuit of happiness," of living in peace and tranquility, fishing along a river or inventing the next new technology, so too do the Jews and Israel.

It is not enough to combat the de-legitimization of Israel's right to exist, the demonization of Jews and Israel or Israeli leaders and the IDF, and the double standards applied to Israel in the media and world forums. (These are Natan Sharansky's famous "3 Ds of the new anti-Semitism,"[13] which I played a small part in developing when I served as a senior advisor to Sharansky in the Israeli prime minister's office.) We need a more assertive, more positive approach to remind humanity—and its leaders—of the legitimacy afforded the return of the indigenous Jewish

---

13   See Natan Sharansky, "Antisemitism in 3-D," *Forward*, Jan. 21, 2005, http://forward. com/opinion/4184/antisemitism-in-3-d/

people to its ancestral homeland, the Land of Israel, by the nations of the world a century ago in the League of Nations Mandate given to Britain in 1922. Such were my thoughts about my fourth goal as I walked along the water.

As if on cue I came to a fork in the river, where a large sign with photographs and explanations almost blocked the path. It was a fascinating display which had been set up so you can stand and compare the photo with the scene in front of you. Today, the fork in the river sits in the shadow of a highway, whereas in the photo, a field stretches behind it. The description of the original "settlers" of Tel Aviv working the land and using the water was stirring, and illuminating. I loved the symbolism, related to my musings, connecting the past and present and future, let alone the environmental protection element. If that wasn't enough of a hint for my next goal, I immediately received another. Walking past the fork, I found myself in a forested area, and soon heard the sounds of children—hundreds of children!—laughing and running and rough-housing.

I had stumbled alongside a huge outdoor challenge course, with climbing and swinging ropes, tree houses and more. I wanted of course to climb the fence and join in the fun, but sufficed with waving back to a few older children who, seeing me and my pack and flag, called out and waved as I passed. As if it was scripted, I noticed the diversity of the group—white and brown and black and blond, tall and short, boy and girl, even (outwardly) religiously observant and less so, various kinds of kippot—in short, a grand spontaneous presentation of the multi-cultural ethnicity of Israel, right there in front of me. The "ingathering of the exiles" indeed.

These two incidents, one after the other—the biblical prophecy coming true, and before that the sign describing Tel Aviv's early pioneers—combined to reinforce that fourth goal. I would work to ensure that a confident and forceful message would be disseminated, and received, across the globe. Exactly how, in what format and through which channels or structures, I didn't yet know. I only knew that I could, and would, act to help others appreciate not only the legitimacy of our country's founding but the beauty and wonder (and justice and morality) of our multi-cultured society as well. I was confident that considering my background, training, and experience, I could find a way to make a modest contribution to this effort.

So with two personal and two professional goals already coalescing, I was curious to see if I could come up with objectives in other areas of interest which I'd pursued over the past few decades.

With the demonstration of the kaleidoscope of ethnic, racial, religious and other identities here in Israel right in front of me, my thoughts went straight to one of my most serious concerns since I moved to Israel thirty years previously. The issue is the relations of Jew to Jew in Israel and between the Israeli Jewish community (and the State of Israel) and the Jewish communities around the world. Here I was, striding along my path in the Jewish state, literally holding in my person some of the most arduous challenges facing us as a people. Who am I? I'm an American Israeli Traditional Liberal Observant Mystical Halachic Feminist Zionist Male Human Jew. All true.

I grew up in a Reform Jewish family, which meant observing some but not most of Jewish traditions, yet with a strong connection to the Jewish people and our history. I was and remain proud to be a descendent of one of the first Jewish families to arrive in the thirteen Colonies, and of the first American-born Jewish community leader, Gershon Mendes Seixas. He was known as "the Patriot Rabbi" for his support of the American Revolutionary War, and was the representative of the Jewish community at George Washington's inauguration as President. Like many good Californians, I explored and experimented with various religious traditions, praying in various churches and synagogues, mosques and Buddhist temples, looking for a spiritual home. In the end, going to study in the Reform movement's rabbinical seminary demonstrated my interest in, and commitment to, my Jewish identity. Its location, in Jerusalem, introduced me to Israel. I quickly fell in love with this brash, young, dynamic, irritating, frustrating, beautiful country, and started to learn more about the centrality of the Land of Israel in my people's identity. Living and studying in the holy city at age 21, I discovered myself even as I explored my historical and tribal links to the country. As I delved further into our past and traditions, becoming more acquainted with Jewish philosophy and thought and more observant of Jewish ritual, I felt that I had finally come home. Still, I retained my affection, respect, love and admiration for the country of my birth, the United States of America, the home of my family for over two hundred and fifty years and the land of opportunity and freedom. I remain a proud US citizen, alongside my Israeli citizenship.

Straddling not only the two cultures of America and Israel but the two worlds of Reform and Orthodox Judaism—let alone Zionist and non-Zionist—gave and gives me a somewhat unique perspective, as well as the ability to understand the different outlooks and to bridge between them. Throughout over thirty years I've lived in Israel, including those working in government service as well as in business, I have been privileged—and able—to help various groups to develop an appreciation for one another, and to recognize the importance of mutual respect and cooperation, for the benefit of all. But it had been a long while since I had taken any action, or written anything, or been involved in any organization, which sought to further these goals.

One of the most pressing issues facing the Jewish world today is reconciling our too-divided nation, meeting the challenges presented by modernity and by the different values and priorities of different streams in Judaism. Not to mention the small matter of running a modern nation-state with its needs to promote defense and security, public welfare, and the continuity of the Jewish people. Nodding at a Haredi strictly Orthodox man walking toward me, just a few minutes after a completely secular young woman had jogged by me (and him, no doubt), I undertook to look into ways I could return to my activism on this front as well. This became my fifth goal.

Unintentionally moving through Rav Kook's concentric circles of affinity, from myself and my goals for love, through my children and family to Israel and the Jewish people, it was a natural next stop to consider Israel's place in the world, and the Arab-Israel conflict. One might ask, "Who the heck does this guy think he is? He got divorced, went on a hike, and now thinks he can solve the world's problems?" I suppose I've always had an interest in problem-solving. In large part, my studies for my masters in international relations at Hebrew University in Jerusalem were focused on conflict resolution and communication. From my days as a student of psychology through my business career, I've enjoyed playing a role in helping to brainstorm ideas and resolve disputes. And I've often had cause to call on what I learned about Gandhi and his methods of "truth-struggles" at UC Berkeley, whether applying them to family disputes or the violence in our region, or everything in between. Basically, I've dedicated the past quarter-century of my career to looking for solutions to our regional predicament.

And so as I walked along the Yarkon my thoughts strayed to considering the past 100 years of Arab hostility to the Jewish national renaissance. A number of basic themes recur in my articles, my public speaking, my time leading MediaCentral, and my years in the Israeli PM's office. These include the need to recognize the complexity of the issues rather than pursue simplistic "solutions," and the importance of acknowledging reality, historical truth, and western legal principles. In addition, the necessity for all parties to really see, recognize and accept the other, as well as Sharansky's insistence on freedom and democracy as a prerequisite for peace, have been central to my outlook. I had spent years looking for answers. How to find a breakthrough; how to convince those on the extremes that there is a middle ground; how to find and promote the moderates on the other side who are interested in real peace? As I wound down my rather spontaneous pondering of the future and what my next steps were to be, I returned to this theme of conflict resolution, wondering if perhaps there might be a contribution for me to make, beyond yet another op-ed or speech. I thought there might be, and I had my sixth goal. It felt a bit pretentious to think I can solve the region's problems, and I laughed at myself, shaking my head.

Walking under the shade of tall eucalyptus trees as I wound my way beside the river, I spotted a vine winding its way up from the dirt. And so as I reviewed my mental list of answers to "Who Am I?" one last time, my thoughts returned to the vineyards I'd walked through and the wine I'd tasted on the Shvil, and thus to my wine-making. After twenty years of hobby experience, learning from my friend and mentor Raphy, I considered the option—the possibility!—of finally opening my own winery. I've grown and produced Cabernet Sauvignon; picked and produced Petite Syrah; bought and produced Merlot, Sangiovese, Petit Verdot. I've played with blends and attempted a (disastrous, undrinkable) rosé—but have never taken it seriously enough to be more than a gratifying diversion. I came out with a few excellent, superb vintages, though unfortunately only 100–200 bottles at a time, and with little clue to why a particular year was better than any other. I knew enough about viniculture to know that I didn't know enough to succeed on my own; but I felt strongly that I have a knack for the art and business of winemaking, as well as an idea for great twist on the running of a winery. Having already begun discussions with one of Israel's leading award-winning young vintners and with a few potential investors, I had laid some of the groundwork. And so as my seventh goal I promised myself I'd put new energy into the pursuit of this dream, as well.

I was pretty much finished with setting goals, and not unhappy with the result; I planned to write them down in my journal that evening. And it was then—as I saw my friend Tally coming toward me on her bike—that I decided to write this book.

I can't say the decision came "in a flash." But at that moment the realization came to me that the sum of these contemplations might be of value. The lessons I'd learned so far regarding success on the Trail and in my life as I moved beyond the divorce were something of a departure from what I'd been exposed to previously. And all I'd learned could not really be expressed in a brief op-ed, or forty-minute talk, or even a magazine article. Certainly not if it were to include the context of the trek, with all the color and experiences of the hike itself lending weight and meaning to the concepts.

Thus I met Tally with a profound sense of purpose, though not yet well thought out, regarding my post-walk near or middle future. I was going to fall in love and find a partner in life; be the best father in the world; bring solar electricity to Africa; promote the legitimacy of our state; save the Jewish people from itself; propose a new approach to regional peace; open my winery; and write a book to help others facing hardship if I could. "No problem," I said to myself as Tally approached. Should take about six months; then I can retire and spend my days growing grapes and making wine.

Tally, a New York transplant high-powered lawyer and an old friend, was continuing a conference call with a client while on her shared ecology-conscious Tel Aviv bike. After a quick hug and update on her personal and professional life (and a laugh about her lawyer-ing while biking), we spoke a bit about the divorce and the Shvil, keeping things light and pleasant. I appreciated her making the effort to come out, and told her that, but we both needed to keep the visit short; she as work was pressing, I as I had yet to decide on a place to camp. Not only that; having made these momentous decisions in the midst of Tel Aviv, I wanted to get back out into a natural, less urban environment to contemplate it all. It was good to see her; I was glad to keep walking on my own.

The path was flat, shady, and not too hot, as it kept with the curving Yarkon, and we quickly left Tel Aviv behind as the trail continued into fields and small groves of trees and bushes: exceedingly conducive to intensive deliberation.

I'm walking along this wide, dark brown dirt path, winding its way alongside the river as it twists and turns its way, meandering east, and I feel like I'm in the wild, though I know I'm still in the middle of metropolitan "Tel Aviv."[14] *I'm in such a good mood, both because I've got this renewed sense of purpose . . . and I'm heading home. I'm thinking and thinking and I feel something surfacing. All my lessons and conclusions seem to be coming together. Humility; acceptance; gratitude; forgiveness; possibilities and now goals: these could form the foundation of an approach that not only helps to overcome person trauma but resolves conflicts as well. I have to work this out.*

I've stopped for a drink at what the sign says is the last water fountain on the path. It seems the Yarkon river recreational area turns from an urban sports and recreation park into a wilderness preserve at this point. I love the transition and am enjoying every step, though it's a bit confusing: Am I in metropolitan Tel Aviv? Am I in a nature reserve? Looking up from the water fountain, to the north I'm unexpectedly taken aback by the sight of a familiar building. It turns out I'm right near a high-tech company I worked at over twenty years ago! It's a strange encounter with both the small size of Israel and the unique history and progress of the area; parts are still literally undeveloped, parts are restored and preserved as a park and recreation area, even cultivated, and parts are 100 percent urban (or urban park)—something I haven't found in San Francisco or NY or elsewhere.

The Trail follows the route of the river, and the river is like a snake: it curves around and back, and sometimes I can see the exact place across the stream where I was just thirty minutes ago. Surrounded by fields and orchards, I pass an occasional ruin (from British, and Turkish, and then Byzantine times, hard to keep track of them all), crossing here a metal footbridge, there a wooden one, and having to take off my shoes and walk through the water once. There are no other people on the trail, and that suits me fine. At a spot under a tree where the dirt is a bit more flat, trees a bit more abundant, and privacy a tad more assured, I begin to set up the tent.

I send the map coordinates to Netanel, and try to guide them as they drive. After about an hour, as darkness falls, I walk out to the edge of the woods and see them bouncing along toward me through a wheat field. Actually, first away from me, then turning toward me again, as they try to navigate terrain not exactly meant for a car. I send a text to Nati—just park there and walk!—but little do I know what they have in the car and why they're intent on bringing the car closer. Not to mention the predictable mentality of a bunch of twenty-five-year-olds viewing it as a challenge by which to prove their manhood (and IDF-trained navigation skills). Finally, after managing to go down a steep ramp into a ditch and up the other side, they drive up

---

14   The city of Tel Aviv itself is rather small, with various cities connected to it, like Los Angeles is to the surrounding cities between which few visitors can really distinguish.

to me—and right by me. They just keep going down the dirt road, bumping away, leaving me in their dust. I can't help but laugh and laugh, not least as Netanel, in the front passenger seat, and Zachy, Nati's other best friend, in the back seat, are having hysterics. I just walk back up; they'd seen the tent just next to and above the dirt path, and having parked are already unloading the car.

Ahhh—"HaMaith!" As I noted back at the Carbolet, Matan "HaMaith" is one of Netanel's oldest friends. He spent many an hour in our home when they were growing up. Lately, when I was living on my own, he had taken to dropping by on a Shabbat afternoon to lose to me in Cribbage, eat chips and salsa, and drink beer though Nati wasn't even there. Considering that he was driving, I should have predicted that sort of practical joke.

It was a night to remember; not only did we laugh our heads off, I finally discovered the wonders of the Israeli tradition called a "Poika," a meal which young Israelis love to concoct on the beach or while camping, or when serving in the IDF and having a night out in the forest with the unit. It's a cross between a stew and a fraternity brothers' drunken attempt to make dinner with no guidance. As I learned that night, it starts with a base of chicken, water, a few carrots and onions and some beans and rice and potatoes, and then goes from there into whatever direction the group feels like (with whatever ingredients happen to be at hand). On this occasion, that included beer, cola (apparently a popular addition), barley, celery and some wine, plus salt and pepper and other spices and a few other things I can't (and maybe don't want to) recall. Needless to say, it was out of this world.

Before we ate, we sat around the fire—a fire which was burning not only the wood I had painstakingly gathered while waiting for the fearless three to arrive, but small logs Matan had taken from my front porch at home. He insisted on burning to the last one, throwing more and more on the fire just to annoy me. (Perhaps you can begin to appreciate what makes HaMaith special . . .) In addition to drinking the cold beer from bottles Netanel pulled out of a cooler (aaaahhh!), we had opened a really fabulous bottle of wine Matan had received from his work, a fine Rechasim red as I recall. It hadn't been his intention, apparently, to open it, but Nati had grabbed it from the car and presented it to me—"Pa, Matan brought this for you!"—and I was happy to play along. Naturally. Sort of paid him back for taking my wood.

The guys wanted stories, which I told them. We caught up on some news of theirs and even talked a bit seriously about marriage. They all had been married recently, and asked for advice, half-humorously, along the lines of "what not to do." I said one main thing: cherish your wife. Make sure she always knows she is your number-one priority, before the kids, before work, before your parents, before (even!) your friends. Funny enough, it wasn't a lesson I learned on the Shvil; it was something I knew from my life with Karen and my observations of friends and family over the years. I think it spoke to them; I'm sure they've forgotten the conversation but I retain some hope the message was indeed absorbed.

Then Zachy asked me to share some lessons from the Shvil; that was a bit easier. Without too much detail, I mentioned a few, very briefly. These included the importance of patience; taking one step at a time; appreciation for all things and especially for the little things, and for the people in your life; paying attention to all the beauty around us; looking back occasionally, for perspective; taking it slow. They all seemed to immediately "get" the application of these hiking lessons to more general life situations. I added the observation, from my early days in the desert, of the relativity of time and space, when going at a walking pace. And finally, pointing to my pack, I reminded them that you truly need very little; that most of the "stuff" in life is just that: stuff.

We ate and reveled in the taste and aroma and texture of the poika. I especially enjoyed this new experience, not least as a most-of-the-time vegetarian who enjoyed the chicken, with no apology. And it never comes out the same twice. Not being a cook, I was amazed that Coke and beer could be so tasty in a dish like that.

Once we'd eaten our fill, Netanel picked up the guitar and played a bit; I videoed some of it, in the dark, and I've treasured occasionally replaying it. He sang a song or two I was familiar with but don't play myself, so it was cool to have the variation; Zacky and Matan joining in, while painful to listen to, was great fun too. Interestingly, I didn't become melancholy at all. I think had the evening been held earlier in the trek I might have, but at that point—with the three of them with me and with just a few days and nights to go—I felt as if I was already home. When they left, they mentioned it was the first time they'd done a "boys' night out" since Nati was married, and I was glad I had given them an excuse of sorts. And though when they left I felt a bit low, kind of abandoned, I soon settled into a pleasant mood, knowing I'd see Netanel and them all again in just a few days.

I slept well, due not least to the bed of pine needles and leaves under the tent, and so wasn't even annoyed when at 6:30 a.m. I was awoken by the sounds of a tractor. Actually, it was an earth-mover, as I saw when I peeked through the zipper to check it wasn't too near to endanger me. Who knows whether in the early morning haze the operator would even notice my tent? I saw him looking at me as I went about my morning tasks, and waved to him as he drove off downstream. Setting out, I thought of how I really was "returning home" in more ways than one. My social calendar had certainly filled up: between Jeremy and Vivian in Herzliya Sunday, Tally and then Nati and friends Monday, arranging to meet up with Aaron and perhaps Yaakov, both of whom work in the Tel Aviv area on Tuesday, let alone expecting to see Meira and Bini on Tuesday evening and staying with kibbutz acquaintances Tuesday night and then with my friends Russell and Adena Wednesday night, I was quite literally using this week to "re-enter" my social milieu. Unplanned as it was, it seemed more than fitting.

I continue to be taken aback by the beauty of this simple nature trail. It's a rather balmy morning, and I'm making good time, so stop to enjoy and take photos frequently. At times, like now, I feel I'm in the Middle East—surrounded by reeds as they tower over the stream and the path, swaying softly in the breeze. And at times I think I could be in California, watched over by tall eucalyptus and other trees full of chirping birds and fluttering leaves. Every now and then, at a turn in the stream and thus the path, I have to stop again to admire the little corners of paradise I discover: here a wider pond in the river, with ducks swimming in a row; there a small embankment where a family is picnicking (how did they get there?); now a shaded wooden foot bridge next to a pumping station. Here, I decide, is the perfect place for a coffee.

Sometimes I can't be bothered: take the pack off, unzip, pull out the pot and burner, coffee and sweetener, matches and cup; set it all up, including something to shield the flame from the wind; wait for it to boil, wait for it to cool down; and finally drink the stuff. And then put it all away and pull the pack back on—feeling it weighs more, not less, than it did 20 minutes ago. But today I'm happy to do it—looking back at all the ascents and descents, the cliffs and rocks, the heat and dust, the cold mornings and nights and loneliness and alone-ness over the past seven weeks plus, I'm appreciating the flat terrain, the pleasant heat of the morning, and the relatively short distance I've planned for the day.

I start to ruminate again, as I sip my hot, thick, dark "mud," the coffee-with-the-grounds-in-it strong mix I've become used to here in Israel, with its wake-me-up-NOW grittiness in your teeth and pungent aroma. "Get a life!" we used to say when I was younger—and how fitting that is, for me and for us all. We all need a sense of purpose; we all need meaning in our life—which is what "life" means, in a way. Eating, sleeping, eliminating, breathing—this is not life. Loving each other, having a family, building community, helping people, learning new things, making the world a better place: this is living. I remember what Viktor Frankl says in Man's Search For Meaning: *it was those with a reason to live who survived the camps. "Katonti" as we say in Hebrew, I say to myself; my "suffering" I put in quotes as it can't be compared to that of those who went through the Holocaust of course. And yet, and yet. THIS is really what it comes down to, for all of us, isn't it? Whether our pain or challenges are personal or communal, it is what we strive for which lends our lives consequence. It is those with reason to live who survive personal suffering, and nations with a reason to live (and not merely the strength to exist) which remain long after their enemies vanish. I'm reminded again of Mark Twain's reflections on the "secret" of the Jews; how the Romans and Greeks, Persians and Babylonians rose up, made a great noise, and are no longer, whereas the Jewish nation endures.*

So what is our secret? It is not—as the anti-Semites would have it—that we think we are somehow more precious to God as His "Chosen People." It is true that we believe we are chosen, but not in that way, as if as a "favorite." It is that we have a role to play in history, in humanity, given to us by God. This is our understanding, traditionally, of the "Chosen" designation: chosen to bring His message, not for special privilege (unless it is a privilege to be hated, resented and persecuted). That message is one of goodliness, of values and morality beyond that of the jungle, of responsibility and accountability, of the equality of all and the obligations of each, according to their standing and ability. And bringing that message is the Jews' contribution to the world, as my friend Rabbi Ken Spiro so succinctly put it in his book, WorldPerfect. *It is the Jews' very special task, and it is this mission which gives our life meaning, and through this the reason and the strength to survive, as individuals, and as a nation.*

Get a life indeed. Even as I talk to myself I put away the detritus of my coffee break, and get moving. Around a corner, just ten minutes later, I'm walking in an orange grove. Oranges! I can't believe it; Israel has stopped growing and exporting those famous Jaffa oranges, as they consume far too much water. This area—once the rural outskirts of Tel Aviv and Petach Tikvah—used to be the main region for growing oranges. Can't believe there are still some here! I couldn't find someone to ask permission to take a few . . . so I take some photos instead. Continuing my train of thought, I see a connection to these groves. The Jews came here to (re-)establish our nation-state, but we had many more goals than merely that national aspiration for independence and sovereignty. One was to revive a Jewish economy, based on the labor of Jews, a return to the Land represented by actively cultivating the soil. And these orange groves are incredibly symbolic of just that. And of course one of our central goals was to demonstrate how a modern society could act, survive, and prosper based on our ancient principles of liberty, equality, and peace.[15]

But now I have to stop and focus on something much more immediate. I'm not be sure whether I'm supposed to enter the gate of the Sources of the Yarkon national park or walk on this path outside the fence! Darn it—the Shvil signs aren't clear. I'll try going in . . .

It was a mistake, and I was angry with myself. I was so wrapped up in my highfaluting deliberations over meaning and purpose in our lives that I wasn't paying attention to the maps or terrain or trail signs. I had been walking for over four hours, winding back and forth across the stream and under highway 5, and I was tired and hot and fed up. So I retraced my steps and approached the Tel Afek national park where I'd arranged to meet my good friend Aaron for lunch. I walked by Kfar HaBaptistim (the Baptists' Village), a "settlement" of unusual provenance, established in the 1950s with roots from before the founding of the State. Passing another *"pinat chemed"* (little corner of charm), I stopped myself from asking "Why haven't I heard before of this place," as there had been so many on this trek. Here too, almost every turn along the Yarkon turned up similar little picnic spots or

---

15   There are many explorations of just what are basic Jewish values, from the most stringent and specific ritual commandments to the most expansive and universal moral imperatives. My ruminations that day focused on the latter, and recalling those musings here accurately is not meant to suggest this is a definitive statement of all aspects of the purpose and "meaning" of Jewish religious and national life. Those interested are encouraged to see Ken Spiro's *WorldPerfect* for a more broad treatment of Jewish thought and philosophy.

swimming holes. (I remain intrigued by the story of water in the Middle East and in Israel in particular, and look forward to returning to the Yarkon Sources national park to learn about the amazing efforts made by the early Yishuv, the British, the JNF/KKL and the Israeli government to promote water conservation and environmental protection—in many ways leading the world.)

Crossing the railroad tracks, I came across a "pill box" from the early mandatory period. These were two-story towers erected by the British to protect main traffic arteries, at the time of the 1936–39 Arab violence. I was amused—and not—at the Red Guide's rather laconic description: ". . . placed here by the British army (1935) to prevent attacks on trains. . . ." I thought, *plus ça change, plus c'est la même chose* and all that. Why don't we learn from history? Einstein's definition of insanity came to mind: continuing to do the same thing, in the same situation, and expecting different results. Why is the West still so devoted to passive means of defense against attacks on our civilians? This was almost 100 years ago (and at a time when Western morality was not very concerned with the ethics of our military operations). One wonders—or at least I did, looking at this round tower with small slits for a rifle barrel to protrude from, one of the many spotted throughout the land, including those I see almost weekly as I drive by them in southern Jerusalem, and near Hebron—what our world and our region would look like today had the British, and then us Israelis, made it clear with decisive force that attacks on civilian transport would not be tolerated.

I'm not advocating, nor was I thinking as I looked at the eighty-year-old structure, standing almost as a monument to Western naiveté, that we should be overly harsh in our defensive military campaigns, nor that we should be indifferent to civilian casualties in our response to such threats and attacks. But it occurred to me, looking at the passive obelisk standing there naked and forlorn, how representative it is of the conciliatory response offered in the face of a century of barbaric attacks on innocents. For over a hundred years, appeasement has not been effective against violence carried out in the name of a fanatic religious interpretation of Islam or of pan-Arab nationalist fervor (or the anti-Semitic opposition to the Jews' return which combines the two).

I was reminded, inevitably, of Israel's security barrier against terror, another passive form of defense; in essence, a modern "pill box" hundreds of kilometers long. Not far from where I was, the fence runs the length of the 1949 armistice line, separating pre-1967 Israel and the disputed territories of Judea and Samaria, where the Palestinian Authority of course rules over 98 percent of the Arabs resident there today. That oft-condemned security barrier has effectively prevented those Arabs wishing to harm our civilians from gaining access to our population centers; but it doesn't address at all the source of their desire to do us violence. The theme of Arab incitement, this "culture of hatred" encouraging their children and youth to hate and stone, stab and shoot and kill Jews and Christians, Israelis and Americans, had been one of my foci for years, in my work with the media and with my moderate Arab and Muslim friends in democracy movements. I have to admit I was reluctant, there on the Trail, to really allow my thoughts to continue down that road. So I promised myself I would address these issues at some point later, and not least the myth that "moderate" is an adjective which can at all be used to describe Mahmoud Abbas and the rest of the "Palestinian" leadership, and much of that of the wider Arab and Muslim world.

Coming into the Tel Afek park, I found a picnic table near a water faucet, under a set of tall eucalyptus trees, and splashed some water on my face. In the ten minutes remaining before Aaron arrived, gave some more thought to the question of what gives meaning to our lives as Jews.

One of Judaism's, and the Jewish people's, other goals—in fact a central goal of our belief system, as articulated three times a day in our prayers—is peace. "Three times?" Actually it's dozens, if you include all the different mentions of peace in our psalms and supplications, in our blessings, our songs, our lullabies, even the names we give to our children and cities, parks and restaurants. (Part of this book was written at "Beit Hashalom," the House of Peace, in Metulla; much of it in the City of Peace, *Ir Shalom*, pronounced *Yeru-Shalayim*—Jerusalem.)

The desire for peace is a central tenet in our worldview, whether internal and personal (psychological, spiritual, emotional), communal (among the Jewish people), or national (with our neighbors, adversaries, or competitors). It is not merely a goal; it is *the* goal, in the pursuit of which all our efforts are directed. Jewish tradition defines paradise, or rather redemption (since the goal is to achieve this form of perfection in human existence in this world, not the next), as a time and place where everything is in harmony, when the lion lays down with the lamb and when swords are turned into plowshares.

Making peace between a man (or woman) and his fellow is considered one of the greatest mitzvot, or commandments, in Jewish life. Aharon, Moshe's brother and the second founding father of the Israelite nation, is described as a *"rodef shalom,"* a pursuer of peace. When a Jew observes/celebrates Shabbat, his/her Sabbath rest is a contribution to world peace. The Talmud is full of anecdotes praising leaders of the Jewish people for making compromises in the cause of peace. And the concept known as "Shalom Bayit," peace in the home/house, is one of the foremost and most basic tenets of both the Jewish religion and the Jewish people as a civilization, stressed in secular as well as observant households.

Examples of this abound in the history of the Jewish people, from Avraham giving the "better" land to his nephew Lot and both Avraham and Isaac relinquishing claims to the wells of Beer Sheva to Abimelech, to King David and King Solomon making pacts with neighboring powers; from Moshe trying to appease Pharoah to the leaders of the Israelite nation trying to appease the Greeks and Babylonians; from Talmudic reports of arguments decided by what will bring concord (rather than what is considered correct) and statements regarding the importance of peace to today's efforts by successive Israeli governments—from

Right and Left—to bring the Arab-Israel conflict to an end. What became clear at the end of this train of thought was that Frankl's principle seems to apply to nations: that a people with a sense of purpose survives oppression and persecution where a nation without that, fades, as per Twain. And whether we define that goal as "peace" or "*tikkun olam*" (making the world a better place) or "redemption," it certainly drives our national spirit forward as Jews and Israelis, both in terms of our striving for innovation and perfection as well as in terms of our willingness to suffer, our capacity to stand strong with our backs to the wall, and our will to survive.

What goal, I asked myself just as my friend Aaron arrived in his car, what purpose, does the Arab/Muslim/"Palestinian" leadership place before their people? This is not the place to explore these ideas in detail; suffice to say that my thoughts that day led to a seemingly obvious conclusion, which I arrived at as Aaron parked a few meters away from where I sat staring through the trees. I shoved those issues to the back of my consciousness and welcomed Aaron, walking toward me with two bottles of ice-cold beer in his hand, with a tremendous smile on his face. His bear hug was even bigger than his smile. He brought me a falafel in a pita, with hummus and tomatoes and pickles; sometimes the simplest foodstuffs can feel like such a feast. We sat, ate, talked a bit, nothing too deep, and caught up on kids and community news. Of course he asked me how the trek was going—having not seen me since that dinner in Ein Kerem four weeks earlier—and I did share a few highlights, and a bit about the transformation I'd been going through. I offered a brief version of the above, lighter in the telling, as well.

When Aaron left—after another very welcome hug from one of my closest and most laid-back friends who reminded me of all that is good in my life—I wandered a bit around the Tel Afek national park. Of course (what did I expect?) there was history here I wasn't aware of, archeological remains going back some 5,000 years—5,000 years of continuous settlement!—which I'd never heard about. I enjoyed climbing up to the hill called Antipatris, where today one sees a fortress built apparently in 1571 (recently, in other words) by Sultan Salim II of the Ottoman empire. I loved seeing the word "settlement" used on a plaque, devoid of political or pejorative reference; inhabited since the Chalcolithic Period, it was the biblical city of Aphek (where the Philistines routed the Israelites led by King Saul, and seized the Ark of the Covenant as described in chapter four of Shmuel Aleph or 1 Samuel) and then was built as Antipatris by Herod some 2,000 years ago in honor of his father. Josephus suggests Antipatris sits on the remains of a village called Kfar Saba—familiar to us as the name of a modern Israeli city nearby.

Stone-age ancients, Israelites/Jews, Romans, Jews again (Herod being "King of the Jews'), Romans, Byzantians, Crusaders, Marmluks, eventually Ottomans, British, and now once again Jews/Israelites/Israelis built and inhabited and used this strategic hill location to protect/dominate the narrow pass between the springs of the Yarkon and the hills of Samaria. This was the Caesarea-Jerusalem road for the Romans, the Damascus-Cairo road for the Arabs and Ottomans, and is the gateway from Judea and Samaria to the industrial and population centers of modern-day Israel. And once again, I marveled at a country and a land so full of powerfully emotive and inspirational sites that in 30 years of living here I could still be not only surprised but moved by a casual encounter with antiquity. And it was beautiful. But I couldn't remain—I had a rendezvous to make with my youngest daughter and her boyfriend.

I set off across the road and, not unhappily, traipsed along dirt roads and fences beside dry wheat fields and dilapidated buildings on the outskirts of the small Jewish villages of Givat HaShlosha and Kfar Sirkin. I found myself within a hundred yards or so of Highway 6, the new and massive freeway running north and south through central Israel. It was hot and getting late, and since I'd slept out the night before I was tired, unwashed and pretty uncomfortable. I was to spend that night with friends at Kibbutz Nachshonim, only about six kilometers further, but it took me over two hours at a slow pace. I reached the overpass south of there just as Bini, Meira's boyfriend, texted me that they were coming off the freeway.

I hurried to the end of the bridge to find a place they could pull over. Just as I reached a spot, they drove up and stopped behind me. Getting out of the car, Meira literally stepped back with a double-take. I guess I looked pretty ghastly: part hobo, part hiker, part madman, I was sweaty and dirty and unshaven, half walking, half stumbling toward her with the happiness of the meeting and the tiredness of the hiking and the last 60 seconds of jogging across the overpass to reach them.

I had to laugh when I saw her face—shock mingled with concern mingled with disgust. Though Mimi had seen me more than once during the trek, she actually hadn't seen me on the Trail in full gear and glory, and it seemed to frighten her a bit. Fortunately, she recovered quickly; after hugs all around, we bundled into the car and headed over to the kibbutz for a trip to the little store for a bit of junk food (and supplies for the next day, for me). Finding a small park/playground with plastic and metal table and benches, we enjoyed a picnic of cheese and crackers, pretzels and Kefli (my favorite Israeli snack) and caught up a bit.

I can't say I loved the house-related news; it had been so refreshing, peaceful, care-free not to have to deal with (or even know about!) the leaky pipes and floods, power failures, illnesses of Sam the cat, unpaid bills or the like over the past two months or so. Discussing some of them simply reminded me how that peace was coming to an end. But sitting with the two of them, on the way to developing a strong and loving relationship, was a real joy, and it filled me with warmth and happiness. Young love does that to you, I suppose.

But more than that, I was content to know that while I was overcoming my own disappointment and pain on the Trail, Meira was moving ahead with her own life without the scars of a divorce which might have left her cynical about her own prospects for happiness with Bini, who himself comes from a divorced family.

Perhaps the informality of it, as if we'd just met for a beer after a days' work and not toward the end of a five hundred mile trek, got to me, but I was sad to have to say goodbye. But this was Tuesday evening and as darkness descended and we had a long hug, I reminded myself that I'd see Meira in just a few days . . . coming home. I managed not to cry; but mainly because just then the phone rang. It was Meir, my host, wanting to know where to pick me up, so that was that.

Meir and Rivkele Merav are the classic kibbutzniks (one who lives on a kibbutz). Not quite my parents' generation but somewhere around two decades my senior, they fall squarely into an almost stereotypical category of socialist, non-observant (or, let's be honest, sometimes anti-religious) Hebrew-speaking salt-of-the-earth Israelis which formed the backbone of the pre-independence and early years of the State of Israel. They are brash, opinionated, extremely Left-wing and pro-"Palestinian" (not necessarily the same thing), anti-Haredi and anti-Likud and anti-Netanyahu. And they are also warm, loving, caring, hard-working, idealistic, romantic and strongly committed to their nationalist/ideal version of Jewish peoplehood and Zionism. All this was reflected a few weeks earlier in their immediate and enthusiastic reply to my initial query whether I could stay with them as my "angels" for that night. Like so many *Chiloni*[16] Israelis, their love for the Land of Israel and connection to our roots means they are among those who are most active in the hiking culture of the country (like the grizzly author of the Red Guide himself, Yaakov Saar).

Rivkele and Meir are dear friends of Karen's Auntie Diana and Uncle Michael. Di and Mike visit them every time they come to Israel, and often come explicitly for their family *smachot*, or celebrations. (Mike and Di spent time themselves on kibbutz in their earlier years; Di was a member of Meir and Rivkele's kibbutz. They share many, though not all, political leanings.) I have such immeasurable love and affection for Mike and Diana that I feel like Rivkele and Meir are family of sorts; and over the years they have been welcoming and kind to us, even if our connection has been intermittent. Coming into their home was almost as wonderful as being with Mike and Diana—and not least as much of our initial conversation was about all the family news. But on their own merit, Meir and

---

16   As noted earlier, Israelis use this Hebrew term, meaning "secular," to identify those not otherwise included in various camps of the more religiously observant, from modern Orthodox and religious Zionists through Haredi strictly-Orthodox groups. I particularly dislike the term, as it ignores the incredible variety of Israelis and Jews who may not identify as Orthodox or even "observant" but who certainly have a religious or spiritual connection with their tradition, culture, people and land. They often observe practices as varied as lighting candles on Friday night or going occasionally to synagogue, circumcising their 8-day-old boys or participating in a Passover "Seder" dinner or fasting on Yom Kippur, the Jewish Day of Atonement, the holiest day of the year—all of which a vast majority of Israeli Jews observe, even while called "Chiloni." I use the term here in that spirit—though still reluctantly.

Rivkele were incredibly hospitable. ("All the news" included the divorce, of which they had heard but wanted more detail on, as well as updates on all the kids and even on Karen, which meant we talked for over an hour before I even went in to have a shower.)

They put a lovely salad and some cheese in front of me, knowing exactly what I could eat since they didn't keep a kosher kitchen, as we chatted about their children and grandchildren, about the Shvil and my observations, and then a little about politics. (We kept it light; Meir is a political cartoonist, whose satirical pen is not usually to my liking, but whose talent and opinions I respect and enjoy.) After my shower, I was too tired to write in my journal (again), and knowing I had a long and hard day ahead, was happy to fall into bed (yay! A real bed, with sheets and pillows and everything!) You'd think I hadn't slept at an ambassadorial residence just two nights prior.

Wednesday morning, I took a brief barefoot meditative walk on the grass of their garden, which included enjoying the vibrant, colorful flowers planted on the edges of their lawn. I loved the look and feel of the kibbutz houses all around: small, squat rectangles with all that one needs to raise a family but nothing more, nothing extraneous, and with much of the stuff of family life taking place outside the home. Not for the first time, looking around me I said, "I could live here" to myself, and meant it sincerely. After a quick cup of coffee and bowl of cereal with Rivkele, I strapped on my pack and headed out. Walking along the perimeter of the Kibbutz, I see the orange, blue and white Shvil markings on the side of a tree, and I feel that I've met up again with my old friend from last night.

I hadn't been hiking for more than half an hour or so, when I crossed from the outskirts of "one Israel" (the secular Kibbutz) into the fringes of "another Israel," the Haredi strictly-Orthodox city of El Ad. The fact that I felt comfortable walking in both means I'm either representative of the wonderful blend of tradition and modernity and Zionism which is the mark of the Religious Zionist community . . . or I'm simply schizophrenic. Either way, my connection with my people and land was in for a surprise when, crossing the entrance road to El Ad, I confronted a small stone building standing alone in a field, with nothing but a rusty old sign to mark it.

Should I take a look? Can't really be bothered; it's just another stone building. Today is to be my longest day on the Shvil (not the hardest—not too many hills to climb or descend—but definitely the longest, with a total of 31 kilometers to schlep through), so perhaps best to push on. But let's take a quick look—not least as I see some sort of design at the top of a pillar which looks interesting.

So I peek inside, I start by checking if there's any indication of a mezuza on the door, looking for that tell-tale sign of past Jewish residence in old buildings, a thing I've had for years whenever travelling. Sure enough, there's an indentation here in the stonework of the door frame, about three-quarters up the side—just where a mezuza would be placed. What is this place? I'm no archeologist but the structure seems pretty

Mazor Mausoleum near El Ad

old. I take a quick look at the Guide, and am completely in shock. I've just stumbled into the oldest and best-preserved building in the country. Is that possible? I decide to turn my phone on and verify what I've read. The Amud Anan app and Google concur: this is the Mazor Mausoleum, from around 300 CE, the only still-standing structure from that time in the entire country. It actually dates back further, to Hellenist (Greek/Maccabean) times! It's well over 2000 years old, it might have housed Jewish heroes (or just farmers or traders even) back then, and here it stands in a field, ignored by the residents and passers-by, drivers and workers, Israelis and tourists and others going about their daily lives. Apparently it served as a mausoleum and then later a mosque; and some hold that John the Baptist stayed here overnight. The cornice which arrested my attention at the very first is indeed original, and no surprise that it reminded me of pillars I'd seen in Athens and Rome. Wow. Just wow.

Why does this little one-room, single-story stone building move me so profoundly? Something about this structure speaks to me. It seems to say: I was here, at least from the time Judah Maccabee defeated the Greeks and Hellenists; I remained, guarding the Via Maris, the primary Roman north-south passage, and I have been present, if not conscious, for all the invasions, battles and upheavals since. From the Crusades through the recent Arab round of violence, here I stood. And here I am overlooking Israel's Route 6 highway today.

I walk inside, then all around the small building; the stones remind me of the Kotel, the western retaining wall of Herod's expanded Temple Mount in Jerusalem, built around the same time. This simple stone edifice serves as a reminder of the

259

mundane endurance of our presence here. It was here then; it is here now; it will be here tomorrow. Like us.

It seems to me that its holiness resides in its very mundaneness, hints of Rav Kook. The Jewish nation, like this strong, quiet, unpretentious structure, has a role to play, in this land. These bricks served as a house, an inn, a tomb; it served its purpose without fanfare, and still stands. We Jews remained in our Land, some, as others were forcibly evicted from their homes and communities and spread far and wide. And those who stayed, as well as those who were expelled but retained their connection, like this building, just simply got on with life, farming, planting, building, learning, creating, existing . . . and returning.

I wonder how many on the Kibbutz, with their farming and tourism enterprises, their modern sensibilities and political leanings, are aware and appreciate the historical significance of this relic nearby, testifying to our roots in this land which they wish to divide again, legitimizing the questionable claims of the "Palestinians" while diminishing the historic and legitimate claims of our own people. And I wonder how many in El Ad, sitting in their yeshivas learning Talmud all day, appreciate the significance of this remnant of the Greek and Roman, Byzantine and Ottoman conquerors who—apparently with God's blessing—were the instrument of our dispersal and the cause of so much of our nation's suffering. As I turn to continue the trek, I'm thinking the latter could learn a bit of humility, and the former a bit of national pride, from this little stone hut. And I wonder whether I'll be able to retain this feeling of awe, this acute sense of the vast sweep of history in one little space and one brief moment. I hope I can.

I started off again, the trail turning east and climbing into a forest. I was happy to see another water post built by the water company Mekorot "for the use of hikers on Shvil Yisrael," and gratefully drank, splashed, filled my bottles and Camelback. It was at that point I saw—or first, actually, heard—the animals. A herd of brown horses were feeding, walking, breaking twigs underfoot and occasionally neighing, not 50 meters from where I stood at a crossroads of two dirt paths. I walked along the trail, which brought me nearer to them; I thought to give them some food—I had a carrot in my pack—and then thought the better of it, both for time and safety. And good that I did: even without food, a young colt started to approach me, and I cheerfully reached out to rub its nose. Suddenly its mother shot out of nowhere, bearing down on me so fast I had no time to react.

Trying to lunge out of the way of her expected head-butt (yes: try to "lunge" with a 50-pound pack on your back: it's more like underwater kicking, all in slow motion). I fell backward and sideways, first onto my left knee, then over on my back. Fortunately, I didn't break my fall this time with my elbow; unfortunately, I broke it with the palm of my hand, and it, and my knee, remained sore and scraped for days. Fortunately, the colt bolted, and so its mother stopped short of trampling me; unfortunately, the mare remained standing close enough that I felt it imprudent to get up.

So I half-sat, half-lay there for a minute or two. I started to shuffle a bit to my right, when it became apparent that the mare no longer saw me as a threat (and therefore no longer of any real interest). I stood, adjusted, and took a few photos of the beautiful (if now slightly scary) pastoral scene of wild horses cavorting and munching in the dappled sunlight under the canopy of evergreens. I walked on, and settling into a decent pace, I found the going tough. Gorgeous though it was, and walking through the shady forests was a welcome break from the previous day's plodding alongside dry fields, it wasn't nearly as flat as I had anticipated. I felt like I was climbing the *Milchan* above Timna all over again! At one point, I calculated the elevations involved: a total of some 600m of ascent and the same on descent. Like a horse speeding up on heading back to its stable (an unfortunate choice of illustration perhaps, but that's where my thoughts led me that day), I guess I was so near home I could feel it, I could taste it, and pushed myself to go faster.

I didn't complain (who is there to complain to? Myself? And about whom? Myself!) but I was certainly aware of the pain and the pressure. Still, I reveled in so many associations as I trudged along. I crossed Highway 6 twice that day, and spent most of the day hiking near it; I passed a number of locations familiar to me. I had spent a month of miluim reserve duty there at the very time the freeway was being constructed, patrolling the seam line marking the 1949 armistice line, in the years of the "Palestinian" Arabs round of rioting and violence in the late '80s and early '90s, which they called the "Intifada." (Their attacks resulted in the limitation by Israel on the numbers of Arabs from the disputed territories— once upwards of 300,000 daily, with no need for registration or authorization— and the requirement for entry permits. This was a decade before the murderous suicide bombings and shootings of Arafat's War against Peace, in the midst of the Oslo "peace process," which led to the building of the security barrier.) I remembered the resentment of having to wake up at 4 a.m. to stake out the dirt road leading down the hill, just around the bend I was now walking through, to catch the vans transporting Arabs illegally crossing over the '49 armistice line from Samaria to work.

That game of cat-and-mouse infuriated me: both that the Arabs had destroyed the slow progress toward accommodation and mutual coexistence that had been building for decades, and that our leaders in Israel found no better solution than forcing reserve IDF battalions like ours to play immigration police for months on end. We caught vans stuffed full of 15 men, young and old; we brought them to wait at the check-point; sent their names in to confirm they weren't wanted terrorists by the Shin Bet general security service (Israel's FBI); and then let them go home. One of my duties was to ensure they had water (once a medic, always a medic), as they sat in the sun. It seemed to me at the time a silly, tactical quandary which might have had a better answer.

I remembered, as I trudged along, two incidents which remain with me to this day. Once, stopping a van at sunrise, our unit's officer found himself confronted by an angry 30-year-old Arab man, who used aggressive language and gestures to argue not only that they should be let go, but that our very actions were unjust. Our officer felt threatened by the menacing actions and lost his cool, raising his rifle toward the man (though without pointing it directly at him nor cocking it to put a bullet in the chamber). I stepped in between them and quietly told our officer "אין צורך ליזה, זה לא מתאים לך"—"This isn't necessary; it's not like you." "They just want to work to support their families," I told him, and told the man we understood this, but that he/they had to find work nearer home and not in Tel Aviv, until they convince their leaders, and their kids, to stop attacking us. I was no *tsaddik* or saint, just a normal guy in the right place and time. As an older member of the unit, with the patina of respectability that comes with being a medic ("Doktor" they call us), I was able to grab my officer's attention. Things calmed down and that was that.

But in recalling the incident as I walked, I connected it in my mind to so many aspects of our life here, and not least to the exaggerated, hostile and agenda-driven misrepresentations presented these days by groups like "Breaking the Silence." Organizations like theirs, Betselem, and Human Rights Watch purport to "expose" misdeeds by the IDF, but serve only to slander and distort the reality which I and the vast majority of other soldiers recognize—complex, challenging and difficult as it is. A pro-"Palestinian" activist could misuse the above anecdote as an example of reprehensible behavior of an IDF officer, when in fact it was and is the daily fodder of a multi-faceted antagonistic environment in which our soldiers almost always act with good judgment and humanity (much more so than any other western nation on earth or in history, as testified by Colonel Richard Kemp, former British commander in Afghanistan).

As I climbed the last hill before heading down to go under Route 6 again, these notions reminded me of a second episode from that time, which occurred at the Rantis junction. An older Arab man—60 or so, I was 30 at the time—came to the checkpoint we manned, and not having a permit was told he couldn't continue. He argued; our officer remained firm in enforcing the regulations. He pleaded; the officer agreed to check with his superior, and then with the Shin Bet, but to no avail; there was no permission to be had. In those early days after the "Palestinians" initiated that period of their attacks, few received permission; from that 300,000 figure at the height of coexistence the numbers fell to some 30,000 a day. Every time the Israeli government eased restrictions, Israelis were killed by terror attacks in our cities. It was not—and remains not—an easy-to-solve predicament, until the Arabs cease encouraging violence. Like the man from the van, this fellow just wanted to work, to support his family. But the world, politics, conflict, his leaders and society (and our leaders too, though defensively) conspired to prevent him.

I felt, at the time, and still feel, that there exists no "right" for someone living in the territories to be given access to the economy of Israel in which to work. This is a privilege, no less than for a Mexican to be able to work in America or a Turk to work in Austria. And Israel was and is justified in taking steps to ensure those who work in our towns and farms are not part of that vicious jihadist ideology set on destroying us. Requiring authorization for crossing the armistice line, or building the physical security fence when the suicide bombings and other attacks escalated in the '90s, are some of these reasonable, defensive steps. And yet watching this older man implore us to simply let him feed his family, I also couldn't accept that we can't find imaginative ways to enable him to do so. On the one hand, I felt the security apparatus should have given my officer more leeway to make exceptions (though this was early days in the long process of radicalization of "Palestinian" society and of the development of our innovative responses to their violence). On the other hand, I was well aware of the many occasions already—including one at our checkpoint, Rantis, just before we took over—where seemingly innocent Arabs had blown up bombs.

In the end, I approached the man, as he became more animated, and took him aside, as if to offer him water and further help. I simply handed him 100 shekels (about $35 or so), the equivalent, I knew, of the pay he'd receive for a day's work on the construction site in Petach Tikvah. He looked at me; hesitated; said no; hesitated again, and then took it. Saying "thank you" quietly, he took the cup of water and walked back up the road. I spent the day thinking about the quandary we were all in, and wrote an article about finding a solution to our conflict soon after. Though I knew I had solved nothing, I felt that I had at least made a small gesture of conciliation, and humanity, in the midst of the madness we found ourselves. Walking in the hills close by where both these incidents took place, I returned to that train of thought, about the power of the individual, acting morally, to affect the world we live in.

It's a very Jewish idea. I wasn't then, and am not now, a "Leftist" as the term is used in Israel. Our sages said, "If you save a single life, you've saved an entire world." And Hillel the Elder said, "It is not incumbent on you to finish the work, but neither are you free to desist from it." And "If not now, when?" And "If I am not for myself, who will be? And if I am only for myself, what am I?" Our moral compass, our universe of values as the people of the Book, as the Holy Nation, has given us strength over 3,500 years and has guided our public policy and private decisions, and has never failed to bring us happiness and success, joy and contentment, yes even in the midst of tragedy and sorrow and horrific suffering. It is this sense of purpose which gives our life meaning, personally and nationally. As Frankl writes, the world can improve only if "each of us does his best."

As I turned my back on the hills around Rantis and headed down to cross under Route 6, I thought of that older Arab man, and wondered what became of him, not least as I was closer to his age now than to my age then. But then, in one of the most unusual non-nature-related sections on the Shvil, I found myself deep beneath the earth, looking at the longest underground passage I'd ever seen, basically a four-sided concrete drainage conduit built specifically for hikers on the Trail. It concentrated my thoughts, as I forgot the implications of Torah morality for our modern life and focused on bending over and not panicking as I continued on through this 200-meter-long tunnel, trying not to bang the top of the guitar or my backpack on its low roof.

In the middle of it I found an incongruous square of light on the floor. I stared up at a square duct above my head, perhaps 100 meters in height. Suffering from a weird form of reverse-vertigo, a growing claustrophobia, and a sudden arachnophobia—with my elder daughter Meravi in mind, not a great lover of spiders, she—I bolted. I managed to get, literally, to the light at end of the tunnel and I flopped down on a small rise covered with weeds, laughing at myself and my tendency for the dramatic, as well as at the contrast of this mundane challenge with that of the philosophical issues I had been struggling with just a few minutes before.

*I start to sing a song of Rabbi Nachman from Breslov—*כל העולם כולו גשר צר" *מאוד . . . והעיקר לא לפחד כלל*"*—"All the world's a very narrow bridge; the main thing is not to be afraid at all." Whether a bridge or a tunnel or a path, I'm thinking, it is indeed often our fear which prevents us from moving across it or ahead with our lives, that's for sure. Shouldering my pack, I head up a small incline on a narrow trail, marveling as I go at the colors of the spring flowers—blues and violets of various hues, pinks and whites and yellows and incredible shades of reds, I wish I knew their names. And then Woah! Coming over the top of the hill, I find myself next to the largest building I've ever seen in my life. It's like a huge rectangular land-bound aircraft carrier—and even though I know what it is, as I've driven by it on Route 6 innumerable times, it still takes me aback.*

I'm gazing up at the furthest edge of the Teva pharmaceuticals manufacturing plant, the largest of a number of big factories right near the freeway. They are so much BIGGER than they look from the road! Can a building, an industrial area be beautiful? I guess it can—when it demonstrates, in all its physical eminence, a kind of power, influence and progress—not unlike, I'm thinking, standing beneath the new Freedom Tower in New York. Of course here it's Jewish development, it's the instrument and reflection of the maturity of the Israeli economy and the ability of the Jewish nation—the people and the nation-state—to triumph, beyond our wildest dreams. So I take some delight in walking the length of four football fields beside this massive expression of Israel's creative energy and the innovation which lies at the heart of our modern economic miracle. Even though I prefer landscapes and wilderness.

Coming down from the built-up area, I stumble on a wine press and building frames on the side of a hill, right next to Route 6, remains of a village some 3000 years old. The Gat suggests there were Jews here, and I see steps down into a small bath-like enclosure, suggesting a mikvah which validates that thesis—but I haven't the luxury to look further. I'm only 17 kilometers or so into the total of 31, and it's well past midday. Just then two young men come along behind me, heading in my direction but walking much faster than me. They stop and we chat a bit. As usual, one of the first items to discuss on the Shvil is how far you've come, how far you have to go that day. When I said I'd come from staying over at friends in Nachshonim, one of the guys says his grandparents live there, and they plan to stay there tonight. Of course: it turns out that Ravid is Meir and Rivkele's grandson! He and his friend are hiking a bit of the Shvil for a few days, and we laugh and laugh at the small world which is Israel. He knows Michael and Diana, naturally, and the warmth with which he speaks of them fills me with pleasure. We walk together for a bit, until we reach Tel Hadid and I'm ready for a rest. They want to make it further before catching a ride back to Nachshonim, so I take a photo and send it to Meir—"Guess who I met on the Shvil?!?"—and take a quick, and somewhat uneasy, look at the map.

I have seriously miscalculated. From Tel Hadid I still have more than ten kilometers to go, including ascents and descents of another 400 meters or so. I'm not worried; I'm near enough to civilization. And my friends awaiting my arrival in the town of Modi'in already offered to pick me up at the trail crossing, so I can always have them collect me at a different point if necessary. I really want to stick with the plan, though. I don't want to skip any part of the Trail here; I don't want to have to add more to tomorrow; I want to watch the sunset from the top of the hill near Modi'in. So I decide to push on.

After admiring a memorial to fallen soldiers at the base of Tel Hadid, I head to the summit. Passing remains from the Bronze Age and the biblical town of Hadid, I look quickly out at the magnificent view of Tel Aviv and the Mediterranean in the distance from the top of the mount, and then start down the hill. I stop to admire the slow ballet in blue and white of the El Al (Israel airline) planes making their wide circle over the Shomron to approach Ben Gurion airport from the East. And I spend the next twenty minutes or so as I bounce down the slope muttering to myself how ridiculous and dangerous it is for anyone to contemplate relinquishing security control over the neighboring hills of Samaria, from which a lone terrorist with a shoulder-held rocket launcher can take down an airliner, not to mention what a trained armed force could do.

About 3 kilometers and less than an hour later, making good time, I arrived at road 443. Or rather, at the messy, confused, torn-up construction site that had become of this part of 443 at the entrance to the Ben Shemen forest. It took a precious twenty minutes to navigate not only across the road (there was a huge and impassable ditch) but to find the lost trail markings. Once at the entrance to Ben Shemen forest, I sat down on a picnic table under the shade of dark green fir trees and took stock—as I watched teenage counselors round up (and clean up after) a bunch of disabled kids on a day's outing. I had about nine kilometers left to go, and about two hours of sunlight. In my most optimistic outlook I could make it before dark, even taking into account that my calculations were notoriously overconfident.

I knew I was kidding myself; it wasn't likely to happen that way, especially as I was already tired. Still, I didn't want to quit. This was my last full day on the Shvil; the next day, Thursday, was to end with my leaving the Trail and hiking over to where I planned to spend my last night, prior to walking home to Beit Shemesh Friday morning. I wanted it to be full, and invigorating, complete and inspiring. And so, rather casually I must say with hindsight, I just got up and started walking, following a bus with screaming kids on it going down a well-travelled hard dirt road (to where? I do not know) and trying to shield my face and nose from the dust. I can't say I finished the deliberations with some calculus of cost-and-benefit or further, more careful reading of the map and terrain. I simply stood up and stepped out. I did, though, remember my experience hiking up from the Machtesh haKatan, the Little Crater, walking that last hour in real darkness. I checked my phone battery and stopped to make sure my headlamp, stored on the very top of my bag in an external pouch, was accessible and working. Then I moved on, through a quiet patch of forest, along a section of the Trail that winded this way and that, becoming more beautiful as the sun descended into its final quadrant and the temperature fell.

Ben Shemen forest, famous for its hundreds-of-years-old olive trees, is a lovely, serene oasis; one that, even though so close to home, I had never walked through before. My eye was drawn to a particularly well-kept KKL/JNF plaque, and it turned out to be a monument or memorial to Ezer Weizman, Israel's seventh president and former head of the air force, who had fought in every war since (and before) Israel's founding. The inscription was moving. I'm not sure why but I feel it is so very appropriate that we have forests—living, breathing, green and beautiful forests—dedicated as memorials all over our country, and not just buildings and stones, monuments and plaques. The rolling countryside unexpectedly reminded me of Sonoma County, near San Francisco, from my childhood. In the sparkling light of the deep azure sky, as the sun began to drop lower on the horizon away to my right over the little village of Gimzo, I started to really move, almost marching, tramping in time to my new songs, with my sticks clacking along with the rhythm of my steps. So I started to sing, first "There's a bright golden haze on the meadow," "Zippidy Doo Dah" and then "I've got six pence" with its refrain about "Rolling home; rolling home, in the light of the silvery moon." I sang my "Clothe me in Love" over and over; even recorded myself singing it, and then filmed my shadow parading along, with the green fields of wheat and barley surrounding me, lit by the shimmering gilded orb just hovering over the horizon. It was an incredible end to a glorious day.

And then the sun began to sink behind the hills; not slowly but abruptly, it seemed to just withdraw the warmth of its embrace without warning. It wasn't dark of course, not by a long shot. The sun hadn't even set yet. I still wasn't worried; I had another two, maximum three kilometers to go, no worries.

Without hyperbole, it was an adventure. Given that I had a headlamp and enough water to last a night if it came to that, I wasn't worried. What I hadn't planned for was losing the trail, and losing power to my phone, let alone for a chill which crept up out of the blue and which made my shoulder hurt more than ever before.

I just keep going—now I'm not singing, but keeping up a rather determined monologue with myself, glad I sent a message to Russell about where and when to meet before losing power but knowing I'll be at least a half hour, if not an hour, later than expected. I lose the trail markings, retrace my steps, find them, lose them again. "Where the heck is it? Which one? Darn it this doesn't make sense!" I keep saying to myself as I begin to climb the 1.5-kilometer ascent to the top of Hirbat Ragav. I literally switch back and forth from looking at the map in my hand to the trails in front of me every few seconds; the hill is criss-crossed with paths and is just a mass of confusion. It seems there's a popular "Single" here, or mountain-bike path, or actually a few together; I notice then a few bike trail markings, but that makes things only more confusing. The fact that I can see, and the Guide points out, many ruins from Roman and Byzantine times only makes it all the more frustrating and difficult. Frustrating, as of course I'd like to investigate them and learn more about them; difficult as I become increasingly afraid of tripping and falling, with rocks strewn across the paths, remains of stone buildings all over the place, and even caves appearing out of nowhere right in front of me.

Then I read this in the Red Guide: "There are several ancient underground water cisterns in the area, take extra caution." Oy! Frustration grows, as does my unease. I can just see it: no injuries alone in the desert, none on the cliffs below Manara, none along the rocks and shifting overhangs of the sea coast or clambering over boulders and streams . . . he falls and breaks something a few miles from home, a day before he finishes the trek. So I step more carefully and, when the time comes, about halfway up the hill, take two decisions: one, to take out my headlamp (an admission of failure of sorts, but what idiot alone on a hill in the growing darkness even bothers to think such thoughts?); the other, to now simply ignore the search for the lost Shvil markings, and just head straight up the hill. I haven't lost the trail so much as I'm deciding to leave it; the markings don't conform to the map and Guide description, and I'd very much like to see the view from the top.

As it gets darker, it gets steeper, and as it gets steeper, my legs scraped and scratched by the sharp branches of the shrubs, I get more determined, and push on harder. I'm basically stomping straight up through the brush, no path. After about twenty minutes of this—which to be honest is just about as much as I can endure—I get to the summit. I could care less about Hirbat Ragav at this point. What grabs my interest is the view, even in the relative darkness. Looking to the east, I see an iridescent reflection of the sunset behind me on the glass of Modi'in's tallest buildings, and for a moment I'm confused—it looks like Oz! Absolutely mindboggling! Turning to the west, I'm equally bowled over by the spectacular beauty of the sunset itself, over the coastal plain cities of Ramle and Lod and the seaside cities of Bat Yam, Holon, and Tel Aviv—the former not at all known for their prettiness. The buildings in silhouette make me think of San Francisco, as seen at sunset from my college town of Berkeley; I stand there homesick all of a sudden for those evenings watching the sun turn the Golden Gate Bridge and the towers of SF a bright shining orange and then sizzling into the Pacific—or so we pretended. I spend a few minutes just taking it all in, savoring this exquisite moment of silence in the world, when no conflict or strife, no questions or hesitations seem to burden me or the planet . . . and then it's gone, and I'm left with a dark indigo sky to the east, a deepening orange and red and yellow horizon to the west, pink and white and gray clouds above, and opaque shadows on the slope beneath me.

Realizing I have to get moving, I head down the hill, stepping carefully, my head-lamp on full. I'm so glad I made it to the top—not just on principle, it feels good to have pushed for another "last thing." It takes a good thirty minutes to get down to the bottom of the hill; and here's Russell, standing by his car parked at the side of the road, right where the Trail touches the street, with a big smile on his face and outstretched arms. I don't even want to know how long he's been waiting; it's such a relief to see him, I just sigh and smile back as I approach him. It's done; this day is over; thank God for this wonderful day.

It was fun to see Russell and Adena and enjoy their company as they put their kids to bed. They were, as I wrote in my journal later, especially affectionate: "Our privilege to be your last מלאכים Angels!" they said. It was a bit weird, too; at dinner they reminded me that the last time I had seen them was also there, at their table, when they had me over for supper, less than four months previously. It was the day I gave Karen the *get* (divorce), which was also the day of Nava's funeral, which was not a good day at all. I remember—and we spoke about—wanting to cancel dinner that night, but then just coming so as not to be alone. They were not only good friends to have me but good people to be with at that time. The had experiences of their own (it being Russell's second marriage) and so were able to offer the sort of companionship and support I needed at the time. Now, at this dinner, as I put it in my journal, "it was so nice—and comfortable—and comforting." Enjoying a very nice 2011 Gamla Merlot with Russell, we talked for quite a while as Adena went out to visit her mom. I slept extremely well that night.

Waking up early, Russell and Adena set up a full and delicious breakfast; then Meira's close friend from high school, Aya, who lived in Modi'in at the time with her parents, came to pick me up to take me back to the Trail. I treated her to a cup of coffee and croissant en route; it was so very very strange to sit at Café Aroma with all the other "normal" customers starting their morning with a *Café Hafuch* latte. I felt like an alien, and sat there looking at the people having their mundane conversations, going about their daily routine, feeling a bit odd and isolated and unconnected. Thankfully, I was with Aya; we joked and laughed and

Sunset over Tel Aviv from Hirbat Ragav near Modi'in

caught up on news, and by the time she dropped me off, with a selfie in the car to send to Meira, I felt much less alone.

And so I set out with a light heart and a spring in my step. Having pushed myself the day before to complete those 31 kilometers, I was left that day, Thursday, with less than twenty to go. That meant also looking forward to a nice evening to put my thoughts together, write a bit, play guitar, and generally relax and get in the mood for coming home. Friday was planned to be even easier and less stressful, about ten kilometers up and over a few hills to Beit Shemesh, with Netanel apparently planning to join me for the few hours that would take. But although the Trail on Thursday was similar to the previous day's, it was a very different experience, both easier and shorter. But mainly, it was my last day walking the Shvil, and that just made it different.

From the moment I left Aya's car, I was singing. First my תפילות prayers, then all my favorites. Walking a few hundred meters above Highway 1, the main Jerusalem-Tel Aviv freeway, which could be seen (and heard) periodically through the trees, I started listening to Jason Mraz, and finished with Passenger—with no tears. I wasn't sure whether that was significant, but it seemed so. Approaching the highway through another field of barley, I took a photo or two. What are these drivers thinking about as they rush from one place to another? What do I usually think about on the freeway? Do they marvel at the significance of this concrete link between the ancient capital and heart of the Jewish people, Jerusalem, and the modern center of commerce and culture of the Jewish nation-state, Tel Aviv? Do I? Do they appreciate, even in their peripheral vision while focused on the road, the extraordinary beauty and majesty of these glowing yellow and emerald fields, dark green and brown olive groves and vineyards, just sprouting bronzed lime-colored vineyards? Do I?

I remembered reading Robin Sharma's *The Monk who Sold his Ferrari* and promised myself not only to read it again, and to re-read Leo Buscalgia's *Living Loving and Learning, Zen and the Art of Motorcycle Maintenance* and all the other books I'd already been exposed to on this theme, but to continue my meditation and to expand and enhance my sense of wonder and delight in all that exists in this amazing world. With that thought in mind, I hoisted my pack and headed through a young wheat field, the breeze flowing through it making "waves" of the sheaves as if to welcome me forward, and headed toward Latrun, the monastery and the fortress, now a museum and memorial to the armored corps of the IDF.

This is all so familiar, but a bit bizarre. I've been here before, more than once, but not like this. I've driven by these fields a thousand times. But I've never hiked around the periphery of Latrun, never stood here by the Shvil Yisrael sign, never crossed the road wearing a hat and a backpack and continued on up into the hills. I have arrived at the foothills of the Judean mountains and I am home. Well, not quite. But I'm getting there. Standing at the Shvil poster, I take photos of myself with the map behind me, making silly faces—and then notice a tall female soldier in an air force uniform looking at me strangely. She's smiling slightly, and I realize it's Avital, daughter of my friends Jonty and Janet! A familiar face, family almost, and it seems natural. Close to home you're bound to run in to people you know, but it seems out of the ordinary to me. I'm still in Shvil mode, so I guess I'm psychologically still far from home.

Up and down the hills, past a Tel with archeological remains from who-knows-when, past so many vineyards I stop counting, into and through a still-young and quite lovely (and quiet) forest and up past Neve Shalom . . . and all of a sudden, before I'm really prepared for it, I've reached the point where I leave the Trail! It's only about 2 p.m. and I'm here already.

Under a grove of gray and brown pine trees at the top of the hill I throw down my pack on a picnic table bench and realize: this is it. I see the Trail markings just ahead: Shvil to the left. But I'm heading to the right. There's a green arrow pointing right, I don't know why, probably left over from some group outing or other, but for me it's an obvious sign, and I take a picture of it.

I sit for a few moments, drink, and eat a banana I happily accepted from Russell this morning. Was that today? Just five or six hours ago? Really? I'm so much back in Shvil mode that their "normal" home seems like another life. It was, it is, another world. Am I returning to that world? Can I?

Looking through the trees, I meditate, seeing and not seeing them. I sit for over an hour, not thinking, centering, closing my eyes once I take in the view of the forest and the fields and hills further off, and allow myself to breath, to accept, to celebrate, to mourn, to delight, to just be. And when I open my eyes, I have tears in them, but tears like I've never had before: tears of joy, tears of gladness, the living waters of life

Wheatfield near Highway 1

just flowing down my face like rain. I'm thinking about the connection between rain and trees and earth and sky and me and my family and Israel and the nations and the oneness of all things under God and in God and as God. . . . I'm glad I'm alone since it's all a bit much.

I laugh—self-deprecating but also aware I'm not that far off-base as these things go—and reach for my pack. I stand for a few seconds in front of those markings, wondering who put that green arrow there for me . . . and then start off, not quite sure which of the many dirt roads ahead I'm supposed to take but heading west knowing I'll get to Mitzpeh Har El, where I'm staying tonight, eventually. I call Netanel to make arrangements for the next day; it turn out that Tehila is joining us, which is great. Sending a message of thanks to Russell and Adena for hosting me, I think of all the family friends—old and new—with whom I connected on this trek. What an assortment! Jews from America and Iraq, England and Cochin, students and ambassadors and software engineers and lawyers.

Are we all simply wandering Jews, I'm wondering as I walk, members of a nomadic tribe here on a temporary rest stop? Is my trek, now that it's coming to an end, just a symbolic demonstration of my people's never-ending search for paradise-on-earth, for home, for peace? It seems ironic that I've chosen to spend my last night at a Bedouin tent, so emblematic of the Tent of Meeting which accompanied my ancestors as they wandered through the desert.

NO. And yes. No, this is no temporary stop in an unceasing migration of the Jewish people through time and space. We have returned to our ancestral homeland, unique in the annals of history, fitting for the people which has defied historical "realities" time and again to re-emerge vibrant and stronger after facing and defeating the most horrific of challenges. Like the Mishkan, *the Tent of Meeting, settled and became the* Mikdash, *the Holy Temple, our tents—from Austria and Australia and Andelusia and Tunisia and Texas—have become homes in Eilat and Metullah, Tel Aviv and Beit Shemesh and of course Jerusalem, and our return is solid and genuine and lasting. And so my return to my home tomorrow is in fact the end of this trek; it is symbolic of my people's coming back to our indigenous land, not of our ceaseless wandering.*

But yes, in another way, this trek is indeed representative of the Jewish nation's eternal quest: not the physical wandering but our search for Truth and peace, a mission which did not and does not end with our entry into the Promised Land, but rather which continues and takes on new impetus with our settling in this Land of Milk and Honey. Our purpose, the meaning inherent in our existence, has only been enhanced by our re-establishment of our sovereignty in our native land, and with it our taking control over our own destiny after two thousand years.

And so too for me: I am returning, and my return embodies and bolsters my own sense of personal meaning and purpose. Tomorrow I'll be going home—"I'm coming home," as the button we were given to wear on the plane when we made Aliya, moving "up" to Israel back in 1985, announced—and that's not at all the end, but rather the beginning, of my new life. I know that; that's why I'm so excited to be here, as I walk into the Orchan Bedouin tent compound at Mitzpeh Har El, a dusty hilltop in the middle of this JNF forest. I'm happy to see picnic tables, an open door to the bathroom hut, and a small grassy area I can pitch my little tent on. I feel at home here, a place where I've spent many a late night over a beer with a friend, so near to home. This is very much "my" forest and hills, and so much "my kind of place"—unpretentious, surrounded by nature, unspoiled and quiet.

At least it seemed to be quiet—until they started the karaoke at 11 p.m. I guess I forgot that every Thursday night, including the Thursday night before the week of Pesach, there's a sing-along under the tent. But that was okay with me. That afternoon, after setting up, I had enjoyed a visit with my friend Yaakov, who stopped by on the way home from work, along with our new friend the camel who escaped his enclosure and seemed to want to join us for a beer. Our conversation was light, and I appreciated that; I had dwelled enough on my own on the meaning and significance of the trek coming to an end as I walked the more and more familiar paths there so near to home. My thoughts and feelings were too complicated and heavy for a casual quick review with a friend; but it was comforting, and enjoyable, to sit with Yaakov, and made the re-entry a gradual thing.

I had a great supper of laffa, labane, and zatar, followed by nana (mint) tea, and I sat and wrote and wrote. I had a lot of catching up to do in the journal, just recording the previous eight days or so! Sitting on my own on a couch in the large Bedouin tent covered with skins and canvas but open on the sides, with pillows and Middle Eastern rugs throughout, was just what I needed and wanted, quiet and relatively empty, but not deserted so I didn't feel alone or lonely. Over the course of a few hours writing I managed to get as far as the previous morning, when I was gently interrupted by a young woman. I had brought my guitar into the tent, and seeing it, she and her friends asked me to play something. That only lasted a half hour or so, but was fun. When they started up the Karaoke, I sat and

Yaakov and the camel at Mitzpeh Har El Bedouin tent

listened a bit, wrote some more, and began to think of heading to bed, though I wondered whether I could sleep with that racket going on.

When the Bedouin bartender called me over, instead of asking me to pay, he asked me to choose a song for the Karaoke. We had spoken, and he had congratulated me on completing the Shvil, so he wasn't too surprised at the song I picked: קום והתהלך בארץ *"Kum v'hitalech b'Aretz,"* "Arise and walk the Land," the old Israeli Zionist standard which I mentioned had become an anthem of sorts for me since Purim. I set up my phone to record it on video (Video 11), did a passable job, managed not to build too much emotion into it, and to a smattering of applause, returned to my couch and cushion at the other end of the tent to finish the night.

I guess it was the song that did it. I returned to finish detailing the last two days of the trek in my journal, and then waxed a bit philosophical. I posted a final Shvil Facebook status, reproduced below. At 1:30 a.m., I figured it was about time to wrap it up. I'll let my final journey entry, from Thursday, April 10, verbatim and unedited, including its closing listing of the main Hebrew passages and poems which accompanied me the entire way, speak for itself, as a fitting ending to my chronicle:

> I really did it! It's a bit overwhelming to recognize what I've done. About 800kms ~ 500 miles! Like Netanel said: there are people who start things, and then there are people who finish. (Michael French.)
>
> I have taken my love for Israel, my love of nature, my love for hiking, my need/desire for release and/or challenge and some sort of deeper recognition of a need for a representation of the transformation my life is going through, and expressed it in perhaps the most powerful, fitting, healthy, uplifting way possible.

Good for me!

Has it been "transformative'? Am I a new or different person that I was 2 months ago? Am I more complete, or more content/happy, or less sad/depressed? I really don't know . . . though certainly the periods of sadness, or misery, or regret, or contemplating the "what ifs" and the like are both less frequent and less intense (and less lengthy).

But I am certainly in a different "place" than I was then. I have, if not "moved on," then at least moved forward. And the forward movement of the Shvil has certainly contributed to that.

So it's 1:30 a.m. . . . . Tomorrow I'll walk home—with Nati & Tehila, which is both fun and comforting to look forward to . . . .

It's late and I really have little to write of any pithy value. Many thoughts and feelings—wrote some on FB, including the conflicting feelings of glad to be going home and wanting to continue . . . .

I will find time to present more articulately those "lessons" learned, especially the "relativity" issues as well as the humility, appreciation/ gratitude, acceptance, forgiveness, & meaning themes.

But that's all for now.

. . . יחבקו אותך דרכיה

[Her paths will embrace you . . . from the
"Rise and walk the Land" song]

היה טוב, וטוב שהיה.

[It was good, and good that it was.]

It's time to return to real life, with all its mess and ups and downs, disappointments and celebrations, magnificence and tragedy, sadness & misery and beauty and wonder.

רבות מחשבות בלב איש

ועצת ה' היא תקום

עצת ה' לעולם תעמוד

מחשבות לבו לדור ודור . . .

[Many thoughts reside in the heart of man
But what God wills is what comes to pass
The plans of God stand forever
The thoughts in His heart for every generation]

צדיק ה' בכל דרכיו וחסיד בכל מעשיו

[God is righteous/just in all His ways,
and gracious/kind in all his actions/doings]

חננו מאתך דעה בינה והשכל

[Grant us from your knowledge, understanding and enlightenment]

... מה רבו מעשיך ה'! מאוד עמקו מחשבותיך

[How incredible/vast are your deeds, God!
Extremely deep are your thoughts/calculations ...]

ברוך שאמר והיה העולם—ברוך הוא
ברוך אומר ועוש
ברוך גוזר ומקיים

[Blessed is the One who spoke and
the world was created
Blessed is He
Blessed is (He) who Says and Does
Blessed is (He) who rules and fulfills his decrees]

מודה אני לפניך

[Thankful am I before You]

אהיה אשר אהיה

[I Am As I Am/
I Will be What I Will be/
I Am That I Am]

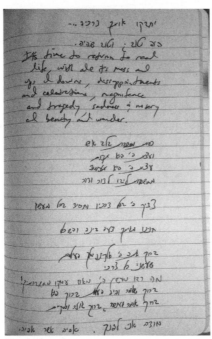

Final journal page

275

Facebook Post Week Eight—Final Night—April 10:

Well . . . This is it. My last night on the trail. It's been almost two weeks since my last update, partially explained by my effort to finish by tomorrow, which required pretty long and hard days this last two weeks. I won't go into detail here, but it was a fabulous, glorious even, conclusion to a phenomenal, extraordinary journey.

In the past 12 days I have walked from the western Galil to the Mediterranean to the Judean hills, up (and down) the Carmel, along the (beautiful restored & preserved) Yarkon river, in and around remains of Israelite, Roman, Byzantine, Crusader, Arab, Ottoman, British, and finally Israeli(te) fortresses, synagogues, mosques, monasteries, farms, fields, villages, baths/mikvaot . . . and wine presses ("gats').

And though my walking was still—somewhat surprisingly—almost entirely solitary, these last two weeks were certainly more social. I met a few people each day on the trail—young and old, Israeli and otherwise, biker & hiker & dog-walker & even a unicyclist. And I stayed or visited or reconnected with many friends, like Judy & Arnold, David & Amanda, Tally, Vivian, מאיר וריבקלה, Russell & Adena, Zachy, Matan, Jeremy, Aaron and Yaakov; and made a few new friends.

Each day brought with it, as it has this entire trek, not a few spectacular moments—incredible views, a variety of flowers, unusual animal sightings (I now have photos of many species of butterfly, let alone a few snakes, horses, cows, jackals, lizards, beetles, many birds, sheep, goats, and now—here outside my tent at Mitzpeh Har El—a camel, to augment the flora I've shot & shared).

I spent a glorious Shabbat on the Sharon beach, commencing with an hour of guitar before sunset on a rock at the water's edge (shades of my youth) and ending with a massive bonfire on Motza"sh with the beach entirely to myself. Though occasionally lonely, I could at least sing every Shabbat song I know without any child of mine begging me to stop. ☺

Had a really special evening with Netanel in Zichron Yaakov (having given up looking for the nearby campsite), and a lovely picnic with Meira & Bini at the end of a long day walking along Route 6—an experience in itself, taking in all the variations in terrain and flora step by step, as the world speeds by, the drivers oblivious to the wealth and beauty of the hills full of flowers and butterflies, caves & ruins & groves & vineyards & wheat fields.

And I finally—finally!—have been initiated into the Secret Society of the Poika. Thanks Nati & Matan & Zachy for a crazy and marvelous campfire and evening—the poika was simply tremendous. And so glad we had enough wood. Good thing my wood-burning stove at home is at the end of its season.

I explored a few of Israel's earliest kibbutzim, swam a few times along the coast—and found a pristine hidden cove (had to jump in of course) on the way down to Herzliya. (I'll reveal the location to anyone who asks, but am not publicizing it. ☺)

I can highly recommend a walk—or bike ride—along the Yarkon river; it's like a long, narrow Central Park and just charming. And the Sources of the Yarkon national park near Rosh HaAyin (which means, for the uninitiated, "beginning of the spring') is a unique and not-well-enough-known oasis of forest, rivers, ponds, paths, shade & water flora.

As I began to approach home, walking through these hills ever more familiar, I realized how much I have missed all that is dear to me—both at home and beyond. And how much I really don't want this journey to end.

I suppose this might be said for almost any peak experience, whether lasting two hours or two months. (On the other hand, yesterday was my longest hike yet, 31 kilometers with a lot more climbs than anticipated—so my feet and thighs and shoulders and back and neck have no such conflict.)

I can only say that I am a bit overwhelmed that I actually did this (Netanel: I finished it!): I'm very, very glad I did, and I'm even more glad that tomorrow I'll be walking in the door of my house for the first time in 55 days . . . hopefully not to leave any time soon (Mimi, you'll finally have me around for a bit).

All of you—friends and family, and friends who are family—have been stupendous. Without your love and constant support I never could have succeeded. This is most especially true of Netanel, Merav, & particularly Meira—I am, every day and always, so very grateful to you and for you. And those of you who helped or encouraged me at the most difficult moments—you know who you are—were and are the true מלאכים Angels of my Shvil. I thank you and love you all.

שבת שלום וחג שמח Shabbat Shalom and Chag Sameach

Chapter Nine

PUTTING IT ALL TOGETHER

[Conclusion(s)]

That final morning—which I haven't included in the last chapter as it wasn't officially part of the Shvil, though certainly it was part of my trek—dawned spectacularly. There's no other word for it. I prayed with special intensity. The sun streamed in from just over the Judean hills to the east, right onto my uplifted face, my head growing warm in its rays, covered with my Tallit prayer shawl and my *Tefillin*. I'm not embarrassed to admit I asked someone to take a photo, a biker who stopped for water and to wash off the mud from his tires, toward the end of my prayers; I just wanted the memory to be preserved. I saw it as opportune that he came by at just the right time while I was in between sections and nearly finished. I was celebrating, singing almost all the passages usually sung on a festival or a Shabbat, taking my time, making it count. I was so happy to be there; so happy to be me; so happy to be going home.

Jason Mraz's song "Lucky" kept running through my mind as I packed my tent away, I just had to put it on: I felt truly "lucky to be where I have been, lucky to be coming home again." Netanel and Tehila arrived, hugs all around, a photo or two, and we were off. In fact, we had a special send-off: Eilon Bar Tov, Yaron's father (from Timna and more), knowing I was setting out that morning from Mitzpeh Har El, had ridden down on his bike from his home in Mevaseret just to see me off. Very kind of him to come (a good hour's ride at least, and twice that on the ascent back up), and fun. Then Nati took my pack—in fact carried it for some of the way home—and,

Last morning Tefila at Mitzpeh Har El

thanking the owner/manager of the Orchan and calling goodbye to my camel friend, we made our way down the dirt road to Route 44, across it and up through Kfar Uriya and down to the wadi leading to the Nachal Sorek valley, past vineyards and fields, a little forest land (but not much), up and down the already dry slopes of the low hills leading home.

It took about two hours to get near Beit Shemesh, walking casually, with Nati stopping frequently to take photos. (It was great to have him, with his professional-caliber camera and keen artistic eye, to document it all). We took a break at "my" winery, which I had discovered on one of my first bike rides on moving to Beit Shemesh in 1994, about 7 kilometers or 4 miles from home. Mony winery is unique in Israel and perhaps the world as the only Muslim-Arab-owned, Jewishly-Kosher winery situated beneath a Christian monastery. Aside from its picturesque setting and unpretentious nature, I loved following its progress as it grew from a tiny and not-so-successful family venture into one of Israel's more prominent smaller wineries. I was lucky enough to have developed a relationship with the owner, Shakib, and his son Nour and grandsons Nassim and Zaki, as well as the young winemaker they brought in years later, Sam Soroka, now one of Israel's leading vintners. They guided me sometimes in my own grape-growing and wine-making, and I frequently brought foreign correspondents to visit the winery, and to go down into its 150-year-old cave/cellar, taste the wine and olive oil and experience a fascinating and unusual slice of life in Israel.

So naturally, as we neared home, Netanel and Tehila and I had to stop and taste the latest vintage as we neared home. Shakib happened to be there, and

Celebrating the return at Tel Beit Shemesh

offered us glasses; standing under the canopy of vines just recently sprouted on the lookout next to the winery, from where you can see the town of Beit Shemesh on the hill to the east, the Sorek stream and valley below, and the coastal plain fading into the distance over the lower rolling hills to the west, we sipped a little of the very nice, if a bit rough, 2012 Reserve Cabernet.

From there, we walked along the road I've so often biked over, before and since, past Kibbutz Tzora, managing to just resist the temptation to pop in to the Tzora winery, another favorite of mine and known for its prize-winning wines reflecting the local and regional terroirs. We crossed through some fields and by the chicken coops, over the railroad tracks and up to Tel Beit Shemesh, our own archeological excavation from the Bronze Age, biblical times and since. Here we took more photos—local boy returns!—symbolic of me standing with the archeological, historical site of my ancestors in the foreground and the modern hometown behind me, and then made our way through the edge of town.

Purposefully, I walked up the stairs and through the cul-de-sac of Rechov HaShita, Acacia Street, where I'd lived for over 12 years when we first moved to the town, and where most of my closest friends in the neighborhood still lived. I hadn't called ahead, so I passed through that one part of "home" mostly unnoticed and unheralded, except for being caught by Esti (who had honked and texted me after driving by on the road to Jerusalem four weeks earlier), who clapped and called from her balcony, and that was nice.

Coming down the street toward my house, Yaakov (from the day before, with the camel), his wife, Shalva, and their children Sari, Elisheva, and Tzvi, my good friends and neighbors, were standing on the street, sweetly and quietly clapping to welcome me home. Nearing home, I saw a red ribbon tied across the entrance gateway (hah! Not a yellow one, appropriately). Netanel was filming as Meira came out of the house and up the walk. It was then that I noticed some music playing, which got louder as I approached; they had put on "Eye of the Tiger," and as it blared, I ran through the ribbon with my hands up.

Fortunately, I didn't trip; that would have been laughable, especially as it was on video (Video 12). Sam the cat nonchalantly rubbed against my leg and allowed me to pet him; Tehila and I took more photos of our arms—mine dark brown from the sun, hers ivory-pink white—as it began to sink in: I'm home. I actually didn't take the pack off immediately; I stood there, as the music played and Nati filmed, and we took a few more photos. Then at the entrance to the house, I paused to read and relish the poster Meira had put on the door. On large yellow coloring paper she had written, "You F#@%*ing Did It," quoting one of our favorite Jason Mraz songs which we listened to and sang together after climbing up Half Dome, and writing the name of the song "A.W.S.O.M.E." out as well. And she wrote the Hebrew words for "welcome," "ברוכה השבה" (or more exactly, "Blessed is he who returns") too. The fact that all three were spelled wrong—even the Hebrew—only made it more perfect and gratifying. I still have the sign.

And that was that. I felt a little like Frodo arriving home—again, without my own Sam to support or comfort or accompany me. But like Frodo I knew I had achieved something miraculous, had accomplished more than what I had set out to. I had hiked the Shvil, yes, but I had learned so much also, about myself, about my people, about my country, about humanity. I walked the Trail but I also found peace in this Promised Land of ours, and my coming home was not an end but a beginning. My grandma Edie used to love to quote that "life is a journey." Though this trek was over—there and back again, as Bilbo had it—my journey was certainly not. A new stage was indeed beginning. At the moment I

Meira's sign on the door

crossed the threshold back into the house, I was thinking of all the incredible possibilities which were open to me in my life . . . and to which I was open, now, here in this land so full of promise, our Promised Land.

One who has read this far can't but help to see the connections. My hike across the length and breadth of Israel renewed for me—and perhaps for others reading this—my love for the history and significance of Israel and the Zionist enterprise, the national liberation movement of the Jewish people. My appreciation of the land, the people, the society and nation was refreshed, in all their complexity and beauty. I had learned a great deal, and gained tremendous inner strength. I discovered, or re-discovered, humility, acceptance, gratitude, forgiveness, and a sense of purpose. But even more than each of these on their own, I developed an understanding of how the linkage between these five elements can help build a life of meaning, pleasure and fulfillment, full of possibilities.

The humility of recognizing our insignificance leads us to tolerate all sorts of situations we otherwise intellectually would see as unfair and treat as unwelcome.

This acceptance of life as it hits us leads to the appreciation and gratitude for all that we have, all our blessings.

Such gratefulness and recognition of the amazing, incredible lives we live and all that's in them then results in a profound ability and willingness to forgive—ourselves and others, including those who have hurt us or we feel have done us wrong.

With the negativity of complaints and resentments out of the way and with our focus on the positive, we are open to seeing that life is chock full of possibilities, and we can turn inward and outward to apply all our energies to achieving whatever personal (or national) goals we set for ourselves. Hopefully, optimally, helping to make the world better for our being in it, as God would have us do.

Jack Canfield, author of *The Success Principles* and originator of the *Chicken Soup for the Soul* series, put a few of these ideas together this way:

> By taking the time to stop and appreciate who you are and what you've achieved—and perhaps learned through a few mistakes, stumbles and losses—you actually can enhance everything about you. Self-acknowledgment and appreciation are what give you the insights and awareness to move forward toward higher goals and accomplishments.

John Ruskin, the nineteenth-century English prolific writer, thinker, painter, and art critic, connected humility, purpose, and forgiveness in his own powerful fashion:

> The first test of a truly great man is his humility. I do not mean, by humility, doubt of his own power . . . [but really] great men . . . have a curious . . . feeling that . . . greatness is not in them, but through them . . . and they see something Divine . . . in every other man, and are endlessly, foolishly, incredibly merciful.

I finished the Shvil ready to move on. But I've also learned that finishing is beginning: I'm now in the middle not only of my life, and of my learning and recovering, but of my very being. "Being is becoming," Hegel suggested, and on the Trail that was always true. You are only really on the Shvil if you're moving on it. Sitting still on it means you're just a visitor. The very essence of human existence is the possibility within, as yet untapped and unexpressed. That contradiction became very much part of me.

There is so much still to be learned, explored, lived: for me, and for anyone seeking solace and direction, comfort and support, for all of us. How? You can take a two-month hike of course. Or you can adopt these tools as part of a life philosophy just by joining me on my journey. And though I often balk at "exercises" in all the self-help books I've read (all of them terrific, and incredibly valuable), I'd humbly suggest that you take a few moments to review your own situation, through the prism of these five elements. You can meditate on it, record it, write it down, or just talk to yourself while driving (or better yet, taking a short hike anywhere with quiet and natural beauty). As I wrote in the beginning, my reference point is often God, as creator and as the powerful and comforting force beside me in my suffering; but these steps can be applied without reference to God.

Start with humility. It's easier than we think (though not quite as simple as saying "We're not worthy!" like Mike Myers did in Wayne's World). Rabbi Simcha

Bunem, a Jewish Hassidic eighteenth-century leader in Poland, was said to carry a piece of paper in each pocket: one with the phrase "I am dust and ashes" (Genesis 18:27), the other saying "I am created "in the image of God'" (Genesis 1:27). Rav Kook in his book *Ein Eyah* echoes this when he notes that real humility is not self-effacement, but rather simple awareness of our place in the universe. Recognizing our true worth, imbued with Godliness, we can understand the nature of reality and see ourselves for what we genuinely are: a collection of atoms held together by a soul connected with God and with all of life.

In Jewish tradition, on completing the Sh'ma (שמע ישראל ה' אלוקינו ה' אחד *Sh'ma Yisrael, Adonai Eloheinu, Adonai Echad*—"Listen/Hear, Israel, the Lord (is) our God, the Lord is One/Alone"), we linger on the last syllable of "One/ Alone," "אחד—Echaaaad." In that extended time we contemplate, and acknowledge, the *unity* of all things. Our place in that one-ness of God is very very small. Crucial, central, momentous . . . but infinitesimal. Reflect on that.

Acceptance of that "nature of reality" flows instinctively from humility, whatever your reality may be. Whatever your unique circumstance—whether you are suffering from illness, divorce, death of a loved one, job loss, or general depression[17]—an important first step is to say to yourself, "It is what it is." Not apathetically; rather, with a considered understanding that we simply have to deal with life as it is, and not spend our time wishing it were different (or complaining how unfair it is). There are so many wonderful popular aphorisms along these lines, we all know them: making lemonade with the lemons; Niehbur's great saying about granting the serenity to accept what I can't change, the courage to change what I can, and the wisdom to know the difference, which we've referred to previously; and one of my favorites, John Lennon's "Life is what happens to you when you're making other plans." They're all true, and a bit of humility makes them easier to believe. Yosef, thrown into captivity in Pharoah's dungeon after being sold as a slave by his brothers to nomadic traders, seems to bear all the events in his life without protest or question, and then explains to his brothers, years later: this was all part of God's plan. *That's* the acceptance we're talking about.

Those first two elements are perhaps the most difficult to practice. The others are simpler to adopt, and to express. Once we've incorporated humility and appreciation into our way of thinking, being grateful for all our blessings is a natural outcome. No matter how difficult life is, we all have things to be grateful for. Gratitude just fills in the spaces that were taken up with anger, frustration and resentment. The subjective listing of your particular reasons for being thankful, for appreciating all the blessings in life, may be one of the most rewarding,

---

17 This is of course not meant to address clinical states of depression, anxiety or the like. It may serve useful as a tool in the process of healing, but my use of the term "depression" is not intended lightly. If you can't get out of bed, cry for no apparent reason, have no interest in work or socializing, feel a constant sense of darkness and/or just don't feel like living: please, call a doctor or therapist. You don't have to—must not—"accept" *that* reality.

uplifting, profoundly moving experiences you'll ever have. Do it. Do it now. In writing or in your head, in word or song or prayer, alone on a hill or with a friend, *just do it*, as Nike urges. And once you do it—even if you've only taken 30 seconds while reading this sentence to review the most basic aspects of your life you're glad for, including perhaps your ability to see, read, think and feel as a sentient human being—I think you'll be surprised how incredible it is, and how incredibly inspiring.

It might motivate you to action—to express your gratitude, to hug someone, to do a good deed for someone else—and I'd imagine it will encourage you to do so more often. Like once a day, or twice a day, or more. Observant Jews express simple gratefulness some three, four, five times a day, since הודיה (*Hodaya*—thankfulness) is a primary theme in our prayers (morning, afternoon and evening) and in the blessings after meals. So the sentiment accompanies us throughout our day and in fact our life. But it is an easy discipline to adopt. Saying מודה אני (*Modeh Ani*—I am thankful) on waking each morning, every morning, is an effective way to start. Or fixing any set time, once a day—at the table, or when going to bed, or while exercising (or meditating)—just take 30 seconds (not minutes; seconds!) to count your blessings. It may transform your mood, your attitude, your day, your life.

The joy which emerges from gratitude leads the way to forgiveness, as it's hard to retain the anger preventing forgiveness when full of such gratefulness. Though as with appreciation, forgiveness is so highly personal that for anyone to address it properly requires deep analysis of an individual's life experience, clearly not within the purview of this work. And yet. Like gratitude, forgiveness is a skill, or a muscle, which can be exercised, practiced, honed, and perfected. Again drawing from the wisdom of ancient Jewish sages, Jewish tradition provides a wonderful guide. Individually, in our daily prayers, we create the forgiving environment in our psyche by asking (demanding? Expecting?) God to forgive us and pardon our transgressions. How can we request such a thing unless we are prepared to forgive others? Indeed, in the month and days and hours leading up to Yom Kippur, the Day of Atonement, Jews seek forgiveness from one another, and offer compassion to others, as a prerequisite to receiving mercy from God on that day.

Once you have humbly accepted your reality, and gratefully acknowledged the gifts we've been given, we've created a stable and suitable foundation on which forgiveness can be offered. It must be sincere, and from the heart. What is critical is that we truly forgive our mother or father, our boss or child, our neighbor or competitor or spouse or ourselves, recognizing that everyone is doing the best with what they've been given in life. And forgiveness can transform our approach to others into one of goodwill and peace. This doesn't suggest we absolve others of responsibility for their actions, or abandon demands for changes in their behavior. But our focus here is on eliminating our own feelings of resentment and bitterness, thus freeing ourselves from negativity to be able to move forward with our lives.

Moving forward with our lives means having goals which give meaning to our existence. Our final element, meaning and purpose, relates to all our goals as individuals. But there is one primary goal, which underlies and enables any other. It is the pursuit of peace and harmony, both internal and interpersonal. In the deepest understanding of our life's purpose, what we all look for—whether in family and friends, money or fame or otherwise—is peace: the peace of a contented, purposeful soul. Such a soul is in touch with not only itself but with the broader "I" and oneness of the universe, as Rabbi David Aaron puts it.

Of course, the meaning in our life comes from many sources, many goals; as Victor Frankl has described it, our reasons to live may be as mundane as the enjoyment of physical pleasures and as lofty as a desire to cure cancer or bring an end to war and conflict, or anything in between. But whatever those purposes may be, they are, in an existential way, making a contribution to our personal, and the world's, peace.

As mentioned earlier, Frankl's *Logotherapy* approach describes three ways of bringing meaning into our lives, within the context of meeting personal challenges. First, creative *actions* (achievements or work); second, *love*, or relationships; and third, personal *growth*, especially overcoming *suffering*. What is amazing—and personally relevant for most of us—is that our lives are unique and constant laboratories for the creation of satisfying, meaningful growth experiences. That is, if we are open to the possibilities inherent in all the opportunities which face us. My divorce was certainly *suffering*. My trek was obviously *action*, as are my work and the very act of making my life in Israel, and all my various other pursuits. I now have *love* again in my life with my new wife Miriam and our children and wider family, and the "family" that are my friends. And the Shvil experience certainly afforded me a great chance for *personal growth* as well. All these fill my life with purpose and meaning, and give me inner peace. This helps to explain the title of my book: hiking the Israel Trail truly helped me to find peace, in all its connotations.

We each can of course determine our own sources of meaning. Whether love, achievement, surmounting pain or mastering our challenges, or a combination of them all, the point is to identify them, elevate them, and pursue them. In *The 7 Habits of Highly Effective People*, Steven Covey's second "habit"—*begin with the end in mind*—focuses on the importance of goal-setting, and then he enhances that with an eighth habit (another book) about finding your unique personal significance, what he calls your "voice." This is another way of expressing Frankl's urging us to seek that which gives our life meaning. What's important is that you do so, rather than either just living day to day or allowing your cultural milieu to dictate that for you. Dale Carnegie presaged Nike's *Just Do It* marketing slogan by almost a hundred years when he wrote, "Inaction breeds doubt and fear. Action breeds confidence and courage. If you want to conquer fear, do not sit home and think about it. Go out and get busy."

"Success" as defined by western society does not fill our lives with meaning. The usual signs of success, whether wealth or possessions, influence or popularity, actually *rob* our lives of real meaning. They restrict our capacity and time for love, relationships, and creative acts. You must define for yourself what will infuse your life with meaning, in terms of experiences, actions, work, self-improvement activities, and personal interactions. Just don't let life just pass you by.

Rabbi Lord Jonathan Sacks, in his *Machzor Rosh Hashana*, the prayer-book for the Jewish New Year, offers a concise summary of the traditional understanding of our purpose in life, which in the process includes aspects of the five elements we've discussed here:

> No people has believed as lucidly or as long as have Jews, that life has a purpose; that this world is an arena of justice and human dignity; that we are, each of us, free and responsible, capable of shaping our lives in accordance with our highest ideals. We are here for a reason. We were created in love and forgiveness by the God of love and forgiveness who asks us to love and forgive.

I hope you've enjoyed walking the Land of Israel with me. If you choose to read the introduction to *My Israel Trail* again, from the perspective of one who now has vicariously accompanied me on my journey, perhaps you can understand more easily how the five elements fit together. And I hope this might enable you to achieve peace within yourself, as well as with those around you. I have found the combination extraordinarily valuable, and I believe others may find it useful in looking for their own sense of peace and harmony. And not only individuals; it may be true for nations as well. But that's a whole different book.

And that, I suppose, is the real conclusion to my journey seeking peace in the land of milk and honey. We are all part of many concentric circles. I am a member of my family and of my wider community, a part of the nation of Israel and a resident of the Middle East, a member of the human race and an infinitesimal speck in the universe. Connected as we all are, if we can bring a sense of inner peace, meaning, forgiveness, gratitude, acceptance and humility to impact our widening circles, perhaps the tranquility I found in my trek on Shvil Yisrael and shared with you and others, can finally bring real peace to our beloved Promised Land and to the entire world.

AND LIFE CONTINUED . . .

There are those who have asked, "And then what? Where are you now?" So for the reader who is interested, a brief afterword. Following my trek, I took many decisions as a direct result of the experiences described here. One was to write this book, which has taken four years. The most important by far was to open myself again to love, and thereby I found Miriam, or rather she found me; we met in August 2014, and married in August of 2015. Our family—"The Brady Bunch on steroids" I call it, with 12 children (including 3 married in), 4 dogs, and Sam the cat between us—fills our life with energy, love, challenges, and happiness. My three children and their life partners continue to blossom as adults; now more than ever I try to support them in every way possible and to be a central part of their lives as they have always been in mine. My relationship with Miriam's six children whom I've "inherited" continues to flourish as well, as we find our own ways to navigate the challenges of a blended family.

In December of 2014, I gave in my notice to MediaCentral, though I have remained involved in helping to guide "my baby," advising and raising funds and maintaining my friendships with many of the foreign journalists in Jerusalem. I did join my friend Yossi and am enjoying my work securing investment for EnergiyaGlobal, a leading renewable energy company bringing solar, hydro and wind electricity to developing African nations. It is incredibly rewarding to be part of a business model which allows us to "do well by doing good," delivering electricity to some of the poorest communities on the planet.

In light of my Shvil experiences, I have increased my efforts to reassert the legitimacy of Zionism and Israel, in my public speaking, writing, social media and other activities. I am convinced that all the misinformation and misconceptions surrounding Israel are not answerable solely through the usual channels of "Israel advocacy" and activism. Rather, a strategic, long-term effort to "Re-Legitimize" Israel is needed, reaffirming the very legitimacy of the nation-state of the Jews, as the indigenous people in our ancestral homeland. These pursuits, along with my continued involvement in activities related to intra-Jewish issues and the Arab-Israel conflict, occupy more and more of my spare time.

And speaking of land, I have made some headway with plans to open a new winery in the Jerusalem hills, turning my hobby (and one of the themes of my trek) into a vocation as well as a calling. Our winery will hopefully not only produce superior vintages (to complement the many other world-class vineyards and wineries in Israel today), but will provide a platform to promote Israel, presenting the story of Israel to diplomats, students, tourists and others . . . through wine. Please look me up if you come to visit Israel/Jerusalem—I'll be delighted to share a glass with you.

Acknowledgments

Writing a book, let alone this book, is an incredibly personal and private experience. But it cannot be done alone, as I discovered in the process.

So too hiking the Shvil; so too coping with an unwanted divorce. I am greatly indebted to so many; my humility and gratitude are boundless.

To me, the word *acknowledgment* is fascinating. It's as if we must actively take what we *know* to be true and to articulate it, in a very public recognition of the contribution made by others. So first and foremost, without embarrassment, I acknowledge the role of God, *Hashem*, in my life at all times, and with humbleness and acceptance I thank him/her for the innumerable gifts in my life, chief among them those who love me and the experiences I've been privileged to have, including taking part in the miracle of the reassertion of Jewish sovereignty in the Land of Israel and the hike across Israel which gave birth to this book.

My children, and especially my youngest daughter, provided unending support both through the difficult times and while I was on the Shvil, and while writing, as did their spouses. Each in their own way, they loved and comforted me, laughed and cried with me, and did so with the sort of empathy, intelligence, kindness, patience, and firmness one doesn't really expect at that age or stage in life. It's what a father anticipates as comfort in his old age; I was and am lucky to have experienced it much earlier. Nothing could make me prouder, or ever has, than my kids growing up into incredible human beings.

My friends-who-are-family gave constant encouragement and help, in word and deed (oh so many words)—Moshe HaLevi in particular, and Deborah, Rebecca and Zvi, you are paragons of patience and understanding, and your counsel was and is always so wise. Aaron & Hadas, Ken & Ruth, Yehudit, Michael, Jeremy & Mandy, Nomi & Yoel, Yaakov & Shalva, Mark & Naomi, Dave & Ahava, Eli & Judy, Leonie & Haim, Mordechai & Monica, Yossi & Susan, Dov & Freda, and many others who I'm sorry I can't keep listing, were unstinting in their generosity and love, and I carry their warmth with me still, as I did on the Shvil. The same must be said of my brother, Mark, whose ear and counsel were and are a constant help.

Zvi, my best friend who has struggled and overcome his own challenges, was by my side in so many ways—including literally, driving down to Eilat and seeing me off, spending a *Shabbat-in-the-Shetach* camping out even though he hates camping, and more—and I remain in his debt not only for his constant help, but for the awareness that he was and is always there, for me and my kids, in case of need, a source of incredible security at all times.

There are so many who helped me in large ways and small, on the Shvil and after, that I can't possibly list them all—among them the מלאכי השביל *Malachei HaShvil* Trail Angels who opened their homes to me and provided not only a bed and shower but food and drink and mostly warmth and encouragement. These Angels included friends and acquaintances I landed upon with almost no warning, who welcomed me literally like angels—Arieh, Ilan, Cheli & Moshe, Avraham & Rutie, Jacob & Haviva, Judy & Arnold, David & Amanda, Meir & Rivkele, Russell & Adena, and of course Viv, the ambassador who's just a normal person (and great fun to boot). In preparation for the hike I received great advice and assistance from Michal and Shani & Shuki (who also lent me their backpack), and gifts which I was grateful for every single day, as noted, from my son and his wife (walking sticks, lantern light, pillow), my youngest and her husband (Leatherman, neck scarf, hat), my brother Mark (Camelback, trail soap, vegetarian freeze-dried meals), my father-in-law (the lightweight *Tallit* prayer shawl I used every day), and even my former wife, who many years ago gave me the small *siddur* prayer book I carried with me. Yaakov Saar, author of the Red Guide, mentioned also in this telling, deserves thanks for his dedication and effort.

I want to acknowledge the contribution my former wife made to me, to my life and to my experiences on the Shvil as well as the lessons I've taken from them. I am who I am today partially due to her influence, and our years together were and will remain part of me, always. Her leaving was sudden, tragic, unexpected, and incomprehensible to me; it was also stimulating, inspiring, and liberating as well. I had wanted to hike the Shvil for over a decade; as noted, after climbing Half Dome with my youngest daughter in August 2013, with the divorce looming, I decided firmly that the time had come. Everything that flows from that point is a result of my former wife's decision, and I am grateful—and harbor no resentment—for it, however strange that sounds even to me.

I could not have hiked the Trail, nor written the book, without the understanding and flexibility offered by Joe Hyams and David Barish at HonestReporting, the parent organization of MediaCentral, and then Yosef Abramowitz and Weldon Turner at EnergiyaGlobal. In the writing of the book, the angels of the Golan, Lilach and Guy of בקתות בערפל (*Biktot B'Arafel*—Cabins in the Clouds, the hostel at Nimrod) played a crucial role, when I told them of my need for a place to write and they instantly said, "Come up!" Their rustic cabin on the hillside overlooking Birkat Ram was a quiet place of solitude in which I was able to return in my mind to those days on the Shvil, almost reliving them as I listened to the birdsong amid the soft rustle of the wind in the trees while I wrote. It was natural for Miriam and me to use it as a getaway after our wedding, and again on our first anniversary. At a crucial juncture when I desperately needed a refuge, my friends Jeremy and Mandy graciously provided one, and it (and their love, and that of all the children too) enabled me to finally complete the writing. For that I am forever grateful—as well as for all the tea and cake and soup (and latkes) . . .

There is no question that my parents, Joan and Don, have influenced who I am and how I relate to the world, and without their love and support I could not—would not—have had the life I have lived, in Israel and otherwise. One significant aspect of this is the strong identity I inherited from them, including their respect for their parents and ancestors, as a Jew—both as a member of the Jewish people and nation as well as a follower of the Jewish religion—and as a proud and fiercely patriotic citizen of the United States of America. I am eternally grateful for the combination of American and Jewish values and principles my mom and dad instilled in me, foremost among them honesty, loyalty, empathy, generosity, reverence for our history, and tolerance and love for all. Another tangible facet of my parents' impact is the love of nature and the outdoors which they instilled in me, whether on excursions across America, camping trips in the Sierras, hikes throughout California and elsewhere, or sending me for years to Skylake Yosemite Camp, where I both enjoyed and learned so much about nature (among other things) and where I worked also for many years.

In this writing, I have benefitted enormously from the guidance of a number of very different but equally accomplished and gifted writers—in particular Gil Troy, Haviva Ner David, Michael Lavigne, and David Ehrlich. I am incredibly grateful to each of them for their insights and suggestions. (You may thank Michael for convincing me to make the tale much more personal; and Gil for his insistence that as much as I wished to convey the hardships, boredom, heat and loneliness of each day, it would in fact present too much of a boring hardship to my readers to repeat them ad nauseum.) I am greatly indebted also to Miriam, my wife and partner in all things, for her editing of the manuscript and offering profound and important suggestions, from a very different and helpful perspective. You are indebted to her as well, not only for reducing the length of the book, but for making it much more readable. It goes without saying (why then say it? It seems to be the tradition . . .) that they bear no responsibility for the style or content of the final product. I thank Daniel Pipes and Asaf Romorovsky and The Middle East Forum for their grant to help put together a website for the book and for their warmth and encouragement.

Last (though to say "not least" would diminish her impact and importance) I have too few words which can adequately express my thanks and appreciation to my wife, Miriam, for the encouragement and support, inspiration and strength she has given me. Miriam: Your coming into my life has indeed both brought to me, and enabled me to express, the "love in my heart, love in my hand" that I sang about in the desert that day. To have "someone who loves me, someone who can" to spend the rest of my life with is the most meaningful source of comfort and inspiration one could possibly imagine. You are indeed *my muse; my worst distraction, my rhythm and blues . . . All of me loves all of you—all your curves and all your edges, all your perfect imperfections. You're my end and my beginning; even when I lose I'm winning . . .* (Thank you, John Legend, your song "All of Me" was clearly written for me/us; when I sang it to Miriam at our wedding in 2015, her mother thought I wrote it, it fit so perfectly. Don't worry: Miriam instantly disabused her of the notion.)

Miriam, it is because of you that I look forward to a future of happiness, meaning and fulfillment; it is you whom I knew I was destined to meet, though I did not know your name. (And we must thank JDate.com, too, for providing the platform through which God worked his inexplicable and subtle magic. Though you get credit for making the first move . . .)

Humility, Acceptance, Gratitude, Forgiveness, and Purpose all have found a home in me, and I acknowledge and celebrate the impact the Shvil has had on my life. I highly recommend the experience to any who wish to explore Israel, our history and reality, the Land, and its people.

Video Index

About the Author

Aryeh Green is a passionate lover of Israel—the people, the land, the country, and the idea. Residing in or around Jerusalem for the past three decades, Aryeh lives and breathes a vibrant and living Judaism, which affects all he does—including serving as chief strategy officer of EnergiyaGlobal, a Jerusalem-based renewable energy platform for Africa; as director emeritus of MediaCentral, providing services for the foreign press in the region; formerly as a senior advisor to Israel's deputy prime minister Natan Sharansky; as a backyard vintner; and as a writer, activist, husband, and father.

Scan to visit

www.myisraeltrail.com